THE

TWELVE

LIVES

OF

ALFRED

HITCHCOCK

THE

TWELVE

LIVES

OF

ALFRED
HITCHCOCK

An Anatomy of the Master of Suspense

Edward White

W. W. NORTON & COMPANY
Independent Publishers Since 1923

Frontispiece: Hitchcock and "Hitchcock," May 1972.

For information about permission to reproduce selections from this book, write to
Permissions, W. W. Norton & Company, Inc., 500 Fifth Avenue, New York, NY 10110

For information about special discounts for bulk purchases, please contact
W. W. Norton Special Sales at specialsales@wwnorton.com or 800-233-4830

Manufacturing by Lake Book Manufacturing
Book design by Chris Welch
Production manager: Anna Oler

Library of Congress Cataloging-in-Publication Data

Names: White, Edward, 1981– author.
Title: The twelve lives of Alfred Hitchcock : an anatomy of the master of suspense /
    Edward White.
Description: First edition. | New York, N.Y. : W. W. Norton & Company, [2021] |
    Includes bibliographical references and index.
Identifiers: LCCN 2020042546 | ISBN 9781324002390 (hardcover) | ISBN 9781324002406 (epub)
Subjects: LCSH: Hitchcock, Alfred, 1899–1980. | Motion picture producers and directors—
    Great Britain—Biography.
Classification: LCC PN1998.3.H58 W545 2021 | DDC 791.4302/33092 [B]—dc23
LC record available at https://lccn.loc.gov/2020042546

W. W. Norton & Company, Inc., 500 Fifth Avenue, New York, N.Y. 10110
www.wwnorton.com

W. W. Norton & Company Ltd., 15 Carlisle Street, London W1D 3BS

1 2 3 4 5 6 7 8 9 0

For public libraries and independent cinemas

Contents

Introduction

I n the spring of 1921, Alfred Hitchcock began his career in the movies. Some months earlier, he had read that the American production company Famous Players-Lasky was to open a branch in London, his hometown, and was looking to recruit designers of intertitles, the story and dialogue cards for silent films. Having spent the last couple of years designing print advertisements for W.T. Henley's Telegraph Works Company, the movie-mad Hitchcock, barely into his twenties, had skills perfectly suited to the job.

The company's first production was to be an adaptation of a novel, *The Sorrows of Satan*. Hitchcock obtained a copy of the book, and—with the assistance of some of his advertising colleagues—designed intertitles for the proposed film. Immediately, he faced a setback. When he submitted his designs, he was told *The Sorrows of Satan* had been scrapped. So, away he went—and returned with new designs for the production that had been announced in its stead. Impressed by the boy's ingenuity, the bosses decided to try him out on a casual, freelance basis. The money wasn't much, so he moonlighted, continuing his regular job alongside his film work, while slipping his manager a cut of the extra income in return for a blind eye. His first assignments went well enough that Famous Players-Lasky eventually offered him a full-time contract. It appears he left Henley's on April 27, 1921. Electrical cabling's loss was world cinema's gain.

The story, told by Hitchcock himself, evinces so much of what would present itself over his sixty-year career in motion pictures. There is his buoyant ambition, his vivid visual imagination, his interest in telling stories with as few words as possible, a reliance on source material, and the use of others to achieve a Hitchcockian end. Perhaps more than any-thing, in telling the anecdote Hitchcock was depicting himself as he was wont to do: an outsider who navigated obstacles with talent, zeal, and cunning.

Within six years of starting his job at Famous Players-Lasky, the hus-tling novice was forging a legend. In 1927, Hitchcock became a sensa-tion following the success of his first three films, *The Pleasure Garden*, *The Mountain Eagle*, and *The Lodger*.* But moviemaking was only half his genius. According to Hitchcock, on Christmas morning that year, sev-eral of his friends and family unwrapped a curious stocking filler: a tiny jigsaw puzzle of the wunderkind's silhouette. The nine-stroke self-portrait—an exquisite Art Deco flourish—was typical Hitchcock, as was the decision to issue it as a Christmas present. From now on, Hitchcock's physical self was to be a promotional tool and a work of art, a walking, talking logo for what critics once called "the Hitchcock touch" but what we might term "the Hitchcock brand," a riveting fusion of his personal fame and mythology and the themes, aesthetics, and atmosphere of his movies. For the next half-century, Hitchcock's persona was the active ingredient in the most celebrated of his fifty-three films,† the way Oscar Wilde's was in his plays, and Andy Warhol's was in his art. Hitch-cock stands alone in the Hollywood canon: a director whose mythology eclipses the brilliance of his myriad classic movies.

Today, Hitchcock is cited as the representative figure of his medium. As the historian Paula Marantz Cohen says, Hitchcock's career provides "an economical way of studying the entire history of cinema." His work spans the silent era, talkies, black and white, color, and 3D; expression-ism, film noir, and social realism; thrillers, screwball comedy, and hor-ror; the cinema of Weimar Germany, the golden age of Hollywood, the

---

* All three premiered in 1926, but it was not until the following year that they were released nationwide.

† Fifty-four if one counts a German-language version of *Murder!*, which he shot simultaneously alongside the Anglophone version.

rise of television, and the ferment of the sixties and seventies that gave us Kubrick, Spielberg, and Scorsese.

But the significance of Hitchcock stretches far beyond cinema. In many senses, Hitchcock was the emblematic artist of the twentieth century—not necessarily the most talented or the most accomplished, but one of vast influence, whose life and genre-straddling, multimedia work vividly illuminate key themes of Western culture from the Roaring Twenties to the Swinging Sixties. A story of Hitchcock is also a story of the emergence of the United States as a cultural behemoth; the insistent rise of feminism; the changing roles of sex, violence, and religion in popular culture; the pervasive influence of psychoanalysis; the growth of advertising and promotion as a cultural force; and the vanishing gap between art and entertainment. He and his work are cultural touchstones, seminal to cinema, television, art, literature, and advertising, as familiar to viewers of *The Simpsons* as to critics of the Venice Biennale. Anxiety, fear, paranoia, guilt, and shame are the emotional engines of his films; surveillance, conspiracy, distrust of authority, and sexual violence were among his most abiding preoccupations. On both counts, his work speaks with urgency to today's audiences. In the 1960s, his films entered academia in the form of film studies; now, Hitchcock is a subject of inquiry in manifold disciplines: gender studies, queer studies, urban studies, fat studies, religious studies, criminal justice studies. While he lived, he could seem a man out of time, a Victorian relic in the thick of the twentieth century. But, decades after his death, this singular person lives among us in many guises.

This book offers twelve of those "lives," twelve close-up portraits of Hitchcock, each from a different angle, each revealing something fundamental about the man, the public entity he crafted, and the mythological creature he has become. This is about the life Hitchcock lived, but also the various roles he performed and inhabited; the versions of himself that he projected, and those that the rest of us have projected on him. Among the dozen diverse incarnations, we will see Hitchcock the irrepressible jester, the lonely and terrified child, the problem-solving innovator, the global citizen who never left London, and the transgressive artist for whom violence and disorder were a creative life force. Throughout the chapters, Hitchcock's peers, those who influenced him, and those who followed in his footsteps will slide in and out of view. An important part of the Hitchcock brand is the idea of Hitchcock the all-powerful creator of his filmic universe. It is both true and not. His talent cannot be denied, but without the intervention of creative collaborators, journalists, publicists, and we, his public, the thing we know as "Hitchcock" would not exist.

Each of the twelve lives flits across the decades, making connections between Hitchcock young and old. The Hitchcock of popular imagination is dominated by his image at the time of his greatest success in the 1950s and early 1960s. But long before the creepy uncle of *Psycho*, there had been another Hitchcock, an impudent young urbanite of the Jazz Age who captured interwar London on screen and brilliantly exhibited ideas and impulses at the core of his later, more exalted work. The economist David Galenson once theorized that there are two poles of genius: the prolific, precocious Picasso, and the ruminative, late-blooming Cézanne, endlessly retreading the same ground. Hitchcock may be the only major artist of the last one hundred years who could convincingly be used as a model for either.

Paradoxically, but perhaps inevitably, this emblematic figure was a complete one-off. His public image, developed and exploited across multiple media, borrowed from Victorian aesthetes, Edwardian music-hall entertainers, Hollywood moguls, and the European avant-garde. He emerged into the public eye as a distinctively English sort of modernist. Steeped in a national culture of nostalgia and tradition, he pursued innovation and new technology while nudging elements of the taboo, the experimental, and the marginal into the mainstream. An interpreter of the modern and the urban, Hitchcock constantly stressed the importance of technique and process, using the camera, the studio set, and the editing room to play with movement, speed, and time. Like all true modernists, he delighted in undermining shibboleths, and shocking respectable sensibilities. He was a flaneur and a mythmaker, who embraced self-promotion as an end in itself; not just a filmmaker but an impresario, an entertainer, and the creator of spectacle, with his mythology at its center. The bigger that mythology grew, the more Hitchcock used it to tease us, with in-jokes, irony, and self-parody. By the time the cultural revolutions of the 1960s began, the modernist whiz kid had morphed into a wily old cynic on the path of postmodernism.

Though Hitchcock often insisted he was a very straightforward sort of fellow, his complex personality remains a source of fascination and contention. He had an enormous ego and fragile self-esteem; his capacity for self-disgust was equaled by his self-regard. While he possessed great surety in his abilities and opinions, he was in constant need of affirmation, from those closest to him as well as from the complete strangers who constituted his audience. He had an unmatched ability for communicating emotional experience, yet he displayed little conscious understanding of his own emotions and seemed to feel always wary of and threatened by other people. Hitchcock promoted competing, contradictory ideas about himself; he asked us to believe that he was both a nervous wreck and a man of sangfroid. He took pride in his refinement and sophistication, at the same time battling to control his appetites. He felt empowered and appalled by his masculinity. Although he saw himself as an ally of women, his name has become synonymous with male predation and abuse of power. He presented himself as full of knowledge, knowingness, and control, but he lived and died baffled by himself, frightened by what he knew about this world and what he didn't about the next.

Such contradictions have encouraged astonishingly diverse interpretations of Hitchcock. The reading of him as lecherous ogre competes with the image of Hitchcock the uxorious husband. Hitchcock the brooding artist is countered by Hitchcock the vaudevillian. The dyspeptic misanthrope identified by some contrasts with the hopeless romantic that others recognize when they delve into the Hitchcock filmography. Since his death, these disparate images have grown like bamboo forests around Hitchcock's name—but, in each case, it was he who planted their seeds. For decades, the question has been incessantly posed: "Who is the real Alfred Hitchcock?" At times it seems more apt to ponder, which Alfred Hitchcock is your Alfred Hitchcock?

Like the lines of his famous self-drawn silhouette, each of these chapters will contribute a different component of Hitchcock's identity. Only when all twelve are seen together will the full picture be complete. But, at the bottom of each is a man and his obsession with every facet of motion pictures: color and costume, the minutiae of production design, the use of music and sound, the writing of the script, the intangible chemistry of a well-chosen cast, the transformations that could be achieved by lighting, and the magic that could be performed in the edit by the judicious use of a pair of scissors. "I've never known any man who enjoys making films more than Hitch," said Norman Lloyd, a good friend and colleague. "It's so much part of him. His enjoyment of it is an example of how life should be." Whether any of Hitchcock's many lives could or should be an exemplar for our own remains a tantalizing question.

THE

TWELVE

LIVES

OF

ALFRED
HITCHCOCK

1

THE BOY WHO COULDN'T GROW UP

A year and a half after the end of World War I, Londoners were used to ghosts walking among them. The absent were present in every street of the capital; lives finished but unresolved, stalking those left behind. J. M. Barrie, the creator of *Peter Pan* and the most celebrated playwright of his day, was one of many who was haunted by his loss: the war had claimed his friend Charles Frohman, the Broadway producer who had been instrumental in his theatrical success, as well as George Llewelyn Davies, one of the brothers on whom Barrie had based the Lost Boys.

In April 1920, Barrie premiered his new play at London's Haymarket Theatre. Unlike Peter Pan, the eponymous heroine of *Mary Rose* is a girl who wants to grow old but can't. As a child she went missing, only to rematerialize three weeks later unaware that more than a couple of hours had elapsed. Years passed without incident, though she remained curiously childlike on the inside. Entering adulthood, Mary Rose goes missing again, reappearing decades later—but without aging a day. When she learns from her family that her baby is now a man, and is himself missing in the Great War, the shock kills her. Her ghost, the sweet girl stuck in a time before everyone's innocence had been destroyed, returns to haunt the family home, searching frantically for her son. Never had one of Barrie's tales of supernatural mystery seemed so earthbound.

Among those who attended the play's first run was Alfred Hitchcock, an advertising designer for an electrical cabling firm, with a dream of making it in the movies. Taking a trip to the West End for a night of spectacle and sensation at the theater was one of young Alfred's great pleasures. Before the war, he went frequently with his parents, though now he tended to go alone, one of the many solitary, immersive experiences that stimulated his intense imaginative life.

In certain ways, Barrie foreshadowed the artist Hitchcock would become. Rambling back and forth across the territory of perennial obsessions, they both told campfire tales of the magical that were more complex and unsettling than they first appeared. Reviews of *Mary Rose* sound remarkably similar to the kind that attended Hitchcock's career. "This eerie and beautiful play," reads one piece filed in London, "holds you spellbound at the theatre, and sends you home with something of a shiver." The writer took a swipe at the snooty curmudgeons who turned their noses up at Barrie's work, as well as those who dredged his plays for hidden meanings, those "people who can see metaphors in scaffold-poles and symbols in coal scuttles," precisely the same complaint that certain critics would one day level at obsessive watchers of Hitchcock's films. Another reviewer complimented *Mary Rose* as a "slice of a delightful cake"; one of Hitchcock's repeated boasts was that while some filmmakers make slices of life, he made slices of cake.

Mary Rose left a lifelong impression on Hitchcock. It so influenced him when making *Vertigo* (1958) that he tracked down the music used in the original production to give to the film's composer, Bernard Herrmann, as inspiration. A few years later, he developed a script for a film adaptation of the play, but it was too offbeat for his studio, and the movie never happened. His connection to *Mary Rose* was strong but intangible, something to do with the transporting strangeness of the theater, the bewitching ethereality of Fay Compton in the title role, and the devastation done when the cocoon of childhood is ripped open. Like so many others in the audience of 1920, the adolescent Hitchcock had experienced loss and grinding anxiety in recent years, intense emotional experiences that never shuffled out of frame. A little like Mary Rose herself, part of

Hitchcock remained a child forever. In his own words, "the man is not different from the boy."

Hitchcock struggled with endings. *Psycho*, with its deus ex machina lecture in developmental psychology, thrown into the filming schedule at the last minute as a way of explaining Norman Bates's murders, is the textbook example. Sometimes the problem was caused by the delicate sensibilities of the censors, or the intransigence of meddling producers. Other times, Hitchcock felt constrained by his audience's requirement for narrative neatness. Rarely did he exhibit such difficulty with beginnings, especially when the story being told was how Alfred Hitchcock became "Alfred Hitchcock."

The basic facts of his early life are plain enough. He was born on August 13, 1899, above his father's greengrocer's shop at 517 High Road in Leytonstone, Essex, east of London. By the time of Alfred's arrival, Emma and William Hitchcock already had two other children: William (after his father) was nine, and Ellen (or Nellie) seven. Hitchcock's father was the type of person evoked by the common nineteenth-century description of England as "a nation of shopkeepers": a man for whom being one's own master was a source of pride, and the ability to convert one penny into two a moral virtue—though it seems he left a good deal of those pennies behind the bar of his favorite pubs. His younger brother, John, was a better example of the breed, with a successful chain of food shops that paid for a five-bedroom home, attended by a small domestic staff, in the well-to-do London district of Putney. Although an extrovert personality with a keen sense of fun, Emma was a redoubtable matriarch. In her home, cleanliness and neatness were insisted on as the outward manifestations of inner goodness. "A wonderful character . . . very forceful," is how Hitchcock's daughter, Patricia, remembered her grandmother. "You can imagine a young person could be scared of her. . . . She made them toe the line."

Despite the emphasis on hard work and self-discipline, the Hitch-

Hitchcock's father with his son William, Alfred's older brother, outside the family shop, c. 1900.

cocks were not puritans. In addition to the theater outings, classical recitals, fairs, and circuses were common family activities. There were also plenty of day trips along the Thames and into the Essex countryside, as well as seaside holidays in Cliftonville in Kent where his uncle John rented a large house in the summer.

Aged six or seven, Hitchcock moved with his parents and siblings to Limehouse, by the Thames in the heart of London's traditional East End. His father bought two fishmonger shops, above one of which the family lived at 175 Salmon Lane. Both Hitchcock parents were of Irish descent. William was brought up in the Church of England, but Emma came from devout Catholic stock. When they married, William converted, and all three of their children were raised in the Catholic faith. The teachings and rituals of the Church played a central role in family life. Borrowing the words of the First Epistle of Peter, Hitchcock's father affectionately referred to Alfred as his "lamb without a spot," while Emma, if Hitchcock's recollection can be trusted, had her youngest boy stand at the foot of her bed each night to confess his sins.

Aged nine, Hitchcock was sent away to Salesian College in Battersea, a boarding school at which the discipline was apparently so harsh and the food so awful that his parents removed him after just one week. From there, he attended Howrah House, a convent school run by the Sisters of the Faithful Companions of Jesus. At the age of eleven, he entered St Ignatius College, a Jesuit school in Stamford Hill, north London, named in honor of the founder of the Society of Jesus, the sixteenth-century diplomat and soldier St Ignatius of Loyola, who wrote a hugely influential handbook of spiritual direction, advocating a chivalric vision of Christianity in which men poured all their mortal energy into fighting for the glory of God. Jesuit schools gained a reputation for austerity and discipline, a reputation that Hitchcock thought just. Punishment at St Ignatius College, as was common in Jesuit schools of the time, included strokes on the hand with a ferule, a foot-long leather-covered rubber strap. The ferule ritual was "highly dramatic," remembered Hitchcock, as "it was left to the pupil to decide when to go, and he would keep putting it off and then he would go at the end of the day to a special room where there would be a priest or a lay brother who would administer the punishment—like sort of, in a minor way, going for execution." When the moment of punishment eventually arrived, the pain was intense. If a boy had been sentenced to twelve strokes of the strap, he would need to "spread it over two days because each hand could only take three strokes" at a time.

The experience contributed to his reverence for ritual and his dread of authority. Those of Hitchcock's generation might have countered that similar acts of corporal punishment were familiar to senior schools of all varieties in England, and those educated in other denominations—Christian Brothers, for example—endured more severe, and more arbitrary, discipline. Even so, it's evident that the experience left a lasting mark. He told some that his fear of the priests and their methods was the "root" of his work. Wittingly or not, Hitchcock would one day pass on the fear of violent chastisement to a little boy in his care. The actor Bill Mumy was seven years old when he played the central role in "Bang! You're Dead," an episode in the seventh series of Hitchcock's highly popular television series of the fifties and sixties, *Alfred Hitchcock Presents*. By the end of a long day filming, Mumy was losing concentration, and fidgeting when he was asked to stay still, prompting Hitchcock to rise from his chair and cross the floor. Mumy recalls Hitchcock's frame, huge to a small child, clad in priestly black and white, descending on him, sweating, and breathing heavily as he whispered into the boy's ear: "If you don't stop moving about, I'm going to get a nail and nail your feet to your mark, and the blood will come pouring out like milk—so *stop* moving." Mumy was petrified, and years later when he worked in the same building as Hitchcock at Universal, he avoided even walking past his office. "It has been a big deal for me for over fifty years," he said in 2013, "tattooed on my id," in the very way that Hitchcock's own encounters with authority figures clung to him throughout his life.

Hitchcock left school a few weeks ahead of his fourteenth birthday, as was the norm for children of his background. From there, he pursued his interest in science, technology, and engineering by enrolling at the London County Council School of Marine Engineering and Navigation. After a year of study, he entered the world of work, in November 1914, at W.T. Henley's Telegraph Works Company, where he was initially employed in the dull task of estimating the sizes and voltages of electrical cable. Eventually he was moved into the advertising department, and he took evening classes in art at Goldsmiths College, University of London. It was at this point, in his late teens, that his creative life began.

Upon this skeleton of facts, Hitchcock's experience of childhood is fleshed out largely by stories that emanate from his own memories. In his mind's eye, he was a timid, solitary, though not unhappy child who sat on the sides, watching rather than participating. Sports, and rough and tumble games, were not for him. "I don't remember ever having a playmate," he recalled, and he was too young to hang on the coattails of his siblings. He thought himself agreeable enough, though, according to one biographer, schoolmates tended to think him strange and teased him for smelling of fish. Lacking friends, he retreated (perhaps contentedly so) into books and maps, indulging a fascination with travel, learning train timetables by heart and tracking the journeys of ships across the oceans. By the age of eight, so he insisted, he had traveled every route on the London General Omnibus Company.

His most vivid memories—or, at least, the ones he publicly declared—were concerned with fear, the fuel on which the Hitchcock juggernaut ran. He claimed to be scared of just about everything: policemen, strangers, driving, solitude, crowds, heights, water, and conflict of any sort, all caused him excessive vexation. "An alarm clock about to go off" is how he described himself to Hedda Hopper, the legendary chronicler of Hollywood. "There's a lot of work going on inside." "It was amazing to see these fears," said Robert Boyle, the production designer on *North by Northwest* (1959), *The Birds* (1963), and *Marnie* (1964), not because there was anything outlandish or weird in the things Hitchcock was frightened of, but because he had such an ability to communicate the physical and emotional experience of being afraid common to us all. "The difference between his fear of authority and his fear of heights is that he could put it up there on screen," said Boyle. He was, as biographer Donald Spoto put it, "a visual poet of anxiety and accident."

Genetics or learned behavior might explain the derivation of his worrisome nature, which sounds a lot like what clinicians now speak of as generalized anxiety disorder. His father, William, seemed to relax only at the theater, Hitchcock recalled. "I think he worried a lot. Selling produce that can spoil in a day must be nerve-wracking." Typical of Hitchcock to find melodramatic edge in the life cycle of a pilchard; even the experience of selling fish, fruit, and vegetables crackled with suspense.

In general, however, Hitchcock preferred an explanation that was simultaneously more pat and more spectacular, attributing his anxieties to the impact of specific moments in his childhood of which he had patchy, but powerful, memories. Principally, these were emotional recollections, strikingly vivid snapshots of unusual moments, which he wheeled out as set pieces over the decades. The best known of these stories is what we might call Hitchcock's genesis myth, the moment he supposedly acquired his fears of authority, abandonment, and the contradictory horrors of guilt and arbitrary injustice—all the unruly emotions that surge through his most famous work. "I must have been about four or five years old," he told his fellow film director François Truffaut. "My father sent me to the police station with a note. The chief of police read it and locked me in a cell for five or ten minutes, saying, 'This is what we do to naughty boys.'" John Russell Taylor, Hitchcock's authorized biographer, stated that Hitchcock's sister, Nellie, confirmed the story was true, but he never directly quoted her version of events.

Certain discrepancies in the story's various retellings encourage one to wonder whether the incident was as fresh in Hitchcock's mind as he claimed. Usually, he said he had been five or six years old at the time, but to Truffaut he suggested that he could have been as young as four, and to the journalist Oriana Fallaci he remembered being eleven. To an Australian newspaper he said, "I'm told I was frightened by a policeman as a small boy, so maybe that's why I like thrills." Perhaps, then, this was a memory inherited from relatives who spoke about the incident, and which his imagination had given form to retrospectively—entirely plausible for one with such a vivid and eventful interior life. Sometimes he claimed to have no clue what infraction had triggered his custodial sentence. Other times he speculated it was because he had followed the tram tracks from his home—captivated, as always, by the adventure and romance of travel—but come sunset, he'd been unable to find his way home in the dark. That his father should respond to the return of a missing child by having him put in prison—albeit briefly—seems astonishing, though surely not a sign of uncaring cruelty. Hitchcock once joked that his father had been riled at having to delay his dinner, before adding, "perhaps he was angry because he was worried about me." If true, it's redolent of the way a middle-aged Hitchcock responded to a similar situation, more than forty years later, when his wife was late for dinner because of heavy traffic she encountered after a Sunday outing with Anne Baxter, the leading lady in Hitchcock's film *I Confess* (1953). "There he was, sitting like Jove, furious at us," remembered Baxter of the angry, stressed man they discovered on their return. "He didn't forgive me for that dinner delay for a long time."

Other, similar stories of childhood trauma became pillars of Hitchcock lore. One time he apparently woke to find his parents out of the house, gone for a walk or to the pub, sending young Alfred into a dread that he had been abandoned. Again, the adult Hitchcock supplied an intense sensory memory: standing alone in the dark of the kitchen, weeping, he pushed slices of cold meat into his mouth in a vain attempt at self-comfort until his mother and father returned. In rehearsing the story in public, he said the episode had instilled in him a fear of the dark (tricky for a man head over heels in love with the cinema) and an unconquerable dislike of cold cuts. In another of his favorite origin stories, he explained that his passion for scaring audiences began before he could walk or talk, when his mother leaned over his cot and said, "Boo!" This one wasn't meant to be taken seriously. It was a neat way of explaining that enjoyment of fear is hardwired into the human brain, and that none of us ever truly ceases to be the mewling infant in the cradle. These were the operating principles of his life in film.

Talk-show hosts and newspaper journalists never tired of giving Hitchcock an opportunity to tell these anecdotes, and Hollywood publicists made sure they were written into his official biographies when materials were sent to press around the release of a latest film. It was as though each new picture was a reliving of Hitchcock's childhood, another chance to paint with the camera the fear that first flowered in the belly of the boy he used to be. Paul Cézanne had Mont Sainte-Victoire to return to time and again; Hitchcock had the dark interior of an empty terraced house and the clank of a prison-cell door.

The factual basis for many of these childhood yarns is impossible to verify. One might hazard that they are a little too perfectly Hitchcockian to be true, or at least to be taken as the starting pistol for Hitchcock's career in shadows and suspense. As his parents had taught him, Hitchcock valued neatness in all things. He stated to others that his idea of pure happiness was "a clear horizon. Nothing to worry about on your plate"; maintaining "a tidy mind" was a goal for which he labored daily. The empirical accuracy of these memories, however, is less important than their emotional tone. Hitchcock was telling us that he associated childhood with fear, uncertainty, confusion, and brief moments that change everything.

In a profound sense, Hitchcock thought there was an irreducible part of himself that remained a child all his life. Not only was it, by his reckoning, the basis of his unusual personality, it was also his source of abundant creativity. His inner child, he believed, provided the dominant themes of his work, as well as the rare talent that allowed him to explore those themes on screen with such fluidity and originality. "I believe it's intuitive to visualize," he explained, "but as we grow up, we lose that intuition," though he fancied himself something of an exception: "My mind works more like a baby's mind does, thinking in pictures." It's an inversion of the traditional romantic myth of the child genius. Rather than exhibiting an uncanny adultness as a boy, Hitchcock's contention was that he maintained childhood qualities that bloomed in adulthood. That he had held on to a childlike nature was evident to many of those who knew him. Russell Maloney of *The New Yorker* observed that Hitchcock worked with the "mind of an intelligent child who gets angry when his adventure story bogs down midway with talk of love, duty, and other abstractions." Others noted his juvenile sense of humor that stayed with him even as he entered his eighties. "I was very close to Hitchcock," said Arthur Laurents, screenwriter of Hitchcock's *Rope* (1948). "He was a child, you know, a very black-comedy child."

In Hitchcock's remembering, there was no meandering path between his childhood and adulthood, only a straight superhighway. "My wife says my design for living is work," he said, "which could be true because I planned my life's work as a child." The novelists, playwrights, and artists he claimed to have adored as a schoolboy remained crucial influences all through his career; he never divulged an old guilty pleasure, some youthful obsession that he later looked back on with embarrassment. Along with Barrie, Hitchcock named the spy novelist John Buchan and a gamut of middlebrow English authors as the great cultural influences of his youth, as well as Edgar Allan Poe, whom Hitchcock discovered as a sixteen-year-old when he read his biography. It was "the sadness of his life," one marked by childhood abandonment, that drew him to Poe's writing. His adolescent reading of Poe's stories revealed to him a truth on which his whole career was based: that people love—need, perhaps—to be scared in safety. "And, very probably," he reflected, "it's because I liked Edgar Allan Poe's stories so much that I began to make suspense films." Poe's work also inspired *The Avenging Conscience* (1914), a film by D. W. Griffith that had a huge impact on Hitchcock when he saw it as a teenager.

Possibly, this was an honest reflection of the person he had always been, someone of unwavering tastes and sensibilities. Aged twenty, he founded and edited Henley's in-house magazine, the *Henley Telegraph*, in which he published a series of his own short stories, mainly melodramatic tales with a comical twist that are reminiscent of his later work, including occasional pieces published under his name in popular fiction magazines. His childhood fascination with timetables, maps, and machines stayed with him, too. In scripting sessions in the 1970s, the final decade of his life, he induced exasperation and amusement in his writers when he would obsess over some seemingly trivial detail to do with the San Francisco Bay Area Transit system, the distance between London landmarks, or at which remote Finnish train station a scene should be filmed.

Hitchcock as a jailbird baby, in *Alfred Hitchcock Presents*.

Ironically, though he attributed his facility as a filmmaker to the little boy within, in his years of greatest fame he presented himself as the type of person one couldn't imagine ever being young. When, as an adult, he encountered children, he often failed to make allowance for their age, as though he had no conception of the ways in which they might have differed from grown-ups. Some of those who visited Hitchcock and his wife at their home noted that their little girl, Pat, was treated as an adult rather than a child, and there are several stories of him doing the same with children who appeared in his films. One day during the making of *The Man Who Knew Too Much* (1956), starring Doris Day and James Stewart, a colleague gave it to him straight: "Your problem, Hitch, is you don't know how to direct children. You use the same language with Chris [Olsen, a child actor] you use when you're talking to Jimmy, Doris, or any adult." In conference on the script for *The Birds*—Hitchcock's famous film about a sedate Californian community suddenly besieged by flocks of vicious birds—Hitchcock questioned whether it was realistic for Cathy, the daughter of the Brenner family, to hug Tippi Hedren's character when thanking her for a birthday gift. "I really don't know much about their behavior. Do they really fling themselves into people's arms?" he asked, sounding as though he were talking about some exotic species he'd only ever witnessed from afar, despite at this point being a proud grandfather of three young girls.

If he did feel distant from children, and experienced some discomfort when looking back on his own early years, it might explain the lack of sentimentality with which he put childhood on screen. Cruelty to innocent children is a recurring theme in cinema, as it is in so much other folk and popular culture. When Hitchcock was growing up, in the very earliest days of motion pictures, there was a rash of wildly popular films of babies and toddlers caught candidly by the camera, sometimes in moments of distress. One was *When Babies Quarrel*, essentially a silent precursor of "Charlie Bit My Finger." Another was *Cry Baby*, in which, as an advertisement for the film explains, a "pretty little fat baby boy is seated on a high chair. The expression on his little round face shows that he is expecting something very good to eat. When he finds out he is not going to get it, his expression quickly changes from disappointment to grief. As he cries, he rubs his eyes with chubby hands and the big tears roll down his cheeks. Very realistic." Hitchcock was plugged into the urge within audiences to see childhood innocence undermined, the crux of every Brothers Grimm tale. *The Birds* is the stellar example: the elementary school pupils of Bodega Bay being chased through the streets by a murder of demented crows is perhaps cinema's most famous depiction of children being hurt or terrorized, and one of its most disturbing; the Child Catcher locked his victims away but didn't attempt to peck out their eyes.

Hitchcock had a history of putting children in harm's way. In 1934, he made *The Man Who Knew Too Much*; the Day-Stewart version was a Hollywood remake, also directed by Hitchcock. Both versions revolve around the kidnapping of a child, but only in the original do we see the act of capture, when Hitchcock gives us a close-up of the face of twelve-year-old Betty (Nova Pilbeam), her eyes wide and desperate as a man's hand smothers her mouth, as bracingly unsettling an image today as it was in 1934. In both films, the children are sucked into the adult world of deceit, betrayal, and violence. But neither is portrayed sentimentally as a vessel of purity and goodness. Indeed, as soon as the opening titles are complete, they create havoc. In the original, Betty causes an accident at a ski-jumping competition, leading to a pile-up of adult bodies on the snow. In the American version, Hank's transgression is less spectacular, but more shocking. On a crammed bus traveling through Morocco, he accidentally pulls off a Muslim woman's veil, sparking outrage among the other passengers and instigating his parents' first encounter with the spy who will tear their lives apart. In every film that features a child in a prominent role, Hitchcock uses them as spinning tops of trouble. They cause complication and insult, spearing adult perspectives, or saying things the grown-ups would rather leave unsaid. One might think of them, per the critic Michael Walker, as Puck to Hitchcock's Oberon; cheery, free-floating sprites sprinkling chaos into their master's otherworldly kingdom. In one of the many cameos that Hitchcock made in his own films, he appears in *Blackmail* (1929) as a passenger on a London Underground train who has his hat yanked down over his eyes by a small boy. Exasperated, Hitchcock flails around but has no idea what to do—he can't strike the child, and he can't appeal for the boy to observe an adult sense of decorum—so is left to harrumph, his dignity diminished. More often, though, the nuisance caused by Hitchcock's children is unintentional, making them more like Barrie's Peter Pan and the Lost Boys, whose mischief is born of naivete not malice.

Hitchcock admires their pluck, appreciates their potential for comedy, and knows they are naturally sympathetic—yet he's wary of children's capacity to scratch off the veneer of our adult, "civilized" selves. In a cameo in *Torn Curtain* (1966), a grandfatherly Hitchcock holds a baby in the lobby of an elegant hotel as the child appears to urinate on his lap. Considering how Hitchcock worried over the small details of life, and worked hard to remove as much uncertainty as he could from his personal and professional environments, it's not hard to see how the unpredictability of children might have made him wary of them. Only occasionally did he stray over the line between blowing raspberries at the sanctity of childhood and being cruel or unpleasant. In a 1972 interview with Rex Reed, a film critic who is himself no stranger to saying the supposedly unsayable, the conversation turned to serial killers. "I loved the tapes I heard made by the moors murderers," Hitchcock said, referring to Ian Brady and Myra Hindley, who killed five children in Lancashire during the 1960s. "They made tape recordings of children screaming as they were buried alive . . . jolly good stuff." Aiming to shock the wholesome Walton within us all, on this occasion his mordant joking came off as callous and juvenile.

Thirty-six years earlier, he had been accused of something similar, this time in his film *Sabotage* (1936, retitled *The Woman Alone* on its US release) in which a boy of twelve named Stevie is killed by a bomb he is unwittingly carrying on behalf of his sister's husband, who is, unbeknownst to Stevie, a terrorist. In a trick he wouldn't try again until Marion Crane got hacked to pieces in the shower a quarter of a century later, Hitchcock bumps off a delicate, sympathetic character shockingly early in the film, and with it goes the very idea of childhood innocence.

Stevie is handed the bomb, disguised as a reel of film, and is told to take it to Piccadilly Tube station before 1:45 p.m.—the time at which the bomb will detonate. He sets off on his fatal errand like a Labrador retrieving a tennis ball, all bouncy eagerness as he works his way through central London. But his innate childishness—blithe, distracted, unpredictable—leads to turmoil. Rather than hurrying straight to his destination as he's been instructed, he stops to marvel at gabby market traders, admires the marching soldiers of the Lord Mayor's Show, and is pulled out of a crowd to take part in a demonstration of a miracle toothpaste. He's running late, and all the while, we know something he doesn't: the package under his arm is a ticking time bomb. In true modernist fashion, time is disrupted but not obliterated; Hitchcock drags out seconds and compresses minutes, but the hands of the clock sweep ever forward. As the moment draws near, the tension grows. Stevie hops on a bus. He smiles at a lady next to him and pets her dog as a percussive tick-tock rises up in the fraught incidental music. The camera gives us close-ups of clock faces as they pass the window; Stevie nervously taps the package. We imagine that a reprieve must be around the corner. Instead, as the clock reaches 1:45 there's an explosion, and a shot of the bus in smoking ruins.

The scene is not among those that have burned themselves on the cultural retina, but it is crystallized Hitchcock, a devastatingly constructed moment of slow-building suspense of the sort that provides a direct link from Hitchcock films of eighty years ago to Hollywood blockbusters of today. Reviews in Britain made a great deal of the bomb sequence. There were those who viewed it through a Hitchcockian lens and praised the director for having the guts to shake us up with something genuinely beastly. "The bomb is exceedingly 'bombish,'" wrote one critic of the scene of Stevie on the bus, and all the characters "happily ignorant. . . . What more does the lover of film suspense wish?"

Hitchcock, however, took more notice of those who thought he had committed an unforgivable crime. C. A. Lejeune, the leading critic of her day, said, "there is a code in this sort of free-handed slaughter, and Hitchcock has gone outside that code" by exterminating a child with whom the audience had complete sympathy. Perhaps influenced by Lejeune, who was usually a great fan of his, Hitchcock looked on Stevie's death as an egregious error. But for him the problem was not moral but technical. He had confused suspense with surprise. As Hitchcock explained countless times to countless interviewers, suspense is what you get when, as in *Sabotage*, the audience knows there's a bomb in the parcel; surprise is what happens when a bomb detonates without warning. "Had the audience not been informed of the real contents of the can, the explosion would have come as a complete surprise. As a result of a sort of emotional numbness induced by a shock of this kind, I believe their sensibilities might not have been so thoroughly outraged." As it was, Hitchcock had robbed the audience of the relief of suspense they expected and needed. Stevie's death, said Hitchcock, was not so much ill-judged as badly executed: "The boy was involved in a situation that got him too much sympathy from the audience, so that when the bomb exploded and he was killed, the public was resentful. The way to handle it would have been for Homolka [Oscar Homolka, the actor playing the terrorist] to kill the boy deliberately."

That Hitchcock didn't treat children like children might explain why he was so popular with them. Starting in the 1950s, and largely thanks to his television show *Alfred Hitchcock Presents*, he became an early iteration of the trend for the shared cultural interests of adults and children—though, unlike today when childhood passions for wizards and superheroes are carried into adulthood, Hitchcock was a decidedly adult figure who found a way of communicating with kids. The director Gus Van Sant is linked to Hitchcock through his 1998 remake of *Psycho*, but his interest began as a little boy in the 1960s, watching *Alfred Hitchcock Presents*. He and his sister were beguiled by Hitchcock's wry, sometimes cartoonish appearances that opened and closed each episode, and riveted by the suspense stories at their heart. Although *Alfred Hitchcock Presents* was never intended as a children's show, many of its episodes possess qualities common to a lot of the most enduring works of children's literature. Six of its episodes were adapted from Roald Dahl stories, and many more of the Hitchcock television shows contain the key ingredients of Dahl's children's novels and his *Revolting Rhymes* short stories: fantastical wickedness running riot, but ultimately defeated by an extreme dose of moral justice, which Hitchcock often delivered himself in his closing monologues—the teacher speaking directly to his pupils.

From the television shows, Van Sant became a reader of the Hitchcock anthologies of mystery stories and the *Alfred Hitchcock Mystery Magazine*. It wasn't until much later that he explored Hitchcock's filmography. Judging from the fan mail Hitchcock received from the 1950s onward, this was a path traveled by many young fans. The publishers of the Hitchcock magazine received so many letters from children that an official fan club was established. For fifty cents, each member received an eight-by-ten photograph of Hitchcock, a brief biography (which featured the story of his childhood incarceration), and a bulletin of the latest Hitchcock news every quarter. Such was his crossover appeal that Hitchcock was approached to lend his name to a series of children's books. *Alfred Hitchcock and the Three Investigators* ran for thirty volumes in the United States, and was published with success in Europe and Asia. Like an anti–Santa Claus, Hitchcock received missives from children all over the world. Some wanted to point out continuity errors in his films; others asked for explanations of plotlines. Many wanted signed photographs, which the Hitchcock office sent out in large quantities. Others, in the grip of their hero's influence, delivered vignettes of gruesomeness that must have tickled and disturbed the secretaries who opened Hitchcock's mail. One fifteen-year-old boy from Texas wrote to say that he had designed gallows on which to give Hitchcock a spectacular send-off. He had even done the sums to ensure the apparatus did its job properly: "a 3 foot 9 inch drop would be sufficient to break your honorable neck."

The year Hitchcock arrived into the world, Sigmund Freud was at work on one of the most important books of the twentieth century. Published in 1900, *The Interpretation of Dreams* decisively shifted the space occupied by sleeping and dreaming in Western cultures. Perhaps more than any other text, it carried Freud's theories of the unconscious into the mainstream, making his ideas commonplace even among those who have never read a word he wrote. The lodestone of Freud's dream analysis is his notion of a dynamic unconscious that whirs away in each human mind, constructed and anchored in childhood. Dreams, according to Freud, are the expression of childhood desires, typically those that have been forbidden or repressed. As the years passed, Freud modified various aspects of his ideas, and his conclusions were challenged from many angles, not least by his protégé Carl Jung who formulated his own comprehensive theories on the psychological significance of dreams and dreaming. However, the cultural significance of *The Interpretation of Dreams* can hardly be understated. Within twenty years of the book's publication, Freud's concept of dreams as a portal into the child-created unconscious had been widely absorbed, established as a major theme of modern art, and would become a strong influence on the films of Alfred Hitchcock.

Many of those close to Hitchcock said he was very widely read and could talk with authority on matters of psychology, politics, and philosophy, as well as almost any field of the arts. Quite how much of Freud's work he read is hard to determine. Freudian ideas crop up in several of his films, but usually in a rather superficial way—he was, after all, making ninety-minute entertainments for mass audiences. But the notion that dreams can help us understand the inner child that is the unconscious mind resonated with him. Those early memories that he cited as the origins of his anxiety—itself a Freudian-sounding conceit—could equally be mistaken for dream recitals, similar to some of those logged and interpreted in Freud's case studies. The majority of Hitchcock films, for at least some portion, have a dreamlike quality, "oneiric," to use the term favored by the academic critics. Characters, such as those played by James Stewart in *Vertigo* and Cary Grant in *North by Northwest*, find themselves dropped into baffling, nightmarish circumstances, battling their way through a valley of the uncanny—another Freudian backdrop—hoping to put the world back on its axis. When Truffaut noted this, he asked Hitchcock whether this was because he had a lot of vivid dreams

of his own. As he tended to do when an interviewer encroached too close
to the perimeter wall, Hitchcock poured cold water on the topic. "Not too
much," he offered; "my dreams are very reasonable." By "reasonable"
he meant a mundane dream of the sort that a respectable person would
have; certainly no sex or violence like the dreams that haunt the characters in his films. Few who knew him would agree with that. About a year
after he'd made that remark to Truffaut, Hitchcock told a colleague that
he sometimes dreamed that his penis was made of crystal, which, to his
considerable distress, his wife repeatedly tried to smash.

In narrative terms also, dreams, daydreams, and hallucinations are
important to Hitchcock films. His fourth picture, *Downhill* (1927), features a sequence that he hoped would break the mold, depicting a dream
in "solid, unblurred images," vivid and intense rather than as something distant and opaque, as though the dream, although deeply odd,
felt somehow more real than the waking parts of the film. He aimed for
similar, discomfiting sharpness in *Spellbound* (1945), in which the psychiatrist Dr. Constance Petersen, played by Ingrid Bergman, uses dream
analysis to help Gregory Peck's character, John Brown, discover his real
identity and clear him of a murder charge. Hitchcock recruited Salvador
Dalí to design a dream sequence that would resemble one of his paintings in dynamic motion. After a close reading of the dream, Brown is
able to locate a violent, guilt-ridden childhood trauma that is the source
of his blocked memory. With the blockage cleared, his mental travails
are ended, he remembers that his real name is John Ballantyne, and he
realizes that he has been framed for a crime he didn't commit. As if by
magic, the spell has been broken, and the prince and his princess can
live happily ever after.

A similar ending is found in *Marnie* (1964), the third of a triptych of
Hitchcock films—the others being *Psycho* (1960) and *The Birds* (1963)—
that are built around a childhood trauma tucked away inside the mind of a
central character, a loss of innocence that leads them into violence, way-
wardness, and emotional retardation as adults. In *Marnie*, the root of the
eponymous character's kleptomania, compulsive lying, and, supposed,
sexual dysfunction is discovered in her nightmares. At the film's con-

Hitchcock terrorizes children in *The Birds*.

clusion, she dredges up a repressed childhood memory of the time she killed a man who was paying her mother for sex. As the long-repressed trauma comes flooding to the surface, Marnie physically regresses into her child self, cowering on the floor and yelping "I want my mama!" in the high-pitched voice of a little girl.

The role of Marnie is played by Tippi Hedren, who also starred as the flighty Melanie Daniels in *The Birds*. Just before the first major bird attack (at a children's birthday party), Melanie reveals to Mitch (Rod Taylor) that she is an abandoned child. "My mother?" she replies bitterly to Mitch's questions about her family, "don't waste your time! She ditched us when I was eleven." In the closing stages of the film, she is savagely attacked by a mass of birds, at which point Mitch's mother offers her the maternal affection she has craved for so long. In an earlier draft of the script, the point was really hammered home, as Melanie, like Marnie, regresses to childhood and calls out for her absent mother. In *Psycho*, Norman Bates relives his traumatic adolescent memory when he commits murder in the guise of his mother, "Norma," whom he killed in a fit of sexual jealousy.

Why Hitchcock's long-standing interest in the repressed child within should have occupied him so much in this trio of very dark films is unclear. One might speculate that serious health scares he and his wife, Alma, endured in the late 1950s concentrated his mind on his mortality and dragged up unresolved issues from his past. *Psycho*'s screenwriter, Joseph Stefano, apparently captivated his director at the start of their collaboration when he told Hitchcock that he was in therapy. "I would go to his office directly from the couch and tell him all about it," Stefano explained. "He was very interested and seemed delighted that I was, I guess, a different kind of animal than he'd worked with before."

Perhaps not entirely different; Hitchcock had previously worked very productively with Ben Hecht, the so-called "Shakespeare of Hollywood," who had written *Spellbound* and was also heavily interested in psychoanalysis, as indeed was the film's producer, David O. Selznick, who hired his own therapist, Dr. May E. Romm, to work as a consultant on the production. Stefano, however, was of a younger Hollywood generation for whom the ideas of psychoanalysis and its language were an integral part of their identity. During the writing of *Psycho*, Stefano happily divulged some remarkable truths about his relationship with his mother that informed the Bates's parent-child dynamic. "I said to Hitchcock one day: 'I could've killed my mother. There were times when I knew I was capable of killing her.'" Such talk gripped Hitchcock, in part because he couldn't imagine being so emotionally honest with anyone, including himself, and certainly not somebody he barely knew. As Stefano saw it, the child-

hood trauma that forces Norman into his murderous acts was not a con-
summated incestuous relationship with his mother as many believe, but
Mrs. Bates's sexual teasing of her son. "I saw his mother coming on to
him and then stopping him," said Stefano of the childhood trauma he
imagined on Norman's behalf.

More than once, Hitchcock observed that the breakthroughs that
Marnie Edgar and John Ballantyne achieve in his films had not happened to him in his own life. Although he had apparently identified
the traumatic childhood incidents that bequeathed him his fears—the
police-cell incident; the time he awoke to an empty house; the forbidding priests of his school days—he still broke out in a cold sweat when
he saw a policeman or heard something go bump in the night. The fairy-
tale logic of his films, of course, doesn't apply to the real world: locating trauma is the easy bit; the hard work comes in dealing with it. And,
although intrigued by the theories, he expressed doubt about the efficacy
of psychoanalysis. "I think I have enough silly hypotheses of my own
about myself, without listening to the silly hypotheses of other people,"
he told one acquaintance—though such dismissiveness may have been a
way of defending himself from searching psychoanalytical readings of
his darker films. In any case, one must be skeptical about the weight he
placed on those memories, even if one accepts their veracity, considering
the much more serious events that occurred in Hitchcock's youth about
which he said relatively little: the sudden death of his father, and London's cataclysmic experience of World War I.

He was fourteen when the war began, nineteen at its close. There's
barely a significant European or American artist of that generation who
wasn't irreversibly affected by it. Yet if Hitchcock ever spoke about his
thoughts and feelings on the outbreak of conflict in 1914, they don't
appear to have been recorded. It's possible he was unmoved; few had
any sense of the prolonged horrors ahead, and many in Europe at first
regarded the war as an intense jamboree of patriotism that could cleanse
and revitalize a continent stymied by the enervations of the modern age.
"Over by Christmas" is what the British are reputed to have told each
other about the war with Germany. If a teenage Hitchcock had any such

notions, he would have been swiftly disabused of them as casualties began to pile up. Then, on December 12, 1914, his father died of chronic emphysema. Alfred, at fifteen and only a month into his job at Henley's, was now pushed firmly into the adult world. Unlike the prison-cell experience, the emotional impact of his father's death was something Hitchcock never broached in public. The closest to a firsthand account we have appears in his authorized biography by John Russell Taylor, published two years before his death. Having been sought out by his brother, who broke the news to him, Hitchcock went to see his sister, Nellie, who blurted out, "Your father's dead, you know," which, Taylor reports, "gave him a surreal sense of dissociation," the kind of psychologically jarring moment Hitchcock would explore on film as an adult.

Within weeks of William Hitchcock's death, the war took a dramatic turn. Germany commenced its bombing raids on England, reaching London in May 1915. The gigantic zeppelins crept across the skyline like lethal black clouds. Londoners were mesmerized and petrified. Nobody had any frame of reference for an airborne war, let alone one that targeted innocent civilians on the ground. The first raid hit Hitchcock's home turf in the East End. Among the casualties were two children, fatally hit while walking home from the cinema. It was the start of three years of trauma and terror. The worst came on a bright, beautiful morning in June 1917, when Gotha bombers carpeted the city east to west, killing 162 civilians, including 18 infants at Upper North Street School in Poplar, half a mile from Hitchcock's home and even closer to his old engineering school. Wounded soldiers returning from the front became a familiar part of the cityscape, and in the war's final year, the influenza pandemic came with them. Sixteen thousand Londoners died of flu between September and December 1918, with the crowded east of the city worst affected.

There's no way Hitchcock couldn't have been shaken by the onslaught of total war on his doorstep. A historian of the conflict has written that "Londoners almost without exception were caught up body and soul in its maw. The war utterly dominated the city's life. It changed everything." Most damaging was not the physical destruction, but four years of "relentless disruption and accumulating strain, built up night after night," the very type of tortuous suspense and grinding anxiety that was the adult Hitchcock's stock in trade.

To interviewers, including Taylor, Hitchcock gave the impression that the war "did not impinge much on him" and that he was relatively unaffected by his father's death. This seems unlikely, especially for someone of Hitchcock's nervous disposition. The Hitchcock household had several narrow escapes, though Hitchcock recounted such incidents for laughs. Downplaying what must have been an utterly terrifying experience, he recalled coming back home one day in the aftermath of nearby bombing and artillery fire, to find his mother in a state of sheer panic in her bedroom, desperately throwing on her clothes over her nightgown. He reprised that memory as a comedy scene in the film *Murder!* of 1930, in which a woman attempts to dress hurriedly as word ripples down the street that a neighbor has been killed and the police are on the scene. *The Birds* also can be viewed as Hitchcock reliving the terror of the air raids: the indiscriminate targeting of children at school and at play; the Brenners recoiling in their home as the assault rains down; the groundbreaking aerial shot of the birds hovering high above the fiery carnage they have caused in the town below; Melanie, in Hitchcock's early draft, crying out for the comfort and protection of a parent who has abandoned her.

It's impossible to think that a man so beholden to anxiety wasn't deeply affected by the events of 1914 to 1918, entering the adult world as he lost his father and as his city was ravaged by an entirely new, utterly terrifying mode of warfare. The lasting impact that *Mary Rose* had on him, with its themes of dislocating death and youthful innocence shattered by inexplicable tragedy, suggests as much. It is surely more than coincidence that in 1964 he pressed ahead with his plans for adapting the play into a movie, immediately having finished a trio of films in which he had engaged with repressed childhood trauma. When viewed in this light, it makes sense that he swerved the topic of his war years, and instead repeatedly talked about his five minutes in a police cell as the source of his internal anguish. For a man who chose never to look too far inside himself, and who valued his "tidy mind," diverting his feelings of abandonment and arbitrary injustice into other, neater tales would have been eminently sensible—especially when those stories were so visually arresting, tailor-made for his public image as the master of suspense.

Childhood evoked strongly mixed emotions in Hitchcock. It was a confounding place of fear, insecurity, at times isolation, a place of the occluded and the unresolved. Simultaneously, it was the fount of his creativity, a time of play, excitement, novelty, and discovery. Children had uninhibited potential but were vulnerable and unpredictable, a cause of joy and anxiety. The duality was expressed in his telling of the prison-cell incident, in which he suggested he'd been punished for embarking on an intrepid adventure, following the nearby tram tracks to wherever they might lead. The legacies of those experiences never left him. As a man of sixty-three, he recorded an eleven-minute message from Stage 18 at Universal City in Los Angeles, for the benefit of a tiny film society in Westcliff, an Essex seaside resort he remembered from vacations as a boy. His decision to take time out of a crammed schedule to perform this act of kindness was "inspired by a touch of nostalgia," he explained with his customary blank expression. He reminisced about his youth, a time simultaneously close and distant, though he discouraged any attempt to work out just how long ago it had been. "Please don't speculate," he deadpanned; "I'm younger than I look."

2

THE MURDERER

A desperate, wretched love has pulled the girl into the water. From the shore, it looks as though she's making a threat on her own life, hoping that the man who spurned her will rush in, save her, and promise never to leave. For a moment, it seems her wish is granted. Seeing him wade out toward her, she beams and flings out her arms in expectation of a tender embrace. Then comes the violent twist. Holding her by the back of the head, his hands find their awful strength and push the girl under, until nothing but her hair and the fabric of her skirt move beneath the surface.

It was the summer of 1925, and Alfred Hitchcock had just committed his first murder, in his debut feature film, *The Pleasure Garden*, a melodrama about the love lives of two London showgirls. After beginning his full-time post at Famous Players-Lasky British in the spring of 1921, things happened fast for Hitchcock. He established himself at the company, which was based at Islington Studios in north London, and he used his spare time to draft outlines for his own scripts. There was an aborted attempt to make a film—*Number Thirteen* or *Mrs. Peabody*—with money scraped together from family, and he codirected a comedy short called *Always Tell Your Wife* when the intended director fell ill. At the studios, he also met Alma Reville, a young editor, who would eventually become his wife and chief collaborator.

When Famous Players-Lasky British folded, Hitchcock fell in with a group of young filmmakers at Islington, led by the producer Michael Balcon, who was impressed by the boy's "passion for films and his eagerness to learn." Originally engaged as assistant producer on a number of pictures, Hitchcock volunteered for everything: screenwriter, art director, costume supervisor. "I'm sure that if he never actually swept the floor at Islington he would have been ready and willing to do so," said Balcon.

In 1924, Balcon recruited Hitchcock for his new production company, Gainsborough Pictures, to work on two Anglo-German coproductions—*The Prude's Fall* and *The Blackguard*—directed by Graham Cutts at the Neubabelsberg film studios near Berlin, a hub of the German expressionist film movement, and where Hitchcock's ideas about the artistic dimensions of filmmaking were first shaped. During this time, he observed the director F. W. Murnau making *The Last Laugh*. This, Hitchcock said, was where he learned the rudiments of expressionist filmmaking: using the camera to tell a story without words, to capture the subjective emotional experience of a character, and to paint the screen with black pools and bright lights, an effect the German film theorist Lotte Eisner says represents "a twilight of the German soul, expressing itself in shadowy, enigmatic interiors, or in misty, insubstantial landscapes."

His own director proved less inspiring. Although some believe that Graham Cutts was also applying expressionist ideas to his work, Hitchcock maintained that Cutts knew little about directing, and he, Hitchcock, grew weary of having to cover for his boss's extramarital affairs that intruded on their working schedule. When Cutts walked out on *The Blackguard*, denouncing his "know-it-all son of a bitch" assistant, Balcon turned to the twenty-five-year-old Hitchcock to finish the picture, and soon after gave him the chance to direct a movie of his own.

The Pleasure Garden was filmed in Germany and northern Italy, and proved to be an object lesson in Murphy's Law. Equipment was mislaid; film stock was confiscated at customs; money to cover location expenses was stolen; actors absented themselves from crucial scenes—everything that could have gone wrong did go wrong. "I can smile about them today," Hitchcock said of the stresses, "but at the time they were ghastly."

Happily, the movie turned out just fine, full of stylistic flourishes he learned in Germany and preoccupations now considered definitively Hitchcockian: voyeurism, guilt, enchanting blondes—and murder. Over the next fifty years, he would dispatch victims in an ingenious array of horrific scenarios. There was a pre-dinner party garroting in a swanky Manhattan apartment, a knife hurled into the back of an international diplomat, and a shootout in a dingy London backstreet. On his word, women were slaughtered in the shower, pushed from a bell tower, hacked to pieces, and buried in flowerbeds; men were set alight, suffocated, and taken out for a little drive, never to be seen again. In Hitchcock's lethal universe, nowhere is safe; violence stalks factories, schools, and churches; bathrooms, bedrooms, and kitchens; windmills, motels, movie theaters—even the children's carousel at the local fairground. To Hitchcock, all life is in murder. If you want to crack the Hitchcock code, there's no better place to start than at the grisly end.

In any discussion of Hitchcock and his murders, there is a blood-spattered elephant in the room. The shower scene in *Psycho*—in which Marion Crane, played by Janet Leigh (and, from the bare neck down, Marli Renfro, her body double), is stabbed to death in a frenzied attack by Norman Bates—is an emblem of postwar popular culture, unceasingly referenced, parodied, and reinterpreted. The movie was born of Hitchcock's desire to captivate a younger generation brought up on television and rock and roll, and to meet the challenge of elevating the slasher genre to the heights of Hitchcockian brilliance. He had also noted, with envy, the critical acclaim that the French director Henri-Georges Clouzot had won for his film *Les Diaboliques* (1955), a psychological horror film with its own scenes of bathtub-bound violence. Clouzot had clearly been influenced by Hitchcock, yet his film was edgier than the Hitchcock of the mid-1950s, who was making Technicolor escapism with Cary Grant, James Stewart, and Grace Kelly. When Hitchcock's assistant Peggy Robertson handed him Robert Bloch's latest novel, *Psycho*, loosely based on the real-life crimes of the serial killer Ed Gein, she had an inkling that the strangeness of the book's violence, replete with cross-dressers and taboo sexual fetishes, would catch her boss's eye. She was right. Hitchcock was gripped by the novel, especially "the suddenness of the murder in the shower, coming, as it were, out of the blue."

On first viewing, many critics trashed the film, and expressed disbelief that Hitchcock could've wasted his talent on such gratuitousness. One ignored Hitchcock's pleas to keep the plot twists secret, saying he had a duty to warn anybody thinking of seeing the film that they would be confronted by "a rotting corpse in a shawl, a maniac in a wig, and that they are going to share the camera's loving preoccupation with the process of swabbing out the bath where Janet Leigh has been knifed." The sneering and shrieking of critics had no effect; *Psycho* was an instant hit, making a gargantuan profit on its $800,000 budget, which Hitchcock had financed himself after his studio of the time, Paramount, declined to fund such a risky project.

As *Psycho* broke box-office records and launched Hitchcock into a new sphere of cultural relevance, some raised questions about what kind of mind could have produced those fifty-two seconds of savagery. In conversation with Dr. Frederic Wertham, a psychiatrist who was alarmed by onscreen violence, Hitchcock insisted that poor Marion Crane was no different from Little Red Riding Hood, that other flaxen-haired damsel killed by a wolf in old ladies' clothing. Neither, Hitchcock swore, did the scene "reflect in any way whatsoever my own private life or my own private mind." Violence, anger, and conflict of any sort were anathema to him, he insisted. In fact, long before *Psycho*, he had expressed distaste for films that resort to "sadism, perversion, bestiality, and deformity" to elicit emotional responses from audiences, a tactic he condemned as "utterly wrong, being vicious and dangerous." Staff of his recalled a time in the 1960s when he stormed out of a projection room when a film that had been recommended to him featured an unexpected scene of animal cruelty, something he considered beyond the pale. Many of those who worked with him testified that his aversion to conflict was so great that he would go to remarkable lengths to avoid "causing a scene," a horror that could be added to his index of phobias. He told, with pride it seems, the story of how he responded when Ingrid Bergman lost her temper during the complex filming of *Under Capricorn* (1949): "I did what I always do when people start to argue. I just turned away and went home." Such tales were intended to evince his imperturbability; he told anyone who would listen—usually journalists—that he never lost his temper because he had no temper to lose. It wasn't true. Hitchcock's capacity for anger made itself apparent on any number of occasions, though it was generally stifled with fits of sulking and brooding. Flouncing away from arguments wasn't a sign of an even temper, but an inability to deal with complex emotions, whether his or other people's, that manifested itself throughout his life.

Frequently he claimed that he would love to make films that weren't edged in suspense and tethered by corpses, but his audience wouldn't allow it. He couldn't make a film of Cinderella, he said, because "people will immediately start looking for the corpse." Yet the notion that violence and murder were purely the by-product of his nine-to-five day as a filmmaker, no different to him than coal to a coal miner, is clearly untrue. Naturally, he had no designs on being a serial killer himself, but Hitchcock had a lifelong fascination with cruelty and violence that fueled his creativity.

Most of his understanding of violent crime, as with so much else in his life, came from reading, fantasizing, and silent observation. "I've spent so much of my life fascinated by crime and the administration of justice," he said in 1977. By fourteen, he was reading G. K. Chesterton and John Buchan, the cream of British crime writing, as well as "all the real-life crime stories I could get hold of." Over the years, he built something of a crime library and developed an in-depth knowledge of several notorious serial killers; he gave copies of relevant books to a number of his writers for inspiration, and to leading men when preparing to play murderers in his films. As a young man, he was also a frequent visitor to the public gallery of the Old Bailey, an extension of his innumerable trips to the theater and the cinema. "I would have liked to have been a criminal lawyer," he said. "Think of the opportunity I would have had to be a great man in court."

Several of his films feature characters who share his armchair enthusiasm for true-crime tales, and who, like Hitchcock, enjoy murder as escapist fantasy. In *Suspicion* (1941), there's Isobel, a bluff crime novelist who talks Cary Grant through the execution of the perfect murder; in *Shadow of a Doubt* (1943), Herb and Joe unwind at the end of the day with amiable chats about poisoning and bludgeoning, as others might talk about baseball or celebrity gossip. Hitchcock made a joke about the link between fictional murders and the inner desires of their creators in "Mr. Blanchard's Secret," an episode of the television series *Alfred Hitchcock Presents*, in which a sunny, suburban writer of murder mysteries expresses her thoughts about her latest victim: "Poor woman. Such a shame I had to kill her off that way. A psychiatrist would probably say I had some hidden homicidal tendencies. . . . Who knows, if I didn't get it off my chest by writing mystery stories I might end up committing a few murders myself."

Rather than expressing anything particular to his own psychology, Hitchcock tended to frame his interest in murder as an inevitable expression of his cultural heritage. As he explained in his conversation with Dr. Wertham, "Many great English literary figures have always interested themselves in crime. . . . The whole thing is examined on a very high plane. Now, this is indigenous, it seems to me, to the English." He believed there to be a "crime mystique in England, and it rubs off on everyone," evidenced by the ubiquity of violence in the English popular culture of his youth. As a boy he likely would have been exposed to the penny dreadfuls and half-penny periodicals, which conveyed gruesome stories of supposed real-life murder and malice to a readership of adolescent boys and young men.

The war brought devastating violence right up to Hitchcock's front step. Immediately after, there was a nationwide panic, nurtured by the popular press, about an apparent surge in everyday violence. "Much perturbation appears to have been caused among the public by the wave of crime which is reported to be sweeping over the country at the present time," ran one story in the *Guardian* in January 1920, which referred to "a series of particularly cruel and ghastly murders and violent robberies which have occurred during the last few weeks." This was the world in which Hitchcock began his movie career. Indeed, he claimed to have a

Hitchcock as victim and murderer, 1955.

personal link to Edith Thompson, one of Britain's most notorious murderers of the 1920s, from whose father he had taken dancing lessons. Thompson was executed in 1923 for manipulating her lover into murdering her husband, the type of strange, complex tale that absorbed Hitchcock. Her case received saturation news coverage at the time, though today her conviction is regarded as an outrageous miscarriage of justice.

Hitchcock believed that not only were the English—whom he often conflated with the British—powerfully drawn to murder, the nature of English violence was a locus of national identity and experience. The first talkie he made, *Blackmail*, features a memorable scene in which a family discusses news of a stabbing. One character is appalled at the revelation: "A good, clean, honest, whack over the head with a brick is one thing. There's something British about that. But knives? No, knives is not right." Hitchcock told the *New York Times* that unlike American murders, which tend toward dullness in their blunt brutality, murders in England reveal its people's understatement, politesse, and "an ingrained racial sense of drama," which he claimed one could trace back to the work of Shakespeare. American gangsters and professional killers with their clinical gunshot murders were of no interest to him because they were professional crooks; it was the fair-play ethics of amateur gentlemen murderers that made for the most gripping crimes. He explained that there was virtually no gun culture in Britain; as the police very rarely use them, "it's a matter of courtesy that the criminals don't." Gun murders are not unknown to Hitchcock films—*The Man Who Knew Too Much* (1934) climaxes with a lengthy gunfight—but are certainly in the minority. Even in *North by Northwest*, when Eve (Eva Marie Saint) appears to shoot Roger O. Thornhill (Cary Grant) dead, it turns out to have been a ruse, her gun loaded with blanks. In the United States, said Hitchcock, "people get blasted all over the place. I prefer my own style."

By his "own style" he meant death by poison and noose, or shoved from the top of a building, in the spirit of his favorite English murders, which were strange, eccentric cases revealing undercurrents of sex, class, and churning, repressed emotions in the lives of outwardly respectable people, often Londoners from social backgrounds similar to his and who shared his emotional reserve. There was the case of Dr. Crippen, which featured adultery and cross-dressing, and that of John Christie, a fantasist and necrophiliac who preyed on young women at 10 Rillington Place, the quiet home he shared with his wife. Hitchcock's favorite, as he mentioned on many occasions, was that of Edwin Bartlett, a grocer from London (an obvious parallel to his own life) who died on New Year's Eve in 1885 from chloroform poisoning. Bartlett's beautiful young wife, Adelaide, was arrested on suspicion of murder, and during her trial the details of a scandalous affair, encouraged by Bartlett, between Adelaide and a local clergyman became public. In a final otherworldly twist, Adelaide was acquitted, because medical experts had no idea how the chloroform could have been administered without causing severe burns to the victim's throat.

The Bartlett case was obviously tied up with things that could not otherwise be discussed in polite society, which raises the question of what Hitchcock—and other English people—talked about when he talked about murder. First, the act of killing provided a vehicle with which to approach taboo subjects of sex. Young viewers today might still find the shower scene in *Psycho* disturbing, but it's unlikely they'd be startled by the film's opening scene in which John Gavin and Janet Leigh are seen in a hotel room, not entirely clothed. In 1960, the year of *Psycho*'s release, it caused almost as much uproar as the shower scene. The *New York Times* film critic Bosley Crowther wrote Hitchcock to ask for an explanation of why *Psycho* began with such an explicit scene, for an article Crowther was writing on "the evident trend towards greater candor about sex in our Hollywood films." Allusions to sex in the moment of death, and vice versa, can be found in many of Hitchcock's films, *Psycho* included. In *Dial M for Murder* (1954), Grace Kelly's character is attacked by a man who has been coerced into killing her on behalf of her jealous husband. Pinned to a desk with her assailant on top of her, she writhes to free herself, before grabbing a pair of scissors and stabbing him in the back. If the audience hadn't already been privy to the murder plot, it would be possible to mistake the attack for an attempted rape. Devotees of the canon would also recognize a nod to *Blackmail*, in which a young woman uses a knife to fight off a rapist. Other Hitchcock murders are loaded with associations with taboo sexual acts: asphyxiation; bondage; homosexuality; transvestitism; incest. As with murder, these were all things that held Hitchcock rapt, but of which he had no—or very little—firsthand experience.

Hitchcock was far from the only English cultural figure of his generation to use murder as a means of exploring a particular idea of Englishness. In 1927, the year that Hitchcock's first movies received widespread release in the UK, Miss Marple made her debut in the decorous pages of *The Royal Magazine*. Sweet old ladies sleuthing in manor houses and rural parsonages was exactly the kind of atmosphere George Orwell evoked in his essays "Decline of the English Murder" and "Raffles and Miss Blandish," in which he cited traditionally "English" homicides—inspired by class resentments and sexual frustration, carried out with good manners and fast-acting poison—as markers of a distinctive sense of Englishness that was being silenced by raucous Americans. From the early to mid-twentieth century, murder was used by mainstream English writers and artists as a statement of their cultural identity. It was comforting, perhaps, for them to think that England's sturdy middle classes could take even the most diabolical manifestations of modern vulgarity and make them genteel, adhering to the manners of an increasingly distant golden age, before the impact of modern America began to make itself felt. Naturally, this reverie of English gentility obscured a more brutal reality. Orwell conceded that "within living memory . . . kicking your wife to death" could have been called "a typically English crime," the kind of sudden blaze of domestic rage to which Hitchcock was also drawn.

Orwell thought that England's "great period in murder, our Elizabethan period, so to speak, seems to have been between roughly 1850 and 1925," the very year, coincidentally, that Hitchcock committed his first murder to celluloid. Hitchcock's killings fused the two things that Orwell considered opposites. With his films of the twenties and thirties he used German art and Hollywood sizzle to hurl the tradition of English murder into the new age of speed, machines, and sensation. Adopting the language of modernist artists of the era, many of whom extolled violence and disruption as a cultural force, he argued that the violence and

peril he put on screen were not desensitizing his audiences but recon-
necting them with the raw reality of human existence. "I am out to give
the public a good healthy mental 'shake-up,'" he said, without which
modern societies "grow sluggish and jellified . . . our civilization has so
screened and sheltered us that it isn't practicable to experience sufficient
thrills at firsthand." In a reversal of the predominant logic of our own
times, Hitchcock was arguing that the best way to live in the moment was
to spend more time in the dark, staring at a screen.

Hitchcock wanted his film murders to affect viewers in the same
way that reading about his favorite domestic murderers had always
affected him, disrupting the humdrum of middle-class daily life. This
is evident in his American work, too, in which a phalanx of fatally char-
ismatic men from respectable backgrounds seek to reshape the world in
their own vision, using murder as their tool. "I certainly admire people who do things," says Robert Walker as Bruno in *Strangers on a Train*
(1951) while plotting a murderous scheme that he thinks will elevate him
above ordinary people. Guy, a handsome tennis player, expresses horror
at Bruno's suggestion that they each commit a murder on behalf of the
other, causing Bruno to plead "what is a life or two, Guy? Some people
are better off dead." When Joseph Cotten was struggling to get inside his
serial killer character in *Shadow of a Doubt*, Hitchcock said it was simple: "To him, the elimination of his widows is a dedication, an important
sociological contribution to civilization. Remember, when John Wilkes
Booth jumped to the stage in Ford's Theatre after firing that fatal shot, he
was enormously disappointed not to receive a standing ovation." Hitchcock may have been appalled by real-life violence, but he understood the
urge to be publicly known for one's audacious brilliance, to subvert reality, with an audience gasping in thrilled disbelief.

As an artistic gesture, the shower scene echoed an event sixty-six years
earlier, when Aubrey Beardsley's illustrations of Oscar Wilde's play
Salomé were published, and the world got its first shocking glimpse of
John the Baptist's severed head dripping thick ropes of black blood onto

the milk-white page. Fittingly, in Robert Bloch's novel, the shower murder isn't a frenzy of stabbing as it is in the film, but a decapitation, the victim's head sliced off by the blade of Bates's butcher knife.

Wilde and Beardsley were prominent among a generation of late nineteenth-century artists who rejected realistic depictions of the natural world in favor of fantasies, dreams, and nightmares, locating beauty in disorder and disharmony. Their work fed the shadows and monsters of German expressionist cinema, which in turn had a profound impact on Hitchcock's films. Hitchcock publicly acknowledged the debt. He said that in his youth he had been so taken with symbolism, the movement of painters that included Paul Gaugin and Gustav Klimt, that their canvases spilled into his dreams. The aestheticism of Wilde, itself directly influenced by symbolism, had a similarly strong impact. *The Picture of Dorian Gray* was one of Hitchcock's favorite novels, and Wilde's dry witticisms, logical inversions, and agreeable iconoclasm all manifest themselves in Hitchcock's work.

The evidence of Wilde's influence seems to have been in Harold Hayes's mind when he wrote to Hitchcock a few months after the release of *Psycho*, asking for a contribution from Hitchcock that would unpack for his readers "those aspects of your technique which give violence a certain sophistication in this day and age" for a forthcoming edition of *Esquire* magazine. Under Hayes's guidance, *Esquire* would become an important voice in the sixties, tapping into the cultural ferment of that decade, and he apparently recognized earlier than most critics that *Psycho* was more than a scary movie. It was, he believed, a marvelous example of Hitchcock's elevated depictions of violence in a world after Auschwitz and Hiroshima; "people have undergone so much in the past 30 years that it takes a particular kind of genius today to shock them at all." The resulting article provided Hitchcock's tips for how to conduct the perfectly sophisticated murder, in distinctly Wildean terms, ironic and playfully goading. On selecting a victim, Hitchcock suggests that "for amusement, choose from among the pillars of the community; for whimsey, have a go at The Common Man."

In certain ways, Hayes was surely right. *Psycho* was the climax of a creative life spent exploring imaginative, novel, often humorous depictions of cruelty, domination, and obsession. Even so, it seems wrong to cite *Psycho* as the apotheosis of Hitchcock's "sophistication." Though Hitchcock was adamant that the shower scene was no more violent than any of his other murders because it was impressionistic, it was a disingenuous view. The whole point had been to film something that the viewer experienced as the most shocking act of bloodshed; the fact that this end was achieved by technical ingenuity is neither here nor there. On top of the terror and agony that Marion Crane suffers, she is humiliated, slaughtered while defenseless and naked, and done so in a way that is also meant to mock the audience. We've spent forty minutes looking at the world through her eyes, listening to her thoughts, feeling her anxiety, and hoping that she'll somehow get away with her theft of forty thousand dollars that began the whole story. We thought we were with her for the long haul—and suddenly she's butchered and tossed away like the carcass of a Christmas turkey. The still image of Leigh's screaming face, her wet hair stuck slick to her head, is a spectacle of horror perpetrated for its own sake, exhilarating but awful. David Thomson writes of "the moment of *Psycho*," how the movie, and especially that one infamous scene, announced the arrival of a thing called "the sixties," intent on raising hell and undermining truths. *Psycho*, he argues, presaged the Zapruder tape of Kennedy's assassination, and the Vietnam War on the nightly news, or at least gave us a visual point of reference to help us absorb the shock of the footage. By extension, one can see it as the prelude to the even more horrifying screen violence of recent years, not just the gorefests of modern horror movies but also the filmed executions by terrorists literate in Western popular culture. No matter how beautifully lit, magnificently scored, and expertly edited—and *Psycho* is all those things—the shower scene isn't a work of sophistication, it's Hitchcock trolling all those he'd spent decades convincing that even murder could be "art"—beautiful, charming, harmonious. Perhaps the shower scene belonged more to the 1970s than the 1960s; anticipating a future generation of Londoners, it was a punk gesture, gleeful in its creative act of destruction.

The world in which Hitchcock grew up had its own "moment of *Psy-*

cho" a decade before his birth, when Jack the Ripper established himself as a defining piece of East End mythology. When given the opportunity to select a story to film for his third movie, Hitchcock chose *The Lodger*, a 1913 novel by Marie Belloc Lowndes, based on the Ripper murders, which had previously been adapted into a stage play that Hitchcock saw as a teenager. The movie—*The Lodger: A Story of the London Fog*, about a young man who is mistakenly identified as a serial killer whose victims are all blonde women—was a huge success with audiences and critics; it was the first great stride on Hitchcock's path to stardom. The lasting afterglow of this triumph was perhaps part of the reason why Hitchcock described *The Lodger* as his "first good film" and "the first time I exercised my style. In truth, you might almost say that *The Lodger* was my first picture." Its numerous similarities with *Psycho* are worth noting. The action in both is catalyzed by a mysterious outsider in search of a hideaway; both balance shocking horror with dark comedy, shot in a way that evokes the unreal atmosphere of German expressionism. Both were also based on novelized interpretations of real killers who committed depraved crimes against women. In *The Lodger*, the murderer is a cloaked figure known only as the Avenger, though partly because of changes to the script insisted on by the film's producers, his identity is never revealed, meaning it's never specified what he's avenging—it could be read as simply a howl against the existence of females who remind him of his crippling inadequacies, in anticipation of Norman Bates, the original incel, and a precursor to Joaquin Phoenix's Joker.

Some believe that through these films Hitchcock was revealing his own torments and dark fantasies. Certainly, he explored submission and domination in his work, and found in moviemaking ways of controlling beautiful young women, which excited him. To Truffaut he mentioned the sadomasochistic connotations that accompany the many handcuffs in his movies, and told of his interest in the various instruments of torture, violence, and restraint he had seen at the Vice Museum in Paris. Strangulation appears in several Hitchcock films, and he posed for various photos with his hands clasped around a female throat, and sometimes his own.

However, the common denominator among Hitchcock's murderers isn't their victims—who are not all women—but male destructiveness, an emotional aberrance that Hitchcock was attuned to, and perhaps felt inside himself, but never truly understood. His murderers hit out at women, but also at other men, a government, or civilization as a whole. Norman Bates's rage tumbles out in explosions of ham-fisted brutality, whereas the Avenger is presented as a fiendishly brilliant criminal with the power to haunt and terrorize an entire city.

Murder as a twisted expression of artistic flair was something Hitchcock repeatedly addressed. "All murderers regard their work as a fine art," he explained, half-jokingly. "The better ones, I mean." The reference to murder "as a fine art" was one Hitchcock made often; it derives from Thomas De Quincey's satirical essay of 1827, "On Murder Considered as One of the Fine Arts," an aesthete's ironically disinterested appreciation of the act of killing, which outlines the ways in which a murder can be beautiful, an idea Hitchcock borrowed in his "Sophistication of Violence" piece for *Esquire*. De Quincey had a deep obsession with the serial killer John Williams, whose slaughter of seven people in twelve days in the East End of London was an early nineteenth-century precursor of the Ripper. Williams's crimes also inspired De Quincey's gothic tale "The Avenger," the name given to Belloc Lowndes's, then Hitchcock's, murderer in *The Lodger*. "On Murder Considered as One of the Fine Arts" had a sizable impact on subsequent generations of British writers, not only in terms of its urbane, acrid irony but also in cementing a cultural association between murder and artistic brilliance.

In Jack the Ripper's day, popular newspapers blurred the lines between fact and fiction as they cast the Ripper as the archetype of a new cultural figure: a genius twisted by the malevolence of the modern city. One mass-market publication described him as "another Hyde," as though either Robert Louis Stevenson's character from *The Strange Case of Dr Jekyll and Mr Hyde* had been flesh and blood, or the Ripper was a work of spine-chilling fiction. Such reporting promoted rumors that the Ripper was Richard Mansfield, the American actor who at that moment was terrifying West End audiences in a stage production of *Jekyll and*

Hyde. A number of other artists have been named as suspects over the last century. In 2002 and 2017, the novelist Patricia Cornwell published books claiming that the Ripper was Walter Sickert, one of England's most important early modernist painters and a member of the influential Camden Town Group. Hitchcock would have been intrigued to read Cornwell's theories; at some point, he bought one of Sickert's *Camden Town Murder* paintings, a series of melancholy depictions of the murder of Emily Dimmock, a London prostitute who had her throat slit by a customer, on her bed, in 1907. Hitchcock's homes were generously decorated with art; this piece hung on a bedroom wall.

The Lodger rebooted East London's murderer-as-artist tradition for the 1920s, and for the new medium of cinema. The first eight minutes of the film are among the most arresting Hitchcock ever made, and perhaps the highlight of his nine silent films. It begins, naturally, with a murder. The opening shot is a close-up of a woman's face, her mouth wide open in a silent scream in the moment of her demise, foreshadowing that famous image of Janet Leigh in *Psycho*. A montage quickly puts us in a time and place, as police officers arrive on the scene and a horrified witness gives her description of the murderer. Nearly a hundred years later, it feels urgently familiar. A crowd gathers; rumors take flight; sick jokes spread within minutes of the corpse hitting the ground. Reporters scramble, and we track the news as it goes viral through the buzz of the latest technology. "MURDER wet from the presses," read the intertitles, "MURDER hot on the aerial."

Like any good murderer who creeps around popular culture, the Avenger leaves a calling card on the person of each of his victims. And, like any good modern artist, the card has a signature flourish: a single triangle, which is incorporated into the design of the film's intertitles and reflects the tense love triangle between Daisy, her family's mysterious lodger, and Daisy's policeman boyfriend, who suspects the lodger of being the murderer. It's as though the evil genius whose killing spree has brought us here is the same as the one behind the camera. The suggestion is reinforced as a man in a newspaper office leans into a telephone. This is Hitchcock in his first cameo, reporting that the Avenger

The murder of an innocent young blonde woman that opens *The Lodger*.

has claimed his seventh victim. He asserted that his screen debut arose simply because there was nobody else to play the role, and in time the tradition of his cameos became part superstition, part running joke. Whether that's quite accurate is debatable. Nevertheless, his appearance in *The Lodger* gives us another premonition of *Psycho*, this time of the publicity campaign in which he took center stage, using his face, voice, and body to disperse the message about his latest unhinged killer.

The link between murder and creativity was one Hitchcock played with for the rest of his career. Cinemas, music halls, performances of ballet and symphonies, are all sites of Hitchcock murders. Sometimes

Janet Leigh in the shower scene from *Psycho*.

the killers, like Hitchcock himself, are those who see their whole campaign of violence in their head long before its execution, planning it with joyful meticulousness. Other times, they are performers, for whom role-playing, disguise, and transformation are their modus operandi. *Young and Innocent* (1937), a lesser-known Hitchcock film, is compulsory watching for any cinephile if only for the astonishing shot—adapted a decade later for a more famous sequence in *Notorious* (1946)—that takes the audience from the back of a large room right into the face of a jazz drummer, a white man in blackface whom the audience, but not the other characters, now realizes is the murderer we've all been searching for. Knowing that his pursuers are closing in, his anxiety gets the better of him: he loses his rhythm, his eyes begin to twitch, sweat erodes his face paint. His disguise ruined, he's apprehended, given away by his own guilty conscience.

Hitchcock's playful parallels between artists and murderers continue to hold our attention. In 2020, his fantastically silly album of easy listening, *Alfred Hitchcock Presents Music to Be Murdered By*, made a return in the form of Eminem's *Music to Be Murdered By*, which references Hitchcock in its concept, on its cover, and in numerous samples of his voice. Speaking on his original 1958 LP, Hitchcock says that the record is intended for thousands of frustrated members of his television audience: "The program seems to have inspired them to murder, but did not furnish the proper atmosphere for it." Hitchcock's album was released before *Psycho*, but Eminem's is unquestionably a post–shower scene record, his vitriolic rhymes intended to lacerate and outrage. That Eminem sees in Hitchcock—"the master, Uncle Alfred," as he refers to him—a kindred soul is not as surprising as it might seem. Both have been accused of crude misogyny and gratuitous invocations of violence that could corrupt impressionable audiences; both insist it's all humor, hyperbole, and role-play, lost on the po-faced and literal-minded. From De Quincey to Hitchcock to Eminem, the art of murder continues to inspire the most incongruous miscreants.

The dominating power of violence was made clear to Hitchcock throughout his life: in the popular culture of the communities in which he was raised, during the savage war in which he came of age, and in the conflagration that stirred just as he established himself as one of the world's greatest filmmakers.

Between 1934 and 1938, Hitchcock released five pictures that tapped into the violence and menace rippling through Europe, a world detached from its moorings. *The Man Who Knew Too Much*, *The 39 Steps* (1935), *Secret*

Agent (1936), *Sabotage*, and *The Lady Vanishes* (1938) were breakthrough pictures for Hitchcock, the first of the spy adventures after which many of his immortal Hollywood films would follow. "My parents were not political," confirms Hitchcock's daughter, Patricia, but that clutch of films reveals that while Hitchcock may never have been interested in ideology or party politics, he was interested in power, and the means by which people use it against others.

Shortly after the release of *The Lady Vanishes*—one of the great Hitchcock movies of romance and espionage set amid the creep of fascism in Central Europe—he explained that his recent work had been fantastical because his desire to show "violent things" could be done only through heightened fiction. The previous decade or so had been a febrile time; Hitchcock had been motivated to capture the "forcefulness and violence" of that atmosphere. When the General Strike of 1926 put tanks on the streets of London, Hitchcock apparently tried to make a film about it. He wanted to re-create "fistfights between strikers and undergraduates, pickets, and all the authentic drama," but producers told him that such explicitness would never make it past the censors. Much the same thing happened when filming *The Man Who Knew Too Much*. When the Home Office learned of Hitchcock's plans to film a siege at the film's climax, Hitchcock was told he could not show the militia on the streets and ordinary houses "surrounded by machine guns. All that I was allowed to do was depict the policemen being handed rifles and shown how to use them."

In September 1939, Britain declared war on Nazi Germany, by which time Hitchcock and family had begun a new life in Hollywood. From the outbreak of hostilities, Hitchcock felt compelled to lend his talents to the war effort. "I was both overweight and overage for military service. I knew that if I did nothing I'd regret it for the rest of my life." On and off for five years, he worked quietly but seriously on several projects designed to support the cause of US intervention and raise the morale of those back home in Britain. Among a community of Brits in Hollywood, he was heavily involved in the development of a propaganda film called *Forever and a Day* (begun in early 1940, eventually completed in 1943), and reedited two docudramas for the American market, *Men of the Lightship* (1940) and *Target for Tonight* (1941), the former about the Nazi bombardment of British installations in the North Sea, the latter about British bombing raids of Germany. American distributors had refused to handle the films as originally cut, considering them far too parochial and pedestrian for American audiences. Displaying his native understanding of popular taste, Hitchcock made both snappier, and less insularly British, and, according to one historian, they became the most profitable of all government-sponsored war films released within the first four years of the conflict. Between December 1943 and February 1944, he then wrote, produced, directed, and edited two French-language films, *Bon Voyage* and *Aventure Malgache*, both in praise of the French Resistance. At only twenty-six minutes long, and made on a tiny budget, *Bon Voyage* has a certain similarity to the *Alfred Hitchcock Presents* episodes, in that it is littered with false memories and mistaken identities, lots of tightly framed close-ups, and not an ounce of narrative fat. Contrary to later reports, the film was shown to the French public, and appears to have been well received. *Aventure Malgache* was a different story. "We realized that the Free French were very divided against one another," Hitchcock explained, and it was these "inner conflicts" around which he decided to spin the film. With nuanced characters and moral gray areas, the atmosphere was pure Hitchcock—but bad propaganda. Failing to tell a simple story about the heroic French people and the dastardly enemy, the film was suppressed for decades.

As the war rolled toward its end, Hitchcock was approached by his friend, the British producer Sidney Bernstein, to help shape the final reels of a film Bernstein was making for the British Ministry of Information, in which there would be no space for ambiguity or playfulness: a documentary about what had taken place inside the Nazi concentration camps. In June 1945, Hitchcock checked in at Claridge's hotel in London, ready to host several weeks of meetings with two writers, Richard Crossman and Colin Wills, and an editor named Peter Tanner, with whom he crafted the most damning testimony of Nazi atrocities, based on hours of raw footage from Dachau and Buchenwald. Hitchcock's involvement in the film was known about during his lifetime, but he refused to discuss it in any depth.

Originally designed to educate the public about the extent of the Third Reich's crimes, the film was ultimately shelved, unfinished. So horrific was its content that the governments of the United States, Britain, and France agreed that its impact on public sentiment may have detracted from the aims of the Marshall Plan. Better to build a new Germany, it was felt, than wallow in the ashes of the old one. Some of the footage was used as evidence at the Nuremberg trials, but after that the film was removed from public sight. In 1985, five years after Hitchcock's death, it briefly reemerged when PBS screened the unfinished portions of it in the documentary *Frontline: Memory of the Camps*. Only in 2014 was the film finally completed, restored, and screened, when it played at the Berlin Film Festival under the original and appropriately sober title, *German Concentration Camps Factual Survey*.

Given the glee with which Hitchcock put people's lives in danger on screen, simply, as he claimed, to thrill his audience, recruiting him to be the guiding hand on a serious testament to genocidal depravity might seem odd. But Sidney Bernstein, who had known Hitchcock since 1925, "thought he, a brilliant man, would have some ideas how we could tie it all together, and he had." Hitchcock was taken by the contrast of the horrifying footage from the camps and that of the tranquil, bucolic towns in the vicinity. He suggested they use simple maps to illustrate how ordinary life ran along with human slaughter on its doorstep. Peter Tanner, the film's editor, credited Hitchcock's understanding of the emotional impact of film technique as having a real bearing on his work. Hitchcock, said Tanner, "was very careful to try to get material which could not possibly be seen to be faked in any way," making extensive use of long takes that could be displayed without cuts. Likewise, Hitchcock also urged that other parts should rely on montage. In one section of the film that Hitchcock helped to structure, we are shown unbearable images of body parts, and piles of personal possessions. The sight of mounds of clothing, robbed of their owners, transforms everyday objects into symbols of true evil. As Jean-Louis Comolli has observed, the "juxtapo-

sition of what is familiar with what is horrible is one of the great Hitchcock themes."

At one point in the section of the film on which Hitchcock worked, the
camera takes us to the threshold of a room with a sign above the doorway:
"BRAUSEBAD," German for "shower bath." At first sight, it looks like a
bathroom, albeit functional and forbidding. Once inside, the brilliant
white of the room is draped by sinister dark shadows. Most viewers today,
familiar with film images of gas chambers in Nazi concentration camps,
will instantly recognize the deception that Hitchcock and his colleagues
are revealing to us. The apertures on the ceiling are not shower heads,
but vents for poison gas. This is not a place of cleansing, but of murder.

Once seen, the visual rhyme with the shower scene from *Psycho*,
as profane as it might appear, is difficult to dislodge from one's mind.
Picture that moment when Hitchcock's camera looks up directly into
the shower head, the water pouring onto Marion's face and chest. For a
moment she looks relaxed, having made up her mind to hand back the
money she stole and return to being the good, honest person we all know
her to be. From nowhere, she is overwhelmed by a force of inexplicable
depravity. Within seconds, she lies dead, destined for an unmarked grave.

In 1965, the critic Robin Wood—who, at the time, had never seen
the camp footage—wondered whether the experience of working on the
documentary had affected Hitchcock's most famous film. "One cannot
contemplate the camps without confronting two aspects of their horror:
the utter helplessness of and innocence of the victims, and the fact that
human beings, whose potentialities all of us in some measure share, were
their tormenters and butchers. . . . *Psycho* is founded on, precisely, these
twin horrors." If *Psycho* had been influenced by the images he spent days
poring over, Hitchcock didn't say. He may not even have been conscious
of it. Peter Bogdanovich recounts the time in the 1960s when he asked
Hitchcock about a scene in his Cold War thriller *Torn Curtain* (1966)
in which Paul Newman and an East German housewife commit the
remarkably slow, drawn-out murder of a Stasi security agent, Gromek,
played by Wolfgang Kieling. Newman and his accomplice wrestle with
Gromek, stab him, and hit him with a shovel, but he clings, Rasputin-

like, to life. It isn't until they drag him across the floor and hold his head in a gas oven that he dies. Bogdanovich asked Hitchcock whether this was an intentional allusion to the gas chambers of the Holocaust. "He seemed genuinely surprised and shook his head no," but a few years later Bogdanovich saw Hitchcock on a television program, where he "quite seriously and at some length explained the symbolism of this murder sequence and how it related to the Germans' gassings of the Jews." This, presumably, was the show in which Hitchcock said of Gromek's murder, "here we are back at Auschwitz again and the gas ovens. The world today is full of brutality."

Perhaps Hitchcock had been keeping something back from Bog-danovich, or perhaps once the possible link had been revealed to him, he came to see its truth. Gimlet-eyed in all things, Hitchcock was always open to suggestion. It was Jane Sloan who once described him as a "sponge, eager to adapt the point of view that would sell, and open to any idea that seemed good, insistent only that it fit his design." Though impossible to prove, it is not at all hard to believe that knitting together the most disturbing real-life footage of human depravity ever captured had, consciously or not, shaped Hitchcock's feel for his own depictions of murder. The Wildean abstractions of art and sophistication had been superseded by the viciousness of the modern world. Whatever the case, the shower scene had announced a new era. Not long after *Psycho*, the American Red Cross approached Hitchcock to do a knowing rehash of the film's trailer for a public service spot in which he would walk around an ordinary home and point out the lethal horrors that lurk in every room—especially the bathroom. Within the blink of an eye, the transgressive violence of *Psycho* had become part of the fabric of American life. Vio-lence and nudity were taking on new roles in our shared existence. There was no going back for any of us, Hitchcock included.

Over the Christmas holidays of 1969, the BBC treated prime-time viewers to an hour of Hitchcock on his favorite subjects: suspense, sex, movies, and murder. It was a recording of Hitchcock's interview with

Bryan Forbes, a fellow English director, before an audience at Britain's National Film Theatre. For much of the evening, Hitchcock had his audience in stitches, his answers capped with double entendres and twinkly eyed, ironic understatement. There was even laughter when the scene of Gromek's murder was played. One audience member, however, struggled to find the humor, and challenged the "nauseating . . . stomachturning . . . unnecessarily tasteless" manner of Gromek's protracted death. Hitchcock replied, "I would say the demonstration of the scene is intended to show how difficult it is to kill a man. Because it is a messy business, it is a horrible business."

In years to come, numerous young directors defended their depictions of murder in precisely the same terms. Sam Peckinpah said that *The Wild Bunch* (1969) was his attempt to counter the Hollywood tradition in which "people die without suffering and violence provokes no pain." After *Torn Curtain*, Hitchcock had one graphic murder left in him, when Barry Foster's charming psychopath is seen to rape and murder Barbara Leigh-Hunt's character, Brenda, in *Frenzy* (1972), a seventies reprisal of *The Lodger*, tying together the two ends of the Hitchcock murder trail, the fantastical legend of the Ripper, and the disgusting reality of his crimes. The scene took three days to shoot and was difficult for both Leigh-Hunt and Foster. "Just another day and a half and we'll be through with this," they said to each other at the halfway point. In the shot that completes their struggle, Foster was struck by the sight of Leigh-Hunt posing dead with her tongue lolling out of her mouth, just as Hitchcock had directed: "the effect is genuinely horrendous. Hitch did experiment with having an extremely close lens at her mouth, getting through makeup, saliva, and blood. Hitch, I think, was trying to plumb the ultimate in horror there." In the practice of the fine art of murder, there is always some fresh hell to be rent from the murky depths of a brilliant imagination.

3

THE AUTEUR

*T**he Lodger* catapulted Hitchcock to a level of public notice that no other British director enjoyed. Two more films produced by Michael Balcon followed—*Downhill* and *Easy Virtue* (1927)—after which the bright young thing of British cinema was lured to British International Pictures (BIP) by John Maxwell's promise of superior resources and a hefty pay rise. At £13,000 per year, Hitchcock was the best paid director in Britain.

None of the first four movies he made at BIP had the strange, compelling power of *The Lodger*, though each explored something that Hitchcock would appropriate as part of his house style—the drama of live spectacle in *The Ring* (1927), the parochial social comedy of *The Farmer's Wife* (1928), the willful child and moralizing parent in *Champagne* (1928), the themes of guilt, shame, and pariahdom of *The Manxman* (1929). Each also gave Hitchcock the opportunity to try out ingenious trick shots and inventive ways of photographing a scene, every little flourish a moving trademark for the man audiences could not see but whose presence was constant and unavoidable.

In 1929, his silent career ended with the release of *Blackmail*, a talkie about the traumatic fallout of an attempted rape. It would prove to be his best, and most important, film since *The Lodger*, and its production at Elstree Studios was graced by a visit from the Duke and Duchess of York, the future king and queen. Ronald Neame, the assistant cameraman on the film, remembered vividly how the event had been a source of appre-

hension for everyone on set—everyone, that is, except Hitchcock. When
Neame had worked with Noël Coward at another film studio at the time
of a royal visit, Coward drilled his crew on protocol and etiquette, "but
Hitch didn't have any of that kind of thing." When the duke and duchess
watched a scene being filmed, they were both keen to explore the mirac-
ulous technology of talking, moving pictures. Hitchcock was happy
to oblige but didn't stand on ceremony. "I saw Hitchcock pull her [the
duchess], literally pull her hat off and give her the headphones, which he
then put on her head." Manhandling a duchess was, to put it mildly, not
the done thing. The message was unavoidable: even when in the presence of royalty, his set was his kingdom. A Hitchcock film was Hitchcock's creation.

Before the mid-1950s, the idea that Alfred Hitchcock was a great artist
was as alien to those who wrote about art as it was to those who spent every
Saturday night at the movies. Even Hitchcock disliked public discussion
of his films as art, especially once he had become a fixture in Hollywood.
"I really hate the word artistic," he remarked in 1952, explaining that his
job was to balance an array of competing commercial concerns—the star
system, audience expectations, the nit-picking of po-faced censors—
cannily enough to make a hit of which one could be proud. "I have too
much conscience to take a million dollars and make a film that would
please only me and the critics," he insisted.

The way the world thought about Hitchcock—and, to a degree, the way
Hitchcock thought about himself—began to change thanks to a group of
young French critics affiliated with the film journal *Cahiers du Cinéma*.
They identified Hitchcock as an embodiment of what we now refer to as
the "auteur theory," a reading of cinematic production that stresses the
centrality of a director's creative vision in the making of a film. Hitchcock, it was argued, didn't simply direct his films, he authored them.
Moreover, his authorship was so rich, innovative, and distinctive that he
was more than a Hollywood hit-maker; he was a bona-fide artist.

His first encounters with the French critics caused surprise and not a little confusion on both sides. At a radiant flower market in Nice in 1954, the founder of *Cahiers*, André Bazin, was permitted to interview Hitchcock during a break in the filming of *To Catch a Thief* (1955). When Bazin floated questions about the themes, symbols, and meanings of his films, Hitchcock equivocated, partly because he disliked being entirely frank with a journalist when he could tantalize and dissemble, partly because he was genuinely nonplussed by Bazin's detailed analysis. For his part, Bazin, always less enthusiastic about Hitchcock's work than many of his colleagues, was astonished by the director's docility on set, slumped silently in his chair looking "prodigiously bored" as the crew worked busily around him. As afternoon turned to evening, Hitchcock suddenly roused himself and began an animated conversation with Cary Grant. Was he concerned about some subtlety of his star's performance, or anxious about the dying light, perhaps? "No, the light is excellent," Hitchcock told Bazin, "but Mister Cary Grant's contract calls for stopping at six o'clock; it is six o'clock exactly, so we will retake the sequence tomorrow." This was Hitchcock, a supposed Napoleonic general of the movies, whose armies of the make-believe were under his unwavering control—yet, to Bazin, he looked more like a competition winner than a director, a guest for the day on somebody else's shoot.

Bazin's reservations didn't deter his colleagues. In 1957, Eric Rohmer and Claude Chabrol published *Hitchcock*, the first full-length critical study of his work. To many in America and Britain, it seemed absurd that the man they'd always seen as an uncommonly accomplished ringmaster was now being hailed as an artistic genius. The new take on Hitchcock—and other Hollywood directors such as Howard Hawks—was the stirrings of something that was larger than film criticism, a reevaluation of popular culture that dissolved the stark barriers between art and entertainment. By the end of the sixties such notions would be pervasive. For now, the Hitchcock reappraisal seemed delusional to some. In the British journal *Sight & Sound* the American critic Richard Roud published a piece about the excesses of French criticism, citing the eulogizing of Hitchcock as Exhibit A. Roud suggested that "one's first reaction might be to conclude that these men must be very foolish," and that Hitchcock himself knew that "this Hitchcock idolatry" was risible.

For Anglo-Saxon unbelievers, worse was to come. In 1962, François Truffaut, a thirty-year-old critic turned filmmaker, arrived in Los Angeles for a lengthy series of interviews with Hitchcock that remains the starting point for most analyses of Hitchcock's life and work. The following summer, Jean Douchet traveled to California for his own piece about Hitchcock. Keenly aware of the publicity opportunities offered by his young French disciples, Hitchcock arranged for a limousine to ferry Douchet to and from his hotel for three days. Douchet's expenses were covered by Universal Pictures, to whom Hitchcock was contracted, excepting a night at the Fairmont Hotel in San Francisco, for which Hitchcock paid.

Perplexed as he may have been by some of the auteurist theories, Hitchcock agreed with the fundamental precept that behind each great film sat a great man in a canvas chair. As early as 1927, he had expressed the opinion that any films worth watching have their director's thumb-prints on the negatives. "They are their babies just as much as an author's novel is the offspring of his imagination. And that seems to make it all the more certain that when moving pictures are really artistic they will be created entirely by one man." It was just such a powerful, creative progenitor that Hitchcock projected himself to be from the start of his directing career, finding various ways to insert himself into his body of work. In his first movie, *The Pleasure Garden*, Hitchcock included his signature in the credits, and in most of his subsequent films he made his famous cameos. A photograph taken during the making of his second movie, *The Mountain Eagle*,* shows him posing as the kinetic hub of his film set, a decisive young man in masterful control of the most modern of media.

The story of how his third picture, *The Lodger*, came to be muddies that image. June Tripp (professionally known simply as June, but also

---

* There is no known extant copy of *The Mountain Eagle*.

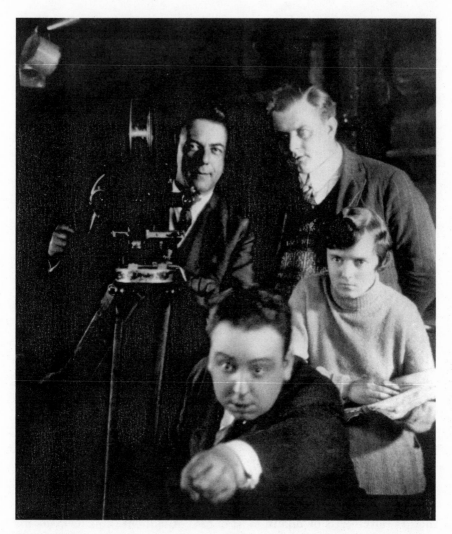

Hitchcock posing as the dynamic young director; Alma Reville looks on, c. 1926.

sometimes referred to as June Hillman), who played the female lead of Daisy, attested that on set Hitchcock was in absolute control. "Fresh from Berlin, Hitch was so imbued with the value of unusual camera angles and lighting effects with which to create and sustain dramatic suspense that often a scene which would not run for more than three minutes on the screen would take an entire morning to shoot." It was draining for the cast, but "his brilliance was patent"—though not to everyone. As producer Michael Balcon told the story, Hitchcock's old director Graham Cutts, perhaps motivated by jealousy at Hitchcock's rapid advancement, "began to tell anybody who would listen that we had a disaster on our hands. Unfortunately one person who listened to him was C. M. Woolf," the distributor. When he watched the film, Woolf, who had already delayed releasing Hitchcock's first two movies because he felt they lacked box-office appeal, said he had never seen such artsy rubbish in his life, and ordered it shelved.

Balcon stepped in and persuaded Hitchcock to work with Ivor Montagu, a twenty-two-year-old polymath, with the aim of enhancing the film's box-office appeal. Montagu thought the situation was "as humiliating for the one as it was embarrassing for the other," but the changes he made saved the day. He slashed the number of intertitles from around three hundred to eighty, shortened some scenes, suggested reshooting certain others, and recruited the graphic artist E. McKnight Kauffer, whose atmospheric designs bolster the brooding expressionism of Hitchcock's movie. Balcon showed the new version to an audience of journalists, whose glowing response persuaded Woolf that it was safe to release.

On one level, this is evidence of the difficulty of expressing a single creative vision in an industry replete with technical, commercial, editorial, and political forces outside a director's control. One of the reasons Hitchcock looked back at his work with Balcon with such fondness is because Balcon tried to remove some of those obstacles and let Hitchcock stay as close to his own path as possible. In America, Hitchcock took a producer as well as a director credit from the late forties onward, but in the first few years in Hollywood he bristled at the involvement of powerful producers, especially David O. Selznick, who considered himself to be the key creative presence in any production that bore his name. In such circumstances, identifying a lone "auteur" can be tricky, if not impossible.

However, Montagu stressed that he inserted nothing of himself into Hitchcock's work; his contribution to *The Lodger* was "in the nature of that which a gallery director makes to a painting in suggesting how it should be framed, where hung and in what light." He loved Hitchcock's original cut and believed that "what the film needed was editing *toward*, not *away from*, its exceptional qualities," emphasizing Hitchcock's influence on the film, those characteristics that Montagu elsewhere described as his "observation of familiar and unfamiliar pictorial detail" and "an artist's eye for meaningful compositions." Montagu tried to locate and enhance the essence of Hitchcock, a method that many of Hitchcock's subsequent collaborators would employ.

Of all those who invested their talents in the Hitchcock legend, the most constant, and perhaps the most important, was his wife, Alma Reville. They were, at first sight, an odd couple. Her small, delicate frame contrasted with his famous bulk. Likewise, her instinct to please and soothe, reflected in the beaming smile with which she greeted the world, differed sharply from Hitchcock's egotism, his tendency to sulk and show off. To quote their daughter, Hitchcock was "a born celebrity" who craved things—attention, public affirmation, a feeling of specialness—that the more retiring Alma seemingly had little use for.

Alma was born to Lucy and Matthew Reville in Nottingham, on August 14, 1899, just one day after Alfred's birthday. The family moved to London when Alma was an infant, after Matthew secured a job in the costume department at Twickenham Studios. As a teenager, Alma dreamed of being an actress, though her father thought it best for her to experience the "seamy side of film life," and helped her land a job as a "cutter." It proved a turning point. Although Alma later took a couple of small acting roles, it was scriptwriting and editing that absorbed her. While Alfred was still at Henley's, Alma's film career cantered ahead. A variety of jobs came her way, but she often doubled up as editor (a more functional job in the tender years of cinema than it is today) and "continuity girl," a member of the crew responsible for recording the details of a take in order to avoid discrepancies in the edit. While still in her teens, she was even hired to work on *Hearts of the World*, directed by D. W. Griffith, the titan of silent films, and one of the few directors that Hitchcock readily admitted he was influenced by.

Though it wasn't love at first sight for Alma, her first experience of Alfred was memorable. It occurred in 1921 at Famous Players-Lasky, where they had both recently begun work. She was amused by his imperious manner, entirely unsuited to his junior standing and baby-faced appearance, and puzzled by the fact that each time their paths crossed, he acted as though she were invisible. Years later Hitchcock revealed that his rudeness was a symptom of his youthful anxiety around women, exacerbated by the fact that Alma was, in career terms, four years his senior and already an editor and second assistant director when he was still sketching intertitles. Alma claimed that as it was "unthinkable for a British male to admit that a woman has a job more important than his, Hitch had waited to speak to me until he had the higher position." That moment came when he was made assistant to Graham Cutts on a picture called *Woman to Woman* and, quite out of the blue, he called Alma to offer her the job of editor. They worked together on a further four films with Cutts, and bonded over their conviction that they could do a much better job than their director. When Hitchcock was handed the reins on *The Pleasure Garden*, his first important decision was to hire Alma as his assistant director.

Both were passionate about cinema, fiercely ambitious, but shy and self-contained people whose social lives as children had been limited. In Alma's case, she had been stricken by Sydenham's chorea (St. Vitus dance), causing involuntary tics, jerking of the limbs, and muscle weakness. She lost two years' schooling because of the disorder which, in the opinion of her daughter, led her to become "extremely self-conscious and sensitive about her lack of formal education," much as Hitchcock had. Alma even had a strange story of childhood trauma to parallel Hitchcock's. Amid the crowds in London attending the funeral procession of Edward VII in 1910, Alma was coming down from her father's shoulders when her hair got caught in the coat buttons of a fellow bystander, and she was dragged to the ground as the man walked past, triggering a lifelong aversion to crowds.

The story of their engagement is one Hitchcock enjoyed revisiting. It happened, he said, on Christmas Eve of 1925, sailing back from

Germany, where he and Alma had been working on *The Mountain Eagle*. Hitchcock entered Alma's cabin with an engagement ring in his pocket and a rehearsed speech in his head, only to find her prostrate on her bunk, green with seasickness. Undeterred, he popped the question. In response, Alma "groaned, nodded her head, and burped." For all its unlikeliness, the anecdote has a ring of authenticity. As observed by Patrick McGilligan, Hitchcock had a hugely quixotic view of rail and sea travel, and probably convinced himself that this was the perfect occasion to fulfill a romantic fantasy. That he was unable to gauge the situation and postpone his proposal for a more appropriate moment says a lot about his social clumsiness, and hints at one of the many things the warmer, more empathetic Alma brought to the Hitchcock partnership.

As with *The Pleasure Garden*, *The Mountain Eagle* had been full of delays and obstructions, caused by the weather and other unforeseen circumstances—a nightmare for a worrier such as Hitchcock. When he recounted these experiences publicly, Hitchcock told them laughingly, but in the way one might retell a peculiar anxiety dream. Barraged by unexpected, time-sensitive problems, he turned to Alma for constant reassurance, and she, "sweet soul, gave me courage by swearing I was doing marvelously." She also came to his rescue by handling delicate issues with cast and crew that Hitchcock couldn't stomach. "Like a man, I left Miss Reville to do all the dirty work," he admitted. Hitchcock told many tales about those times in Germany, but he always cast Alma in the same role: a sunny-natured dynamo of winning optimism, "standing four-foot-eleven in stockings and a trifle more in high heels," who never ceased to tell him he was "the snake's hips and the cat's pyjamas." She acted as his battery as well as a protective layer between him and the daunting unpredictability of other people, oiling the Hitchcock machine with diplomacy and emotional intelligence. Over the ensuing decades, Alma worked, formally and informally, in a variety of roles on Hitchcock films: development producer, assistant director, writer, casting producer, script supervisor, all-around editorial adviser. Aptly, she was sometimes simply credited as "continuity."

It's been said that Hitchcock's idea of the cinematic strongman was something he acquired in the film culture of Weimar Germany. However, his view of himself as a precocious expert was manifest years before his time at Neubabelsberg. Aged twenty-one, and only three months into his first full-time job in the film business, he had an article published in *Motion Picture Studio* magazine on the secrets of how to create good intertitles. Exhibiting a self-confidence out of step with the anxious, socially awkward youngster he was away from filmmaking, he criticized "one or two of the leading directors in the States [who] have made a practice of illustrating all their titles. The result of illustrating a spoken title can only confuse the reader," he warned, and urged his peers to avoid repetition. "The hour glass and the scales of justice, their day is ended." A neophyte in the movie business, and he was already disparaging the visual sensibilities of established directors, sniffing at their reliance on hoary cliché.

From the late twenties, he kept his name in the press in this way, sharing his expertise in articles for numerous publications, and entertaining journalists at his flat on Cromwell Road, west London, where he was in the habit of being interviewed in silk pajamas. He went so far as to establish Hitchcock Baker Productions Ltd., a company dedicated to curating his public image. In 1936 he published a five-part series of biographical articles in the popular British magazine *Film Weekly* titled "My Screen Memories," as though he were a grand old man of the business, rather than a thirty-six-year-old on the rise. Yet readers were left in no doubt about the qualities Hitchcock most wanted to stress in those pieces: youthfulness, dynamism, and a sense of mission. The final installment ended with Hitchcock declaring that the nostalgia suggested by these articles was really not his thing: "my most interesting picture is always my next one. I have enjoyed delving into the past in these reminiscences. But the future is much more fascinating."

As the fame of Hitchcock's films spread, so did the celebrity of their director. In March 1939, he was invited to lecture a class at Columbia University on his specialist subject: the distinctive work of Alfred Hitchcock. Speaking in his unmistakable voice—"I have some notes here that are mixed up with a letter from my mother"—he caused ripples of laughter from his young audience as he glided his way through the life cycle of a Hitchcock movie, from conception to projection. It reminds one of how Wilde and Dickens constructed their profiles in America, as well as the recent lecture tour of Gertrude Stein, back home after many years in Europe, during which she wrapped the novelty of her work in the homespun eccentricity of her delivery, pitching herself somewhere between a modernist iconoclast and America's favorite aunt. All three of those august names exploited their looks and demeanor, in concert with their singular voice, to establish themselves as a cultural presence. Hitchcock, as no filmmaker before him had done, followed in their footsteps.

When Hollywood success came his way in the 1940s, his agent—at first Myron Selznick, then Lew Wasserman, perhaps the most important commercial figure in the movies after World War II*—brokered what were essentially licensing deals, attaching the Hitchcock name to a variety of side projects and spin-offs, based around Hitchcock as the personification of his film work. There were books of suspense stories, supposedly compiled by Hitchcock, though his involvement was negligible. In 1947, Hitchcock put his name to an adaptation of Frances Iles's novel *Malice Aforethought* for a proposed ABC radio series, *The Alfred Hitchcock Show*.† Though not picked up, the pilot contained the germ of what would become *Alfred Hitchcock Presents*, the instant popularity of which led to an Alfred Hitchcock magazine, further books for children and adults, and various other Hitchcock-branded ventures.

The television shows were produced by Norman Lloyd, who had appeared in *Saboteur* (1942) and *Spellbound*, and Joan Harrison, a Hitchcock protégé who had worked with him in a variety of roles between 1933 and 1941, before striking out on her own. They had Hitchcock's complete trust and were allowed to take the lead in finding, developing, and pro-

---

*   Hitchcock was also briefly represented by Leland Hayward and Taft Schreiber.

†   Hitchcock had been attached to another ABC radio pilot, *Once Upon a Midnight*, in 1945. The pilot episode was also an adaptation of *Malice Aforethought*. A series was not commissioned. In 1940, Hitchcock oversaw a radio adaptation of his film *The Lodger* as the first episode of the long-running series *Suspense*.

ducing the two dozen stories needed for each season. At various points Hitchcock would offer criticisms and suggestions, but generally he allowed the series to work not according to his diktats, but in his image, which, by the time the first season aired in 1955, was well established. Hitchcock's television output is generally considered the destitute relation of the Hitchcock movies, with little of value to say about his work. Yet *Alfred Hitchcock Presents*—and *The Alfred Hitchcock Hour*, which followed it—distills the spirit in which his most successful collaborators approached their work, especially from the late 1940s onward. To Harrison and Lloyd, Hitchcock was also "Hitchcock," not just a man but an entity, a totem pole, and a guiding spirit. Despite his infrequent involvement, his tastes, sensibilities, and personality loomed over every stage of the shows' production. Speaking publicly about the series, Harrison channeled Hitchcock: "We don't show much violence. . . . Our kind of murderer is polite. We like to suggest rather than show." "Let 'em suffer," she said, talking of the delightful pleasure of torturing an audience. "Let 'em become participants in the show and twist and turn with every twisting and turning."

Wherever he could, Hitchcock worked with the same people over and over, those who knew that working successfully on a Hitchcock production meant pouring one's talents into a Hitchcockian mold, intuiting the vision of the man in charge. For a short time, the designer and illustrator Saul Bass was just such a contributor, designing the title sequences that beautifully augment *Vertigo*, *North by Northwest*, and *Psycho*, as E. McKnight Kauffer's had done on *The Lodger* decades earlier. Bass claimed that he'd done such a good job in storyboarding the shower scene in *Psycho* that Hitchcock allowed him to direct it, only to deny him his due credit once the scene gained its fame. Pretty much everybody connected with *Psycho* rejected Bass's claim. "Alfred Hitchcock was right next to his camera for every one of those seventy-odd shots," declared Janet Leigh, the woman on the other side of the lens. When asked why nobody else remembered the shoot as he did, Bass said that Hitchcock's decision to hand him the reins was "*spontaneous*, not something he planned, discussed, or organized. At that time, nobody paid much attention." More

important, "Hitch was always there and his 'presence' naturally dominated the set. As far as everybody was concerned, including me, he was
in charge whether he said 'action' or 'cut' or not." Even in staking a claim
to a headline piece of Hitchcock's legacy, Bass did so by putting Hitchcock's ineffable influence at the center of the story.

In the months he spent working on the screenplay for *The Birds*, Evan
Hunter wrote excitedly to friends and family that Hitchcock planned on
telling the world that the movie was a joint vision. "This is our picture,
Evan," Hitchcock had told him. "I want this to say 'Alfred Hitchcock's
THE BIRDS, written by Evan Hunter' and that's what we're going to sell."
In reality, there was only one name that the public would associate with
the picture, as Hunter discovered when he tried to tell his young son's
friend that he was the man who wrote the screenplay. "No, you didn't,"
said the little boy, eager to show that he wasn't so dumb as to believe an
obvious lie, "Alfred Hitchcock did."

It is often assumed that, as is the case with Ingmar Bergman, Quentin Tarantino, Woody Allen, and many other so-called auteurs, Hitchcock hammered out his own scripts. In fact, on only one of his films, *The
Ring*, did he take sole writing credit, and even on this he had uncredited
assistance from Eliot Stannard, one of the leading British screenwriters
of the silent era. But with Hitchcock, the notion of authorship was slip-
pery; when opportunity presented itself, he confirmed that though he
may not have sweated over the dialogue within each scene, the creative
credit was, morally, his. Sidney Gilliat, cowriter of *The Lady Vanishes* and
Jamaica Inn (1939), was aggrieved when *The New Yorker* reported that all
Hitchcock films are "about 99.44-percent Hitchcock." Hitchcock swore
that the figure quoted in the article had not come from him, but it does
sound very much like the sort of thing he would have said. Years later,
in a deposition regarding a copyright dispute over *Rear Window* (1954),
Hitchcock told the court that in the writing of Hitchcock scripts, "I dictate the picture," and that the *Rear Window* screenplay should therefore

be regarded as "eighty percent Hitchcock," despite it being officially adapted by John Michael Hayes from a Cornell Woolrich short story.

When it came to screenwriting, Hitchcock relied on the talents of others—though for most of his career, one of those talents had to be a capacity to digest and express what was called the "Hitchcock touch." The "biggest trouble is to educate writers to work along my lines," he once complained. Perhaps Samuel Taylor, screenwriter of *Vertigo* and *Topaz* (1969), put it best: "I can't really say where Hitch's input began or ended. When you worked with him on a film, you wrote a Hitchcock picture."

Usually, the process started with a novel, a short story, or a play. What constituted a suitable source for a Hitchcock film is hard to define. Sometimes it was a question of what was available, or what was urged on him by the studios, into which he tried his best to insert his vision. By the 1960s, at the height of his powers, the search for new movie material was an industrialized effort involving Alma, his secretaries, his agent, employees at his production company, and various people at Universal, all looking for some inarticulable mix of suspense, melodrama, and humor. Original scripts were sent in by both established and untried writers, and lists of promising talents were collated by his staff, tantalizing future generations with hypothetical Hitchcock collaborations with Harold Pinter, Tom Stoppard, and Gore Vidal, among many others.

Given the time and effort dedicated to identifying it, Hitchcock could be remarkably dismissive about his source material. "I never read a book through if I am considering making a picture of it," he asserted in 1937, lest "I get so saturated with the novel that I cannot discard easily what often must be discarded to make a real film and not a mere photographic reproduction of a book." Hitchcock drove notoriously hard bargains when buying the rights to material, and frequently did so anonymously to avoid having to pay a penny more than he absolutely had to. In transcripts of his meetings with Ernest Lehman, the writer of his final completed picture, *Family Plot* (1976), Hitchcock made uncharitable remarks about the movie's source material, *The Rainbird Pattern*, whose author, Victor Canning, was "a very lucky man" for having his work associated with the Hitchcock name. "These fellows," grumbled Hitchcock, refer-ring to the writers of his source material, "you know what happens—they re-release the book with our new title on it."

The resentment is palpable, though one wonders at its derivation. Was it because Hitchcock felt exploited by those profiting from his work? Certainly he had form on that front: for years he silently fumed—not without reason—after learning that the mogul who brought him to Hol-lywood, David O. Selznick, made several times his own fee when Hitch-cock was loaned to other studios. Or, perhaps what stung was the fear that it was he, not the writers, who was the dependent in these relationships.

Of course, the origins of Hitchcock's stories shouldn't lead anyone to doubt his talent or distinctiveness as a filmmaker. Indeed, his achieve-ment in creating such a recognizable cinematic style is all the more impressive considering the discrete origins of his raw material, and that he had so many parties—actors, producers, audiences, critics—to nav-igate. There's also the issue of time: between 1925 and 1960, he made forty-seven feature films, on a treadmill of development, production, postproduction, and publicity, not including any of his radio, televi-sion, or print endeavors. With that schedule, it would have been virtually impossible for Hitchcock not to have collaborated with a host of writers. At least part of the reason for his coolness toward source material was that he didn't seek a book or a play to fall in love with, just something to heave the propeller of his imagination. That needn't be a narrative, but a character, a situation, or simply a particularly arresting image.

North by Northwest began in just this way. Ernest Lehman, best known at the time for having written *The King and I* screenplay, had agreed to work with Hitchcock on adapting Hammond Innes's novel *The Wreck of the Mary Deare* for MGM. Lehman was keen to work with Hitchcock but was stumped on how to turn the novel, much of which is set in an English court of law, into Hollywood entertainment. "The first scene was good: 'ship found in a channel with nobody on board,'" Lehman recalled, but "that was the only good scene in the whole novel." Still, he pushed those doubts to one side, persuaded by Hitchcock's confidence that all the problems could be sorted.

Hitchcock had no hard-and-fast system when collaborating with a writer. Depending on the type of source material being adapted, the writers he could find, and the time available, the process could be tweaked. Usually, however, there was a crucial initial period during which Hitchcock and his writer would meet day after day to thrash out the story they wanted to tell and block its key scenes. Hitchcock believed the best way to solve a script problem was to allow oneself to stumble on it. Frequently, that meant abandoning the writer's room for a pub, or cocktails at home, a restaurant, an expedition down the Thames, or a drive into the California countryside. "Certain writers want to work every hour of the day. . . . I'm not that way. I want to say, 'Let's lay off for several hours—let's play.'"

It was in this circuitous way that work on *The Wreck of the Mary Deare* began. They convened daily for meandering discussions about any number of subjects, anything other than how to turn this uncinematic novel into box-office gold. Lehman began to worry that he would soon be left to bash out a two-hour movie script without the faintest idea of what would go in it. When he shared his concern, Hitchcock told him to relax: he would charm MGM into letting them get to work on something else altogether. They began afresh, working around a single idea: a chase finale across Mount Rushmore, a notion that Hitchcock had toyed with for some time. Six years earlier, the journalist Lawrence Greene reported that Hitchcock's "unrealized ambition is to have Good contend with Evil in the shadow of Mount Rushmore." With the working title *In a North-westerly Direction*—and, for a time, *The Man in Lincoln's Nose*—they pieced together an adventure story about a man who is mistaken for a spy and is forced to go on the run after being framed for murder, that took its protagonist from New York to South Dakota. Hitchcock pitched countless unconnected ideas. In one scene, he envisaged an Eskimo fishing in frozen waters, when a hand suddenly jabs through the ice. Another would track a car being built piece by piece on a production line, with a dead body rolling out of it at the end. "They were all wonderful," said Lehman of Hitchcock's torrent of ideas, "and I took them all down, and I never used most of them."

Hitchcock performing for the camera, 1942.

When constructing a script from their jumble of scenes, Lehman "tried to develop a Hitchcock frame of mind. I became like Hitchcock, and I tried to think like him." His aim was to achieve the Platonic ideal of a Hitchcock film, adventurous, suspenseful, witty; "a Hitchcock picture to end all Hitchcock pictures." Lehman told the press that his script had been written not for Cary Grant, but for another "very special kind of star—the director, Mr. Hitchcock."

Even so, Lehman came to resent that his part in one of Hollywood's greatest movies had, in his view, been obliterated by the legend of Hitchcock's lone genius. Before his death in 2005, he made something of a habit of upbraiding those whom he felt hadn't given him his due. He told an interviewer in 1999, forty years after the film was released, that he was in the midst of "writing a bitter letter to Peter Bogdanovich for writing a paean of praise to *North by Northwest* . . . and mentioning everybody connected with the picture, except me."

Beyond what Lehman and Hitchcock remembered, there is no detailed record of those scripting sessions. But, seventeen years later, when the pair worked on *Family Plot*, Hitchcock recorded their conversations; the transcripts are a privileged insight into a collaboration between two legends* of mid-century Hollywood. The project wasn't as happy or successful as *North by Northwest* had been, but the basic dynamics that defined their relationship are on display: Lehman constantly trying to hold the structure of the film in his head as they move from one scene to the next; Hitchcock firing out thoughts as they come to him, enjoying the occasional digression into Watergate, or some other bit of news or gossip. Images frequently flash into his mind: a sniper's bullet smashing into a gravestone; a man dressed as a woman entering a San Francisco nightclub; a character on the run, clinging to the roof of a moving train. At one point, he muses that perhaps they should read *The Taking of Pelham One Two Three* to see whether anything could be pilfered from it. "My God, how can we," protests Lehman at the prospect of stealing from a fellow writer, "it's still on the bestseller lists." Hitchcock was unfazed. To him, almost all ideas, no matter their origin, would become Hitchcockian when placed before the eye of his camera.

It was Lehman's job to wrangle Hitchcock's parade of unconnected scenes into some coherent narrative shape. The same was true for most of the writers Hitchcock worked with. To concede this is not to minimize the achievements of those writers; writing in the voice and style of another person is a rare and valuable skill. Charles Barr, a chief authority on Hitchcock's early career, dug into the work of Eliot Stannard, the writer who took official writing credit on seven of Hitchcock's first nine films. Barr analyzed *Writing Screen Plays*, Stannard's slim how-to guide

---

* Lehman eventually racked up six Academy Award nominations to Hitchcock's five; neither won any, though both received honorary awards from the Academy.

in which he identifies the chief problem with silent-era screenwriting in Britain: "too many scripts are a series of exciting incidents and nothing else; melodramatic, improbable and often impossible situations followed each other in bewildering rapidity, but I sought in vain for any central motive or theme." As Barr points out, that sounds much like the experience of every writer who ever worked on a Hitchcock script. In 1986, sixty-six years after Stannard's book was published, Samuel Taylor said Hitchcock was "the master of the situation, the master of the vignette, the master of the small moment. He always knew what he wanted to do with those. He did not have so much of an overall view of the story he was going to tell . . . it was like a mosaic. . . . Now, if he didn't have a good writer, there were going to be pieces missing."

After Stannard, Charles Bennett was the next writer who had a decisive impact on Hitchcock's work. Bennett had written the play on which Hitchcock's first talkie, *Blackmail*, had been based, and he shared writing credits on the run of five movies—from *The Man Who Knew Too Much* in 1934 to *Young and Innocent* in 1937—that made Hitchcock synonymous with witty, picaresque spy thrillers. Theirs was an immensely productive relationship; Bennett and Joan Harrison were nominated for an Oscar for their work on the script for Hitchcock's *Foreign Correspondent* (1940). But Bennett was bitter about the lack of praise Hitchcock afforded him over the years for what he says was the crucial part he played in creating the very thing that Ernest Lehman identified as "a Hitchcock picture."

Writing in his memoirs, unpublished until 2014, Bennett accused his former partner of being "completely vain," though he acknowledged that Hitchcock was "brilliant, very brilliant—as a *director*." It rankled Bennett that Hitchcock had fostered an idea of himself as a creative antenna whose films flowed directly from his own imagination without passing through the filter of other creative artists. Bennett's grievance also reminds us that the distinctive one-man brand of Hitchcock's Hollywood heyday didn't spring from the soil fully formed. Especially as a young director, he learned from the highly accomplished people he worked alongside, primarily Balcon, Stannard, and Bennett. "We were a *writer*-director partnership," stated Bennett, "but his vanity could not credit me. He credited no one but himself." As Herbert Coleman, one of Hitchcock's most devoted employees, bluntly put it, " 'Thank you' was not part of Hitch's vocabulary."

Hitchcock might have countered that this was all so much sour grapes. Bennett had a lacerating tongue and a sizable ego himself; "I'm not being conceited," he wrote in his memoirs, "but I was awfully bloody good." However, Bennett expresses sentiments voiced by many of Hitchcock's other collaborators. So often the work would begin amiably, the writers overjoyed to be working with Hitchcock and beguiled by the free-roaming conversations that would commence their collaboration. Evan Hunter was unimpressed by Hollywood when he relocated there to write *The Birds*, but felt the "cheerful side is that working with Hitch is an exhilarating, thoroughly professional, New York style experience," by which he meant perfecting the work for its own sake, rather than the commercial dividends that might follow. But once his draft was finished, Hunter balked when Hitchcock wrote him a lengthy letter explaining that "the script has also been read by a number of other people . . . probably not more than 8 or 9 in total." Some of those were important figures working on the film, but others were writers such as Hitchcock's friend Hume Cronyn, and V. S. Pritchett, whom Hitchcock would later task with refreshing portions of the script's dialogue. There was nothing intentionally cruel in this, and unquestionably Hitchcock's only goal was to improve the script. Yet he either failed to grasp—or simply didn't care—that a writer was likely to take exception at having their work passed around like a bag of potato chips. Hunter felt as though each of those given the script had "stuck his finger in the concept and his foot in the whorehouse door."

John Michael Hayes had similar frustrations. He was recruited by Hitchcock to write a script for *Rear Window*, based on the short story "It Had to Be Murder" by Cornell Woolrich and a treatment by Joshua Logan. Having mapped out the essential design of the film together—in which a man confined to his apartment with a broken leg begins to spy on his neighbors and sets out to prove that one of them is a murderer—Hitchcock left Hayes to get on with building character and crafting dialogue. Hayes couldn't have been happier: "He essentially left you, the writer, alone to do your work . . . he didn't bother you constantly for pages in order to summarily reject them," as Hayes had experienced with other filmmakers. With the draft finished, Hitchcock came back on board to scrutinize the material, going through the whole thing shot by shot. To Hayes, it felt like a true partnership, each man lending his own talents in a thoroughly complementary fashion. They ended up with arguably the best script Hitchcock ever worked with: lean but layered, witty, clever, with a flawed but likable central character, and a gripping suspense story pulling us through from beginning to end. *Rear Window* was the first of four consecutive movies Hayes wrote for Hitchcock, the others being *To Catch a Thief*, *The Trouble with Harry* (1955), and the second version of *The Man Who Knew Too Much*. All but *The Trouble with Harry* did terrific business at the box office, and each chimed with Hitchcock's playful, urbane eccentricity.

According to Hayes, the problems began in April 1955 when he got the attention he deserved for the *Rear Window* screenplay, in the form of the Edgar Allan Poe Award from the Mystery Writers of America. Hayes had never won an award before, and he showed it off the following day. Hitchcock's only response was, "You know they make toilet bowls from the same material."

Viewed on its own, a quip like that doesn't seem much; ill-judged, perhaps, but not malicious. When clustered with other tales of Hitchcock's apparent refusal or inability to praise those with whom he worked, a definite pattern emerges. According to Hayes, he was approached by the *New York Times* to write a piece about the experience of working with Hitchcock. Probably assuming that a self-promoter like Hitchcock wouldn't object to having his praises sung in the pages of the *Times*, Hayes wrote the article, and as a courtesy showed it to Hitchcock before he submitted it. As Hayes told the story, Hitchcock was furious, tore up the article, and said, "Young man, you are hired to write for me and Paramount, not the *New York Times*." Hayes had been unambiguously put in his place—"young man"—and reminded that no mere writer should consider himself a creative peer of Hitchcock's; he was not a collaborator but an employee.

Such a dramatic response also makes one wonder whether Hitchcock's main anxiety was to keep control of his mythology. In Britain, America, and elsewhere, he'd published articles under his name—though not always written by him—that shed light on his creative process in a way that enhanced his contributions and diminished those of his colleagues and collaborators, with the exception of Alma, whose contribution to the Hitchcock project he seemed to enjoy highlighting. To allow somebody to gain a public profile by detailing the ways in which they influenced his work was damaging not only to his ego but to his reputation. "He wasn't for a moment willing to allow anyone to believe he couldn't do it all on his own," was Hayes's ultimate judgment.

The Hayes-Hitchcock relationship imploded when—ironically, considering his complaint of Hitchcock's inability to give "credit where credit was due"—Hayes took umbrage at Hitchcock handing a cowriting credit to the writer Angus MacPhail for *The Man Who Knew Too Much*, a script Hayes insisted should be credited to him alone. Hayes told an interviewer many years later that he had strayed too far from the path of Hitchcock for the master's liking. "I had a viewpoint and a unique way of working . . . that was my downfall, because it was too recognized, and Hitch resented it." Long-standing members of the Hitchcock team accused Hayes of wildly inflating his importance, and claimed it was his ego, not Hitchcock's, that ended their association. Whatever the precise burden of blame, Hayes was cast out of the Hitchcock enterprise. At various points over the coming years when Hitchcock was in need of a writer to enliven a script, those around him recommended bringing Hayes back in from the cold; their talents and sensibilities had so complemented each other, a reunion made perfect sense. Hitchcock would never countenance it.

Hitchcock's most celebrated films were not based on equally celebrated sources. In the 1930s, he adapted Seán O'Casey's highly acclaimed *Juno and the Paycock* (1930), and *The Skin Game* (1931) by John Galsworthy (a Nobel Prize winner in 1932), but he felt he brought little to either play, constricted by the weight of their reputation. In their interviews, Truffaut asked Hitchcock whether he'd ever consider adapting *Crime and Punishment*. Unthinkable, said Hitchcock, as the novel was already considered a classic, implying that he preferred to work with obscure or mediocre literature that he could elevate to the level of Hitchcock.

He did, however, make repeated efforts to recruit exalted authors to work on scripts with him. The most successful of these ventures was with Thornton Wilder, whom he hired for *Shadow of a Doubt* (1943), a troubling tale of American innocence shattered. Wilder had no particular interest in writing films but accepted the job as he was soon to depart for war service and was keen to earn some quick money for his family. For both men, it proved a richly satisfying project. Not long after starting the assignment, Wilder wrote his sister telling her how much fun he was having. "For hours Hitchcock and I with glowing eyes and excited laughter plot out how the information—the dreadful information—is gradually revealed to the audience and the characters." He concluded the letter with a line that would have delighted Hitchcock: "There's no satisfaction like giving satisfaction to your employer."

For the rest of his life, Hitchcock spoke glowingly of Wilder and their working experience. He said that although many writers sneered at the work he did—Graham Greene among them, who publicly criticized Hitchcock's films and turned down the opportunity to collaborate—Wilder never did. "He wasn't like a big shot. . . . He allowed me to direct him and I was grateful for that," said Hitchcock. In return, he treated Wilder as an equal. "My relationship with him was respectful, and this is the important part: He wasn't treated like a hack movie writer, at all. He was treated as he should have been." Inadvertently, Hitchcock was admitting that he didn't necessarily afford the same courtesy to all his writers.

Wilder had approached his work with Hitchcock with little ego or expectation—the best, perhaps the *only*, way to happily write for Hitchcock. Though he was delighted with Wilder's contribution, Hitchcock still recruited another writer once Wilder had departed, to give the script bounce and sparkle. This was frequent practice with Hitchcock;

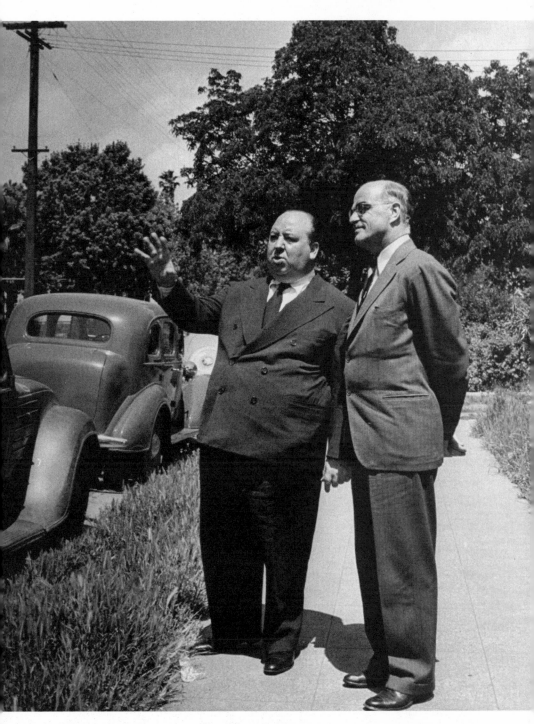

Thornton Wilder giving satisfaction to his employer, 1942.

he employed writers as though they were specialist tradesmen renovating a house. Some were used as constructionists, some as writers of dialogue, others to give "polish" to a final draft. He tried where possible to keep them separate, too, so the only beam running the whole length of a writing project was himself. Wilder never regraded *Shadow of a Doubt* as a true collaboration; he was investing his energies into a Hitchcock project, and it was the entity of Hitchcock that he had to channel, rather than trying to put his stamp on the Hitchcock brand, as Hayes and Hunter had attempted to do.

This was not the case with the next great American writer with whom Hitchcock worked: John Steinbeck. A few months after the United States entered World War II, Steinbeck wrote a lengthy outline for Hitchcock's idea for a film set entirely on a lifeboat in the aftermath of a German torpedo attack.* Presumably, Hitchcock had hoped that Steinbeck would prove as compliant as Wilder. It was a serious miscalculation. Steinbeck's story is an ideological tract in which each character personifies a different constituency within American society: the working-class characters are good, honest, and heroic, while the politician and the captain of industry are superficial, deceitful, and irresponsible. Joe, the story's one black character, is inserted by Steinbeck with the laudable intention of defying racist assumptions—yet he is so thoroughly good and admirable, in a way that no real person could be, that he is less a character than a polemical device. There are other unmistakably Steinbeckian flourishes, such as when a traumatized woman attempts to revive her dead baby by holding the child to her exposed breast.

The political invective was of no interest to Hitchcock, and it's unsurprising that the characters and their relationships were changed substantially by Hitchcock and screenwriter Jo Swerling. The congresswoman—Steinbeck's symbol of cynical ambition—was turned into a writer, played in the film by Tallulah Bankhead, transforming the political into the cultural, which was always surer territory for Hitch-

---

*   Hitchcock's first choice, Ernest Hemingway, declined the offer.

cock. Steinbeck was infuriated with the changes and was particularly aggrieved at what became of Joe, although Hitchcock's—admittedly dull—character is more believable than the one drafted by Steinbeck. More important, Steinbeck delivered a template that told far more than it showed, featuring relatively little that Hitchcock could film; thoughts occur inside the narrator's head, or are carried within dialogue, offering little potential for the camera. Yet one wonders what Hitchcock expected. Steinbeck was not a screenwriter, was hardly famed for his amenability, and there was nothing in his past work that might be described as Hitch-cockian. He was enraged by what he deemed to be Hitchcock's haughty dismissal of his work, branding him one of many "incredible English middle class snobs who really and truly despise working people," perhaps unaware of Hitchcock's unspectacular origins.

There was similar rancor a few years later when Raymond Chandler was engaged to adapt Patricia Highsmith's *Strangers on a Train*, about a psychopath who drags an innocent man into his deranged double murder plot. One biography of Chandler describes Hitchcock as "hard to work with," though the description given of their relationship puts Chandler in a much worse light. He refused to work at the studio but resented it whenever Hitchcock visited him at home, threatened by what he thought of as Hitchcock's encroachment on his territory, physically and metaphorically. He was also frustrated by the open-ended conversations with which Hitchcock began their conferences and hit out in strikingly unkind ways. Chandler became "sarcastic and disagreeable," in the words of his biographer, and balked at ideas that Hitchcock threw into the mix. As Hitchcock emerged from his car before one of their meetings, Chandler mocked him as a "fat bastard," not caring that Hitchcock was within earshot. Chandler finished his draft, but said his sanity had been tested by working within Hitchcock's idiom—"trying to make a dream look as if it really happened"—a task he considered a waste of time.

Hitchcock had Czenzi Ormonde do a complete redraft. Ormonde recalled that in their first meeting, Hitchcock made a performance of holding his nose while dropping Chandler's script in the trash. When he saw the finished film sometime later, Chandler was dismayed—and perhaps hurt that so little of his work had made it on screen. He thought the script consisted of "a flabby mass of clichés, a group of faceless characters," and substandard dialogue. He also made a dig at Hitchcock for being a filmmaker who believes "camera angles, stage business, and interesting bits of byplay will make up for any amount of implausibility in a basic story." He wasn't the first or last writer to complain that Hitchcock lacked interest in character and narrative coherence, but this is too much. What he dismissed as visual gimmickry is the substance of Hitchcock's skill as a visual artist whose primary objective was to express atmosphere and emotion through the gaze of a camera. Criticizing him on those grounds is rather like accusing Sergei Prokofiev of destroying the poetry of *Romeo and Juliet* because he removed all the words and replaced them with music.

In the end, Chandler concluded that it was pointless for any writer to work with Hitchcock, as "there must be nothing in a Hitchcock picture which Hitchcock himself might not have written." In truth, a Hitchcock picture *couldn't* be all Hitchcock; without collaborators, writers especially, his films wouldn't have been made. But during his peak years between the mid-1940s and the early 1960s, Hitchcock was irrefutably the heliotropic force on any Hitchcock project, the source of its energy and the light to which all things grew. So clear on this issue was Hitchcock that he had no compunction assuming credit for the work of others. When he spoke to Truffaut about *Vertigo*, Hitchcock claimed that he had to battle studio executives to allow him to reveal to the audience the film's dramatic plot twist—that Madeleine and Judy (played by Kim Novak) are the same person—long before James Stewart's character learns the truth. It sounded plausible; after all, allowing the audience to stay a step ahead of the characters was Hitchcock's definition of suspense. However, in postproduction Hitchcock had been strongly *against* revealing the twist so early, and was persuaded into it by his associate producer and Paramount executives. It might be that in the five years between cutting *Vertigo* and talking to Truffaut, the memory had become blurred in his mind. Or, perhaps he felt entitled, compelled even, to take possession of the decision that fitted so snugly into his mythology and his need to be at the center of all things, lest he be eclipsed by a satellite in his orbit.

The auteur theory was exceptionally influential in shaping the way Hitchcock was perceived through the sixties and seventies, solidifying his reputation as a film artist. In 1963, the Museum of Modern Art held a Hitchcock retrospective, followed by the first English-language books about his work. The new appreciation seemed to affect Hitchcock's filmmaking, too. In November 1964, he reached out to Vladimir Nabokov, as deified for his prose style as Hitchcock was for his cinematic technique. Hitchcock floated two embryonic ideas. The first was about the wife of a Cold War defector, along the lines of what would become his next movie, *Torn Curtain*. As he explained to Nabokov, "the type of story I'm looking for is an emotional, psychological one, expressed in terms of action and movement and, naturally, one that would give me the opportunity to indulge in the customary Hitchcock suspense." The second idea was one he had played with for a long while and attempted with other writers: a story about a teenage girl who realizes that the hotel run by her family is a front for an organized-crime operation. "As I indicated to you on the telephone, screenplay writers are not the type of people to take such ideas as these and develop them into responsible story material. They are usually people who adapt other people's work. That is why I am by-passing them and coming direct to you—a story-teller." Intrigued by the second idea, Nabokov replied that he was sure he'd be able to rustle up a fine screenplay—though, naturally, he'd require absolute freedom to take the story where he pleased. That was a warning of jagged rocks ahead. Demands on both men's time meant the collaboration never happened, but if it had, one wonders whether it would have stood a chance of avoiding the acrimony that befell the Steinbeck and Chandler projects.

Evan Hunter thought *The Birds* was the moment when Hitchcock tipped his hat to the highbrow critics and attempted to make an "art" film. When Hunter read Hitchcock explaining to journalists that the birds "symbolized the more serious aspects of life," he was incredulous. "This was utter rot, a supreme showman's con. . . . While we were shaping the screenplay, there was no talk at all of symbolism." The production files back him up: in one of his letters to Hunter, Hitchcock had predicted that "we are going to be asked again and again, especially by the morons, 'Why are they doing it?'" Ernest Lehman mirrored Hunter's exasperation when he was asked about the theory that *North by Northwest* was a conscious remodeling of *Hamlet* for the Atomic Age. "It's those damned French critics, the *auteurs*. They're always coming up with all kinds of pretentious crap that has no basis in reality."

Rather than an out-and-out lie, perhaps Hitchcock had arrived at his decision about what the birds signified only once the film was finished; plenty of art is created with gut instinct rather than intellectual calculation. But if Hitchcock was joining the auteur school in trying to figure out the film's hidden meaning, he was only pitching in with the rest of his audience. In the months and years following the release of *The Birds*, Hitchcock received letters from the public asking what the film was about, specifically why the birds had turned. In 1969, as the one-year anniversary of Martin Luther King's assassination approached, one viewer felt compelled to write Hitchcock to say they had just divined what the film was really driving at. The birds, this person wrote, might be seen as members of an oppressed race, who, after years of being "shot at, caged up, eaten, and literally taken for granted . . . couldn't endure the degradation any longer!" Sometimes Hitchcock responded to such letters with something along the lines of the explanation that Hunter had read, or a claim that the film was inspired by a real-life case of rabid bats in New Mexico. Just as often, though, he told them he hadn't the faintest idea why the birds attacked. "Why should I? I am not omnipotent." Strictly speaking, it was "omniscience" he should have denied; in the filmic world of Hitchcock, power over all life ultimately rested in his hands, even when it confounded him as much as the rest of us.

4

THE WOMANIZER

"Hitchcock's genius is being frittered away on triviality and pettiness." So stated one British critic in 1931, as Hitchcock's career began to falter. After the triumph of *Blackmail*, he applied himself in several directions: adaptations of two serious stage plays (*The Skin Game* and *Juno and the Paycock*), a crime thriller (*Number Seventeen*), a comedy-drama about a bored married couple in search of adventure (*Rich and Strange*), and two versions of a whodunit, filmed simultaneously (*Murder!* for Anglophone audiences and *Mary* for the German market). Each had its merits. None was first-class Hitchcock. There was also *Waltzes from Vienna*, a delicate drama from 1934 based on a musical about the writing of *The Blue Danube* and perhaps the trough of Hitchcock's career.

He only regained his footing when he paired up with the writer Charles Bennett and reunited with Balcon and Montagu to make *The Man Who Knew Too Much* for the production company Gaumont-British, the first of a glut of espionage thrillers that revived his reputation and brought him to the attention of American studios. In 1939, feeling he had reached the limits of what he could achieve in Britain, Hitchcock packed his bags for Hollywood, on a seven-year deal with the producer of *Gone with the Wind*, David O. Selznick.

Having discarded an initial plan for a movie about the sinking of the *Titanic*, Selznick handed Hitchcock the task of adapting *Rebecca* (1940), a modern riff on *Jane Eyre* by the English author Daphne du Maurier. It was a canny choice; the novel inhabits territory familiar to the best of Hitchcock's British output: menace, secrets, and the torment of a beautiful young woman. Despite a tussle for creative control between director and producer that set the tone for their future relationship, *Rebecca* was a success, fusing Selznick's glamour with Hitchcock's atmospheric suspense. Recognition at the Academy Awards followed; the film (and therefore Selznick) won Best Picture, while Hitchcock earned his first nomination for Best Director.

Joan Fontaine was also nominated for her performance as the unnamed heroine. Casting the part had been an arduous process. Hitchcock and Selznick traded strong opinions about the many auditionees, each trying to steer the production in the direction of his vision. "Too big and sugary," Hitchcock said of one actress; "Too Russian looking," of another. "Grotesque" was all he had to say about a third. Fontaine, always favored by Selznick, got the part but had a fraught time with her director. "We liked each other," she believed, "and I knew he was rooting for me," but he had "a strange way of going about it." Hitchcock wanted Fontaine to act like the anxious, lachrymose wreck described in the script, and he went to remarkable lengths to ensure she did. He told her that other cast members didn't like her, and that her leading man, Laurence Olivier, thought her role should have gone to his wife, Vivien Leigh. When Fontaine struggled to cry during one scene, Hitchcock asked if there was anything that might help. She ventured that if he slapped her in the face, that might do the trick. "I did," recalled Hitchcock, and Fontaine "instantly started bawling."

Rebecca announced Hitchcock in America as a director of "women's pictures" but also as a director of women, a man with a rare talent for creating, and re-creating, female stars. In December 1940, one magazine told its readers that Fontaine was not a "gorgeous genius" but a "puppet, walking and talking exactly as her Svengali Alfred Hitchcock demands!"

Perhaps no other male artist of the twentieth century dedicated as much time and effort to exploring the lives and identities of women. Certainly no aspect of his legacy is so heatedly contested. Caught between feelings of admiration and resentment, identification and estrangement, an instinct to worship and a desire to control, Hitchcock had a complex, contradictory set of ideas about women and his relationship with them. He surrounded himself with women, sought out their friendship, gave them responsibilities and opportunities that few men of his station did, and proudly championed their work. At the same time, it was through women that he revealed the darkest, most discomfiting parts of himself—and embodied the culture in which he existed, as a filmmaker and as a man.

Hitchcock's life spanned a remarkable period of change in the lives of women. Born in the age of Victoria, he was raised in the era of the suffragettes, when the popular newspapers that carried those tales of curious murders which he devoured also gave blanket coverage to the "suffragette outrages" of the 1910s, in which campaigning women cast off gender norms in acts of violent civil disobedience. In London, grand locations became scenes of disorder and terrorism, anticipating the way in which Hitchcock would use world-famous landmarks as the venue for perilous climaxes: in the National Gallery, Mary Richardson took a blade to Velázquez's *Rokeby Venus*; bombs were planted in St Paul's Cathedral and the Metropolitan Tabernacle; Egyptian mummy cases were smashed at the British Museum, the very place where Hitchcock staged his first great chase scene, at the end of *Blackmail*, one of his several films about the travails of a preyed-upon woman. The response of officialdom to the suffragettes' actions included brutal reprisals that had a hint of Hitchcock about them: imprisonment, beatings, the forced feeding of hunger strikers, carried out to punish lawbreakers and to humiliate those who transgressed the social code by not being sufficiently ladylike.

Cinema, in its fledgling state, gave space to women that more traditional industries and art forms did not allow. Charlie Chaplin first appeared as "The Tramp" in a film of 1914 costarring and directed by Mabel Normand, an instrumental figure in his breakthrough success. When the American publisher Houghton Mifflin published a book titled *Careers for Women* in 1920, it contained a chapter about the job of film director. Of course, the film business was never a haven of equality; even at this early stage, exploitation and marginalization of females was endemic. Yet women made themselves a crucial part of the landscape, as creators and audiences. For young women with increasing freedoms and disposable incomes, movie theaters were places of entertainment and empowerment, where images of their own lives, as well as projections of their fears and fantasies, could be enjoyed. Often, they would go to see stars such as Mary Pickford, a global phenomenon whose movies made her both rich and powerful.

Indeed, Pickford was a turbine that powered Famous Players-Lasky, the Hollywood production company. When Hitchcock started his career at the firm's London branch, he worked alongside, and beneath, many women, including those who dominated the scenario department. One of those women—identified in some places as Anita Ross but named by Hitchcock as Elsie Codd—wrote the script for *Number Thirteen* (alternately titled *Mrs. Peabody*), Hitchcock's first attempt at film directing, which fell apart during production in 1922. In his predirectorial days, the films he worked on were also heavily focused on female characters. One of those, *The White Shadow* (1924), starring the American actress Betty Compson, was thought lost until three of its six reels were discovered in New Zealand in 2011. Identifying precisely what contribution Hitchcock made to the film is difficult. The publicity that followed its discovery claimed he was assistant director, screenwriter, art director, and editor, though the British Film Institute gives the credit of editor to Alma Reville, and Hitchcock's writing work was tweaking and polishing a screenplay already drafted by Michael Morton. Even so, a twenty-four-year-old Hitchcock was heavily involved in the production. The movie is far from a classic—even Balcon admitted that the production team was "caught on the hop," as it tried to capitalize on the recent success of *Woman to Woman*, also starring Compson. Still, the surviving reels are intriguing, as they contain themes we now associate with Hitchcock's directorial work: doubles, mistaken identity, and the danger that lies in wait for young women who will not be tamed. The story concerns twin sisters: Georgina, a chaste, biddable girl, and Nancy, a bobbed-haired rebel "without a soul" who smokes, drinks, gambles, and flirts with men. When Nancy runs away to live a bohemian life of excess, the saintly Georgina protects her sister's reputation by assuming her identity. Frustratingly, the extant reels end just as the search for Nancy homes in on the Parisian nightclub she frequents. However, the scene is set for moral redemption; when Georgina unexpectedly dies, her soul possesses Nancy, who reforms her ways.

When Hitchcock's screenplays became more sophisticated—at least partly because he engaged better screenwriters than himself to craft them—the distinction between the good girl and the bad girl was blurred in complex female characters. An early draft of this character came in Hitchcock's silent film *The Manxman* (1929), in which Kate, played by Anny Ondra, wrestles with the competing binds of familial duty, social respectability, and individual fulfillment. Perhaps the best example of the type is Ingrid Bergman's Alicia Huberman in *Notorious*, written by Ben Hecht. Alicia is the fast-living daughter of a convicted traitor who is persuaded by the American spy Devlin (Cary Grant) to infiltrate a coterie of Nazis in Rio de Janeiro. As part of her mission, she seduces and marries Alexander Sebastian (Claude Rains), who possesses vital secrets about Germany's nuclear weapons. The hypocritical American intelligence officers who have recruited her look down on Alicia as "a woman of that sort," but Devlin, who is hopelessly in love with her, comes to understand her bravery and her moral worth. At the movie's climax, Devlin saves Alicia from being killed by the Nazis—and in so doing realizes that Alicia has also rescued him. The "fat-headed guy, full of pain" has been taught how to love by the virtuousness of a promiscuous woman.

Characters such as Alicia were crucial to Hitchcock's success; his identity as a filmmaker rested on his relationship with women, and he held as an article of faith that his audience was predominantly female. In 1931, he said he chose his leading ladies "to please women rather than men, for the reason that women form three-quarters of the average cinema audience." It was a contention he never abandoned; "80 percent of the audience in the cinema are women," he remarked in 1964. "Even if the house is fifty-fifty, half men, half women, a good percentage of the men have said to their girls: 'What do you want to see, dear?' So, men have very little to do with the choice."

The need to create movies that women would flock to see was one of the reasons his filmmaking team had a strong female presence at its core. Joan Harrison, the producer of *Alfred Hitchcock Presents*, was a twenty-six-year-old Oxford graduate when Hitchcock hired her to be his secretary in 1933. As often happened with those whom Hitchcock liked and trusted, Harrison's role quickly grew; she was asked to vet and appraise source material, and soon became part of his scriptwriting team, relocating to the United States when the Hitchcocks moved there. Peggy Robertson came into the fold in the late forties as a script supervisor but became a high-powered assistant, performing tasks more typically associated with a producer or a production manager. Aside from those pivotal figures, there was a roster of female writers, from famous names such as Dorothy Parker, who lent her talents to *Saboteur*, to the big-screen novice Czezni Ormonde, Ben Hecht's associate whom Hitchcock engaged for the post-Chandler rewrite of *Strangers on a Train*.

Principally, there was Alma, variously an assistant director, writer, unofficial coproducer, and a ubiquitous adviser whose opinion Hitchcock trusted unwaveringly. Alma was also the hub of Hitchcock's private life. In Britain and America, the couple very often mixed business with pleasure by hosting cocktail parties and dinners—cooked by Alma, a marvel in the kitchen—for the latest Hitchcock collaborators. In his pomp, Hitchcock was a regular at fashionable Hollywood restaurants, such as Chasen's, Perino's, and Romanoff's, but usually sat beside his wife. With the exception of his mother, he doesn't appear to have been particularly close to any woman until he and Alma began to work together in London and Germany, though he openly declared that he preferred the company of women, and particularly disliked being part of a big group of men. Being "one of the boys" sat uncomfortably with him; since childhood he had felt unnerved or diminished by competitive masculinity, something that imbued—in his mind, at least—a kinship with women. Donald Spoto has described Hitchcock as a loner who "never had the gift of friendship," yet a sincere and deep friendship is precisely what Hitchcock formed with Alma, in whom he found somebody who shared his sense of humor as well as his artistic and commercial ambitions, understood his fears and insecurities, knew how to buoy him up, but was also prepared to speak her mind when she thought he was in error. One writer who interviewed the Hitchcocks in their old age was impressed by a "fruitful kind of friction passing between them, as Alma interrupts one of Hitchcock's professorial monologues to interject her own peppery opinions."

Early and sustained success as a filmmaker gave Hitchcock extensive control over his working environment. Women therefore played a more prominent part in his life, professional and private, than might have been the case had he stayed in advertising, or pursued some other career. Hitchcock's films repeatedly latched on to what he thought were women's giddiest hopes and deepest fears: the fantasy of romance and adventure; the terror of rape and murder. In the process, he turned to Alma and the women around him for advice and insight. Yet the experience of watching some Hitchcock movies is that of observing a man trying to divine what he thinks are the endless mysteries of womankind, especially in matters of sexuality. "Although I think Hitchcock's camera was sympathetic to women," said Jay Presson Allen, one of the women who wrote for him, "I don't believe he necessarily understood them."

In relation to women, Hitchcock can sometimes appear like a curious brew of J. Alfred Prufrock and Benny Hill: English repression meeting English bawdiness, which may be two sides of the same coin. Shyness and insecurity in his physical appearance prevented Hitchcock from having romantic or intimate relationships with the women whose company he so enjoyed. At various times, he said he was very sexually inexperienced, and that he had lived much of his life in a state of impotent celibacy. Of the many things that he and Alma gained from their relationship, sexual fulfillment was not among them. Hitchcock told some that he'd had sex just once in his life, and joked that he'd had to use a fountain pen on the night Alma conceived. His occasional outbursts of "outrageousness" on set with his leading ladies—slapping Fontaine during *Rebecca*, for instance, and apparently exposing himself to Madeleine Carroll on *Secret Agent*—were done with the justification of getting

Alma and Hitchcock aboard the SS *Mary*, on a trip to America, June 1938.

an emotional response to aid their performance. One wonders whether, along with his stream of dirty jokes and innuendo, they were also his substitute for physical intimacy.

According to his own testimony, he was unusually cosseted at the time he took the reins on *The Pleasure Garden*, aged twenty-five, having never been out with a woman, not even Alma. During the filming of the drowning scene, he was baffled when the woman playing the victim refused to go into the water. It was left to the cameraman "to tell me all about menstruation. I've never heard of it in my life!" It might strike one as an unlikely story; Hitchcock was a movie director during the Roaring Twenties, "not a backward, pre-adolescent country boy from an earlier century," in the words of one skeptic. Yet such ignorance is not entirely inconceivable. After all, E. M. Forster confessed to the pages of his diary that only at the age of thirty—a year after the publication of *A Room with a View*—did he learn "exactly how male and female joined." Forster's powers of observation were at least as formidable as Hitchcock's, and his learning was immense; if he could have gone through his twenties in such a state of obliviousness, then why not the equally shy, socially awkward Hitchcock?

Regardless of its truthfulness, the tale speaks to his feeling that women were an exotic and unknowable species. It seems that even with Alma, there was some part of her being—her sexual self—that existed frustratingly beyond his ken. The bewilderment, fascination, and longing women caused in him were all diverted into his films. The ultimate manifestation of this is the fabled Hitchcock "blonde." His interest in blonde women is first hinted at in *The Pleasure Garden*, then confirmed by *The Lodger*, in which all the Avenger's victims are fair-haired, while Madeleine Carroll, star of *The 39 Steps* and *Secret Agent*, was the woman Hitchcock pointed to as the first true Hitchcock "blonde." Though taxonomized by their coloring, the definitive characteristic of these women is ineffable mystery. Like a scratched record, Hitchcock recurrently expressed a dislike of "women with sex hanging all over them like baubles," favoring instead "a woman who does not display all of her sex at once—one whose attractions are not falling out in front of her . . . she ought to maintain a slightly mysterious air." "Anything could happen to you with a woman like that in a taxi." He evoked this image of a reserved woman turning into an insatiable nymphomaniac on the back seat of a taxi so often that it's possible it stemmed from a real-life experience that, as Hitchcock told friends and colleagues, happened to him after a Christmas party in the twenties or thirties. Equally, it could have been a morsel of risqué gossip of the sort he loved to hear, and spread, about colleagues; or, simply the reverie of a frustrated, inexperienced man, with an immensely vivid interior existence. Without explaining how he came to formulate the theory, he repeatedly avowed that Latin women, though famed for their supposed hot-blooded passion, had little interest in sex, while the "typical American woman" is "frigid" and "a tease, who dresses for sex and doesn't give it—a man puts his hand on her and she runs screaming for mother." The most sexual women of all, he opined, were those of northwestern Europe, the Germans and Scandinavians, and especially the straitlaced English: aloof, decorous, and passionless on the surface, but quivering with hidden passions—Hitchcock could've been talking about himself.

The quintessential incarnation of this type of woman was Grace Kelly, who starred in three of his films, *Dial M for Murder* (1954), *Rear Window* (1954), and *To Catch a Thief* (1955). Interpretations of Hitchcock's behavior around actresses and his motivations in casting them differ, but his infatuation with Kelly is beyond dispute, as it had been with Ingrid Bergman the previous decade. The appreciation was mutual: Kelly and Bergman both declared themselves smitten with Hitchcock, his gracious manners, his humor, and his talent. In all three of her films with him, Kelly encapsulates the notion of femininity that exhilarated her director: the ice maiden concealing a volcanic sexuality. In *To Catch a Thief*, she is even given her own "back-of-a-taxi" moment when her lady-like character, Frances Stevens, abruptly steals a kiss from an astonished John Robie (Cary Grant) before shutting her bedroom door in his face. Hitchcock was thrilled to learn that in real life "the snow princess," as he called Kelly, appeared to embody his fantasy. "She fucked everyone," he is reported to have said on the set of *Dial M for Murder*, including "little Freddie the writer," referring to a dalliance between Kelly and the screenwriter Frederick Knott, which, as the author Steven DeRosa notes, might tell us as much about Hitchcock's view of writers as it did his views on sexually active women.

In each of her three films there is something extraterrestrial about Kelly's characters. She doesn't enter *Rear Window* so much as she manifests, from nowhere in the pitch black, as though beamed in from another dimension. Having roused her crochety boyfriend (Jeff, played by James Stewart) from his sleep with a soft, slow kiss, she switches on three lights, with a ritual recitation of each one of her three names—"Lisa. Carol. Fremont." Now she is illuminated: an angelic visitation in evening gown and high heels. And, lo, she delivers a miracle of a gourmet meal, transported fresh from one of Hitchcock's favorite Manhattan restaurants, turning a fusty bachelor pad into an oasis of midtown opulence.

In Hitchcock films, men and women are separated not only by biology but also by plains of experience: men—excluding the insane ones—inhabit a world governed by fact and rationality, while women, as Richard Allen argues, have access to mysterious reserves of instinct and intuition. In *Spellbound* and *Notorious*, Bergman's characters have an abundance of this quality, as do Daisy in *The Lodger* and Blanche in *Family Plot*, the director's third and fifty-third films, respectively. Throughout *Rear Window*, Lisa performs small miracles. Even Stella (Thelma Ritter), the nurse attending to Jeff's broken leg, showcases the mysterious powers of female perception when she tells Jeff how she predicted the Wall Street crash when she was nursing a director at General Motors. "When General Motors has to go to the bathroom ten times a day, the whole country's ready to let go." "Well, Stella," replies Jeff, "in economics a kidney ailment has no relation to the stock market." "Crashed, didn't it? I can smell trouble right here in this apartment. . . . I should have been a Gypsy fortune teller instead of an insurance company nurse." Like Midge, Barbara Bel Geddes's character in *Vertigo*, and Jane Wyman's Eve in *Stage Fright* (1950), part of Thelma's role is to embody "ordinary" womanhood. Arguably, these women reflect the women Hitchcock knew best, Alma in particular, those on whom he relied but who did not represent his ideal of feminine sexuality. Yet even these "ordinary" women have something unfathomable about them.

Hitchcock was one of a vast roll call of twentieth-century male artists who wondered aloud about who women are and what they want. What's unusual in Hitchcock's case is the eagerness with which our culture adopted him as an authority on the subject. During his most high-profile years, from *Notorious* to *The Birds*, his opinion was sought by interviewers—male and female—on various aspects of women's lives. How should they dress? How should they speak? Do they possess the necessary qualities to be good film directors? Do their fears differ from men's? On one

Hitchcock with Ingrid Bergman, during the filming of *Notorious*.

occasion, asked to distill the essence of femininity, he submitted that as he wasn't a woman, he probably wasn't best placed to answer. Usually, however, he was only too happy to give his two cents. He once claimed, without any apparent mischief, that it was a "very well known fact" that if "a woman is surprised in the nude, what does she do? She covers her breasts. Why not shield the area between her legs first? Never. Always the breasts." On another occasion, he offered tips on how women should dress in order to bag themselves a husband. "A woman who wants to subdue a man would do well to subdue herself first," he offered before getting into specifics: "Never dither about a color. Try it against the face

Hitchcock at work on *Rear Window* with Grace Kelly and script supervisor Irene Ives.

and contemplate the effect. . . . The new lilacs and mauves are very becoming, but do make certain that you get the *shade* right for *you*."

Only rarely did an interviewer ask where the maestro got his information. More commonly, his attunement with the feminine disposition was accepted as a self-evident function of his work. It led to a great many pieces by or about Hitchcock in women's magazines, and various invitations to support an array of causes linked, in one way or another, to women. In the sixties and seventies, there were multiple overtures from the organizers of beauty pageants, such as Miss World, Miss California, and Miss Zodiac, entreating Hitchcock to preside over the judging. He was also sounded out about becoming the owner of a franchise in the first iteration of women's professional basketball in 1978. Hitchcock swerved all such offers, but the notion that he had a powerful, sympathetic connection with women was a key part of his mythology. "It's easy for him to make a woman say 'yes,' " wrote the interviewer June Morfield in 1962. "You see, he has a way with them . . . once a woman gets involved with Hitchcock, she's rarely ever the same again."

Accompanying the image of Hitchcock as an expert on femininity was his reputation as a creator and controller of women. On May 10, 1958, a piece titled "Hitchcock Gives Free Rein to the Gentle Sex" appeared in *TV Guide*, with a nod to that week's episode of *Alfred Hitchcock Presents*. A mocked-up photograph displayed seven actresses from the series as puppets, each having their strings pulled by Hitchcock, their puppeteer. The day before that piece was published, Hitchcock attended the premiere of his latest movie: *Vertigo*, about male obsession and female objectification, in which James Stewart's retired police officer John "Scottie" Ferguson attempts to remold his lover, Judy, into a replica of Madeleine, the deceased object of his desire. Only in the final tragic minutes of the film does Scottie come to realize that Judy and Madeleine are the same woman (both played by Kim Novak), and that he has been unwittingly embroiled in a murder plot. Each generation of the last century has had its own "Pygmalion" movies about men trying to create their perfect woman: *My Fair Lady*; *Weird Science*; *Pretty Woman*; *Ex Machina*. The distinction between those films and *Vertigo* is that the director of the latter had for many years proudly boasted that transforming women was one of his great achievements. In this role, he likened himself not to Henry Higgins but, with tongue in cheek, to Svengali, the malevolent character from George du Maurier's novel *Trilby*, who not only turns a young woman into a star but exploits and abuses her in the process, possessing and controlling her in a way that robs Trilby of the person she once was.

A critical and commercial disappointment at the time of its release,

Vertigo is now widely regarded as one of Hitchcock's crowning triumphs, and the definitive statement of his interest in women. In Scottie, some see a stand-in for Hitchcock himself, a wry, witty, self-contained man whose life is governed by phobias and anxiety, and who becomes fixated with turning a girl-next-door into a ghostlike vision of feminine mystery and cool sexuality. In the years immediately preceding *Vertigo*, Hitchcock had been in search of a new blonde heroine. He'd been stung by the departure of Ingrid Bergman, who moved to Italy with the director Roberto Rossellini, and then by Grace Kelly's decision to ditch her film career in order to marry Prince Rainier of Monaco in 1956. In 1957, after directing her in *The Wrong Man* (1956) and "Revenge," the first episode of *Alfred Hitchcock Presents*, Hitchcock signed Vera Miles to a five-year deal. The contract forbade any commercial engagements requiring her to dress in swimwear, lingerie, or anything Hitchcock considered beneath the dignity of a lady. Hitchcock had her lined up to star in *Vertigo*, but his ill-health forced the production to be pushed many months back. By the time the wheels were ready to roll again, Miles was pregnant and no longer able to participate. Ultimately, he gave the female lead to Kim Novak, whose excellent performance is integral to *Vertigo*'s peculiar charm, but Hitchcock complained both during production and for many years after that "it was very difficult to obtain what I wanted from her because Kim's head was full of her own ideas."

Hitchcock next turned his attentions to Eva Marie Saint, an Oscar winner for her role in *On the Waterfront*, and seen at the time as the antithesis of the demure Hitchcockian blonde. Hitchcock reveled in the task of refashioning her for his purposes, inhabiting the role of a "rich man who keeps a woman: I supervised the choice of her wardrobe in every detail." The success was tinged with sadness. "I took a lot of trouble with Eva Marie Saint," he vented to Hedda Hopper, "grooming her and making her sleek and sophisticated. Next thing she's in a picture called EXODUS and looking dissipated." He was referring to Saint's performance in Otto Preminger's epic about the founding of Israel, after which she appeared in an equally earthy role as the downtrodden Echo in John Frankenheimer's *All Fall Down*. Saint's decision to take these parts seemed to cause Hitchcock genuine distress. In a passage of their interviews that did not make its way into François Truffaut's book, Hitchcock explained the effort required to transform an actress—even a highly accomplished Oscar winner—into a Hitchcock blonde: "you go to work on these girls and teach them how to use their face to convey thought, to convey sex, everything." All too often, however, his creation was sullied by some other director, unworthy of the siren he had made: "all the heartaches I've had, and the pain, and the emotion I've poured into the thing, ends up nothing . . . the effort: completely wasted."

This was the measure of Hitchcock's possessiveness, as well as the belief he had in his ability to realize female perfection. In this way, he sounds less like a dirty old man angling for the fulfillment of a sexual fantasy, and more like certain male fashion designers who come to see their muses as flesh-and-blood mannequins on whom to project aesthetic ideas only tangentially connected to the person beneath the fabric. It's a type of male relationship with femininity that Paul Thomas Anderson explores in *Phantom Thread*, his 2017 film about the fashion designer Reynolds Woodcock, who bears some striking parallels with Hitchcock beyond their similar surnames, including a gargantuan appetite, a loyal partner named Alma, and a penchant for stitching messages into his garments as a physical sign of himself in each of his works. To realize his narrow vision of feminine beauty, Woodcock relies on the diligent efforts of a talented and industrious team, mostly the women we see busily walking up and down his spiral staircase, an allusion—intentional or otherwise—to the chorus girls running down a set of stairs in *The Pleasure Garden*, the opening shot of Hitchcock's first film.

In Anderson's movie, Woodcock's career as a maker of new women is threatened by changing tastes of the wider culture, a shift in ideas about women and female beauty. When Hitchcock gave his confession to Truffaut, he was facing something similar. His work with Grace Kelly coincided with Marilyn Monroe's rise to stardom in films such as *Niagara*, *Gentlemen Prefer Blondes*, and *The Seven Year Itch*. In her book *American Beauty*, Lois Banner identifies Monroe as the apogee of two distinct types of femininity that dominated in the 1950s: voluptuousness, which connoted a certain sexual brazenness, and girlish, garrulous naivete. Both of these identities were anathema to Hitchcock's idea of the perfect woman. In a draft of *The Trouble with Harry* from 1954, John Michael Hayes details a vapid blonde bombshell character, ultimately excised from the shooting script, that resembles the Marilyn stereotype, that combination of hypersexuality and innocence identified by Banner. In the months and years after Monroe's death, Hitchcock proffered the opinion that "poor Marilyn had sex written all over her face." It was, in part, to counteract the rise of the brasher sexual identity projected by Monroe that Hitchcock persisted with his model of the cool, elegant blonde, to the extent that he cast the unknown Tippi Hedren to play Melanie Daniels in *The Birds*. In clinging to his ideal woman, Hitchcock was asserting himself on the movie industry and the wider culture.

According to Hitchcock, it was Alma who first alerted him to Hedren, whom she had seen in a television ad. In appearance, Hedren was a facsimile of a Hitchcock heroine: slim, with a pale complexion, a bone structure of Palladian exactness, and, of course, a head of shimmering blonde hair. Equally important, she had the "high-style, lady-like quality which was once well-represented in films by actresses like Irene Dunne, Grace Kelly, Claudette Colbert." Hedren was thirty-one and had never acted before. To most directors, this would have been a serious concern, but to Hitchcock, Hedren's inexperience had its advantages; she would certainly be more pliant in his hands, and he would not have to undo bad habits inherited from previous directors. Without meeting her or even seeing her act in anything other than her commercials, Hitchcock offered her a five-year deal, on the relatively modest sum of $500 per week. Hedren accepted, assuming it was television work that Hitchcock had in mind. A few weeks later, the director had her perform an expensive three-day screen test in full costume, acting out scenes from *Rebecca*, *Notorious*, and *To Catch a Thief*. Hitchcock then invited her to join him, Alma, and his agent Lew Wasserman for dinner at Chasen's, the Hitchcocks' favorite restaurant, where he told her that she was about to become a movie star. "Shortly after our drinks arrived, Hitch turned to me and without a word, handed me a small gift box," recalled Hedren many years later. "I opened it and found myself staring at an exquisite, delicate pin—gold and seed pearls, crafted to depict three birds in flight," Hitchcock's way of saying that the lead role in *The Birds* was hers. "I was stunned. I'm sure I gasped." Telling a story that she had heard many times before, Pat Hitchcock says, "Tippi started to cry. Alma cried. Even Hitch and Lew had tears in their eyes." Hedren's account is virtually identical, with one difference. According to her, Hitchcock's "eyes were dry. He just stared back at me—very, very pleased with himself."

For different reasons, *The Birds* was a difficult shoot for Svengali and his Trilby. Hitchcock fretted about the pressures of making the film through his own production company, as he had done with his previous movie, *Psycho*. Unlike that film, *The Birds* was a vast logistical undertaking, the most formidable of his career, exacerbated by the fact that he had cast an acting novice in the lead role. Having been led by Hitchcock step by painstaking step through the entire script, Hedren navigated the filming well, and produced a remarkably accomplished debut performance in a film that migrates from romantic comedy to shrieking horror. But in the infamous scene in which Melanie Daniels is savaged by birds in an attic, Hedren experienced genuine trauma. Before filming had begun, she had been assured that no live birds would be involved in the action; the most terrifying thing she'd have to contend with were a few mechanical ravens. But as the day approached, it became obvious to Hitchcock and his team that it would be impossible to capture the realism and intensity they were after without the use of real animals. As Hedren remembers, she found out about the change of plan on the morning of the shoot. "It was brutal and ugly and relentless," she says of the five days she spent on the floor of the set while birds were thrown at her head. The crew members who have spoken about it over the years attest that they all, Hitchcock included, felt bad about the situation. In 1980, Hedren said it was "very hard for Hitch at this time, too. He wouldn't come out of his office until we were absolutely ready to shoot because he couldn't stand to watch it." However, she now suggests that the episode was part of Hitchcock's effort to dominate her.

In the publicity for the film, Hitchcock boasted about the way he had invented 'Tippi,' insisting—without explanation—that her name from now on be held between inverted commas. Hedren was introduced to journalists with a brief biography and details of the exacting tutelage that Hitchcock had provided, including the twenty-five thousand dollars that had been spent on her screen tests, conducted with the exactitude of a real Hitchcock shoot. Even when Hedren spoke to America's teenage girls through the pages of *Seventeen* magazine, Hitchcock was with her to explain to the interviewer Edwin Miller how seriously he took building a character and, in this case, the actress cast to play her.

The minute attentions paid to her acting and the creation of her public persona elicited no complaints from Hedren: "He was not only my director, he was my drama coach, which was fabulous." The problem was that the 'Tippi' project strayed beyond the film set; Hitchcock inserted himself into Hedren's life in ways she could not accept. He left food he wanted her to eat outside her front door, sent her a peculiar Valentine's message, and peppered her with requests for her to join him for dinners, lunches, and drinks. When alone, he told her dirty stories and jokes, likely the same ones he told Grace Kelly and Ingrid Bergman, though Hedren wasn't anywhere near as amused as those two women appeared to have been. Worst of all, she alleges that one afternoon Hitchcock "threw himself on top of me and tried to kiss me" in the back of a limo directly outside their hotel. "It was an awful, awful moment I'll always wish I could erase from my memory." Hedren says the incident was never mentioned by either of them for the rest of the production.

The situation worsened during the filming of Hitchcock's next movie, *Marnie*, in which Hedren took the title role, originally intended for Grace Kelly. Hitchcock's unwelcome attentions continued, though some cast and crew members felt he had an old man's hopeless crush on an ingenue, nothing more. Things came to a head when Hitchcock forbade Hedren from traveling to New York to receive a *Photoplay* award from Johnny Carson on *The Tonight Show*, which infuriated Hedren, and which she interpreted as part of his broader strategy of controlling and possessing her. In the aftermath of this, an ugly encounter occurred between the two that abruptly ended their professional and personal relationship. Hitchcock spoke very rarely about what went on, and when he did his comments were elliptical and evasive. The most he revealed was that Hedren had crossed a red line and "referred to my *weight*."

Hedren's version of events alleges that Hitchcock sexually assaulted her. The first inklings of this story landed in the public consciousness in the early 1980s, in Donald Spoto's biography of Hitchcock, a book derided by some of Hitchcock's most faithful collaborators as fanciful and malicious. A further account was published by Spoto in 2009, on which the movie *The Girl* (2012) was based, enlarging the image of Hitchcock as a sadistic misogynist who deliberately humiliated Hedren to satisfy his lust and assuage his feelings of inadequacy. Then, in 2016, Hedren published her story in her own words. "I've never gone into detail about this and I never will," she writes of what occurred in Hitchcock's office. "I'll simply say that he suddenly grabbed me and put his hands on me. It was sexual, it was perverse, and it was ugly, and I couldn't have been more shocked and more repulsed."

Hedren's book was met with fierce criticism from those who maintain that Hitchcock adored women and prided himself on behaving like a gentleman in their presence. Doubts and questions—of a type very familiar to us from recent controversies—were raised. Why had her story shifted over the years? If Hitchcock had been guilty of sexual assaults, why hadn't she reported them to the police? How could she have previously spoken glowingly of a man she now claimed had abused her? Factual inaccuracies in Hedren's account were also highlighted. Hedren contends that Hitchcock was intent on ruining her career as punishment for rejecting him, and she alleges that François Truffaut had wanted to cast her in *Fahrenheit 451* but was dissuaded from doing so by Hitchcock. Truffaut's daughter, Laura, has said this is untrue. John Russell Taylor spoke for many skeptics when he accused Hedren of desperate attention-seeking: "How else is she going to stay in the eye of the public than by coming up with increasingly sensational stories about Hitchcock?"

Hedren's memoir was published a year before the torrent of allega-

Hitchcock instructs Tippi Hedren on the set of *Marnie*.

tions against Harvey Weinstein and numerous other powerful media figures catalyzed #MeToo. The sharpened focus provided by that phenomenon impels even those unconvinced by Hedren's allegations to take heed of the ways in which Hitchcock was known to have behaved around at least some women during his years in the film industry. Brigitte Auber, who played Danielle in *To Catch a Thief*, valued the friendship she struck up with Hitchcock, somebody she looked to as a kindly mentor. One evening in Paris, after the two had met for dinner, they sat in a car outside the apartment where Auber lived with her boyfriend. Hitchcock lunged at her, kissing her on the lips, though she immediately pulled back, stunned, much as Hedren claims to have done during the filming of *The Birds*. He was instantly contrite and embarrassed, and attempted to revive their friendship in the coming years, though Auber was unable to see him in the same light ever again. "It was an enormous disappointment for me," she told biographer Patrick McGilligan. "I had never imagined such a thing. The quality of our relationship was entirely different." McGilligan rejects the darker characterizations of Hitchcock, yet he acknowledges that the director was "capable of questionable behavior" and claims that Hitchcock "had at least two friendships with actresses" turn sour in the mid-1950s in similar fashion, but only Auber was prepared to speak publicly about her experiences. McGilligan also describes Hitchcock's penchant for groping women and for "thrusting his tongue inside [a woman's] mouth."

Despite the protestations of Hitchcock's ardent defenders, it's difficult to see why Hedren would have fabricated the entire story, and taken the trouble to keep it alive more than half a century later. Hitchcock spent decades publicizing the pleasure he took in possessing and molding beautiful young women; the fact that many of those women had nothing but good things to say about him—and several of them continue to talk fondly of him to this day—does nothing to mitigate the experiences of others who felt preyed on. Hitchcock alone bears responsibility for his acts of predation, though his behavior was thoroughly facilitated and normalized by the culture within which he lived and worked, one we are only beginning to fully reckon with. Socially awkward, self-absorbed, and sexually frustrated, Hitchcock made passes at and assaults on young women because he failed to control his urges, but also because in the environment he inhabited, men of his standing were afforded license to behave in that way. In Hitchcock's case, this latitude enabled his pursuit of a fantasy version of himself—the suave, sexually successful alpha male with women in his thrall—in denial of the obnoxiousness or the absurdity of his conduct. Those who were around him in his dotage at Universal were aware of unusual arrangements he had with at least one of his young secretaries, who would disappear into the boss's office for lengthy spells. One Hitchcock biographer alleges that the woman was shaken by "ugly, intimate demands" of an unspecified nature and left Hitchcock's employ in distress. Others offer a different perspective. One former colleague, the screenwriter David Freeman, remembers asking her what she was up to behind the closed door; "I'm being erotic for Mr. Hitchcock," she replied. Precisely what occurred, and what degree of coercion was involved, is probably impossible to prove at this remove. Money may have changed hands, either as a token of affection or as an inducement for silence. When the woman concerned arrived for work in a flashy new car, colleagues drew their own conclusions about how she had managed to pay for it. At least one of her contemporaries believed that she appeared unfazed by the whole thing, and maybe thought it worth the effort considering the remuneration she received.

Perhaps. But even if this more benign version of events is accurate, that for a time this was a known part of Hitchcock's office routine evinces the huge allowances that were made for his behavior. In the sixties and seventies, he was a living institution at Universal, its third-largest shareholder, and widely regarded as "a god of cinema." Indulging a peccadillo in the privacy of his oak-paneled office was considered no more than the old boy deserved. "It was a different era," said David Freeman, a much younger man who wrote Hitchcock's final script in 1979. "People would keep their mouths shut about it. Certainly the people on the staff. Peggy Robertson ran that company and she knew what was going on and she knew also that no one would benefit from the world knowing this."

Robertson was indefatigably loyal to Hitchcock the man and the entity, and would hear no criticism of his treatment of women. But from personal experience she knew that powerful men in the movie business had license to indulge themselves. Decades after the event, she recalled starting her career on a film directed by Gabriel Pascal and being horrendously embarrassed by Pascal's insistence that she sit next to him in restaurants while he fed her. Though it gave the crew "lots of laughs and sighs of relief that they weren't the ones who were getting fed," she hated it. "But there was nothing I could do, you know? Who was I, the lowest person there, lower than the clapper boy."

A longtime friend of Hitchcock's, Marcella Rabwin, described him as "absolutely charming. He was so sweet. He was so nice. He did everything right." Yet she also knew he was indulged in various ways because he was considered brilliant: "He was sarcastic and he was cruel and he was many of those things, and we all overlooked it." Rabwin had experience of other such brilliant and domineering men, having been assistant to David O. Selznick, the "woman's film" impresario who launched Hitchcock's career in Hollywood, and who also thrived on controlling and changing actresses. "Every relationship my father had was a Pygmalion relationship," said Selznick's son, Daniel, but none more so than with the actress he eventually married, Jennifer Jones. Daniel thinks the filming of the Selznick movie *Duel in the Sun* was the "apotheosis of David's fantasy of Jennifer. At one point during the filming, he had her go to some place outside of Tucson and crawl across sharp pebbles so that her knees got completely bloodied. In a hundred and ten degree heat. And she was prepared to do whatever was required." As the last few years of revelations and reckonings have taught us, this dynamic is not only part of Hollywood's distant past but its present, too.

If the events of the filming of *Marnie* have gained piquancy in recent years, the same is true of the movie itself. At the time of its release in 1964, critics were not kind. A reviewer for the *Tatler* found fault in the principal characters, Sean Connery's Mark Rutland embodying "the vanity of men," while Hedren's "properly cold Marnie left *me* properly cold, too." The *New York Times* was similarly put off by casting and characterization, as well as by the "glaringly fake cardboard backdrops" and an "inexplicably amateurish script." In the subsequent half-century, the film has undergone an astounding shift in reputation. Today, many critics consider it Hitchcock's purest work of art, a complex, textured film in which technique and thematic preoccupations combine without commercial compromise. Robin Wood, the doyen of Hitchcock critics, said, "If you don't like *Marnie*, you don't really like Hitchcock . . . if you don't love *Marnie*, you don't really love cinema."

Adapted from Winston Graham's novel of the same name, *Marnie* is about a brilliant but damaged woman who thieves her way around the country, robbing huge sums from her duped employers before leaving town and relocating under a new identity. In Philadelphia, a mutual attraction develops between Marnie and her new boss, the dashing but arrogant Mark Rutland. What Marnie doesn't know is that Mark has an inkling of her criminal past. When she steals from him, he quickly tracks her down and blackmails her into marrying him. They take a honeymoon on a cruise ship, where their bond develops, but Mark becomes infuriated by Marnie's complete aversion to sex—although it's hard to imagine many women rushing into bed with a man who has coerced them into marriage. In their cabin one night, Mark is overcome with lust and frustration, and pulls Marnie's nightdress down. Seemingly ashamed of his actions, he apologizes immediately and wraps his dressing gown around her. Marnie is now frozen, catatonic, as Hitchcock women often are in the wake of a traumatic experience. Mark begins to kiss her, and then he rapes her. The next morning, Marnie attempts to drown herself in a swimming pool but is saved by Mark at the last minute. From here on in, Mark, by turns caring and obnoxious, makes it his objective to cure Marnie of her kleptomania and her sexual phobias, which he seemingly does in a melodramatic final scene in which Marnie locates the childhood trauma that has disordered her mind.

Even by Hitchcock's standards, *Marnie* is an ambiguous, polarizing film. When working on his first draft, Evan Hunter questioned the rape scene, arguing that it was dramatically unnecessary and bound to ruin any sympathy the audience had for Mark. Hitchcock was undeterred: "Evan, when he sticks it in her, I want that camera right on her face!" When Hunter submitted a version of the script with the rape omitted, he was let go soon after. His replacement, Jay Presson Allen, later told Hunter that she thought the rape was Hitchcock's "reason for making the movie." It presaged events more than a decade later when Ernest Lehman objected to Hitchcock's plan to begin the script of *The Short Night*—his final, unfinished film—with a rape scene. Lehman was ultimately replaced by David Freeman, who had no such qualms. Likewise, Allen had no worries about how Hitchcock's female audience would respond to *Marnie*. "I'm very fond of Evan," she remarked in 1999, "but I think he was psychologically a little naïve. There's a vast audience of women out there who fantasize the idea of rape." In another forum, she told an interviewer that writing the scene "didn't bother me at all . . . I just thought she [Marnie] was kind of a pain in the ass and I didn't blame him [Mark]." That, coming from the film's scriptwriter, might be the kind of sentiment that the writer Bidisha detected when, in an article in the *Guardian* in 2010, she cited Mark's treatment of Marnie as a crystalline example of Hitchcock's "full-on misogyny, rampant woman-blaming and outright abuser apologism."

Other critics argue that *Marnie* is actually a conscious attack on the patriarchy, the most forceful example of Hitchcock's compassionate respect for female suffering at the hands of traditional masculinity, an identity from which he had always felt alienated. Mark Rutland, argues the academic William Rothman, "has a singular bond with women . . . a capacity to identify with women, no less than to desire them, that he has in common with Hitchcock himself." Moreover, Rothman questions "whose will, if anyone's, is being imposed on whom" during the "so-called rape." Marnie's total inertia, her complete lack of any emotion after Mark rips off her nightdress, "gives him grounds for believing that after his sincere apology she now trusts him, and gives us grounds for believing, as he does, that he is making love to her, not raping her." That opinion seems hard to square with what we know of the film, and what we know of rape. Marnie is, to use Rothman's words, "entranced, turned inward," and totally unresponsive when Mark takes hold of her; that she's not screaming and scratching his eyes out does not indicate she's consenting.

Similar debate has been had—though less frequently, and less passionately—about the scene in *Blackmail* in which Alice stabs Crewe as he forces himself on her. It seems to have been filmed unambiguously as an attempted rape, but certain critics have expressed doubts. That Hitchcock's films cause such debate about the simple facts of what is shown to us on-screen could be attributed to their director's commitment to ambiguity, his aversion to a black-and-white world of easy answers. It also reflects the gap between attitudes of our own time and those of Hitchcock's filmmaking prime. In the 1980s, Robin Wood posited that audiences of that decade might struggle to fully comprehend Hitchcock's classic films of the 1930s, because assumptions about gender and sex had shifted so much. Something similar could now be said of Hitchcock's films of the sixties. One need only read the Truffaut interviews for evidence of how the critical atmosphere has changed in the last sixty years. At several junctures, Truffaut analyzes Hitchcock's female stars in a notably sexualized way. Of Teresa Wright's performance in *Shadow of a Doubt*, he says her "portrait of a young American girl was outstanding . . . she had a lovely face, a nice shape, and her way of walking was particularly graceful." He's even more effusive about Kim Novak in *Vertigo*, whose "carnal qualities" and "animal-like sensuality" were perfectly suited to the role. "That quality is accentuated, I suppose, by the fact that she wears no brassiere."

This does not mean that the debate about Hitchcock's treatment of women, on-screen and off, is merely twenty-first-century political correctness. In 1972, on the release of *Frenzy*, the *New York Times* pushed back on the reams of positive reviews with an article, "Does *Frenzy* Degrade Women?" As early as 1935, *Film Weekly* ran a piece in which Barbara J. Buchanan asked Hitchcock, "Why do you hate women?" The question was prompted by Hitchcock's recent film *The 39 Steps* in which Madeleine Carroll is handcuffed to her costar Robert Donat and hauled around the Scottish countryside as he tries to clear his name and uncover a nefarious spy ring. Buchanan said this denied Carroll "her dignity and glamour," a suggestion that, ironically, if judged solely by today's standards might be construed as more than a little patronizing toward women. Hitchcock denied that he hated women—though he did, jokingly, call them "a nuisance"—and said Carroll was put through the mill in order to strip away the surface layers and reveal the real person beneath. "Nothing pleases me more than to knock the ladylikeness out of chorus girls!" Paralleling his situation with Fontaine on *Rebecca*, and Hedren on *The Birds*, stories also spread—some by Hitchcock himself—that he had deliberately caused Carroll upset when the cameras were off, pretending to have lost the keys to the handcuffs, meaning she was cuffed to Donat for a large chunk of the first day of filming. He assured the public that his scheme was all in aid of improving her as an actress, and she "entered into the spirit of the whole thing with terrific zest. . . . I remember, though, that she had a friend watching on the set one day, who came up to me and reproached me for my rough handling of her!"

Putting a woman through an ordeal was certainly something Hitchcock relished, and which he wove into his public profile. Quoting the playwright Victorien Sardou, he said the key to good drama is to "torture the women!" He knew that statement was provocative, just as he understood that it was essentially true. More than a century on from the *Perils of Pauline*, our screens are still saturated with graphic depictions of violence done to women at the hands of men, for our entertainment. Hitchcock didn't create our culture's appetite for that, but he knew better than anyone how to exploit it—and taunted us for our perversity in enjoying it.

Moreover, rarely do women in his films emerge diminished from their trials. Hitchcock's heroes are often obstinate and emotionally stunted, their glaring defects softened by wit and charisma. The women have their flaws, too, but grit and constancy usually see them through the worst that men, full of their anger and violence, can hurl at them. Roger Ebert wrote that "sooner or later, every Hitchcock woman was humiliated." He was only partially correct. It's true that Grace Kelly, as Margot in *Dial M for Murder*, is subjected to a terrifying attack in her own home. But as Lisa in *Rear Window* she puts Jeff to shame by acting with physical and moral bravery, proving Thorwald's guilt and her own fortitude in the process. In *Under Capricorn* and *Notorious*, Ingrid Bergman plays women who are drugged and held captive in their own homes. But they are survivors, whose qualities transform the self-absorbed prigs in their midst. We, the audience, are encouraged to celebrate the strength, tenacity, and guile they display in staying upright in a wind tunnel of masculine hostility. The men who become dangerously besotted with women in Hitchcock films are usually rather weak and pathetic characters; we're not meant to admire but pity Scottie in *Vertigo*, Gregory Peck's Anthony Keane in *The Paradine Case* (1947), and Jonathan Cooper, played by Richard Todd, in *Stage Fright*. In *Marnie*, Hedren's character takes the awful responsibility of shooting her horse to end his suffering after a bad fall. In so doing, she displays a capacity for courage and selfless love entirely beyond the possessive, controlling Mark. William Rothman may be wide of the mark in questioning whether there is a rape in *Marnie*, but he's surely correct that Mark thinks he is acting like a perfect gentleman— because Mark is a self-obsessed oaf unable to appreciate the pain he's causing the woman he professes to love.

Such is the strange, contradictory nature of Hitchcock's relationship with women—redolent of Hollywood's bifurcated treatment of women over the last century. His working life was spent thinking of ways to charm and unsettle female audiences, giving them heroines they would simultaneously aspire to emulate and dread becoming. Yet he used those same opportunities to effectuate his fantasies of control and specialness, making exploitation of women not only a theme of his work but a methodology, at times, even the work itself. "When one is reading criticism defending or attacking Hitchcock's treatment of women," writes Tania Modleski, one of Hitchcock's most thoughtful critics, "one continually experiences a feeling of 'yes, but . . .'" This is probably how Hitchcock felt, too.

5

THE FAT MAN

"I don't know who you employ to time your scripts, but whoever did it is misleading you horribly. I will even go so far as to say disgracefully." In August 1943, Hitchcock found himself immersed in one of his least favorite activities: repelling the encroachments of a Hollywood producer. Several months earlier, Selznick had loaned his star director to Twentieth Century-Fox, who were keen on Hitchcock's bold idea of making a wartime movie set entirely in a lifeboat. The scripting process for *Lifeboat* (1944), involving John Steinbeck, had been challenging; now, with filming already under way, Darryl F. Zanuck was insisting that Hitchcock's finished script was fifty percent too long. Hitchcock was infuriated by this eleventh-hour intervention, especially as he knew Zanuck was incorrect; meticulous in his planning for every movie, Hitchcock had a very firm grasp of schedules and timings. When Zanuck saw a hastily assembled rough cut of the first reel, his tune changed completely: "It has tempo, interest, and a feeling of being very much on the level."

Despite garnering Hitchcock his second Oscar nomination, the film did not do well at the box office, and was criticized by those who thought Hitchcock had made the American characters look lazy and chaotic in comparison to the steely, resourceful German U-boat commander played by Walter Slezak. Slezak raved about the experience of working with Hitchcock: "Hitch knows more about the mechanics and the physical technique of acting than any man I know." He was less complimentary about his fellow cast member Tallulah Bankhead—he thought she was a narcissistic fool; she referred to him as a Nazi—and morale among the actors was rarely high. Filming lasted nearly three months, during which the cast was confined to a small boat floating in a huge water tank. When they weren't feeling seasick, they were drenched, freezing, and struggling with colds. Hitchcock had limited sympathy. As he told one cast member during the production of a previous film, "there's no law that says actors have to be comfortable."

In such circumstances, it was not immediately obvious how Hitchcock would perform his customary cameo. The solution he hit on was pure Hitchcock: clever, funny, and in the service of his personal mythology. Twenty-four minutes into the movie, the character Gus reads aloud from a newspaper; on the page facing the camera is an advertisement for a fictional weight-loss product, the Reduco Obesity Slayer, with photographs of two Alfred Hitchcocks, one his familiar three-hundred-pound self, the other a much slimmer man. This was life intruding on art. Since January 1943, Hitchcock had been on a severe diet, and he used *Lifeboat* as a way of advertising that fact to the public. The world knew Hitchcock as "a fat man," and he often played the role for them; he'd been debasing himself by putting fat gags in his publicity articles for years. In an industry filled with the slender and the chiseled, his appearance made him memorable, a way of distinguishing himself from the crowd. It could also act as a masking agent, obscuring the person beneath the flesh. Both had their advantages and disadvantages. Neither gave him what he really craved: control of his own body, materialization of the Alfred Hitchcock who lived inside his head.

Within the shifted reality of the Hitchcock universe, it takes a brave or foolish person to trust the evidence of their own senses. Observable truth is a false friend; there is no steady fact of existence that cannot be undermined. The treachery extends even to food and drink. In *Notorious*, Ingrid Bergman's heroine is poisoned to the verge of death by a cup of coffee; homebodies in *Rich and Strange* (1931) and *The Man Who Knew*

Too Much feel their discomfort in foreign lands because of the exotic food they are fed. In mid-twentieth-century America, nothing could be more wholesome and nourishing than a glass of milk—except when it's handed to an unwitting guest at the Bates Motel as part of her final meal. In Hitchcock's initial design for *Suspicion*, another glass of milk, glowing like lily-white kryptonite, was delivered by Cary Grant to Joan Fontaine not as a restorative tonic but as a poison-laced murder weapon. Maybe the best episode of *Alfred Hitchcock Presents*—his favorite, and one he directed—has a woman serving the leg of lamb with which she killed her husband to the policemen investigating his disappearance. As the cops blithely dispose of the murder weapon, a delicious home-cooked meal doubles as the execution of the perfect crime.[*]

For most of his eighty years, Hitchcock felt the same unease about comestibles, which were both friend and foe, the source of joy and companionship, disgust and shame. The moral and physical complications of eating and drinking were subjects of daily contemplation for him, and oozed into his work as plot points, potent thematic symbols, and vital insights into character. He resented the impact that consumption had on his body, that unruly mass of flesh that could not be compelled to do his bidding. He could "accidentally swallow a cashew nut and put on thirty pounds right away," he explained on his struggles to make himself the size and shape he longed to be. When the cameras rolled, lissome bodies were prone to follow his every command; a shift of Tippi Hedren's eyebrow, or a flick of Eva Marie Saint's hair, would happen only if he desired it. Even some obstinate method actor like Montgomery Clift could be made to tilt his head in the way his director said it should. No amount of self-denial or wishful thinking ever gave Hitchcock the same control over his own form. As he was reminded incessantly throughout his adult life, he was "fat," a term that denoted not simply a physical characteristic but a way of being in the world. The distress his weight caused him—or, more important, his inability to control it—can hardly be overstated. "I don't feel comfortable in my fat," he admitted to a journalist

---

[*]   "Lamb to the Slaughter," written by Roald Dahl.

Hitchcock at Oktoberfest, Munich, September 1960.

in 1964. Not one friend or colleague believed he had ever been anything other than profoundly unhappy about his appearance since childhood. He spoke of his relationship with his body in Kafkaesque terms, a hostage within a captor's grotesque shell. "I have all the feelings of everyone encased in an armor of fat," he complained, convinced that his weight made others see him as something less than fully human.

Hitchcock being Hitchcock, he found a way to profit from his grievance, by pouring his appearance into his personal mythology and making it a marketable commodity. And, as people uncomfortable in their own skin often do, he pretended to find the whole subject hilariously funny, making a joke of himself before anybody else had the chance. In a speech he recycled on several occasions in the sixties and seventies, he addressed the question interviewers had asked for decades: "Who is the real Alfred Hitchcock?" First, he told his audience, the "real Hitchcock" is not the person your eyes tell you he is; that fat man is an impostor. In a characteristically deadpan riff, he said the confusion initially arose when he'd asked for a stunt double to perform his first cameo. "The casting department, with an unusual lack of perception, hired this fat man! The rest is history. He became the public image of Hitchcock." The misconception lingered until some years later he gave "an accurate and detailed description of my true self," and the casting department hired Cary Grant, although the public still considered him to be the short, tubby man with a bald head and dour, emotionless face.

As sensitive as he was about his appearance, Hitchcock had a deep-seated desire to be seen; he invested creative effort in publicizing his face and body, and appreciated that his distinctive looks could be made to work to his advantage. On one level, the jigsaw of his silhouette that he dispatched as Christmas gifts in 1927 (the year in which he first became a celebrated public entity) might be read as a self-deprecating joke; in nine strokes of a pen, he rendered himself—the round-shouldered blob that he saw, and despised, every time he looked in the mirror—worthy of artistic reproduction. Yet it was also a revealing display of self-promotion. From that moment, Hitchcock commandeered his body to help curate his public image, creating for himself a new, semi-fictional persona, a character more layered and complex than most of those that appeared in his films. At the peak of his celebrity, he dashed off the silhouette when approached by autograph hunters—including Andy Warhol, who had him draw his profile on a batch of Polaroid photos when the two met for lunch in April 1974. Warhol, like Hitchcock a former ad man, would have appreciated the savviness with which Hitchcock reproduced and exploited his silhouette, which was also used to publicize many of his Hollywood films and was seen at the start of every episode of *Alfred Hitchcock Presents*.

He was pained not only by his size but also by his shape, the "cottage loaf" body that he said he inherited from his mother. A photograph of one of the Hitchcock boys shows in all likelihood his brother, William, on a horse next to his father outside the family shop; it displays the same physique Hitchcock lamented: stocky, large head, round torso, and limbs just a little less than proportionately long. The boy in the photo is perhaps eight or nine, roughly the same age at which Hitchcock would relish the aroma of the local bakery, where he'd be given free biscuits, a treasured memory he retrieved as an old man. It was also around this time that a schoolmate told him he was "funny-looking." Whether or not the child meant to cause harm, it lanced right to the bone. Hitchcock never developed the emotional robustness that would allow him to brush negative comments aside. Iffy reviews, rejections, and sleights—real or imagined—burrowed their way inside and stayed there, even at the height of his success. On this occasion, young Alfred went home and stared into the mirror, turning his head to one side to inspect the contours of his face. When his mother came up to him, he asked her whether she agreed that he looked odd. "You'll grow out of it," was her simple, devastating response.

The sense of existing within a body that was not truly his might have emanated from this exchange, as did his fixation with his profile. The habitual drawing and redrawing of the silhouette was an attempt to bring this disruptive impostor under control, and an inversion of the Hollywood cliché of being photographed only on one's "good side." He publicized his "funny-looking" profile relentlessly, even though he could be cutting when those around him expressed a similar fixation with their appearance. One of the anecdotes he enjoyed sharing with journalists was of the time a young actress, knowingly beautiful, asked which he thought was her best side. "You're sitting on it," Hitchcock replied.

Sometimes, he tried to convince Americans—and perhaps himself— that it was only Hollywood's unattainable standards of beauty that made him seem physically unusual. There had never been a time in his life when he could have been described as slim, but "in England, everyone looks as I do, and no one would remark on it," he said in 1979. That was a characteristic exaggeration, provably false but resting on an import- ant kernel of truth. The England of Hitchcock's infancy was a place and time that cast larger bodies as models of good health. "Plumpness" was the word; in the East End of 1899, razor-sharp cheekbones and catwalk builds were generally associated with poverty and tuberculosis. Both Queen Victoria and her son Edward VII were renowned for their heft and their gargantuan appetites. Like Hitchcock, who "was not one to toy with his food," Victoria chomped her way through meals at an astounding clip, and she and Edward both gorged on rich multicourse meals. The era also experienced a transformation in British dining, especially in Lon- don, led by chefs such as Auguste Escoffier, who introduced what is now considered classical French cooking, service à la Russe, and the model of the modern restaurant. There wasn't much haute cuisine served up chez Hitchcock, which was a household of potatoes, roast meat, and fish and chips that they sold from one of their outlets on Salmon Lane. Yet Hitchcock would always regard this pre–World War I moment as a culi- nary high point, not because it was gluttonous but because it seemed to him the ultimate in simple sophistication, an ideal he cherished in all aspects of life. As one colleague put it, "his pleasure was in artistic effi- ciency." He collected menus from the period and enjoyed reading them, a practice that seemed like some refined form of torture when he was on one of his periodic spells of dieting. When he threw a dinner party for Joan Harrison and her husband, novelist Eric Ambler, the food was re- created from one of his favorite menus, dating from 1892.

Despite anything he may have said to the contrary, his size and shape very obviously marked him out from the crowd in England. The bird-like Alma was always worried about his weight, and periodically went on his diets with him, a sign of the love and dedication she invested in all things Hitchcock. "He is much too heavy," she said in 1972. "He tries to diet now and again, but it is awfully hard for him. He does so love ice-cream." In 1917, his exemption from military service was possibly on the grounds of his obesity, which must have been a source of simultaneous relief and embarrassment in an environment of nationalist fervor when all young men were expected to prove their masculine worth. Any sense of estrangement would have been even more marked in the 1920s, when slimness for both men and women became the ideal as never before. In the artistic world of Weimar Germany, where Hitchcock began his directing career, the slim line was revered. Even the monsters in German cinema were tall and slender. The shadow cast on the wall by the creeping figure of Nosferatu, an image to which Hitchcock referred so often in his own work, stretches up, not out; his limbs are as long and spindly as Hitchcock's were short and stubby. If Hitchcock felt he was a thin man trapped inside a fat man's body, he may also have felt like a twentieth-century man trapped in a nineteenth-century shell.

In day-to-day life, rather than a modern machine that powered him forward, Hitchcock experienced his body as an anchor. In 1938, a short report appeared in London's *Daily Herald* about a cricket match he played in, presumably for a team representing Shamley Green, the Surrey village where the Hitchcocks had a cottage. The journalist was struck by Hitchcock's imperious demeanor on the pitch, noting that he bowled the ball with a languorous underarm action, "feet planted firmly on the ground, from which position he did not move. The ball was brought back to him by hand." Aside from the incongruous image of Hitchcock decked out in white flannel on a sports field, this is instantly recognizable as the Alfred Hitchcock of Hollywood fame, rooted to the spot, haughty and immobile as others buzz around him. It sounds remarkably similar to descriptions of him in other situations requiring some degree of physical exertion. He and Alma spent many Christmases in St. Moritz, where Hitchcock contented himself with watching others having fun in the snow. "Hitch insists on getting into ski pants," explained Alma, "which takes him about an hour, and then he sits on the porch smoking the whole time!" The writer Whitfield Cook recalled going to a nightclub in Los Angeles with the Hitchcocks and Grace Kelly. "I danced with Grace and Alma . . . Hitch just sat and watched." Others remembered Hitchcock's tendency to arrive at a party, plant himself in one spot, and wait for others to approach him. In all those settings Hitchcock developed a particular social style to accommodate his weight, one of nonchalant mastery in which ordinary folk flitted this way and that while he stood—or sat—like a lone molecule of calm.

In the first few years as a director, before he became heavily obese, he had been keen to present himself as a rather dynamic figure, braving exotic locations, being loud and busy in the studio. From the mid-1930s, when his weight rose as high as three hundred pounds, his style changed to the point where he was routinely observed to be looking inert, or downright bored by the whole business of filming, even falling asleep during takes, a habit he eventually developed at dinner, too. "He does not deliver a mass of instructions in a loud voice and he does not rush from one part of the set to another," reported one journalist who had been granted access to the set of *The 39 Steps*. "It is hard to tell whether he is annoyed or not. . . . He is a mystery to most." A decade later, a journalist for *Good Housekeeping* encountered a relatively slim Hitchcock, yet still made note of his size, shape, and mobility as he contrasted the physicality of the director and Ben Hecht during the story conferences for *Notorious*. While Hecht would pace about or "sprawl artistically on the floor," Hitchcock, "a 192 pound Buddha (reduced from 295) would sit primly on a straight-back chair, his hands clasped across his midriff, his round button eyes gleaming."

The turn against Victorian plumpness was arguably even more dramatic in America than it was in western Europe. In the late 1890s, Charles Dana Gibson's illustrations of the so-called Gibson Girl captured a picture of willowy beauty that would influence representations of female perfection for the next hundred years or more. Male bodies were also reshaped—metaphorically and literally—by the example of the heavy-weight world champion James Corbett, and by Bernarr Macfadden, the father of bodybuilding. By 1920, the eradication of fatness had become a lucrative industry and something of a moral crusade. If people know one thing about William Howard Taft, president between 1909 and 1913, it's probably the humiliating story of the time his three-hundred-pound naked body got wedged in the White House bathtub. The tale is almost certainly untrue, but it has persisted because it allows us to mock the man for his weight. In the entertainment world, the public censure of fat was obvious. In 1909, Lillian Russell, once celebrated for her voluptuous-ness, gave interviews on how she fought the flab, revealing the details of her calorie-burning morning workout. When the German soprano Olive Fremstad made her feted debut in New York, critics praised her voice but ridiculed her size and shape. A few years later, another soprano, the Ital-ian Luisa Tetrazzini, spoke of her surprise at how much attention Amer-ican journalists paid to the weight and appearance of opera singers.

Hitchcock felt the pressure of that same critical gaze when he first set foot in the United States in 1937. At this point, he had yet to sign a deal with an American studio, and he treated his visit as part fact-finding tour, part publicity campaign to raise his profile. As had been his habit in London, he arranged to conduct a couple of interviews over food and drink. He looked on mealtimes as opportunities to get important work done with journalists, actors, writers, and executives. They were also occasions when he was at his most accessible. Over several years, Peter Bogdanovich built a relationship with Hitchcock through lunchtime con-versations, as did John Russell Taylor, the man Hitchcock entrusted to be his biographer. "Working with Hitch meant eating with him," explains Shirley MacLaine, star of *The Trouble with Harry.* "I wasn't blonde, thin, ethereal, so he didn't want to jump on me"; instead, he lavished her with food and drink: "breakfast was pancakes, fried eggs, fruit, toast, and jam. My lunch was worse because the desserts were heaven, and dinner was something I had to learn how to eat with him: meat, potatoes, appe-tizers, seven-course meals and Grand Marnier soufflés." The dining table was a place where Hitchcock felt comfortable and powerful, a fixed setting that encouraged familiarity, sharing, and conviviality while still having the barriers of table and chairs to prevent genuine intimacy, a safe space and a venue for performance.

When he arrived at the 21 Club in midtown Manhattan for his interview with H. Allen Smith, one of New York's best-known celebrity interviewers, Hitchcock had surely approached it as an opportunity to charm, and to display himself as a bon vivant of an irrefutably English variety, in line with his idiosyncratic films. Instead, America viewed him as a glutton. If Smith's account can be believed, Hitchcock devoured a lunch of three steaks and three helpings of ice-cream parfait, supplemented by three pots of tea and some post-blowout brandy. Perhaps the gorging had been an act. Hitchcock loved to stage elaborate practical jokes at dinner parties, designed to baffle and disgust his companions. It's not completely unthinkable that the 21 Club lunch had been intended as something of this ilk. If so, the joke got lost in translation. He was reported to have been unhappy that his capacity for consumption, not his filmmaking brilliance, dominated the coverage of his American debut. Eight days after Smith's article was published, the *New York Times* ran a piece that likened Hitchcock to Falstaff, describing his hail-fellow-well-met personality at the dining table, which probably got closer to the Rabelaisian side of his character that he had been hoping to transmit. But it was accompanied by a mocking description of his body: "His free-floating, unconfined waistline is a triumph in embonpoint. . . . When he smiles, his chins all smile with him, one after another." It set the tone for the next forty-three years in which American journalists used Hitchcock's body as a creative-writing homework task, each endeavoring to sketch with words the most gratuitous depiction of his physical form. Writers compared him to Disney characters, clouds, four-legged animals, and various inanimate objects. One declared that "Alfred Hitchcock has a posterior like those London busses on which his characters so often flee," while another went for an extended nautical metaphor, likening Hitchcock's profile to the "forepart of a sailboat with a balloon jib set. His mast, or backbone, is tilted slightly to the rear to balance the

weight of his flying belly and he moves forward in a unique waddle. . . .
His red face floats like a pennant at the forepeak, cushioned on three
ample chins."

In her 1943 article, "300-Pound Prophet Comes to Hollywood," for
the *Saturday Evening Post*, Alva Johnston split her wonderment for Hitchcock's moviemaking skills with the memory of how his peculiar body
had transfixed the public on his arrival. "The newcomer was a sensation
with his cycloramic torso, setting-sun complexions, round, wonder-
struck eyes, and cheeks inflated as if blowing an invisible bugle. People reacted to him like children at sight of balloon giants in Macy's
Parade. . . . He drove about a tiny Austin which fitted him like a bathing
suit." Nearly twenty years later, at the apex of Hitchcock's commercial
and critical standing, another writer for that same publication claimed
that the director "holds two distinctions on the movie-TV industry—
one centered on his odd physiognomy, the other on his impudent vocal
cords." Apparently, *Psycho*, *North by Northwest*, *Vertigo*, *Notorious*, *Shadow
of a Doubt*, and all his other outstanding achievements over the preceding decades were overshadowed by the sight and sound of a man who was
written about as though not an entirely real person, halfway between a
forbidding mythical creature and a children's cartoon character.

Even his employers joined in. The critic Casey McKittrick has mapped
how David O. Selznick and his employees actively encouraged promotional materials that emphasized Hitchcock's size in his early years in
Hollywood. McKittrick's study of Selznick International Pictures official
records—dominated by Selznick's long-winded memos that exasperated
Hitchcock—lead him to believe that the company's top brass used Hitchcock's sensitivity about his weight to force him to "comply with their
wishes and to shame and disarm him when contract disputes arose."

Rather than trying to ignore or fight against these things, Hitchcock
took possession of his body and guided America's interest in it, starting
in 1943 when he went on a lengthy and very public weight-loss regimen.
In various conversations, Hitchcock cited different triggers for this,
including a story that he had caught sight of his reflection in the window of a shop in Santa Rosa during the filming of *Shadow of a Doubt* in

1942. For a second, he wondered how this fellow could have allowed himself to grow so big—and then realized that he was looking at himself. He voiced disgust at his own body in a very Hitchcockian way, noticing how the flesh around his ankles had started to spill over the top of his socks, a tiny detail that conjures an arresting image. However, the issue of his size had become much more than aesthetic: he was experiencing chronic back pain and struggled to get insurance because of his obesity, he had an abdominal hernia (a problem he refused to have corrected until 1956) and, most alarmingly, a heart that was sixteen percent enlarged. His physical health surely contributed to his supposed impotence, too. Pressures to slim began to accumulate. In late 1942, his mother passed away, and in the first week of 1943, he received the news that his brother had also died. Suicide was ultimately found to be the cause of William's demise, but initially Hitchcock was told that he had succumbed to a heart attack. The shock of those two bereavements—even though he and William were never especially close—could only have sharpened his sense of mortality, especially now that he was forty-three, no longer anyone's idea of "the boy director."

The year 1943 proved a turning point for Hitchcock, personally and professionally. A week after William's death, *Shadow of a Doubt* was released, a film that Hitchcock had shaped as producer as much as director. *Lifeboat* followed, and was in many ways the most ambitious project he had undertaken. In between, he lost an enormous amount of weight and would never be so big again. In shedding something of his old self, he birthed another new life of Hitchcock: The Dieter.

Hitchcock remarked that when audiences saw the mocked-up ads for Reduco in *Lifeboat*, he received numerous inquiries about where this miracle weight-loss treatment could be obtained. The truth, of course, was that Reduco, rather like *Lifeboat* itself, was a fictional product based on the general flow of real-world events. To lose the pounds, Hitchcock had not turned to a miracle cure but to a course of abnegation, skipping meals and denying himself the treats that gave him such pleasure. His was something of a crash diet, in which he essentially missed breakfast, save for a cup of black coffee, and restricted himself to the same at lunch or, at most, a minute steak (just the one) and a green salad, with something similar for dinner. No space was made in his schedule for exercise of any sort, but he cut out various things he blamed for his rotundity, especially potatoes and his beloved ice cream. His Achilles' heel was alcohol, as it had been for his father and his brother. Joel McCrea, the star of *Foreign Correspondent*, said that he saw Hitchcock down a pint of champagne at lunch breaks in 1940. Around the same time, Samson Raphaelson was taken aback by the great quantities of gin and orange Hitchcock got through as they worked on the script of *Suspicion*. When he wanted to lose weight, Hitchcock was able to cut back on the booze, but he admitted that his taste for it made controlling his weight an uphill struggle. His wife knew it, too, and guests saw him sneaking drinks when he thought Alma wasn't looking.

The daytime sustenance of coffee and steak remained his default menu for long periods of the rest of his life, though dinner was a different story. Those who lunched with him often felt it was expected of them to follow the ritual. Anthony Shaffer, the screenwriter of *Frenzy*, grew sluggish after several days of midday steak and suggested that they might try something different the next day. Twenty-four hours later, Shaffer was presented with an extensive array of dishes. Hitchcock was joshing, but perhaps the joke was also meant as a rebuke for what Hitchcock inferred as criticism of his eating habits. Shaffer went back to the daily steak and never mentioned it again.

Hitchcock wasn't the first or last Hollywood star to deliberately change their body shape, but nobody had publicized it in quite the way he did. Not only did he crowbar the subject of his weight loss into a film about wartime calamity on the high seas (in which the survivors risk dying through thirst and starvation), he also put it into living rooms across the United States in the form of a spread in *Life* magazine, which comprised a series of photographs before, during, and after his reduction from two hundred and ninety-five pounds to two hundred and thirty-eight pounds over an eight-week period. And, as the text in the article makes clear, the story was to be continued: by time of publication, Hitchcock was down to around two hundred pounds, and his ultimate goal was one hundred and sixty-eight. The photos are very Hitchcock-ian in their execution. In each shot he poses with his trademark blank expression—one that manages to convey dourness and flamboyance simultaneously—next to a potted plant; as the plant grows in each snap, so Hitchcock shrinks. Aside from being terrifically clever and funny, there's also a feel of great contemporaneity in these photos; they could be ripped from the pages of a modern supermarket tabloid, or an Insta-gram story published by a social media influencer. This piece, which was ultimately incorporated into his *Lifeboat* cameo, was planned months in advance of the film's release, suggesting that from the time he decided to lose weight, Hitchcock had mulled the publicity opportunities, thinking of how he might use his body to deepen his relationship with the Amer-ican public.

From then on, Hitchcock incorporated his weight struggle into his public reputation. Nearly five years later, he penned an article about his latest movie, *Rope*, in which he announced that for his next cameo the "Hitchcock countenance will appear in a neon 'Reduco' sign on the side of a miniature building," seemingly sure that his readers would instantly understand the reference. Until the end of his days, Hitchcock's weight would hit peaks and troughs; a period of gain would be followed by a spell of self-denial. The fluctuations were spotted by the press, and Hitchcock was available for comment.

As Jan Olsson notes, Hitchcock's was "one of the most written-about bodies in the twentieth century," as scrutinized as any of the actresses whose appearances he obsessed over. But among his generation he was rare—possibly unique—in being a famous, powerful man whose attempts to maintain a healthy weight and find peace with the way he looked became a topic of public discussion and part of his public image, even while he lived. The cameos and the wry news pieces sometimes gave the appearance of a man with a rhino-thick skin, for whom the subject of his obesity was a bit of fun. That was evidently untrue. He was com-fortable with ridicule, but only so long as he was directing it. Whitfield Cook recorded in his diary the sight of Hitchcock performing "the breast

Hitchcock reveals his weight loss, January 1943.

ballet," a dinner-party turn in which—under the influence of much red wine—Hitchcock would whip his top off and gyrate his pectorals for the amusement of his guests. He also did "the whistling sailor," a ventriloquist's gag achieved by drawing a face on his naked belly, with the mouth around his navel; then, in the words of one who witnessed it, he "whistled, at the same time wobbling and shaking his stomach, and the big pink visage below his red face seemed not only to whistle but to change its expression." Those who saw these performances found them hysterically funny; knowing Hitchcock's talent for performing, they probably were. Yet, knowing also how sensitive he was about his appearance, it's difficult not to find the idea of Hitchcock presenting himself as a big fat joke more than a little sad.

In other people, he always found fatness a matter of humor and ridicule. Before the filming of *Torn Curtain*, Hitchcock tinkered with a scene in the script in which the erratic behavior of a member of the public threatens to have the lead characters captured by the East German authorities. As originally written by Brian Aherne, this disruptive member of the public is a small woman, scrawny and disheveled, but Hitchcock found the scene comedically lacking. Under his correcting pencil, the skinny woman became obese, the implication being that fat bodies are inherently funny in a way that thin ones are not. That overweight people struggled to be taken seriously was a lesson he had learned over and again. "I don't look like an artist," he pondered aloud when asked why he had never won an Oscar. "I don't look like I've starved in a garret."

An ironic concomitant of the consumerist boom of the Truman-Eisenhower era was rapid growth in the weight-loss industry. Hitchcock's apparent switch from prewar feaster to postwar faster gave him a connection with millions of other Americans, especially women. In 1940, he was still telling journalists that he ate "simply but a lot." By the 1950s, he was speaking of himself as a gourmet who was also an inveterate calorie counter, carefully planning his meals in order to make sure he had space for an evening martini. Discernment, restraint, and matchless self-discipline now became a key part of his public image. In 1955, for example, the *Los Angeles Times* published his tips for getting rid of "that turkey and eggnog waistline," and he provided the paper's *West* magazine with a list of his favorite Los Angeles eateries, all of which he said were chosen purely on account of their culinary sophistication. For the popular women's magazine *McCall's*, he raved about the brilliance of Escoffier, spoke nostalgically about the dining habits of his Edwardian childhood, and hammed it up for the cameras, sitting glumly before a meager plate of food, which, as Jan Olsson has outlined, became a common pose for Hitchcock during the fifties. The days of ice cream for breakfast and six-course lunches were gone. In fact, he suggested, they had only ever existed within the minds of mischievous or gullible American journalists who had reported his quips about liking steak à la mode as if fact. In moments of self-criticism, he blamed his lack of willpower for not being able to lose weight permanently. Other times, he proffered more forgiving theories. "I don't get the jitters; that's why I'm overweight," he once claimed. "I don't work or worry it off." On several counts, that explanation was patently false.

The persona of a gastronome tortured by his passion for food and drink wasn't simply invented for publicity purposes. Those around him on location in the south of France for *To Catch a Thief* recall Hitchcock's tussle between abstention and excess. As Grace Kelly remembered it, "He used to diet all week in anticipation of having a glorious meal on Saturday evening. He'd spend all week just thinking about it." Her partner of the time, the fashion designer Oleg Cassini, joined them for many of those meals and was struck by how Hitchcock directed the occasions with an energy few recalled seeing in him in any other setting. "We would gather at the restaurant of his choice for the precise meal of his choice. We always ate in restaurants rated three stars or better. Still, Hitchcock would review everything in advance: the wines, the soup, the fish, the meat, the sorbet between courses, the dessert, the fruit and the cheese. He would preside over it all, like an emperor, savoring each morsel. I've never seen anyone enjoy a meal more."

Hitchcock transmitted the idea that, for him, dinner with company at a fine restaurant was a total and immersive creative experience, similar to the making of a film. Though he always stressed his preference for well-cooked, simple food, the serving of a meal gave him an opportunity to express the extravagant and theatrical aspects of his personality, dominating the situation by stage-managing it. Marcella Rabwin observed this when Hitchcock threw a dinner party for her at a Los Angeles restaurant. Hitchcock planned the whole menu, and had ingredients flown in fresh from around the world, at a time when such a thing was a great extravagance. There was woodcock from Scotland, beef from Japan, limestone lettuce from Kentucky, and, of course, several bottles of the finest champagne. "It was a meticulously timed event," recalled Rabwin, remembering how staff at the restaurant shuttled back and forth to collect food from the airport, at tremendous expense. His expenditure on food and drink was vast. In his first year in America, he spent $2,459.30 in restaurants, more than $40,000 in today's money, and a further thousand dollars each on groceries and liquor.

Knowing how Hitchcock bloomed during the course of a dinner party, Grace Kelly threw one in his honor on their return from filming *To Catch a Thief*, at which she served the dishes from France that he had most enjoyed. Edith Head, the acclaimed costume designer, thought the gesture revealed a profound similarity between Kelly and her director, both of whose lives were guided by the pursuit of sensory stimulation. "Grace was never THE ACTRESS; she liked acting, and did it well, but it was just another experience; she was a girl who believed in life. She loved beauty, loved prettiness, and wasn't afraid to tell you so." Food was also a point of bonding between Hitchcock and Ingrid Bergman. "I loved to visit the Hitchcocks," Bergman said. "Alma was one of the best cooks in the world. I always had second helpings of everything, especially dessert."

The center of Hitchcock's gastronomic universe was his home, where he and Alma teamed up to make elegant consumption an immovable part of their daily routine. When Alma unofficially retired from her work on Hitchcock's movies in the 1950s, she invested her time and creative energies in cooking, something she'd always loved and at which she excelled. She experimented with new recipes, preparing meals for guests or, more commonly, making dinner for Hitchcock and her to share after he came home from the studio. Pat remembers that her father would frequently phone home after lunch to discuss what he could look forward to later that evening; it was over these dinners that Hitchcock would work through script or production problems with his wife. Invariably, the table was beautifully laid, the wine thoughtfully selected. "They took their time," Pat recalls, "and at the end of the dinner, after a cup of coffee, Hitch stood up, put on an apron, filled the sink with water, sprinkled the soap, and did the dishes."

In the early 1960s, the Hitchcocks overhauled the kitchen at their Bel Air home to allow Alma a bigger canvas on which to create. The renovations—which apparently cost sixty-five thousand dollars, more than the original cost of the entire house—included the latest and best in terms of kitchen hardware, utensils and gadgets, as well as an enormous walk-in refrigerator-freezer, and a wine cellar that held as many as sixteen hundred bottles, fitting for a man who had recently been awarded the prestigious title of Grand Officer of the Burgundian Order of Tastevin. In his excellent writing about the shifting significance of food to Hitchcock's public profile, Jan Olsson explains how members of the press were invited to capture this shrine to fine dining in a number of photo-heavy pieces—usually timed to promote a new Hitchcock film— the first being in Look magazine, August 1963. Twenty years earlier, an article like this might have opened with a comment on Hitchcock's hind quarters, the girth of his belly, or the ruddiness of his cheeks. Instead, the first words quote Hitchcock on the similarities between cooking and filmmaking. "Food, like pure cinema, is putting pieces together to create an emotion. . . . Independently meaningless, together they mean something." Look presents Hitchcock as front of house, the haughty but humorous maître d'; back of house was Alma, a homely force of creativity who shared with readers two of her recipes, including a dish she called "Terrine à la Hitchcock." Olsson points out that the Hitchcocks' rebrand as the neighborhood Francophile sophisticates was well timed, and not only because it mirrored Hitchcock's emerging reputation as Hollywood's *artiste sans pareil*. Julia Child's *Mastering the Art of French Cooking* had been published two years earlier, in 1961, and the first season of her television show *The French Chef* ran between February and July of 1963, concluding only a month before the publication of the Hitchcock piece in *Look*. Child's influence helped demystify "fancy" French food, finding a spot for souf-flés and consommés in ordinary American kitchens. This is precisely the way in which the Hitchcocks' interest in food was covered in the last two decades of their married life. When Pat Hitchcock published a short book about her mother in 2003, she devoted fifty-one pages to Alma's recipes and menus. It reads like one of Child's books, albeit with the occasional English treat among the French classics—Yorkshire pudding, pheasant with bread sauce, roast lamb with mint sauce, all Hitchcock favorites.

From the mid-sixties on, the references to Hitchcock's weight dra-matically reduced in the pages of the American news media, or at least they were sublimated into the image of Hitchcock as serious connois-seur, an image he was careful to maintain. In 1966, he sent a disgrun-tled telegram to a press officer in London, complaining about a letter that had appeared in *London Life*, a new and very fashionable publication. The offending missive had referred to Hitchcock ordering steak and kidney pudding when it should have been steak and kidney pie. Unhappy that he might appear to be ignorant of the difference, Hitchcock pressed to have a correction issued.

By the seventies, the decade in which America's "obesity epidemic" began, Hitchcock's body no longer seemed as unusual as it had at the end of the Great Depression. Surely, his advanced years and stellar rep-utation had earned him a break from the gossip, innuendo, and ridi-cule. Nevertheless, the long struggle with his weight had taken its toll. Hitchcock's final ten years were a slog. He suffered from excruciating pain in his arthritic joints, likely exacerbated by years of supporting so much weight and his fanatical opposition to exercise of any sort. Weekly checkups with the doctor had been part of his life since 1942, but in 1965 these increased to two, sometimes three, times a week. He had a pace-maker fitted in 1974, and took pleasure in showing people the machinery he had to connect to himself when sending the hospital his latest read-

Gourmand and gourmet; Hitchcock at the 21 Club in Manhattan, 1956.

ings. Boozing was not advised in this condition, but the more his health faltered and his productivity declined, the more he reached for liquor to stem the anxiety. He tried to be subtle about it. He'd ask a secretary to bring more ice for his drink, her cue to break out a cube of frozen vodka; the maid knew that when he requested orange juice, he really meant something more medicinal; he'd find a way to bring afternoon drinks into the morning, and he secreted a bottle of brandy in his bathroom for emergency swigs. He was in no condition to make films, and Alma, who fell victim to her own debilitating health problems in the seventies, was too frail to cook. The two cherished pillars of their creative lives, cinema and food, had been knocked away from beneath them. In a couple of heartrending letters to friends and family in the late seventies, Hitchcock chose to express the emotional difficulties both were experiencing in terms of the impact it was having on their diet.

> Lunch usually consists of a sandwich of thin bread, one we enjoy most is a roast beef spread, and we always keep a ham. She has a toast breakfast, afternoon tea with a chocolate biscuit and then dinner. If Pat doesn't provide it, I go out and with the help of the day nurse usually prepare something like a fillet steak or half a chicken, which is easy to handle. . . . This is a very sad letter, but there's little else I can tell you. Naturally, she never leaves the house, but I try to take her out one night a week to our favorite restaurant, but manoeuvring her is quite a business. That is why she can only manage it once a week.

Ultimately, though, Hitchcock kept control of his body and ensured that it lived beyond the grave. While his television shows aired, the silhouette of his profile was as recognizable to viewers across the Western world as Mickey Mouse's ears, Marilyn's hourglass figure, or Elvis's curled upper lip. In 1956, a year after *Alfred Hitchcock Presents* premiered, and several years after their association had ended, David O. Selznick requested permission to use the silhouette to promote some Hitchcock movies that Selznick wanted to re-release. Hitchcock refused. Later, a PR executive suggested that they freshen the image and create a new silhouette design. Again, Hitchcock said no.

In June 1972, the audience of *The Dick Cavett Show* applauded as the host, in imitation of Hitchcock, appeared in silhouette at the back of his set. He held the pose for a few seconds, at which point Hitchcock emerged from the opposite direction, just as he did at the start of his own programs. The studio erupted with cheers and whistles. Facing a svelte, debonair man half his age, Hitchcock knew the body being celebrated was his. Traitorous, deceptive, and unreliable though it may have been, it could not have belonged to anyone else.

6

THE DANDY*

Of the ten movies that Hitchcock made during his seven-year contract with Selznick, only three were produced by the mogul who brought him to Hollywood: *Rebecca*, *Spellbound*, and *The Paradine Case*, starring Gregory Peck, Ann Todd, and the Italian actress Alida Valli, whom Selznick hoped would be his next great female star. On paper, *The Paradine Case* seems promising Hitchcock material: the story of a suave English barrister whose infatuation with the woman he's defending in a murder trial imperils his marriage, his sanity, and his client's life. Selznick, however, wasn't content for Hitchcock to shape it as he saw fit, and intervened at every crucial juncture, rewriting James Bridie's script, vetoing Hitchcock's ideas for shooting the crucial courtroom scenes, and excising roughly an hour from Hitchcock's cut. It was one of the most stressful and chastening experiences of Hitchcock's career.

The movie was the last he was obliged to make under the terms of the Selznick deal, and it was with relief and excitement that he went on to his next project. *Rope* was produced by Transatlantic Pictures, a production company newly established by Hitchcock and his old friend from London, Sidney Bernstein. To underline his sense of agency, Hitchcock

---

* This chapter owes a particular debt to Thomas Elsaesser's essay "The Dandy in Hitchcock," which was itself written in response to Raymond Durgnat's thoughts about Hitchcock's aestheticism and dandyism.

made a radical departure from his familiar shooting and editing techniques in favor of a series of unbroken long takes, artfully cut to make it appear as one fluid, unbroken piece of film. It was an exceptionally ambitious scheme, which pushed the technology of the day to its limits, and the merits of which are keenly debated. To some, *Rope* is a technical masterstroke. Others think of it as a moment when Hitchcock betrayed the principles of his art. "It's inherently uncinematic" is the implacable opinion of fellow director David Fincher. "It's not a movie."

Hitchcock's other major production decision was to shoot in color for the first time, a visual leap perfectly suited to the film's content. *Rope* centers on Phillip and Brandon, a couple of dandies who attempt to execute the perfect murder for the aesthetic pleasure it will bring them. They are two of Hitchcock's murderers as artists, for whom everything in life—including the effectuation of death—is an opportunity for creative perfection. "I've always wished for more artistic talent," says Brandon. "Well, murder can be an art, too. The power to kill can be just as satisfying as the power to create."

All the action takes place in their beautifully appointed Manhattan apartment, a place that can only be understood in color. Theirs is a world of well-cut clothing and fresh-cut flowers; antique furniture and crystal glassware; rare books, piano recitals, and dinner parties. Even the stunning view from their living room window, the New York skyline of sunsets, skyscrapers, and electric lights, would lose its power if painted in black and white. It was a material existence that Hitchcock understood, for it mirrored his own. It was he who guided the selection of the artworks to be hung on the apartment walls; he who stipulated the color of Phillip and Brandon's suits. Despite looking like a staid British bank manager, Hitchcock apportioned great depth to the surface of things. He wasn't showy or decorative in his dress, but he was committed to the perfection of appearance as a way of exerting control over himself and the world around him. In his work and through the living of his life, he reconciled the two strands of the nineteenth-century figure of the dandy, and in so doing asked questions about what it means to be a man in the modern world.

———————

Perhaps the reason it seems so peculiar to discuss "Hitchcock the dandy" is that the common conception of dandyism has drifted quite some way from its roots. Type "dandy" into a search engine, and one is given the definition "a man unduly concerned with looking stylish and fashionable," augmented by a use of the word in a sentence: "*his floppy handkerchiefs and antique cufflinks gave him the look of a dandy.*" The dandy evoked here is a descendant of the fin de siècle variety typified by Oscar Wilde, flamboyant young men let loose in the dress-up box. No sartorial flourish was too extravagant for these aesthetes: hats, capes, and scarves, all in bright colors and fancy fabrics, decorated by jewels, trinkets, and feathers. Wilde, the unignorable poster boy for 1890s dandyism, first made a name for himself in America by proselytizing a new dawn in male clothing. He urged men to cast aside somber formality and dress themselves with verve and imagination.

Foppish Wilde set in train an eye-catching lineage of extrovert dandies across the twentieth and twenty-first centuries, particularly among the English—Quentin Crisp, Brian Jones, and Russell Brand all qualify. But Wilde's image was an unconventional elaboration of the original dandy, Beau Brummell, a social-climbing celebrity of Georgian Britain who, ironically, had helped to establish the masculine uniform against which Wilde rebelled.

In Brummell's philosophy, sobriety and austerity were key; there was no place for flashy adornment or garish color. Exquisiteness, not extravagance, was the watchword. Brummell used his body not as a playground for his imagination, but as a mannequin on which to perfect the male ideal by obsessing on tiny details. He was known to spend hours in front of the mirror fussing over the knot in his cravat and the tilted angle of his hat. His look was predictable but flawless.

Like Wilde, Brummell looked to the example of the ancient Greeks for his idea of the perfect man, embodied by the long-limbed, muscular silhouette that proliferated in their art. In the seventeenth and eighteenth centuries, English country dress had emphasized the belly, narrowed the shoulders, and shortened the legs, favoring those—such as Hitchcock, as it happens—with John Bull–like frames. Brummell tossed tradition aside and redesigned gentlemen's clothing to make the chest, shoulders, and legs the key male attributes. Under his influence, the template of the modern men's suit was created, and, by extension, something of the modern man: a machine for civilized existence.

Brummell and Wilde represent two distinct traditions of dandyism; Wilde was Bowie's Ziggy Stardust to Brummell's Thin White Duke. However, beneath the differences in attire they were united by the belief that the perfection of outward appearance reflects an inner spiritual mastery, and that manners and style are vital to the living of an elevated, hygienic existence in the modern city, a place in which you're only ever a misstep away from the sewer. Hitchcock displayed kinship with both traditions, including in his physical appearance: not just the clothes he wore, but how he wore them. Whether consciously or not, his daily routine was remarkably in step with Brummell's precepts for the well-lived masculine life.

The two schools of dandyism rear their heads in *Jamaica Inn*, the last film Hitchcock made before signing with Selznick. Falling between two Hitchcock classics, *The Lady Vanishes* and *Rebecca*, the film gets little critical attention and is generally regarded as noteworthy only because of Charles Laughton's performance as the deranged villain, Sir Humphrey Pengallan. "We can't recall when we've ever held a monster in such complete affection," stated the *New York Times* reviewer back in 1939, although one of the leading experts on Hitchcock's English period is not alone in believing Laughton's face-pulling histrionics to be "virtually unwatchable." Peter Ackroyd might be correct when he says that *Jamaica Inn* is "Laughton's picture, not Hitchcock's." Even so, it articulates something about style and masculinity highly germane to its director.

The film features a character called Dandy, a member of Pengallan's criminal gang. On the page, Dandy could be read as a flamboyant Wildean—proudly showing off his new lace cuffs in his first appearance—though there's no hint of lavender in Edwin Greenwood's performance. Pengallan is closer to a Brummellian dandy, an aging Georgian rake who, echoing the real Brummell's biography, ridicules his erstwhile friend, the newly crowned King George IV, as "a painted bag of maraschino and plum pudding." Outwardly respectable, Pengallan lives by a moral code that rejects mainstream concepts of law and order in favor of a dandyish sense of his own superior being, foretelling the attitudes of Brandon and Phillip in *Rope*. On surveying booty spirited from a recent shipwreck, he outlines his worldview to his oafish henchman:

> Look at this exquisite stuff. Worth the miserable lives of a hundred rum-rotten sailors. It's perfection of its own kind. That's all that matters, Merlyn—whatever is perfect of its own kind. I'd rather transport all the riff-raff in Bristol to Botany Bay just to save one beautiful woman from a headache. And that's something you don't understand and never will, because you're neither a philosopher nor a gentleman.

Hitchcock wouldn't have shared the social elitism of that speech. But the idea that life finds its apogee in "whatever is perfect of its own kind" encapsulates very neatly his idea of style, in objects and in manners.

Barely into adulthood, Hitchcock resolved to dress the part of the man he felt was waiting within, obscured by that "armor of fat" and "cottage-loaf" shape. While still working his entry-level jobs in his teens and early twenties, he acquired the sharpest suit he could afford, cultivated a thin mustache, wore a natty homburg, and, whenever finances allowed, forwent homemade sandwiches for a proper lunch at an upscale restaurant on the Strand. His friend and collaborator Samuel Taylor saw this as evidence that Hitchcock had always known "the kind of human being and the kind of character he was going to be." With an unerring sense of occasion, he relished any event for which he had to dress up, whether a work function, an opening night of a new play, or a boxing match. Reminiscing about some of the fights he witnessed at the Albert Hall in London in the interwar years, he marveled at the aesthetic incongruity between the brutality in the ring, soaked in bodily fluids, and the sophistication of the watching crowd dressed in evening gowns and black tie. What a con-

The young dandy at work. Hitchcock c. 1926.

trast, he remarked in 1962, to "the Hollywood people" of the present day: men who go out at night in "a shirt . . . without a tie . . . and a light suit, and a woman goes in an evening dress—that awful combination." When his income leaped during the second half of the 1920s, Hitchcock took himself to Savile Row and Jermyn Street, where Brummell had been a century earlier, to set in place what would constitute his "look" for the rest of his days: dark business suit with white shirt, dark tie, and highly polished black shoes.

A true dandy believes that good taste is timeless; Brummell and Wilde both disregarded fashion, which Wilde described as "a form of ugliness so absolutely unbearable that we have to alter it every six months." With the exception of silly getups he wore for a few of his television shows and the odd publicity shoot, these bespoke suits were the only clothes the public ever saw Hitchcock in. Even those closest to him could be caught off guard at the sight of a dressed-down Hitchcock. While on a family vacation in Hawaii at some point in the 1970s, he emerged from his hotel room in what seemed to the rest of his clan like a new skin: a mint-green shirt. Seeing the stunned reaction from his daughter and granddaughters, Hitchcock explained that Alma had bought it for him. He didn't seem thrilled to be venturing into uncharted territory at this stage of life, and Pat wondered whether her mother hadn't bought it as a practical joke. One Hitchcock biographer observed that Hitchcock's commitment to his suits, even when sweltering under a blazing sun or studio lighting, made his clothing a kind of "disguise," a fancy-dress costume similar to the eccentric clothing favored by other imposing directors such as Cecil B. DeMille and Josef von Sternberg. True, dark suits became a trademark for Hitchcock in the way other modern artists developed sartorial identifiers—Picasso with his Breton shirt, Dalí and his waxed mustache. Yet Hitchcock's clothes were the opposite of a disguise. They were a visual statement on how he approached living and filmmaking: with precision, rigor, and efficiency, and with as much understated elegance as he could muster. In the words of Philip Mann, a biographer of some of the great dandies of the last hundred years, "The dandy does not wear his clothing as fancy dress. . . . It is a uniform for living."

The academic Thomas Elsaesser believes the essence of Hitchcock's dandyism isn't in the design of his suits, which were entirely prosaic, drab even. Rather, it's the fact that Hitchcock "*always* wore them, in every climate, in his office, on the set, in the Californian summer, in the Swiss Alps or in Marrakesh." Certainly, Hitchcock's commitment to correctitude over utilitarianism is vital to his sense of style, but if one thing makes him a dandy, it's his unswerving attention to tiny details that nobody but he would ever notice. One friend, permitted to peek inside the Hitchcock wardrobe in the 1970s, discovered a row of what seemed to be identical suits. On closer inspection, however, there were slight differences between them; some were black, others a shade of blue so dark as to make the difference negligible, and there were slight differences in measurements and cut, too, to mitigate his yo-yoing weight. Hitchcock sometimes said he dreamed of buying an off-the-rack suit but that he was prevented from doing so by his irregular proportions. It's unlikely he really meant it; the last thing Hitchcock wanted to be was a middle-of-the-road everyman. As Roland Barthes put it, the true dandy thinks of his suit as a "uniform in its essence, yet adaptable in its details," enabling him to stand out from the crowd while appearing to remain predictably unchanged. It's a notion that could apply to many of Hitchcock's films as well as to his sense of dress.

Appointment books kept by his secretaries from the mid-1950s on give an insight into Hitchcock's daily routine that we don't have for earlier periods. Listed among the meetings, viewings, and scripting sessions are regular and frequent haircuts and shoeshines in the office, and multiple measuring and fitting sessions with a tailor. For a while, the tailor was Frank Acuna, who had made clothes for Cary Grant, too, though at the time Hitchcock used his services he was best known for designing Liberace's outfits, which, naturally, were at the other end of the dandy spectrum from Hitchcock's, though Liberace claimed Brummell as his sartorial godfather. "Whenever I need some new ideas," Liberace told the *New York Times* in 1970, "I invite Frank over for a screening of the movie 'Beau Brummell,' starring Stewart Granger. . . . When I see something I like, I say, 'Make that!'"

The real-life Brummell, however, would have appreciated Hitchcock's restraint far more than Liberace's peacocking. Hitchcock's approach to dressing was as Brummell had intended: a rational, efficient means of obliterating dirt and disorder. The conquest of the modern and the measurable over backwardness and uncertainty.

When color films began to be produced in the 1930s, Hitchcock repeatedly said that he was keen to work in the medium, but only for "dramatic and emotional effect, as a symbol of action and thought." One of the many half-truths about *Psycho*, perpetuated by Hitchcock himself, was that his decision to shoot the film in black and white stemmed from his belief that the sight of Marion Crane's blood gurgling its way down the shower drain would have been distasteful in color. In fact, the decision was motivated more by practical concerns regarding budget, but the power of vivid blood-red was something Hitchcock had thought about for years. As early as 1937, a decade before he shot his first color film, he imagined "red drops of blood dripping on to a bunch of white daisies—just that would bring out the stark horror of a murder much more strongly." Or, how about a girl with a lipstick who "smears her lips and you see her face take on an artificial health from the rouge she puts on it." In *Spellbound*, shot in black and white, Hitchcock stained two frames in red at the moment Dr. Murchison turns his gun on himself and commits suicide. Proustian flashes of red were likewise incorporated into *Marnie*, the color triggering a sense memory of the killing she committed as a child.

When it came to costume, Hitchcock planned color schemes early in the scripting process, with a view to expressing psychological and emotional truths about his characters that would aid the storytelling. Edith Head, the legendary costume designer who worked on eleven Hitchcock films, beginning with *Rear Window*, said, "Hitchcock thinks in terms of color; every costume is indicated when he sends me the script. . . . He's absolutely definite in his visual approach, and gives you an exciting concept of the importance of color." Taking his dandyish instincts for clothes to the screen, Hitchcock gave Head what she termed "an education in restraint." When he identified Vera Miles as his new protégé, it was through the color of her clothing that Hitchcock worked to transform her into the movie star of his imagination. "She's an extraordinarily good actress," he told Edith Head, but "she uses too much colour. She's swamped by colour." On his instruction, Head compiled an entire wardrobe for Miles, solely in black, white, and gray. In costuming his female stars, Hitchcock applied the same basic rules that governed his own dress. He forbade garishness and favored "classic" looks over the latest fashion, resisting an actress's personal taste if he found it unsympathetic. His concerns began and ended with what best communicated unspoken information to the audience. The most famous example occurred during the shooting of *Vertigo* when he insisted that, in the Madeleine part of her dual role, Kim Novak would wear a gray suit. Novak was not keen, and told Head that she was happy to wear any color except gray. Head explained that "Hitch paints a picture in his films, that color is as important to him as any artist," but Novak was not persuaded. "Handle it, Edith," was Hitchcock's unequivocal response. "I don't care what she wears as long as it's a gray suit." Ultimately, Novak relented—she didn't have a great deal of choice—and saw the benefit of having Madeleine dressed so differently from Judy, the second character she played in *Vertigo*. The gray suit created a barrier between the two characters and "helped me stand so straight and erect . . . it helped me feel uncomfortable as Madeleine," a sensation that is almost palpable in Novak's performance.

Hitchcock was rarely happier than when dressing his female stars, an activity that for him, as for James Stewart's character in *Vertigo*, held a sensual pleasure equal to undressing them. Being aware of the avid interest Hitchcock took in women's clothing, Eva Marie Saint made a conscious effort to dress in a demure outfit she had heard would please him, a beige dress with white gloves, on the occasion of their first meeting to discuss her potential role in *North by Northwest*. Hitchcock didn't ask for a screen test, but he did have her perform lengthy tests for her hair, makeup, and costumes, which was an unprecedented experience for Saint. "I think Hitchcock was the only one who demanded that every bit of everything—whether it was the hair, makeup, the whole look— would be tested on camera." Unhappy with what he saw—Helen Rose, not Edith Head, designed the costumes on this production—he and Saint flew to the Bergdorf Goodman department store in Manhattan, where they picked out every item of clothing she would need. Saint was struck by Hitchcock's attention to cosmetic detail. "He had such an overall look for me, for Eve Kendall," she remarked half a century later. "But it wasn't just the clothes. It was the accessories, the hair, definitely the hair, the makeup, the beads around my neck and that sort of thing. And the shoes. I loved all that and the fact that he cared that much. It helped me as an actress to conjure up what he had in mind for Eve Kendall." Saint had her own ideas for her costume design, too, which Hitchcock accommodated. It was she who picked out a black dress covered with swirls of red roses, one of the most memorable outfits in *North by Northwest*, a movie full of beautiful clothes.

Unquestionably, Hitchcock paid vastly more attention to female clothing than male. Even so, he understood the power that clothes had to frame a man's identity—as one might expect of someone who had Liberace's costumier make his suits. One of those playing alongside Eva Marie Saint in *North by Northwest* was Martin Landau in his first screen role, as Leonard, the dandyish sidekick of James Mason's villain, Phillip Vandamm. Hitchcock thought it important that Leonard be dressed almost identically to Cary Grant's character, so he arranged for Grant's tailor, Quintino, to make Landau's wardrobe. In Chicago, Landau was summoned by Hitchcock to LaSalle Street Station, where he was filming a scene with Cary Grant. "Martin, put on one of the suits you are going to use in the movie—I'd like to see it being worn in the surroundings." That he requested to see Landau wearing the suit on location before filming is a sign of Hitchcock's dedication to clothing, but also of his teasing sense of humor. He guessed that Grant would not be impressed to see a supporting cast member—one who had never even been in a movie—wearing suits made by his tailor, cut identically to his own. On location, somebody approached Landau: "Excuse me, Mr. Landau, but Mr. Grant wants to know where you got that suit." When Landau replied that it came from the Universal costume department, he was told, "Mr. Grant says that's impossible." Apparently, Grant could tell just by looking exactly who had tailored Landau's suit, and he was not pleased about it.

Grant needn't have worried. The suit he wore for virtually the entire movie has passed into dandy folklore. In 2006, *GQ* magazine voted it the best man's suit in Hollywood history. "*North by Northwest* isn't about what happens to Cary Grant," writes Todd McEwen, "it's about what happens to his *suit*." Dragged thousands of miles across the country, it takes a beating but never needs more than a light sponging to restore it to its crisp, elegant best. McEwen wonders whether making Grant look scruffy was the only atrocity Hitchcock would refuse to commit on film:

"Perfection of its own kind." Hitchcock with Cary Grant during the filming of *North by Northwest*.

"it would be too traumatic to see this suit getting totaled, that would be way beyond Hitchcock's level of sadism." A decade after *North by Northwest*, Grant gave *GQ* his thoughts on how to dress well, while protesting, with blatant false modesty, that he wasn't at all well dressed and barely had any interest in clothes. He insisted he had never "gone to any special trouble to acquire clothes that could be regarded as noticeably fashionable or up-to-date . . . simplicity, to me, has always been the essence of good taste." An entirely Hitchcockian sentiment. Edith Head noted a similarity between Grant and Hitchcock's instinctive feel for color, too. In preproduction for *To Catch a Thief*, Grant planned a color scheme for his own costumes around the plans Head and Hitchcock had made for Grace Kelly. "She's wearing a pale blue bathing suit for the beach scene? Good, I'll wear plaid shorts. She's wearing a gray dress? How would it be if I wear a dark jacket and gray slacks?" Hitchcock was happy to allow Grant to dress as he chose; some believe that his leading man embodied Hitchcock's fantasy version of himself. He once described Grant as "the only actor I ever loved." Grant agreed that something special existed between his director and him, "a rapport and understanding deeper than words," which manifested itself in their shared tastes, manners, and sensibilities.

One might say that Grant became an avatar for an inner Hitchcock that could not be outwardly expressed. He had a body shape that fit the dandy ideal—slim, long-limbed, with a broad chest and shoulders—and also expressed a confidence in his looks that was entirely alien to Hitchcock. In both *To Catch a Thief* and *North by Northwest* a fifty-something Grant was happy to film scenes in various states of undress. Baring his mahogany-tanned body in the beach scenes of *To Catch a Thief*, Grant displayed more naked flesh than any star in any Hitchcock film.[*] Hitchcock expressed a career-long aversion to making films that starred middle-aged men. He cited this as the reason why he never made a film of the Dr. Crippen story, and why he stopped casting James Stewart after *Vertigo*. But the rule didn't apply to Cary Grant, whom Hitchcock seemed to look on as

---

[*]   Janet Leigh in *Psycho* and Barbara Leigh-Hunt in *Frenzy* both had body doubles.

entirely unique, ageless, and timeless. Enviably handsome and youthful though he was, Grant clearly looks older than the thirty-odd years he's meant to be in *North by Northwest*, and on first viewing it can be confusing to see him referring to Jessie Royce Landis as "Mother," when they look more like brother and sister. Hitchcock never lost faith in Grant's ability to defy the aging process, and hoped to cast him as the leading man of future films, too. As late as 1979, long after Grant's retirement, Hitchcock wrote to him asking whether he might "have the privilege of photographing you again one day, because you can be, you know."

The importance of clothes on a Hitchcock production strayed beyond the gaze of the camera. Male technicians who arrived on set wearing short-sleeved shirts, or—heaven forbid—lacking a tie, would receive a message that such slovenliness was not permitted. The same applied to writers, though Hitchcock would rarely brave the subject himself, it being a little too close to confrontation for his liking. At the end of Evan Hunter's first day on *The Birds*, Peggy Robertson appeared at his side in the parking lot. "Hitch thinks it might be better if you didn't dress for work quite so casually." Either an urgent conversation had been had the moment Hunter exited the boss's office, or Robertson, expert Hitchcock whisperer that she was, had intuited the situation. Either way, the next morning Hitchcock was pleased to see Hunter had left his sports jacket at home and had a tie around his collar. Neckties were important to Hitchcock; without one, a man seemed as good as naked. When one fledgling director asked him for some advice, Hitchcock looked the kid up and down and said, "Real directors wear ties."

The imposition of his tastes and standards in clothing was a way of infusing the atmosphere with a sense of himself, making everybody work toward the goal of realizing the same Hitchcockian end. "Look Hitchcock, think Hitchcock" was the ostensible goal, but it was also evidence of his strong manipulative streak, reshaping those around him by pushing them through the filter of his personality. Peggy Robertson felt the force of Hitchcock's cosmetic expectations, and she admitted to basing at least some of her wardrobe choices on what she thought he would or would not like to see her in, much like Eva Marie Saint had done on the day of their first meeting. Speaking many years after Hitchcock's death, Robertson recalled one occasion on which she bought a sober navy-blue dress, thinking it would please him, but was crestfallen when he paid her a compliment in a tone of voice that she inferred to be a criticism. Another time, she bought a pair of sensible brown shoes that Hitchcock seemed to genuinely like when she wore them to work for the first time. "I was so thrilled by this," Robertson remembered, "that I went out the next weekend and bought about three pairs of these terribly expensive shoes, just glowing with happiness that I was getting some approval." But, ever wary of dispensing praise to those he thought were searching for it, the compliments dried up immediately. "He never said another word about my shoes in my life. Not one. He knew, he could tell." It's testament to the power of the myths that Hitchcock spun around himself as being a man of unmatchable taste and talent that important members of the Hitchcock enterprise would go to such lengths to gain his approval—especially when they knew it to be a virtually impossible task.

The dandy attitude of perfecting life through devotion to small details seeped into every part of Hitchcock's existence. The Californian homes he kept with Alma were decorated and furnished without typical Hollywood ostentation, but with an immense attention to particulars. When Hitchcock remodeled one of his bathrooms in the 1950s, he gave workmen the most precise instructions and was insistent about the use of a particular type of green-and-white marble he had sourced in Vermont. The artwork that studded his walls was deliberately chosen to reflect the Hitchcocks' public and private selves, a mixture of their premodern English heritage and their very modern present; the grittily figurative balanced with the exuberantly abstract, works by Utrillo, Epstein, Klee, and a Picasso that, to Hitchcock's irritation, turned out to be counterfeit. A look in the Hitchcocks' cutlery drawers and china cupboards would reveal not only beautiful implements of the finest Sheffield steel, Waterford crystal, and Delftware, but something antique and silver to cater for any conceivable dining need.

There were asparagus servers, grape scissors, cream ladles, and butter spreaders; teaspoons and demitasse spoons; spoons for sugar, berries, ice cream, after-dinner coffee, and salt; nut picks, berry knives, butter knives, and fish knives; forks for salad, fruit, luncheon, and dinner; pie slicers, cheese planes, and cake breakers; carvers for roast meat, and separate ones for game and poultry. These are just a few entries from an eleven-page inventory of silverware drawn up in 1962 for one of the Hitchcocks' two homes.

That there was a right way of doing things, and a thousand wrong ways, seemed axiomatic to Hitchcock. On the set of *North by Northwest*, he appeared genuinely affronted when he saw Eva Marie Saint pour herself coffee into a Styrofoam cup. In all seriousness, he pointed out that such conduct was incompatible with being a movie star. "Someone should bring it to you in a china cup and saucer." More indecorous behavior occurred the night Paul Newman came to dinner in the early 1960s. Not only did Newman take off his jacket and hang it on the back of his chair the moment he reached the table, he declined the offer of the wines Hitchcock had paired with the food and asked instead for a beer—which he drank *straight from the can*. This was not leading-man behavior; Cary Grant would have rather been seen dead than swigging beer from a can. Hitchcock's opinion of Newman never entirely recovered.

Ritual, performed with easy, understated style was crucial to his public image. His tendency, which he followed most insistently after his break from Selznick, of starting and finishing filming at civilized hours kicks against our culture's dominant notion that to be successful in any given field one must be gripped by "drive," "passion," and "inspiration," all of which eat up the clock. Hitchcock's timekeeping was a dandyish display of effortless mastery; he was in charge of his production, not the other way round. "It's only a movie" became something of a catchphrase of his, an expression intended to convince us that at the core of Hitchcock was an unruffled insouciance. "I've come to believe that a hidden future is one of God's most merciful and exciting gifts," he once wrote, expounding his theory of never taking anything too seriously. "We can live in a state of chronic despair, or we can live with faith in the future, even though it is hidden from us." Of course, this is completely at odds with the other things that he spent half a century telling us about himself, that he was a bag of nerves, terrified of everyone and everything. It also runs counter to his obvious obsession with his work, one that he took home with him and chewed over every night. In describing his routine during filming, he said he would rise early to think through the challenges of the day ahead. His family recalled that this tended to occur about three in the morning, not the sign of a pacific mind.

But the dandy is an identity born to the English leisure class, populated by soft-handed playboys. Beau Brummell's family were stinking rich with "new money," and to compensate for his lack of aristocratic genes, Brummell made a fetish of idleness. In the democratic age, this poses a problem for dandies whose identity has been constructed through industriousness and aspiration. Hitchcock got around the problem by building inactivity into the fabric of his hard-working life. He affected a pose of boredom in his director's chair, and teased interviewers with flippant answers to serious questions. "Let's play" was the attitude he communicated to his screenwriters, despite the fact that he demanded unstinting professionalism and dedication from anyone working for him. Herbert Coleman, his assistant director and associate producer in the 1950s, wrote in his memoirs that his marriage was put under great strain by Hitchcock's expectation of total commitment to the project of "Hitchcock." Coleman was aggrieved when Hitchcock told a colleague that Coleman "knows more about producing a movie than anyone I've ever known. . . . But he has one fault. He thinks more of his family than he does his job." Ernest Lehman was of the opinion that the dandyish loafing was a strategy of self-deception designed to take Hitchcock's mind off the carousel of demands that his filmmaking entailed. Hitchcock made films, so Lehman reckoned, "to keep the franchise of his reputation, his fortune and his lifestyle. But his greatest pleasure, his true raison d'être may have been just to feel comfortable, to sit and spin tales and play with ideas, to be at ease, eating, drinking, sans anxiety—and let's face it, making movies was hard work and produced considerable anxiety in him."

The leading men in Hitchcock's films often have a relaxed attitude to work, or find themselves in a situation of enforced inactivity. In the four movies he appeared in, Cary Grant plays a grifter sponging from his wealthy wife; a secret service operative who spends his time eating, drinking, and riding horses; a retired jewel thief luxuriating in his ill-gotten wealth; and a louche advertising executive. In the latter of those roles, the ad executive Roger Thornhill, he exhibits an industrious streak, but that's glimpsed only in the opening scene in which he steals a cab while off-loading work to his secretary. In these roles, Grant replicates the ideal of the high achiever who never breaks a sweat that Hitchcock aspired to be. His characters could be described by Thomas Elsaesser's feeling that Hitchcock lived his life as a "protest, the triumph of artifice over accident, a kind of daily victory over chance, in the name of a spirituality dedicating itself to making life imitate art."

Sauntering hand in hand with the dandy's disregard of effort is his denial of emotion. An "unshakable resolve not to allow himself to be moved" is how Baudelaire phrased it. In his perfect state, the dandy succumbs to neither sadness nor anger nor joy; he is dispassionate and aloof in all circumstances. It is the most distinctively English part of the dandy's take on masculinity, one that Hitchcock embodied in the expressionlessness of his public persona. Home-movie footage used in a 1999 BBC documentary shows Hitchcock at home in the 1930s, fooling around in front of the camera, pulling faces and pantomiming, at one point pretending to be a baby in a playpen, his fist wedged in his mouth. On first viewing, it's a peculiar sight; despite being one of the most photographed people of his lifetime, the images that have come to define him are those in which he stares into the camera unsmiling, devoid of emotion. For a similar reason, the ending of the *Alfred Hitchcock Presents* episode "The Case of Mr. Pelham," about a man tormented by his doppelgänger, is strangely gripping viewing. As the camera cuts from the final scene of the drama, and back to Hitchcock in the studio, we see him writhing in the grip of two identical-looking medical orderlies. "I'm Alfred Hitchcock! I am, I can prove it . . . I insist!" he shouts, his face twisted in fear and anger. It's an eerie sight, the world's most imperturbable man suddenly all at sea. As this hysterical Hitchcock is led off, another Hitchcock, the blank canvas we all know, walks into the frame, reassuringly deadpan. He apologizes for this unseemly eruption of emotion and explains that the gentleman being removed was an obvious fraudster. Off camera, there is a gunshot. Hitchcock remains unmoved. "Poor chap. If you'll excuse me, I need a moment to pull myself together."

For practically the entire length of his career, Hitchcock extolled the virtue of what he called "negative acting, the ability to express words by doing nothing." Naturally, this had much to do with the technique of filmmaking. "The screen actor," he said in 1937, "has got to be much more plastic" than the theater performer. "Mostly he is wanted to behave quietly and naturally . . . the best screen actor is the man who can do nothing extremely well." Consequently, Hitchcock considered one of his most important duties as a director to cleanse an actor's face of all but the most essential display of emotion. Working with Kim Novak had been a challenge, he told Peter Bogdanovich, because she communicated an array of extraneous emotion through her face. "You have got a lot of expression in your face," he told Novak. "Don't want any of it . . . it's like taking a sheet of paper and scribbling all over it." Speaking shortly before his relationship with Tippi Hedren broke down, he said that controlling her every facial gesture was one of his key achievements on *The Birds*. The evidence of that is plainly apparent in Hedren's close-up reaction shots in the early scenes of the movie, in which the blankness of her expression communicates her character's inscrutability. Some critics have suggested that, despite their gender, Melanie Daniels and Marnie Edgar are two of Hitchcock's most successful dandies—stylish, enigmatic, and as distant as the moon.

In violent, disturbing ways, Hedren's emotionally frozen characters are thawed out, leading to their apparent salvation at the movies' conclusion. The puzzle of how to make the emotionally unavailable available was a big part of Hitchcock's films, especially those led by Cary Grant and James Stewart, each of whom represents a different part of Hitchcock's idea of maleness, perhaps of himself. Grant is a fantasy of charm and sexual confidence; Stewart captures men as people struggling with fear, obsession, and guilt. Uniting them—with the exception of Stewart's married character in *The Man Who Knew Too Much*—was their remote bachelordom, a dandy persona concealing the tender emotional self beneath. By the end of each of the Stewart and Grant films, that brittle exterior has been breached, for good or ill. This is a crucial point about Hitchcock's portrayal of dandyism: it offers its own critique. Unlike masculine types of the same era played by Humphrey Bogart or John Wayne, for example, it's not at all certain whether we're meant to approve of Hitchcock's dandies. He wants us to care about them, but we're nudged to ask ourselves whether all this studied superficiality and hard-fought urbanity is really worth it.

It was a question Hitchcock asked of himself. Wouldn't it be a happier life if he dropped the dandy act and opened himself up to others, even if in doing so he risked some form of self-diminishment? In private moments, he sometimes complained that on set he felt as though he were riding through a desert on top of a camel, unreachable and alone. Wasn't it ridiculous, he asked, that people should always call him Mr. Hitchcock, almost in the same breath as insisting that standards be maintained? "One cannot become too familiar with the people with whom one has to work," he remarked in his later years. "One can't take the risk of exposing oneself as just an ordinary man." John Landis was at the very start of his movie career in the 1970s when he met Hitchcock, and he described the experience as like encountering a mythological creature, such was his reputation and his bearing. Likewise, David Freeman thought meeting Hitchcock was akin to visiting the Eiffel Tower for the first time. "You hear about it all your life, and when you finally see the damn thing, it looks so much like the postcards that it's difficult to see it afresh." On occasion, some brave young soul insisted on treating Hitchcock like a regular person. Bruce Dern claims that on the first day of working on *Family Plot* he sat next to Hitchcock and said, "I don't give a shit if you like this or not, but I'm sitting next to you for ten weeks." Apparently, the brazenness went down well, and Dern believes Hitchcock felt hurt when he wasn't approached on set, despite his tendency to surround himself with a huge invisible wall of unapproachability. He was torn between protecting his specialness and yearning to be one of the gang, something he never mastered. "A lot of people think I'm a monster," he said. "I've had women say, 'Oh, you're nothing like I thought you were.' I'd say, 'What did you expect?' They'd say, 'Well, we thought you'd be very unpleasant and this and that' . . . a complete misconception. . . . I'm just the opposite. I'm more scared than they are." Being misunderstood is an occupational hazard of the career dandy, who must always remain the same on the outside, irrespective of what springs and swirls within.

The conversation between the seen and the unseen, the surface and the subterranean, is the core of *Rope*. The story of an audacious attempt at the perfect crime mirrors Hitchcock's own impudence in attempting to make a movie that appears to be filmed in one continuous take, revolutionary at the time. Both schemes are exercises in exquisiteness achieved through hidden effort, in one case painstaking, in the other sadistic.

Seen but unseen—or, to be more accurate, unspoken—a gay subtext runs through the film. Loosely based on the real-life murderers Leopold and Loeb, the film's central characters, Phillip and Brandon, are partners in an unspeakable crime, a nudge and a wink at their homosexual relationship, the joint enterprise that the censors of the time considered even more harmful to public morals than the annihilation of an innocent life. The code of their sexuality was in the casting: with glee and knowingness, Hitchcock arranged that the two leads were played by gay men: John Dall as the manipulative Brandon and Farley Granger as the easily led Phillip. The screenplay was written by Arthur Laurents. Barely in his thirties at the time, Laurents was as open about his gayness as one could safely be in the late 1940s, a time in which the harassment and criminalization of gay men was pursued with vigor, following years of relative tolerance between the world wars. As both men detail in their respective memoirs, Granger and Laurents were an item during the production of the film, a fact that Hitchcock knew but decided to keep silent about. Indeed, Granger, Laurents, and Dall were all certain that the gay theme of the story held a strong attraction for Hitchcock, who "built sexual ambiguity into his presentation of the material," though he never spoke a word of it to any of them.

Screamingly obvious to modern audiences, but apparently not to those of 1948, the crude coding is most evident in the style of these young aesthetes' lives, the way Brandon fusses over the placing of candlesticks, the extreme refinement of their manners, the intensity of their homosocial world, even the execution of their murder. As the camera enters their apartment, the screen is filled with the face of their victim, David, at the moment of his asphyxiation, a shot that evokes the opening shot of *The Lodger*. The sexual connotations of that scene are obvious here, too; David's face, and the breathlessness of his murderers, are unsubtle parallels with some other intense physical act, and Brandon can't wait to light a cigarette the moment it's all over. When David's body is tossed into the chest, he lies there throughout the rest of the film—like the beating heart beneath the floorboards in Poe's "The Tell-Tale Heart"—a suspenseful reminder of the secrets these gadflies have lurking in the private spaces of their home. The moment of murder isn't seen—only heard—in Patrick Hamilton's play on which the film is based, but Hitchcock insisted it be added to hammer home the disjuncture between Phillip and Brandon's sophistication and brutality—the flimsiness of civilization that Hitchcock's murderers always reveal.

Hitchcock and Laurents built the script with Cary Grant in mind as Rupert Cadell, Phillip and Brandon's darkly witty former tutor who uncovers their crime and is horrified to discover that his ironic reproaches of conventional morality have been taken seriously by his young students, and inspired their crime. The inclusion of Grant would've made this the dandiest, and gayest, film Hitchcock ever made. But both he and Montgomery Clift, originally in line for the role of Brandon, passed on the opportunity. "According to Hitchcock," wrote Laurents in his memoirs, "each felt his own sexuality made him too vulnerable to public attack." Laurents was disappointed to hear of Grant's refusal to participate, as he felt Grant was "always sexual" in his acting and would have added an extra dynamic between the characters. That mightn't be quite the right judgment on what Grant offered. "Not once was Grant sexual on screen," observes the critic David Thomson. "Instead, he knew that watching was erotic, that the glow of imagery was suggestive, but no one was actually going to *do it*." Perfect for a Hitchcock film. Stewart's interpretation lacks the sparkle and ambiguity that Grant surely would have brought to the role, the qualities he gave to all his best performances. Hitchcock recognized Grant's capacity to simultaneously seduce and confuse an audience, apt for this film about forbidden male desire. As one of Grant's biographers notes, when he soared to fame in the thirties and forties, the public asked itself questions about this exotic creature: was he "a new kind of man, or not a 'man' at all?"

Similar questions hang unanswered in several Hitchcock films. Handel Fane masquerades as a woman in *Murder!*, while the person imitating the cat burglar John Robie in *To Catch a Thief* turns out to be a teenage girl. In *The Lodger* and *Downhill*, Hitchcock had great fun toying with the ambiguity of Ivor Novello's masculine identity. Novello was a pinup in Britain, Wales's answer to Rudolph Valentino, but his homosexuality was an open secret in the entertainment world. "I'm glad he's not keen on the girls," says Novello's love rival in the film, a reference to the misogyny of the woman-killing Avenger, as well as Novello's sexual ambiguity. In one scene, Novello appears in a shot with a flowerpot in the background that seems to be resting on top of his head. "It was just too tempting," said Hitchcock of his unsubtle joke. "Anyway, with that profile, why should Ivor mind having a flowerpot on his head once in a while." The homosexual subtext of *Strangers on a Train* is also plain, as Farley Granger's Guy is stalked by Robert Walker's flamboyant Bruno, like a less-clever cousin of the boys in *Rope*. The screenplay for *North by Northwest* is fairly explicit in the homosexuality of Martin Landau's character, Leonard— he of the sumptuous suit—who is described as having "a soft baby-face, large eyes and hair that falls down over his forehead. His attitudes are unmistakably effeminate." Alarms rang when the censor read that. Hitchcock received a letter warning him that "if there is any inference whatever in your finished picture that this man is a homosexual, we will be unable to approve it under the requirements of the Production Code." Yet Landau intentionally played Leonard as though he were in love with

Vandamm and jealous of Eve Kendall, the woman with whom Vandamm is infatuated. All that, however, is conveyed through Hitchcock's "negative acting," in glances, gestures, and tone of voice. Landau had previously played characters full of machismo, and only in the theater, but Hitchcock was sure that he had the ability to play a complex, unspoken masculine otherness, assisted, of course, by the principles of negative acting and well-chosen clothes. "Martin," he assured Landau, "you have a circus going on inside you. If you can play that in the theatre you can play this role."

Hitchcock's gay dandies suggest a narrow, stereotypical, and pretty bleak idea about gay lives. Almost all of them are marked by psychopathy, mental illness, loneliness, or misery. Perhaps, though, he used them to acknowledge and explore ambiguities of his own identity. His Brummellian style of dandyism—the detached, unemotional, precision of the cultivated English gentleman—lived next door to the more ostentatious Wildean tradition, which had queerness among its many layers. The membrane between the two can seem porous, and there has been speculation about Hitchcock's sexual orientation. An "odd, weird, little faggish man" was how Samson Raphaelson summed up Hitchcock, a description he meant fondly. Others noted a decided effeminacy in his movements, a lightness of foot that was apparently unexpected because of his size and his reputation for unsmiling immobility. Rodney Ackland, a gay man who wrote Hitchcock's *Number Seventeen* (1932) during his London period, claims Hitchcock once told him that had he not met Alma in the early 1920s, he might have "become a poof." The phrasing is intriguing, as if Hitchcock conceived of gayness as a style that one could adopt, and one that was close to his own. There's no evidence that he was attracted to men in the way he very obviously was to women; his interest in gayness was likely a manifestation of his masculinity, a feeling of estrangement from dominant ideas of what and who men were meant to be. Hitchcock was forever stimulated by the sight of men and women slipping out of their conventional roles of sex and gender. There is a frisson between Annie and Melanie in *The Birds*, as there is between Patsy and Jill in *The Pleasure Garden*—"sapphic overtones," to quote Pat-

Hitchcock as Lady Agatha, the Countess of Windblown, 1957.

rick McGilligan—which Hitchcock said was inspired by a lesbian couple whom he, as a wide-eyed virgin, encountered in Berlin in 1924. "In the hotel room they made several propositions, to which I stolidly replied, '*Nein, nein.*' Then we had several cognacs, and finally the two German girls got into bed. And the young girl in our party, who was a student, put on her glasses to make sure she wouldn't miss anything." That incident might have been an influence on a multilayered gag in *The Lady Vanishes* when Caldicott and Charters—two inseparable old public schoolboys— are panic-stricken to find themselves in a tiny room with a young woman who cheerily undresses in front of them.

Men in drag have a long history at the heart of British popular culture. In the 1920s, Hitchcock entertained friends by prancing around as "Mabel," a flapper in a slinky dress, high heels, and a string of pearls. Around the same time, Alma had trouser suits made for her by the same tailor who fashioned Hitchcock's clothes. Walking through the lobby of a grand hotel one day, a trouser-clad Alma caused necks to crane in disapproval. "They are all talking about your trousers," Hitchcock said in a booming voice, unable to hide his delight at his wife's taboo-breaking. Norman Bates's cross-dressing mirrored Hitchcock's own enjoyment of posing, often for the camera, in a dress. Once he did a turn as Queen Victoria, and dressed up as the lady of the manor, one of numerous roles he played in a mock murder mystery story printed in *This Week* magazine in 1957.

All this sophistication, this knowledge of the parts of life that happen only in the shadows, jars with the other face that Hitchcock showed the world, that embarrassing twin brother, a fearful and superstitious square who knew nothing about the world beyond the movies. Perhaps the doubles, decoys, and lookalikes that litter his films were a recognition that within himself there were competing identities in constant, noisy conversation. He was simultaneously the artist and the crowd-pleaser, the timorous virgin and the man women couldn't resist—and the fat misfit and the dandy, elegant and precise, for whom obtaining "whatever is perfect of its own kind" was the closest he got to a philosophy of life.

7

THE FAMILY MAN

The gang of three were all together, the talented Hitchcocks on tour. In the spring of 1951, Alfred, Alma, and Pat, now twenty-two, took a trip across Europe. In hired cars—neat and nimble European models, not the lumbering limousines that Hitchcock relied on to ferry him around Los Angeles—Alma and Pat took turns behind the wheel. Averse to driving, Hitchcock indulged his love of maps and assumed the role of navigator.

Europe held a host of associations for all three Hitchcocks. Transatlantic Pictures, the company Hitchcock had founded with Sidney Bernstein after ending his relationship with Selznick, had closed following the relative commercial failures of *Rope* and *Under Capricorn*. Hitchcock dusted himself off, signed a new deal with Warner Bros., and returned to familiar territory, making *Stage Fright*, starring Marlene Dietrich, and *Strangers on a Train*. Pat had played small roles in both films, the former cowritten by her mother and partly inspired by Pat's time at the Royal Academy of Dramatic Art in London. This vacation was her chance to see the wider continent, particularly the great cities in which her parents had learned the craft of filmmaking and the art of coupledom more than twenty years earlier. For Alfred and Alma, the trip offered an unusually long stretch of relaxation, warm with sunshine and old memories, but clouded by melancholy reminders of the war. "Florence we just loved," Alma wrote to Hitchcock's secretary Carol Shourds, despite the damage wrought by bombing, but Munich "was really very sad. As you know, we lived there some time. It has been smashed up badly."

Alfred's letters to Shourds gave fewer details of the experience of continental travel and more about the brass tacks of business, namely his latest search to find new source material. He sent a report back to Los Angeles titled "Journal of Mr. Hitchcock After His Explorations Through the Jungle of Story Agents and Tellers of Tales," detailing his responses to a mound of plays, novels, and short stories sent his way by eager writers and their representatives. One that had been highly recommended to him he dismissed because Alma read it and said she "couldn't make head nor tail of it," the swiftest possible route to Hitchcock's wastepaper basket.

Blending the personal with the professional was standard practice in the Hitchcock household. Hitchcock didn't simply take work home with him; the work was emotionally and creatively grounded in his family's domestic existence. People have often compared his approach to work with that of Shakespeare and Dickens, but both those men used their careers as a means of putting distance between themselves and their families, leading double lives of pen and hearth. The opposite was true of Hitchcock, for whom the boundary between domesticity and creativity was not just permeable but invisible. He once said it was his ambition to put murder back in the home where it belonged. At his address, it had never left. In every sense, "Hitchcock" was a family enterprise.

The movie Hitchcock most frequently cited as his favorite was *Shadow of a Doubt*, his definitive effort at wreaking havoc among a nice, normal family. The film tells the gothic tale of a suave thirty-something serial killer named Charles Oakley (Joseph Cotten) who has earned himself a small fortune by fleecing and murdering wealthy widows out on the East Coast. When the police pick up his scent, Charles flees to Santa Rosa, the uneventful Californian town in which he was raised, to stay with his older sister, Emma Newton, and her wholesome family, a Norman Rockwell painting made flesh. He is hero-worshipped by another Charlie, his eighteen-year-old niece, played by Teresa Wright, who thinks her uncle has been sent by some mysterious force of the universe to enliven her family's mundane life and bring them closer together. Only when two undercover detectives arrive in town does she discover her uncle's murderous secrets. Once Uncle Charlie learns that the girl is on to him, he attempts to kill her, first by suffocation, then by having her fall down a flight of stairs. On the day he leaves town, he tries to push the girl from a moving train, but in doing so he accidentally kills himself.

By dragging his villainy right across the living room rug of his own family home, Uncle Charlie might be Hitchcock's most diabolical creation. Cotten is creepily brilliant in the role, projecting a dark charisma that makes us warm to this psychopathic misanthrope who snuffs out human lives as though they were candles. His sister, her husband, and their children are simple, unsuspecting people whom he seduces much like he seduced the women he murdered. He lavishes gifts on his family, but these are all things that corrupt their purity, symbols of his dissipated life: he brings alcohol to their abstemious dinner table, and invests a huge sum of money at the tiny bank where his sister's husband works—every cent of it pilfered from the dead. His brashest attack on familial goodness is the relationship he cultivates with his niece, the innocent girl with whom he shares a name. We first meet young Charlie as she lies on her bed, the same bed she gladly gives to her uncle during his stay. In a private moment in the kitchen, Uncle Charlie looks unswervingly into the girl's eyes and slips a ring on her finger, a present, he says, bought especially for her, though it's actually a trophy wrenched from the finger of a woman he killed. The suggestion of incest is never explicit—Hitchcock enjoyed flirting with taboos more than embracing them—but the tension between them makes the two Charlies Hitchcock's most unsettling doubles.

Shadow of a Doubt is usually identified as the moment Hitchcock discovered America, cinematically speaking, after four years of living and working there. It was the first time that he made what reads as a truly American film, locatable in American society. An alternative title could have been *A Nightmare on Main Street*, a Hitchcockian twist on a modern

A murderer in the family. Joseph Cotten and Teresa Wright in *Shadow of a Doubt*.

American artistic tradition, in the vein of Sinclair Lewis and Theodore Dreiser, and the man who wrote the screenplay, Thornton Wilder, who had recently won the Pulitzer Prize for his work of experimental theater, *Our Town*. Hitchcock and his collaborators researched the setting for the film assiduously, drilling into minute details, and they decided to film the majority of the production on location in Santa Rosa, at a time when very little filming took place away from Hollywood studios. When Wilder finished his draft of the script in June 1942—en route to performing military service—Hitchcock called in another writer, Sally Benton, to provide a modern edge to the town. According to the patter of what became one of Hitchcock's most frequently told stories, he told Wilder that while he loved the script, their Santa Rosa was "like a town without neon signs." It was Hitchcock's intention to capture something of the unpalatable truth about small-town America, creating the perfect stage on which to set his fairy tale of domestic darkness.

As much of a milestone as it was in terms of building Hitchcock's reputation in Hollywood, *Shadow of a Doubt* is a point of continuity between the two halves of his career. For all that he talked about his terror of police and our collective nightmares about murder, mayhem, and the bomb under the table, the most insistent theme of his work is a seemingly happy home cruelly torn asunder. It's the connective tissue between *The Lodger* and *The Birds*, *The Manxman* and *I Confess*, *Young and Innocent* and *The Paradine Case*, and both versions of *The Man Who Knew Too Much*. It's also the substance of *The Wrong Man*, starring Henry Fonda and Vera Miles. Hitchcock developed the film from an article he read in *Life* magazine about the true story of Christopher Emmanuel Balestrero (known as Manny), the victim of a case of mistaken identity who was sentenced to prison for a spate of robberies he did not commit. Although he was eventually set free when the real culprit was identified, the stress took an immense toll on Balestrero's family, leading his wife, Rose, to a breakdown and a rupture in their marriage. The case fascinated Hitchcock, who decided to shoot the film as though a dramatized documentary, building the story solely on the facts and basing the dialogue on interviews with those involved. Throughout research and writing, Hitchcock stressed that depicting Rose's mental decline would be the hardest and most important part of the script to perfect. As Manny, Henry Fonda's anxious bewilderment is unerringly convincing. But it's Vera Miles's performance as Rose that provides the emotional center of the film, the chilling awfulness of seeing a family unravel when subjected to a sudden, arbitrary assault from the vicious universe outside the front door.

The terror to which Hitchcock subjected his ordinary families may be rooted in his own experience. The sudden loss of his father at the end of 1914, and the instant changes in his family's circumstances, pushing him more fully into the adult world, may well have rippled through his work. Domestic life turned suddenly sour is a staple of his British films. The comedy *The Farmer's Wife* is all about a widower in search of love once his daughter has flown the nest, and *Champagne* sees how a millionaire father and his galivanting daughter survive financial ruin. More gravely, *Sabotage* and *The Skin Game* both deal with appalling family secrets that lead directly to a tragic death: Stevie's murder in the former, the suicide of Chloe (played by Phyllis Konstam) in the latter.

Shadow of a Doubt was made around the time Hitchcock lost his mother in late 1942. Her name was Emma, as is the Newtons' hardworking matriarch in the movie. In subsequent films, damaged or overbearing lone parents—plainly malevolent in the case of Anna Sebastian in *Notorious*—became a noticeable and important fixture in Hitchcock's work, perhaps evidence, whether he consciously intended it or not, of the filmmaker exploring his own familial attachments on screen, communicating what life had been like after his father's passing. There were complex feelings of resentment and frustration in the family home of his adult life, too—yet that place was also a happy refuge and an artistic springboard.

It would be difficult to overstate the importance of home in Hitchcock's life and work, and above all the person responsible for that was Alma. She provided not just creative partnership but also emotional ballast, tethering her husband's neuroses and protecting his large, delicate ego. To observers of the Hitchcocks' marriage, it seemed that Alma's sense of ambition was sated by her extensive involvement on the films that bore her husband's name. But there are traces of dreams she had for herself. There was her nascent acting career—one of her roles was the daughter of David Lloyd George in a biopic of the former prime minister—which ran in tandem with her work in cutting and continuity, pursued with the same enthusiasm that Hitchcock evinced in his entry-level jobs. Mirroring Hitchcock's precocious instructions on how to write good intertitles, a twenty-three-year-old Alma wrote an article for *Motion Picture News* about the secrets of "cutting and continuity," which she averred were "art indeed, with a capital 'A.'" By 1925, the year she accepted Hitchcock's proposal of marriage and first worked as his assistant director, she had enough of a reputation to be profiled in a London magazine. "Alma in Wonderland: A woman's place is not always in the home" revealed what it called "two deadly secrets" about her: she owns "horn-rimmed glasses" and "she has never had the time to get married!"

That changed soon enough. Alma and Alfred married on December 2, 1926. Hitchcock's depiction of married life on screen could be rather bleak. During an argument in *Secret Agent*, Madeleine Carroll slaps John Gielgud, her supposed husband, across the face; he immediately slaps her back. "Married life has begun," she says. It's startling to a modern audience, but such scenes were meant as jokes, a version of cliché gags about the misery of being married that are still a staple of sitcoms and stand-up routines. Hitchcock drew immense strength from his union with Alma, though he sometimes failed to give as much as he took. He admitted that when Alma was in labor with Pat in July 1928, he found it so stressful that he took himself off for a walk, returning hours later to find the baby already born.

Being a wife and mother didn't halt Alma's career. In 1928, a movie she wrote, *The Constant Nymph*, was one of the biggest hits at the UK box office. Over the next several years, more of her work made it to the screen without Hitchcock's involvement, including *Nine till Six* (1932), a film set in a women's clothes shop, featuring an all-female cast. Her calling card was the experience of ordinary British women, prompting some researchers to speculate that it was through Alma that Hitchcock developed his interest in strong, rounded female characters and the domestic settings of so many of his films, especially in the first half of his career. When asked what advice she had for other young women hoping to build a career behind the camera, she was succinct: "Be interested," and be prepared to put the job before everything else. Drive and dedication brought rewards that women of previous generations could have only dreamed of: "I've been almost all over Europe," she marveled, and knew her homeland much better "than most girls get to know this country."

As her husband's name grew, so Alma's involvement in the wider industry receded. It seems she made the decision to concentrate her attention on Hitchcock, in whose career she naturally felt both person-

ally and professionally invested. Alma may have also had the sad, prag-
matic realization that scampering up the ladder would be twice as hard
for her as it would be for a man of equal capabilities. As her early suc-
cesses demonstrate, cinema held opportunities for talented women—
but the glass ceiling was real. In the late twenties, her own husband had
told a journalist that although Alma was of the "utmost value so far as
the story, and even the action went, some of the more unwieldy depart-
ments of film producing were difficult for her to control," which he took
as evidence that men were immanently more suited to being film directors, even though the majority of filmgoers were female. "Would you
expect a girls' school to be built by girls?" he asked the interviewer.* The
chances of fulfilling her ambitions—creative and financial—were higher
if she poured her skills and energy into a man with abundant talent, and
equally abundant deficiencies for which she could compensate.

History is replete with such pairings; the shrewd and steadfast woman
facilitating the success of a talented but fragile man is so familiar as to
be drab cliché. What's important about the Hitchcock-Reville marriage
is that Hitchcock energetically advertised the centrality of their union
to his work, deliberately weaving his private life into his public image
as the patriarch of a bourgeois family of unique distinction; just like
the next-door neighbors, but simultaneously very different. In August
1930, Hitchcock wrote several hundred words for a popular magazine to
publicize *Murder!*, a movie he describes as "the product of the Hitchcock
combination—Mr. and Mrs.," and which demonstrates that Alma knows
"more about scenario writing than I am ever likely to." The piece reveals
Hitchcock's working methods at the same time as showing us the Hitchcock family, including the cute toddler Patricia—"who is two and regards
me as a joke"—their maid, their secretary, their "little cottage hidden in
five acres of coppice," their swish London flat on Cromwell Road, and
even their car, nicknamed Blackmail.

---

* The article was written by Roger Burford and delightfully illustrated by his wife,
Stella, another talented young husband-and-wife team who had found a distinctive
way to collaborate.

The Hitchcocks on their wedding day, December 2, 1926.

The "little cottage" was in fact a rather large Tudor dwelling, fitted out with luxurious modern bathrooms and kitchen, in the Surrey village of Shamley Green. Ostensibly, this was the Hitchcocks' domestic sanctuary from London, the film industry, and the pressures of work. Yet, as with their flat on Cromwell Road, it was also a venue in which Hitchcock performed for journalists. According to one reporter who wrote a feature on it, the cottage was "imbued with the atmosphere of the Middle Ages, together with all the comforts of these Modern days," a reflection of the Hitchcocks themselves: a wholesome, traditional English family at the cutting edge of twentieth-century urban culture. Another journalist was greeted by a smiling Alma—"delightfully vivacious and a charming hostess"—while young Pat introduced her to the pony and the Old English sheepdog. Hitchcock could be seen "parading the garden" in his pajamas, dressing gown, and slippers, a homely, if odd, man of the house.

At the time, this display of contented domesticity—especially his fulsome praise of Alma's talents—made Hitchcock seem a bourgeois eccentric; now it gives him the look of a far-sighted critic of traditional masculinity. For a male artist of the interwar era, Hitchcock's warm public embrace of hearth and home made him an atypical figure. One of his contemporaries, the critic Cyril Connolly, famously wrote that "there is no more sombre enemy of good art than the pram in the hall." Female artists still searching for a room of one's own might have advised Connolly to count himself lucky if parenthood had encroached only as far as the hall, but Connolly's epigram articulates a widely held belief among male modernists. The poet Wyndham Lewis married his wife, Gladys Anne Hoskins, in 1930 but kept her existence a secret, even from close friends, so certain was he that a feminized domestic environment was anathema to artistic productivity. "I have a wife downstairs," he remarked to one visitor, having never mentioned her during the previous two years of their friendship. "A simple woman. But a good cook." Hitchcock's affectionate public take on family life is closer to that of Arnold Bennett's, the exceptionally popular, middlebrow English novelist who was the bête noire of Connolly, Lewis, and other English highbrows. However, Hitchcock's involvement in the modern medium of cinema, his interest in the avant-garde, and his determination to introduce elements of it into his work places him in a unique spot, as does the disconnect between the image of the blissfully calm family life he presented to the public and the families he put on screen—disordered, dysfunctional, or embattled. To Hitchcock, "the pram in the hall" was not a blockage, but a portal to what some have described as his "chaos world," that nightmarish place into which his characters descend.

Right up until the end of his life, Hitchcock publicly asserted that his happy marriage was the girder of his career. Yet it's uncertain how much of the Hitchcocks' marriage made it on-screen. Hitchcock was notoriously evasive on what of himself he put into his films, and Alma left scant public record of her thoughts on anything. As Donald Spoto has noted, perhaps the closest we have to a depiction of Alfred and Alma are Emily and Fred Hill, the lead characters in *Rich and Strange* (1931). Adapted from a novel of the same name by Dale Collins, the film both mocks and celebrates young adults of the Hitchcocks' generation who are encouraged by movies, magazines, and advertising to believe that happiness is only a spending spree away. Bored stiff with their humdrum domestic routine, the Hills splurge a financial inheritance on adventure abroad. After travels through exotic foreign lands, studded with temptations that almost end their marriage, and dangers that almost get them killed, they discover that excitement and glamour are not for them, and they are relieved to slide back into their sedate lives.

As a pair of thoroughly modern young fogies, Fred and Emily read like a riff on Alfred and Alma, despite the fact that the film is largely faithful to its source novel. In Paris, the Hills find themselves in the Folies Bergère, aghast at the gyrating flesh, a scene apparently modeled on the Hitchcocks' own experience of the venue, which they visited while working on the script. At some point in the evening, Hitchcock asked a fellow audience member where he and Alma might see some belly dancing. To their astonishment, they were led to a brothel. "In front of my wife, the madam asked me whether I would like one of the young ladies. Well, I've never had anything to do with that sort of woman. . . . So we had been behaving exactly like the couple in the book—two innocents abroad!" When he discussed *Rich and Strange* with Peter Bogdanovich, Hitchcock described the end of the film: "After it's all over, they [the Hills] meet me in the lounge. This is my most devastating appearance in a picture. They tell me their story and I say, 'No, I don't think it'll make a movie.'" The original script, cowritten by the Hitchcocks with Val Valentine, does feature a scene with the character of an unnamed filmmaker, but, as pointed out by the historian Charles Barr, it does not appear in the extant film. Perhaps Hitchcock's active imagination had blended fact with fiction for the sake of a good yarn to tell Bogdanovich, or maybe he'd misremembered because the characters had always seemed like a version of himself and Alma. Possibly, the initial idea had been for Hitchcock to play the role, in what would have been a witty way of referencing how close the married couple in the film were to their creators, but it proved too unwieldy or unconventional an ending. In any case, the Hills are sober people with hidden passions, fantasies, and yearnings, who ultimately learn the joy of settling. Rather than chase unattainable objects of desire, they embrace domestic stability. The comforts of home and faithful interdependence trump any desire for passionate release. For Alfred and Alma, this was a cherished precept, the cornerstone of their partnership—and a source of frustration that quietly rumbled through their married life.

When Hitchcock left for New York in March 1939, he faced the photographers with Alma and Pat, now aged ten, beaming broadly by his side in a pose of familial happiness they would repeat countless times over the next forty years. Once in America, Alma and Alfred made it their mission to re-create a slice of southern England in southern California. For *Life* magazine, Hitchcock set out his requirements. "What I want is a home . . . a snug little house, with a good kitchen, and the devil with a swimming pool. Only try to find one here." Californian houses, he felt, lacked homeliness; the article featured a photograph of him looking forlornly into a small fireplace, not a patch on the great hearths he was used to back in England. A "snug little house" doesn't really describe the eighty-five-acre ranch the Hitchcocks bought up among the redwood forests and orange groves of Scotts Valley, beneath the Santa Cruz Mountains. Alma's green thumb cultivated an impressive garden. One friend said she was reminded of Alma's flowers on a visit to Nottingham, Alma's birthplace, the city center decorated with colorful hanging baskets.

"The Ranch," though, was just a country getaway. For Monday-to-Friday living, the family at first made a comfortable makeshift home in a house rented from Carole Lombard, whom Hitchcock directed in *Mr. and Mrs. Smith* (1941), a screwball comedy about a married couple whose tempestuous relationship is equal parts hugs, kisses, and smashed dishes. Lombard's sudden death in a plane crash in January 1942 necessitated a permanent relocation for the Hitchcocks. Ultimately, they found what they were looking for at 10957 Bellagio Road in Bel Air, a newly built house that is often described as being modest by Hollywood standards, which Pat remembers as being calm, cozy, but always immaculate.

Just as the London flat and the Surrey cottage had been before the move, these tranquil family homes became the epicenter of the Hitchcock endeavor where so much of the important work happened: scriptwriting, story conferences, thinking, debating, planning—and auditioning for Hitchcock's favor. Those who were asked to visit the ranch knew they had been given special access and were rewarded by seeing Hitchcock in his natural habitat. When Frederick Knott adapted his play *Dial M for Murder* into a script for Hitchcock, he was invited to stay, along with Grace Kelly, the star of the movie. The blurry snapshots that Knott took of the trip are beautiful in their incongruity, revealing a wide-eyed Kelly shoving an enormous hamburger into her mouth, and, even more unusually, Alfred Hitchcock in his garden tending to the roses, wearing a pair of slacks and a white polo shirt. "When Hitchcock liked you . . . you became part of his extended family," said Arthur Laurents, who felt like an adopted child during the time he worked with Hitchcock, eighteen years his senior. He adored the Hitchcock home—"it was lovely being with people who loved each other"—but being subject to Hitchcock's domineering charm sometimes felt a little like "Oh God, I have to go to Daddy's." He learned that paternal favor was not unconditional. When Laurents told Hitchcock he didn't want to work on *Under Capricorn*, he realized he had done more than turn down an offer of work; he had erased himself from the inner circle. Being accepted into the Hitchcock team as a close creative collaborator was also an acceptance into Hitchcock's private world. A rejection of the former was frequently taken by Hitchcock as a snub to the latter. "It wasn't like a big studio," Peggy Robertson recalled, "it was more like a family." If a member of the family decided to move on, as happened when Herbert Coleman pulled away to take up his first directing job, the patriarch felt wounded. By 1955 Coleman had become such a trusted part of Hitchcock's life that when the director left town while renovations were done to his house, Coleman was named as the person to field any questions from the contractors. Hitchcock "was very sad about it," explained

Robertson of Coleman's decision to leave, "feeling Herbie was deserting him. But that's what he wanted to do." It took a lot for Hitchcock to let people in; coming and going as one pleased was rarely allowed.

Social events at the Hitchcocks' could be riotous fun; food and drink were always plentiful and sumptuous, and the guest lists sometimes glittering. When Pat graduated high school, her parents threw a party at Bellagio Road, with Cary Grant and Ingrid Bergman among the attendees. Notwithstanding Alma's total command of the kitchen, Hitchcock directed life at home much as he directed the work of a movie, to the extent that he arranged Pat's wardrobe as though she were one of his leading ladies. When Pat reached adolescence, the very age when most fathers step back from such things, Hitchcock took her shopping for clothes, usually without Alma. "He had very definite ideas for me," says Pat, "of what was appropriate to my personality."

It was around this time that Pat had her first involvement in a Hitchcock film, running lines with Edna May Wonacott, the little girl who played the Newton family's youngest daughter in *Shadow of a Doubt*. In that same year, 1942, Pat was cast in the Broadway production of *Solitaire*. Two years later she landed the lead role in *Violet*, a comic play by Whitfield Cook, which received a lukewarm critical reception and was not a hit with the public. Cook's agent wrote him to say that the sparkling writing was let down by the disappointing child cast in the lead role. Several reviews suggest the reverse was true, and that the fifteen-year-old did an admirable job with flimsy material. "Papa Hitchcock will have no scolding to do for Pat whoops it up like a seasoned trouper," wrote one reviewer.

Naturally, the Hitchcock connection was the source of much publicity. In October 1944, Hitchcock joined Alma at a performance of the play in Boston, immediately before he went to work on his war propaganda films in England, where he experienced the nerve-shredding tail end of the Blitz. As usual, reporters couldn't resist remarking on what an unusual-looking couple Pat's parents were, Alma being much shorter than her husband and not even half his weight. Of Pat's acting ambitions, Hitchcock said, apparently playfully, that although he did not approve,

Alfred, Alma, and Pat out for a walk with their dogs, Edward IX and Mr. Jenkins. Beverly Hills, 1939.

"her mother does thoroughly.... I'll put off as long as possible having to direct my own daughter"—a clear indication that he knew it was only a matter of time.

The occasion came in 1949 when he cast Pat in the role of the absurdly named Chubby Bannister—one of Hitchcock's teasing little jokes—in the movie *Stage Fright*, again written by Whitfield Cook. The script was based on the novel *Man Running* by Selwyn Jepson, but it was Alma who suggested making the protagonist a student at RADA, the august acting school in London at which Pat studied. To develop the treatment and write the screenplay, Hitchcock recruited Cook to collaborate with Alma and him. Since their first association in *Violet*, the Hitchcock family and Cook had grown increasingly close. From 1945 on, he was a frequent guest for dinner or cocktails, and would often meet one or more of them for nights out at restaurants and the theater. In 1948, Cook and his mother even spent Christmas at the Hitchcocks' home, returning the favor the following week by hosting the family at his New Year's Eve party. It was clear that a strong bond formed among all of them, and Hitchcock rated Cook as a writer; prior to engaging him to work on what would become *Stage Fright*, there was talk of collaborating on a vehicle for Shirley Temple. A short story that Cook wrote, "Happy Ending," includes a tableau about a man with a "late-Victorian sense of humor," his wife and their daughter, which, although not modeled on the Hitchcocks, is remarkably similar to many people's descriptions of the family at the dinner table:

> Every evening he'd bring home some joke or story or problem to be brought forth with the dessert. Sometimes the stories were vulgar. Risqué, Mrs. Prann called them. "Percy," she'd say, "don't be risqué. Remember Dora." And Percy, looking coy and drawing his chin down almost inside his high, illfitting collar, would say, "Oho, Dora knows a thing or two; she's a big girl now." And Dora would give a sickly smile.

The scene sounds very much like one Arthur Laurents detailed in his memoirs, in which Hitchcock handed Laurents a cocktail that Hitchcock said was "gin and menstrual blood." Alma responded, "Oh, Hitch!" Pat exclaimed, "Oh, Daddy!" "Both giggled indulgently and he was beamish." At times, though, Hitchcock's schoolboy jokes, heavy drinking, and showing off, especially in front of women half his age, could embarrass Alma and test her patience. Several acquaintances witnessed her sending withering looks and sharp words in his direction.

Cook may have become more than a family friend. In the fall of 1948, Alma returned to Los Angeles from England, where Hitchcock was filming *Under Capricorn*, and embarked on what appears to have been an affair with Cook, one that may have lasted just a few weeks in Hitchcock's absence, or possibly carried on for many months. When Patrick McGilligan first mooted this possibility in 2003, it was met with bafflement from previous Hitchcock biographers, who had never found any sense that Alma was much different from the ever-dutiful companion to the great genius that she presented to the press. But Cook's diaries support McGilligan's suggestion of something more than close friendship.

Cook, at this point a single man, appears to have had a very active romantic and sexual life, and he logged his encounters with Alma in an elliptical, lightly coded fashion, similar to the way in which he recorded assignations with other partners: "Unexpected evening!"; "Chez moi later." One entry, however, seems unambiguous: "Dinner with A at Ready Room. Sex later complicated by overseas call," perhaps, as McGilligan thought, with Hitchcock on the other end of the line. McGilligan also notes that on the evenings they met in September that year, Cook and Alma steered away from their usual LA nightspots, once driving all the way to Santa Barbara for dinner, suggesting that they were keen not to advertise the time they were spending together.

If this was an affair, it seems to have been one born not of a great shared infatuation but of some emotional unease Alma was experiencing—though exactly what is a mystery. In a diary entry from October 1948, Cook perfunctorily describes an evening out with Alma, ending simply with "Tears later." It's possible she had grown despairing of Hitchcock's current infatuation with Ingrid Bergman, with whom he was working on *Under Capricorn*. Hitchcock told a select few—mostly writers on his films—that Bergman had once attempted to seduce him, an unlikely sounding story he related with such conviction that it was hard to know whether it was true or not. Either way, it's easy to imagine how Alma would have felt sidelined, humiliated even, whenever one of Hitchcock's obsessions with a young actress took hold. Tippi Hedren claims that Alma once apologized to her for Hitchcock's smothering possessiveness, though it's not evident whether she had any knowledge of the assault that Hedren alleges. Charles Bennett's memoirs claimed that the Hitchcocks' "married life was a happy one—until a second woman became a part of it," yet Bennett names no names, and no corroboration seems to exist. There have been similar suggestions that Hitchcock had an affair with Joan Harrison, but, again, there's no concrete evidence. The following summer, 1949, when Hitchcock was away once more, Alma wrote Cook to tell him she was feeling "very lonely this week, and recovered my equilibrium—or I thought I had until the day's mail arrived," perhaps because she had received a letter from her husband that knocked her off course. A few weeks later, she again reached out to Cook for emotional support when terrible reviews came in for *Under Capricorn*. The press, particularly in the United States, was savage, taking aim at the script for which, despite her name being absent from the credits, Alma felt partly responsible. The *Washington Post* called the dialogue "unintentionally hilarious."

It might be that Alma's relationship with Cook resulted from a collision of feelings she had for Hitchcock her husband and those for "Hitchcock" the entity for which she had worked so hard over the years. Or, perhaps she found herself yearning for a more intense, physical connection than she had come to experience in her marriage. Cook, ten years her junior, described Alma as "extremely attractive" because of "her intelligence and her warmth," and it's understandable why she might have turned to this vivacious younger man at a moment of unease. The record is frustratingly silent, though one clue might be found in another of Cook's short stories. In "Her First Island," Clara Henderson, "a very conventional woman," begins an affair with a man named Ted during a two-week period in which her husband, Norman, is overseas on business. Though she adores Norman—"a truly warm and fine thing she had with Norman. No one could ask for a better marriage"—she is drawn to Ted because he represents excitement and abandon, and he has no associations with her usual roles and routines. When Norman and Ted meet, they get on terrifically, despite being polar opposites. Ultimately, Clara is pleased to draw a close to her fling, because "Norman symbolized solidity and roots and strong anchors and all those firm attributes one is supposed to have in one's life. Norman was comfort; Norman was protection." It's unclear quite when Cook wrote this and if he intended it as a comment on his relationship with Alma. Even if not, it's an interesting articulation of the dynamics of a triangular relationship and the way Alma may have been feeling about her marriage as she approached her fiftieth birthday. It also nudges one into asking what Alma got out of her relationship with her husband. As Hitchcock outlined in his acceptance speech for the American Film Institute Lifetime Achievement Award in 1979, Alma swaddled him in "affection, appreciation, encouragement, and constant collaboration." In return, Alma found an outlet for her considerable talents, but also stability and uxorious comfort. When they were apart, Alma wrote letters to Hitchcock—and his secretaries—asking whether he was looking after himself, eating properly, sleeping well, and going for his checkups. In return, Hitchcock had a habit of making small but frequent romantic gestures, calling ahead to hotels where Alma was staying to make sure that a fresh bouquet of her favorite flowers would greet her on arrival. On the whole, theirs was a profoundly strong partnership. But at times it was difficult for Alma not to feel overlooked by Hitchcock and "Hitchcock."

It's possible Hitchcock thought Cook was gay: Cook's diaries reveal he had relationships with men and women, and in the months before his apparent fling with Alma, he seems to have become involved with Douglas Dick, an actor who played a role in *Rope*, adding further depth to Hitchcock's interest in the film's theme of coded homosexuality. It's also possible that Hitchcock knew about Alma and Cook, and that she knew he knew, but nothing was ever said about it. Unflinching self-examination was not highly valued in the Hitchcock household. Alfred was a master of dissimulation when it came to his emotions; Alma had an extreme aversion to talking about herself and her past. "There was a primary motivation in our small family to never look back but only ahead," remarked Pat. It was an attitude that allowed Hitchcock to bounce back from failure and disappointment with astounding success—but it also allowed resentments to fester, and damage to remain unrepaired.

The Hitchcocks and Cook remained good friends for years. In 1950, Cook was a witness at Alma's American citizenship ceremony, and a few years later they were witnesses at his wedding. Cook also worked happily on *Stage Fright* as well as on the next Hitchcock picture, *Strangers on a Train*, which featured Pat again, this time in a larger role that made excellent use of her comedic talents. Soon after, Cook made a small but important contribution to *Rear Window*. Pat dialed down her acting career when she married in 1952, and she had the first of her three children a year later. Subsequently, she took on a few roles in *Alfred Hitchcock Presents*, though her only other appearance in a Hitchcock movie was her turn as the cattily amusing Caroline in *Psycho*. Hitchcock said he and Alma were relieved when their daughter decided to favor motherhood over her career. Yet Pat remained part of the broader Hitchcock enterprise, and was on the payroll of the *Alfred Hitchcock Mystery Magazine* for several years, as associate editor, though her formal duties seem to have been minimal.

Once *Stage Fright* was complete, Alma never took a credit on another Hitchcock production. She remained his champion and continued to exert an influence, but crossing the streams of personal and professional may have become too much. As her husband's worldwide fame increased in the fifties and sixties, Alma inched further away from the spotlight, but the significance of her advice never lessened in Hitchcock's eyes. Into the 1960s, Hitchcock still sought Alma's opinion on how he might adapt source material into a new film. With John Buchan's *The Three Hostages*, she pitched a list of highly Hitchcockian scenes, including one of a man being drowned by having his head held under the water of the Ganges River, sparking memories of Hitchcock's first murder in *The Pleasure Garden* and anticipating the slow suffocation of Gromek in his next movie, *Torn Curtain*. She also gave her husband a document outlining the exciting scenes in the book that should be carried over into the film. The page was blank—a lovely example of this aging couple's shared sense of humor and Alma's instinctive understanding of what made Hitchcock and "Hitchcock" tick.

Alma's words could be used to convey praise—Hitchcock offered no higher compliment than saying Alma approved of one's work—as well as condemnation. When Hitchcock wanted to detach himself from a television project with Richard Condon in 1964, he used Alma's opinion as justification. "I had Mrs Hitchcock read the script," he said, as though Condon would naturally accept Alma as the ultimate arbiter on scriptwriting, "and her only comment to me was that she has just read *Infinity of Mirrors* [Condon's most recent novel] and thought it was so beautifully written and asked me why the script could not have the same quality." Should Hitchcock himself ever be on the receiving end of Alma's critique, he felt crushed. After viewing a cut of *Vertigo*, she had just one criticism: "that shot of Kim running. Her legs are so fat. It looks awful." Hitchcock despaired. "Alma hates the film," he told those around him, and returned to the edit to excise the offending shot. About three weeks before the release of that movie, Alma was diagnosed with cervical cancer. Ultimately, she made a full recovery after surgery, but Hitchcock was petrified at the prospect of losing her. When Alma was in the hospital, he traveled there "weeping and shaking convulsively," pushing his fear down into the pit of his stomach and pretending to be perfectly calm as he sat with her. Away from the hospital, he broke down in front of colleagues and wondered aloud whether there was any point in carrying on should the worst happen.

Alma was vital to Hitchcock and "Hitchcock," yet she remains enigmatic. Like Doris Day's Jo in *The Man Who Knew Too Much*, did she itch with unfulfilled ambition, having sacrificed her career in order to better support her egotistical husband? As with Gay in *The Paradine Case*, and Midge in *Vertigo*, did she soldier through the upsetting thought that she, the dutiful, homely companion, couldn't compete with the glamorous object of her beloved's wild fantasies? One suspects both these might be true, but she maintained a deliberate strategy of leaving little record of herself that wasn't mediated through the entity of Hitchcock. In 1966, a branch of the British government wrote to ask whether Alma would share her memories of working in the film industry in the twenties, but she demurred. She was also approached to be interviewed for a book titled *Women Who Made the Movies*; Hitchcock had recently been involved in a similar book and television project, *Men Who Made the Movies*. Hitchcock responded on her behalf, saying, "Mrs Hitchcock and I have given a great deal of thought to your letter," but Alma would not be participating, as she had only ever been "a technical writer of scripts which was definitely not part of the creative process . . . she would assemble a script in its purely technical sense." This wasn't so, but the letter had seemingly been written with Alma's assent. It's possible she didn't feel well enough for an interview at this time, or perhaps she was carrying out her self-assigned duty to create the circumstances in which Alfred was always the star. As Hitchcock once said, the only drawback for a man married to a woman of such discretion is the risk that he "will never be talked about in public," creating in him an "egoistic need to write about himself. I'm sure I prefer it that way. I suspect Alma knows that too."

This was as true in 1925 as it was in 1979, when Hitchcock was working at home on the script of *The Short Night*. Things were progressing sufficiently well for the script to be stress-tested under the weight of a Reville critique. David Freeman, with whom Hitchcock was writing, was amazed to see the old man suddenly animated. He gesticulated and switched voices, performing each of the characters. The doleful, immobile Hitchcock whom Freeman had come to know over the preceding weeks had vanished. Alma, herself ailing from old age and ill health, was rapt. "It was like watching two people on a first date that was going *really* well, and at that point they'd been married fifty years," recalls Freeman. "I think he wanted to show her how clever he was, and more importantly that there was hope, a future. And he desperately wanted her approval." The old Hitchcock—or, to be more exact, the younger one—was back, and Alma couldn't have been happier.

8

THE VOYEUR

In 1953, Hitchcock was treading water. *Stage Fright* and *Strangers on a Train* were followed by a third black-and-white film for Warner Bros., *I Confess*, an unusually sober movie about the trials of duty and conscience starring Montgomery Clift. Then came *Dial M for Murder*. It was a hit, but, as Hitchcock admitted, he coasted through the production; it was only his third color movie, but was otherwise Hitchcock-by-the-numbers and took just thirty-six days to film—five of which were dedicated to the scene in which Grace Kelly is violently attacked in her nightgown, which left the actress bruised and sore. During production, two things kept Hitchcock buoyed: his ardor for Kelly, who he was directing for the first time, and the prospect of his next movie, for which he had the highest hopes.

This forthcoming picture was to be made for Paramount, with whom Hitchcock had recently signed a highly lucrative deal. Under the terms of the contract, he was obliged to make nine films, the rights to five of which would become his after eight years. The first of these films was *Rear Window*, for which he was having a marvelous set constructed: a block of thirty-one apartments, eight of them furnished and fitted with everything but running water. Not that the audience would ever enter any of them; all they'd get was a voyeuristic glimpse through the windows at the good and evil that thrives behind closed doors.

Though its plot is pure fiction, *Rear Window* could count as sensory memoir. A film about the nature of films, a festival of watching and projecting, it is the closest we will ever get to experiencing the world as Hitchcock saw it. Hitchcock was aware of the ethical murkiness of watching, but he never let that diminish the joy it gave him. He spent eighty years never being able to look away, his vision unobscured even when his eyes were closed.

From its inception, cinema has been bound to the act of looking at women's bodies. In 1915, Audrey Munson became the first woman to appear fully nude in a mainstream American movie. The film was *Inspiration*, in which Munson played an impoverished New Yorker, rescued from her drudgery by a sculptor who makes her his muse. When she leaves him, he is crestfallen, and in a plotline that coincidentally foreshadows Scottie's hunt for Madeleine in *Vertigo* more than forty years later, the artist wanders the streets in search of her perfect form among the city's statuary. Despite its shots of nudity, *Inspiration* was unchallenged by the authorities because of its artistic theme, and because in real life Munson's body had provided the template for dozens of statues around Manhattan, many of which survive to this day. She made three further films, but the public soon lost interest in looking at her. The work dried up, debts accumulated, followed by serious mental health problems. On her fortieth birthday she was committed to an insane asylum where she stayed, with hardly a visitor, until her death sixty-five years later.

Hitchcock was acutely aware of the centrality of the watched woman in the history of his medium. The very first shot in the Hitchcock canon is of the bare legs of a group of dancers running down a spiral staircase, evoking Duchamp's seminal painting, *Nude Descending a Staircase*, which itself trailed a pioneering time-lapse photographic study of a naked woman walking down a flight of stairs that Eadweard Muybridge published in 1885. Of course, all these images fit into a far lengthier artistic tradition, stretching back centuries, in which Hitchcock was well versed. When Norman Bates has his "what the butler saw" moment, spying on Marion undressing in her motel room, his peephole is concealed beneath a framed print of Willem van Mieris's painting *Susannah and the Elders*, an image of two men preying on a naked woman while she bathes. The pointed significance of the painting is underlined in the movie's trailer when Hitchcock stops in front of it and says it is of "great significance," before feigning discomfort and changing the subject. Is the painting significant purely because it reflects what Norman does to Marion? Or, do the dirty old men on the canvas signify the one behind the camera? Or, are we, in our enjoyment of looking, either at *Psycho* or at a Renaissance masterpiece, as guilty of voyeurism as any artist?

In conversation with Andy Warhol, another artist who spent a great deal of his career silently staring at bodies in intimate situations, Hitchcock claimed he had glimpsed pornographic films only once in his life, and that was after the age of sixty, and by way of happenstance. It occurred after a steak dinner during a publicity trip to Tokyo, he said, when he was led blithely "into this upper room and there they had a screen that showed these awful films," the specifics of which he didn't divulge. However, he daydreamed about including acts of sexual voyeurism in his films. The story of Adelaide and Edwin Bartlett, which Hitchcock frequently cited as his favorite true-crime tale, entailed the willing cuckoldry of Edwin by Adelaide and a young clergyman named George Dyson. In 1953, Hitchcock published a magazine piece about the case in which he explained—with, as the scholar Sidney Gottlieb has also identified, an intriguing but perhaps unintentional, parallel to his situation with Alma and Whitfield Cook—that the Bartletts' marriage "had been entirely platonic. Except for one occasion which resulted in a stillborn child, they lived together as friends and nothing more. . . . He had encouraged her friendship with George Dyson, and he urged them to become affectionate. In effect, he had 'given' her to Mr. Dyson." Later, Hitchcock imagined making a film about the case, and explained how he would shoot the scene of the parson "making violent love to the young woman while the husband, sitting in his rocking chair and smoking his pipe, looked on." In the first drafts of *The Trouble with Harry*, Jennifer—Harry's widow, played by Shirley MacLaine—confesses that her late husband insisted on hanging a photograph of his brother over their marital bed, to create the impression that he was watching them make love. That risqué element was ultimately dropped, but approaching eighty and working on his final script, Hitchcock imagined a strange act of voyeurism that nobody had ever put in a Hollywood movie: a man and a woman exposing themselves to each other, a prelude to him combing her pubic hair.

Beyond the graphically or explicitly sexual, Hitchcock's preoccupation with looking, its motivations, and its consequences, is one of the most fascinating aspects of his work and one that ensures its enduring relevance to our culture. It was three Hitchcock films—*Rear Window*, *Vertigo*, and *Marnie*—that formed the basis of Laura Mulvey's argument that Hollywood movies display the world through the "male gaze," favoring male desires and experiences, reinforcing the notion that women exist only to please men. Mulvey's term, and its underlying concepts, have drifted into common parlance and, in certain quarters, have helped to solidify Hitchcock's reputation as the supreme auteur of patriarchy. Doubtless, there is abundant evidence in Hitchcock to sustain Mulvey's theory of the privileged male gaze, but it's also true that Hitchcock's male voyeurs are rarely gleeful in their obsessive looking. Often, their ogling causes them either guilt or regret, and hastens their downfall in some way. In that opening scene of *The Pleasure Garden*, Hitchcock shows us the dancers hurrying their way to the stage before cutting to a panning shot across the front row of the audience, a line of supposed gentlemen leering at the women before them. We then see through the binoculars of one particularly lecherous fellow as he stares at Patsy, the film's heroine. After the show, hoping to make a fantasy come true, he approaches Patsy, only to be mortified as she removes her blonde wig—she's a natural brunette—and laughs in his face. Within the first five minutes of the first Hitchcock film, the male gaze is presented, critiqued, and ridiculed.

Unease with a compulsion to look is what makes *Rear Window* so compelling. Not since the experimental *Rope* seven years earlier had Hitchcock found a project that so enthused him; despite various claims to the contrary that have been made over the years, he was heavily involved in building the script from the template of its source material. As the historian Bill Krohn notes, the drafts of the scripts feature so many small touches evocative of earlier Hitchcock—"the little people who inhabit

Hitchcock on the set of *To Catch a Thief.*

it, and the way the man at the rear window becomes involved in their lives"—that they surely came from him rather than from a writer. An initial treatment for the film by Joshua Logan—written before Hitchcock had bought the rights to the story—begins with the camera surveying the windows of the various apartments, not unlike the opening sequence of *Rear Window.* However, Hitchcock had already filmed something very similar more than twenty years earlier, a shot at the start of *Murder!* in which the camera pans down a row of houses, allowing us to peer inside at private lives as lights come on and people respond to a commotion outside.

Rear Window stars James Stewart as Jeff, a globe-trotting photojournalist, confined to his Greenwich Village apartment while he recuperates from a broken leg. Bored and frustrated by his incapacitation, Jeff begins to spy on his neighbors, one of whom, Lars Thorwald, he suspects of having killed his wife. Although disturbed by his voyeurism, Jeff's physiotherapist, Stella, and his glamorous young girlfriend, Lisa, help him investigate the murder, eventually bringing Thorwald to justice. Jeff never leaves his apartment (apart from one brief moment of defenestration), and the camera stays with him throughout. Exhibiting Hitchcock's love of the subjective camera, almost all the action is told from Jeff's perspective. We receive clues, red herrings, and revelations along with him, save one scene in which we see Thorwald exit his apartment with a woman while Jeff dozes in his chair.* We see Jeff's pleasure in spying on the woman he calls Miss Torso as she exercises in front of her window. But we also see his shame as he watches Miss Lonelyhearts being assaulted by a man she has invited into her home, and as she later contemplates suicide. When Thorwald discovers Lisa in his apartment— where she has been looking for incriminating evidence—Jeff is reduced to pathetic impotence, barely able to watch.

Rear Window is Hitchcock's definitive film. It draws together various strands of the Hitchcock touch: ingenious production design; perfect casting; a taut, sparkling script; thrilling entertainment interwoven with dark, unsettling themes; beautifully judged use of colors and clothing. There's also something inspired, in a gently subversive, Hitchcockian way, about the construction of the Greenwich Village apartments where the whole film takes place. In a period in which studios splashed vast sums creating epics such as *Quo Vadis*, *The Robe*, and *Ben-Hur*, Hitchcock persuaded Paramount to spend more than eighty thousand dollars— a vast sum in 1953—on a single studio set for a movie that takes place inside a nondescript apartment, where a middle-aged man sits in his pajamas, spying on the neighbors. Robert Burks, the film's cinematographer, likened it to a DeMille production, though, as the historian John Belton points out, the themes of *Rear Window* hearken back to the earli-

---

*   This, of course, is following another of Hitchcock's favorite tricks of allowing the audience to stay half a step ahead of the protagonist, replacing mystery with suspense.

est days of cinema when films were "more concerned with exhibition, presentation, and display, than with narration." Hitchcock maintained that he was at his best when he adhered most strictly to the principles of silent filmmaking, as was the case with *Rear Window.* Ironically, the film also features some of the best dialogue of any Hitchcock movie. John Michael Hayes was chiefly responsible for that, but he conceded that in the process of writing the script, "Hitchcock taught me about how to tell a story with the camera and tell it silently."

"Of all the films I have made," reflected Hitchcock in 1968, "this to me is the most cinematic." Today, the word "cinematic" is frequently used as a superlative, a synonym for something visually stunning. Hitchcock used it in its strictest sense, meaning the core principles and techniques that differentiate cinema from other visual arts. This has relatively little to do with cinematography, and a lot to do with editing. "Galloping horses in Westerns are only photographs of action, photographs of content," explained Hitchcock. "It's the piecing together of the montage which makes what I call a pure film." Hitchcock's template was laid down by early pioneers, especially Griffith, Eisenstein, Pudovkin, and Kuleshov, the latter of whom conducted an experiment to demonstrate the almost magical properties of film assembly, which Hitchcock referenced in explaining his own technique. "Show a man looking at something," he ventured, "say a baby. Then show him smiling. By placing these shots in sequence—man looking, object seen, reaction to object—the director characterizes the man as a kindly person." But replace the shot of the baby with a girl in a bikini, and the sequence is transformed. "What is he now? He's a dirty old man." A sequence just like that appears in *Rear Window* as Jeff ogles Miss Torso, stretching and twirling in her kitchen. But elsewhere in the film, Hitchcock adds an extra element: the voyeur as unreliable witness. In Kuleshov's experiment, our opinion of the man is manipulated by the nature of what he has seen; in *Rear Window*, Jeff thinks he's witnessing a man getting away with murder—but he can't be sure whether he's being deceived by his own eyes.

It's a feeling shared by Scottie in *Vertigo*, again played by Stewart, who is driven mad by silent watching and the obsessive pursuit that fol-

Hitchcock and the art of looking: James Stewart in *Rear Window*.

lows. If Cary Grant was Hitchcock's favorite man of action, some heroic, imaginary version of himself, Stewart was surely his favorite man of reaction, expressing through his silent gaze unsettling things about being an ordinary man that Hitchcock felt but rarely articulated. Stewart explained that his role in *Rear Window* "largely consisted of reacting. First Hitchcock would show what I was seeing through my binoculars. Then he'd show my face, and I'd reflect what I saw. I spent an astonishing amount of time looking into the camera and being amused, afraid, worried, curious, embarrassed, bored."

It is in their dumb staring that Jeff and Scottie are at their loudest. Hitchcock's original ending for *Vertigo*, only restored on its re-release in the 1980s, was not the dynamic chase up the bell tower that ends with

Judy's fall, but its aftermath: Scottie sitting in a chair, mute, gazing into space. His voyeurism has led him to misery; the male gaze has become an ugly hall of mirrors.

Secrets and unspoken truths permeate Hitchcock's work. Like Jeff and Scottie, Hitchcock was an assiduous observer of people, and he was convinced that everybody had something to hide. Tippi Hedren acknowledged that one of her debts to Hitchcock was the way he encouraged her to drink in her surroundings as a way of developing her craft. "I watch, I observe, I observe people in situations all the time, and I put things back in my memory and say, 'Oh, that would be wonderful to do, to put into a character.' And that I learned from Hitchcock."

This was natural enough for the greatest maker of spy movies in history, especially one who spent the first forty years of his life immersed in a society that valued secrecy in the way that people of twenty-first-century America value disclosure. The profusion of British spy fiction in the early 1900s influenced Hitchcock profoundly and supplied him with much source material. It emanated from a period of rapid growth in state-sponsored espionage, which sat atop a pervasive culture of secrecy that one former cabinet minister called "the British disease." Peter Hennessy, arguably the greatest living historian of the uses and abuses of Westminster power, believes that "secrecy is as much part of the English landscape as the Cotswolds. It goes with the grain of our society." Hitchcock himself said that he "always felt that espionage stories are fairly tricky to do in America," as its openness means it "carries no real menace with it. You always feel you can go to the nearest policeman and complain that the Communists are after you."

Hitchcock adhered to the British code of secrecy, and he formed close personal and professional relationships with those who had extraordinary secrets of their own. His friend and collaborator Ivor Montagu was a Soviet double agent during World War II, while his brother, Ewen Montagu, masterminded Operation Mincemeat, a plot in which the British intelligence services invented an entirely fictitious Royal Marines officer to fool the Nazis into believing that the Allies' plans to invade Sicily were fake. In 1953, Ewen Montagu wrote an account of the plot, *The Man Who Never Was*—a possible allusion to *The Man Who Knew Too Much*, on which his brother had worked with Hitchcock. The book was adapted for the screen three years later, directed by Ronald Neame, who had started his career on Hitchcock's *Blackmail*. An innocent man mistaken for a nonexistent spy is, of course, the central premise of *North by Northwest*, and that idea was first floated to Hitchcock in the early 1950s by the journalist Otis Guernsey who had heard about a wartime tale, similar to Operation Mincemeat, in which the British invented "a fake masterspy" in the Middle East. Ernest Lehman was adamant that neither Neame's film, nor any other real-life story, was in his mind when he scripted *North by Northwest*, but given the spiderweb of associations, it may well have been in Hitchcock's.

Lore has it that not only did Hitchcock have an intense interest in looking and watching, he possessed remarkable powers of observation and foresight. Frequently, he cast actors and recruited writers based on his hunches, reading them over the course of a twenty-minute meeting, or a lunch during which they talked about everything but the film ahead of them. Some colleagues and associates told stories that suggested his abilities approached the preternatural. He could, apparently, grasp a person's character and motive in an instant, second-guess them, and spot lies immediately. Considering how socially maladroit he could be, it seems a little hard to believe, but those who knew him best insist "he had an extraordinary sixth sense." Even some of those who never had the honor of meeting him were of a mind to agree. Recounting the time when he crept onto the set of *Family Plot* in a vain hope of meeting his idol, Steven Spielberg said, "It was as if he sensed an intruder in his reverse vision. He couldn't have seen me but he leaned over to an assistant director and whispered something." Immediately, the assistant director approached Spielberg and escorted him off the set. "That was the closest I came to Hitchcock. I learned that he had eyes in the back of his head . . . very eerie."

The legend of Hitchcock's third eye has been perpetuated at least partially because Hitchcock's ability to visualize is so central to his professional reputation as a director. He often claimed that he would "never look at the script again once it's written, because it's all been done," and by that point, he could see the entire film in his head, shot by shot. "The general method that is used by, might I say, the average director," he boasted, "is to shoot what we'd term plenty of material and then cut. I personally don't use this method. . . . I aim at getting a complete vision of my film before it goes on to the studio floor." All that remained was to go through the tedious process of committing the thing to film, which he did with the aid of detailed storyboards that told cast and crew exactly what was in his mind's eye. He shot only the tiniest amount of footage that didn't appear in the final cut, and reshoots were as rare as hen's teeth. "Films," he said, "are made before they are shot." Once the process was complete, he didn't need to see the finished product with an audience because he knew how they would react. He understood how people worked. He could press their buttons and pull their levers at will. Not only could he see a whole film in his mind, he knew how to project it into ours as well.

It is a remarkable testament to his unmatched visual genius—except it's not *entirely* true. Scripting was clearly a highly stimulating process for Hitchcock, in which images solidified and pieces of the story slotted together. His preproduction planning was also rigorous, but it was an attempt to remove uncertainty and quell his nerves—a safety net rather than concrete walls from within which his films never escaped. On movies such as *Topaz*, *The Birds*, and *Shadow of a Doubt*, new pages arrived well after the cameras had started to roll, with Hitchcock adjusting his designs accordingly, giving the lie to his assertion that he never glanced at the script after the first day of filming. The usual equanimity of a Hitchcock set was frayed in Morocco during the filming of *The Man Who Knew Too Much* when the shooting script failed to materialize on time. Well after principal photography had begun, the assistant production manager, Hugh Brown, noted that the crew was receiving fresh pages each morning and having to work on the hoof. Robert Benchley, who both wrote dialogue for and acted in *Foreign Correspondent*, had a similar experience. From the set, he wrote his wife that "Hitchcock is a good director but an exacting one. . . . The picture isn't written yet, and one of the most important roles isn't cast. . . . They're shooting the stuff that's written, and then, when changes in the plot make that obsolete, they shoot it over."

Neither did Hitchcock storyboard a whole movie in advance, only key scenes, and sometimes not even those. When MGM asked him to provide sketches of the famous crop-duster scene for publicity reasons, he acquiesced—even though no sketches of the scene had been made before filming. Bill Krohn explains that "tracings of each still [from the shoot] preserved among his papers show that Hitchcock, or someone, gave it a try, but what he seems to have done finally was ask a production illustrator to draw a storyboard" retrospectively, based on the action that was filmed. By this stage in his career, Hitchcock's storyboards had become part of his public image, eye-catching props that purported to show us genius flowing through the nib of a pencil. Krohn posits that it began in 1942, when Universal's publicity department placed an article in *Theatre Arts* magazine that reproduced drawings from Hitchcock's latest picture, *Saboteur*, as a behind-the-scenes peek at the Hitchcock methodology. But, even earlier, in publicizing the very first Hollywood Hitchcock movie, *Rebecca*, the *New York World-Telegram* ran an article featuring four sketches that Hitchcock had made during the making of the film, hailing Hitchcock as "a Pattern Designer," whose movies skip from the chambers of his imagination to the page, then onto the screen, in quick, clean strides. Many years later, drawings from *Saboteur*'s Statue of Liberty sequence were put on display by the Academy of Motion Picture Arts and Sciences, which those who worked on the film believed had actually been drawn after production had wrapped.

Hitchcock clearly had an impressive visual imagination. Farley Granger declared himself amazed when he visited Hitchcock's office before filming *Rope*. "Every wall was covered by eight-by-ten-inch drawings from ceiling to floor. I was completely absorbed in this visualization of the script." Yet it is going too far to say that Hitchcock had a film edited in his head, down to the last camera angle, before filming began—not least because by the time he was experienced enough at filmmaking to have developed such a skill, he would have also been experienced enough to understand the advantages of embracing the unexpected, which is a part of the creative process in every medium. Robert Burks confirmed that Hitchcock did exhaustive planning for each shoot, and tended to give camera operators rough sketches for each planned shot on the day of shooting.* "But he never nails you down to those sketches," Burks told an interviewer. "If, after discussion, Hitch finds that we can achieve better results in another way, he has no hesitancy in rewriting the action or dialogue."

Jack Cardiff was a director and Oscar-winning cinematographer who shot *Under Capricorn*, arguably the most complex of all Hitchcock's filming assignments. Cardiff was struck by Hitchcock's certainty about the images he wanted, and his faith in the technicians' ability to get them. "He hardly ever saw the rushes of the day's work," recalled Cardiff. "The editor would keep him closely informed, but Hitch knew exactly what he was getting on the screen. From the moment he had drawn pictures of the camera set-ups, he had it all firmly in his mind." That someone of Cardiff's talent, skill, and experience was impressed by Hitchcock's ability to visualize is telling. Clearly, he had a rare gift. However, Cardiff's description of Hitchcock's behavior during shooting also suggests that Hitchcock made something of a performance of his reputation as the all-seeing genius with an editing suite in his head, and who found filming a terrible bore. "He had his back to the actors," said Cardiff of Hitchcock during one of *Under Capricorn*'s lengthy takes, "aimlessly looking down at the floor, and at the end, when he had said 'Cut,' he made only one comment to my camera operator Paul Beeson: 'How was that for you, Paul?' On Paul's nod, he would signal his acceptance of the whole reel." There's a quiet ostentation in the inactivity described here, the decision to look away from the very thing he should have been looking at; it's

---

* His quickfire sketches were highly effective; he even used them to communicate with the deaf artist A. R. Thomson, when sitting for his portrait. "Language in Pictures," *Gloucestershire Echo*, April 26, 1933, 4.

tempting to believe that on Hitchcock's set the act of directing—of *being* Alfred Hitchcock—was itself part of the spectacle.

It coheres with the broader image that grew around Hitchcock from the mid-1940s: a great man who was defined by his unique ability to see what ordinary people cannot. In his reminiscences, his talent for seeing a film unfold in his head made itself obvious before he'd even begun directing his own films. When working as art director on *Woman to Woman* in 1923, he built the set of the entrance to a Park Lane mansion with nothing at the top of the stairs, much to the consternation of Graham Cutts when he arrived to direct the day's filming. "They were expecting to do the conventional shot from the door looking up the stairs," remembered Hitchcock, "with the balcony and the hostess at the top, and the people going up. I said, 'No. You take the shot from the *top* of the stairs, looking *down*.'" He then explained to his superior that as the scene belonged to the hostess, the action should be seen from her perspective. "I was, in a way, a small martinet. I said, 'this is where the shot is to be done,' and the director was helpless." The common or garden-variety movie director's lack of visual imagination was a subject Hitchcock spoke on from the very beginning of his career, and he never let up. "Not enough people have a visual sense," he moaned in 1976. "They cannot project. See, I don't even look through the camera; I can visualize it on the screen."

Indeed, he consistently professed a total lack of interest in other directors' work. In their many off-the-record conversations about films and the film industry, Peter Bogdanovich can't remember Hitchcock talking about any other filmmakers, with the exception of Orson Welles "because he knew I was doing an interview book with Orson, so he asked questions . . . just a few." Despite his suggestions to the contrary, Hitchcock was assiduous in keeping up with the latest cinema. His appointment books reveal that he made viewing films part of his weekly work schedule. This was especially the case once he signed for Universal in the early 1960s and set up his own suite of offices at the studio. A PhD thesis could be written about the movies that made it onto Hitchcock's viewing schedule at the Universal projection rooms. *Woodstock, A Clock-*

work Orange, Marat/Sade, The Wild Angels, The Pink Panther, The Graduate, Rosemary's Baby, What's Up, Doc? were among the many English-language films watched soon after release, along with dozens of films by leading foreign directors. It was after watching Michelangelo Antonioni's *Blow-Up* that he felt inspired to push into bold new territory in the late sixties. "These Italian directors are a century ahead of me in terms of technique!"

Such admissions were not intended for public consumption. In interviews, the grand old man of cinema was more likely to speak of his work by way of metaphor, likening himself to architects, composers, writers, and especially painters. Cézanne was one name Hitchcock invoked on a couple of occasions, as was his favorite artist, Paul Klee, because of what Hitchcock thought was their similar use of color. "I'm not self-indulgent where content is concerned. I'm only self-indulgent about treatment," he said in 1972. "I'd compare myself to an abstract painter." Story was what he had writers for; the real essence of Hitchcock, the field in which the auteur made his mark, was, he suggested, his inimitable eye. In that same conversation, his interlocutor attempted to tease out Hitchcock's opinions on his peers. Of Ingmar Bergman, Hitchcock offered nothing more than "he has indicated on one occasion that he learned a lot from Hitchcock" in terms of his visual approach, and pointed out that the same was true of Truffaut. Of Vittorio De Sica's *The Bicycle Thief*, he said that the Italian's masterpiece of neorealism was "very good," but that his own films did more with the form.

In fairness to Hitchcock, he would not be the first or the last artist disinclined to discuss his contemporaries' work. But the fact that he chose to explain his style by placing it in the lineage of another, more rarified field of the visual arts indicates he wanted us to believe that his mastery of "pure cinema" put him in a category separate from even the most accomplished filmmakers of the day. One could argue that it expresses an insecurity about his own status as a commercial filmmaker, and about cinema as a whole. If so, it's one shared by plenty of others; there is no shortage of critics who have praised Hitchcock's talents by way of comparing him to other types of artists. Dolly Haas, who played the role of the murderer's wife in *I Confess*, was so fascinated by Hitchcock's visual flair that she concluded he "was actually an architect. I thought, 'My God, the man should have been a visual artist or an architect,' because he drew every close-up and every scene from the left blank page of his manuscript."

It's intriguing that a successful film actress apparently didn't consider filmmaking to be a branch of the visual arts, but Haas hit on an important point. The writer Gavin Lambert once made the brilliant observation that many of Hitchcock's most memorable scenes "could be titled like surrealistic paintings: Human Being Caged by Bird, Cigarette Extinguished in Fried Egg [*To Catch a Thief*], and as a presentation of the extreme not even Dali has gone further than, Young Man Dressed as His Dead Mother Knifing a Naked Girl under a Shower." So strong was his visual motivation that Hitchcock does at times resemble a conceptual artist, one who liked to capture shocking, witty ideas in those images that were so often his initial motivation for making a film. This sensibility is perhaps why his work has appealed to and inspired so many visual artists in other fields, many of whom have responded to Hitchcock's voyeurism in their own creations. For example, Douglas Gordon's 1993 video installation *24 Hour Psycho* slows the Hitchcock movie down, stretching it to last an entire day. So elongated is each shot that, even in the frenetic moments of the shower scene montage, the audience is no longer looking at Hitchcock the filmmaker, but Hitchcock the still-life artist.

The work of the English artist Cornelia Parker has certain parallels with Hitchcock's—bracing images laced with a playful wit, ingeniously executed, communicating an idea or a sensation, rather than a narrative. For her best-known work, *Cold Dark Matter: An Exploded View*, she persuaded the British Army to detonate a garden shed full of everyday objects, then used the remains to reconstruct the shed in mid explosion, suspended in midair, with a single light bulb at its center, creating expressionist patterns of shadows all around it. Parker says that one artwork she wishes she had made is Jeremy Deller's *Sacrilege*, an enormous replica of Stonehenge in the form of a bouncy castle, the type of jaunty undermining of solemn reality that Hitchcock would have appreciated, and which he executed himself with his replicas of Mount Rushmore (*North by Northwest*) and the Statue of Liberty (*Saboteur*) that turned famous monuments into jungle gyms. In 2016, Parker installed on the roof of the Metropolitan Museum of Art in Manhattan a structure she titled *Transitional Object (PsychoBarn)*, a replica of the Bates family home made from the reclaimed materials of a dismantled red barn. In recreating the most terrifying house in American history in the blood-red colors of an architectural icon of American wholesomeness, Parker intended to reflect her observations of the United States, in the way that Hitchcock used his outsider's perspective as a lens through which to look at the American west. Hitchcock's own inspiration for the Bates house, moldering next to a highway that represents the speed and transience of modern America, is thought to have included *House by the Railroad* by Edward Hopper.

Parker watched *Psycho* repeatedly and in freeze-frame, poring over tiny details. It was only in doing this that the artifice of Hitchcock's set became apparent to her: this was not a real house but merely a painted facade, one of the many clever tricks that Hitchcock played on our eyes, confident that, unlike him, audiences rarely look closely enough to differentiate reality from falsehood. It was Hitchcock's contention that almost every shot will be on screen for less than five seconds, nowhere near enough time to pick apart the trickery of moviemaking.

He may have been happy to bend the truth on screen, but Hitchcock's approach to what he called "filling the tapestry" of a film was based on an unbending attention to detail. Though he took pride in declaring his films slices of cake rather than slices of life, he also aimed for realism in his work. Realism in the sense Hitchcock meant it had nothing to do with logic and plausibility, things in which he had only the vaguest interest. Instead, he felt it vital to place the Brownian motion of his plots within a sturdy, immutable chamber. "I avoid out-and-out fantasy because people should be able to identify with the characters. Making a film means, first of all, to tell a story. That story can be an improbable one, but it should never be banal." More succinctly, Robert Boyle described the idea as "fairytales played against a realistic environment." If one played an outrageous event in a convincingly ordinary setting, the emotional impact on the audience would be that much greater. Thus, while one could drive a horse and cart through some of the holes in Hitchcock plots, the mise-en-scènes of those films are remarkably detailed.

Fittingly, the pedant's gaze seemed to reach new heights on *Rear Window*. In creating the right set, he instructed his team to scan Greenwich Village for granular visual details. Doc Erickson, the production manager, was charged with fulfilling Hitchcock's wish for the neighborhood to be thoroughly photographed. Research images were taken of numerous apartments, and several courtyards were captured at different times of day, in different light, from different angles, and at different points of the compass. For the moment in the film when Lisa has an indulgent meal of lobster and champagne delivered to Jeff's ratty apartment from the 21 Club, Hitchcock insisted on sourcing a wine bucket, two dinner plates, and six napkins from the restaurant, as well as a waiter's uniform to ensure that the fabulous implausibility of the scene was accurate in every material detail. It wasn't only Hitchcock's eyes that needed to be satisfied. The sounds of Greenwich Village traffic and street life had to be recorded, this before Hitchcock had taken the decision for the camera to remain within Jeff's apartment for the entire film. The older Hitchcock got, the more interested he became in perfecting such details. A few years later, in the preproduction stage for *Vertigo*, that other exceptional film about obsessive watching, he had the film's art director, Henry Bumstead, research the apartments of single, retired police officers in the San Francisco Bay Area to get an acceptable model for Scottie's home. On Hitchcock's instruction, Herbert Coleman commissioned the portrait of Carlotta Valdes, a prop used early in the film. Coleman had to engage artists in Italy, England, and the United States before he found one to meet the boss's expectations. Coleman wrote to Paramount's point man in Rome with very specific feedback on one iteration of the portrait, including the need to "eliminate the blemishes on the girl's skin below the neck" as well as a vein that was visible on her wrist. The Hitchcockian attention to detail perhaps reached its peak during postproduction for *Frenzy* when the director requested that a member of his team take a trip to the Coburg Hotel, one of the film's settings, and record the noise of its elevator in operation, lest any erroneous whirring and clunking make its way onto the soundtrack.

Hitchcock obsessed over such minutiae because it brought him sensory satisfaction, just as much as having the right colors and costumes. In this sense, his assertion that his films were made to please his audience was false; observing and capturing the facts of the world, then reordering them in a configuration of his choosing, was an ineffable pleasure of which he never tired.

A portion of Hitchcock's audience, however, shares his obsessiveness. They pore over Hitchcock films in the way art historians look at Renaissance paintings, with the certainty that nothing incidental is contained within the frame. Writing in the *Village Voice* in 1960, Andrew Sarris recommended his readers watch *Psycho* three times: first, to be thrilled and shocked; second, to enjoy the humor; third, to drink in "the hidden meanings and symbols." To Hitchcock watchers, as dedicated to his films as Jeff is to the tableaus of life beyond his apartment window, there is bounteous significance in everything: staircases, light bulbs, milk, glasses, parallel lines, eggs, birds, brandy, water, hats, basements, shoes, doors, hands, musical instruments. No other filmmaker receives quite such close viewing. Before he published his book *The Art of Alfred Hitchcock* in 1976, Donald Spoto had watched *Vertigo* twenty-seven times—this when Hitchcock had removed the film from circulation and it was therefore exceedingly difficult to obtain—and still found he had more to learn about it. In 2005, the scholar Michael Walker published *Hitchcock's Motifs*, an academic study of more than four hundred pages devoted to decoding the significance of objects, images, character types, and narrative patterns within the Hitchcock universe. The book has plentiful sharp insights and reminders that Hitchcock did indeed attach symbolic meaning to many details. But Walker advises caution. Paraphrasing Sigmund Freud, he concedes that "sometimes a corpse is just a corpse."

D. A. Miller writes of his experiences watching Hitchcock films in the way others might of staring into the flames of a fire, high on peyote. After years of repeated and intense viewing of Hitchcock, Miller had an epiphany when he found himself watching *Strangers on a Train* very late at night in a "semi-unconscious mode of viewing," seeing all sorts of hidden threads in Hitchcock's tapestry. In this state, he stops paying attention to the foreground that usually grabs an audience's attention, and instead fixates on background details, what we might label "deep Hitchcock." Even continuity errors—a boom mic briefly in the corner of a shot, a coffee cup in a marginally altered position—seem rich in meaning; they form extra layers of "mistake, confusion, and nonsense that permeates Hitchcockian cinema." This is what Miller calls being "the too-close viewer," a phenomenon that fortifies the experience of watching Hitchcock but also leads one down a rabbit hole of obsession, confusion, and self-doubt of the type traveled by Jeff and Hitchcock's other neurotic watchers. Like Iris in *The Lady Vanishes*, Miller sometimes asks himself, "Do I see what I think I see, what the others say isn't there?"

Among the hidden minutiae that Miller upturned in his free-frame scouring are brief appearances that Hitchcock made in his films, other than the famous cameos. If one looks very closely at the early scenes of *Strangers on a Train*, one can see that Guy is reading a copy of *Alfred Hitchcock's Fireside Book of Suspense*; a few minutes later, Bruno's feet can be seen resting on *Suspense Stories*, another of Hitchcock's anthologies. It's an eminently Hitchcockian touch: a tiny self-referential in-joke— but also a wink to future generations, like a wad of chewing gum left on the underside of a school desk, or graffiti scribbled beneath a layer of wallpaper.

Peter Bogdanovich believes the academic scrutiny of Hitchcock's oeuvre "amused him, and delighted him in a certain way," though it sometimes left him scratching his head. In the early 1970s, the eldest of Hitchcock's three granddaughters, Mary, took a college class on his films in which the tutor stressed the vital importance of the number seven to the thematic coherence of Hitchcock, a notion that meant nothing to the filmmaker himself. Mary asked for her grandfather's help on an assignment about the style and substance of his work. She got a C.

———

Hitchcock knew the power one could command by looking—and by denying others the opportunity to look. In his old age, the rights to five of his films returned to him, including *Rear Window* and *Vertigo*. Never voicing his reasons, he withdrew these movies from public circulation. In the seventies, academics and administrators from grand institutions asked to have prints of the films, for scholarly use only. Most times, Hitchcock refused, without explanation. Perhaps he sensed that depriving the world of his masterpieces while he lived would ensure that their fame continued after his death. Three years after Hitchcock's passing, both *Rear Window* and *Vertigo* were re-released by the Hitchcock estate, and subsequently subjected to vital restoration work. Thirteen years later, *Vertigo* was re-released in cinemas across the US and the UK. The reviews back in 1958 had been lukewarm, at best; now they were rapturous. In 2012, *Vertigo* was named the best film ever made by a poll in *Sight & Sound*, the magazine of the British Film Institute, knocking *Citizen Kane* off its perch for the first time in fifty years.

Yet it is *Rear Window* that speaks most eloquently to the twenty-first century. Hitchcock had an instinctive appreciation for the sleight-of-hand trick that cinema plays on us, zooming in on the lives of others while simultaneously reinforcing the solitude of watching. "Our lives are lonely but not private," is how Raymond Durgnat boiled down the fundamental message of *Rear Window*. That seems truer now than ever before. As we observe Jeff gazing across his courtyard, we could replace the glass pane of his window with the black mirror of an iPhone, his sleep-deprived eyes peering into each one of his neighbors' lives through the aperture of social media. "We've become a race of peeping Toms," says Stella to Jeff as she walks in on him prying on the neighbors. "What people ought to do is get outside their own house and look in for a change." A sound piece of advice, maybe, but one that Hitchcock doubted we'd ever follow.

9

THE ENTERTAINER

"Good evening." With that bland but unmistakable greeting, Hitchcock began a new life on the night of October 2, 1955, as the star of his own television show, *Alfred Hitchcock Presents*.

Each week, he appeared before millions of families like a comic-strip character come to life. Against a stark white background, he popped into the camera's eye in a little world of his own and began his introduction to that week's story. Roughly half an hour later, when the episode had finished, Hitchcock reappeared, said his sardonic goodbye, and the cameras cut away. There, it seemed, he stayed in stasis until the cathode tubes awoke him seven days later to perform his next turn, perhaps armed with a tea set, or a deerstalker cap, or a giant pipe that blew bubbles from its chamber.

His stint on television with the thirty-minute episodes of *Alfred Hitchcock Presents* (1955–62), followed by *The Alfred Hitchcock Hour* (1962–65), coincided with what is often described as Hitchcock's "golden age," the years between 1954 and 1963 in which he made *Rear Window*, *To Catch a Thief*, *The Trouble with Harry*, *The Man Who Knew Too Much*, *The Wrong Man*, *Vertigo*, *North by Northwest*, *Psycho*, and *The Birds*. But it was television success that elevated him to new heights of fame, where he was stopped in the street by children in search of autographs, and he became a recognizable face, voice, and body in most households in the United States and beyond. In his weekly turns before the camera,

Hitchcock the entertainer.

Hitchcock exhibited many parts of his public and private identities: his Englishness, his dandiness, his fatness, his devilish lust for murder and disorder. Most clearly, they showed Hitchcock the comedian and the people pleaser, a Hitchcock whose only intention was to raise a smile, albeit without offering one himself. It was what he referred to as "that degrading side of me—the actor." The television Hitchcock was a show-off whose adventure in film had been a prelude to the moment when all eyes were fixed on him, the acclaim of the audience filling his ears.

Some of those who had toiled alongside Hitchcock on his greatest movies, who knew how much of himself he gave to his film work and who appreciated the depth and breadth of his talents, were a little disappointed to see him play a pantomime version of himself on the small screen. Most understood his reasons for doing so. First, television had Hollywood running scared. According to figures from the US Census Bureau, weekly attendance at the movies dropped from ninety million in 1946 to forty million in 1960. To stem the flow, studios lurched to gimmicks, including 3D movies. Hitchcock was handed one of these in 1953, *Dial M for Murder*, and found shooting for 3D a waste of time and effort. The film performed well at the box office, though, as Hitchcock predicted, most screenings exhibited the film in two dimensions.

An alternative way of engaging with the threat of television was to embrace its possibilities. Hitchcock was persuaded of this approach by Lew Wasserman, his agent and the president of MCA, the media company that represented a roster of stars and had already made great inroads into the new medium. Wasserman arranged a deal that Hitchcock couldn't resist: $129,000 per episode in return for his opening and closing monologues and minimal involvement in production, directing two or three shows each season. After years of feeling underpaid—in Britain because the business there lacked the resources of the United States; in Hollywood because moguls such as David O. Selznick had the power to strike deals in their favor—Hitchcock felt he was finally getting his due.

The remaining factor in Hitchcock's entry into television was his yearning for attention. It was a curious aspect of his personality that while he guarded his privacy and had great belief in the rightness of his decisions, he craved the approval of strangers. Almost overnight, *Alfred Hitchcock Presents* gained him the kind of public acknowledgment he'd always desired. From being a widely recognized film director in the early fifties, by the end of the decade he was one of the most famous men in America. "People swarmed out of nowhere to see him," Pat Hitchcock remembered. "It was like being with Elvis Presley."

The series was almost as big a hit internationally as it was in the US. As he liked to say, he recorded his opening and closing monologues in "French, German, English, and American," ensuring he was an A-list celebrity across the developed world. He became accustomed to the stardom and relished it. Herbert Coleman and Samuel Taylor accompanied Hitchcock on a reconnaissance of locations in Finland, where he was thrilled to be mobbed by a group of schoolchildren and to receive an impromptu standing ovation from the patrons of a roadside diner. Coleman spent a lot of time traveling with the Hitchcocks in the fifties and sixties and registered how Hitchcock basked in the attention he received. When they flew to Rome in late 1956, Hitchcock was delighted by the number of photographers waiting to greet him at the airport, but he was puzzled as to why he couldn't find any of the photos in the newspapers the next day. According to Coleman, the event had been arranged by Paramount Studios, which had been unable to raise any interest in covering Hitchcock's arrival because his visit to the city a short time earlier had been extensively reported. Mindful of not upsetting their cherished asset, Paramount had paid some photographers to work their flashbulbs without any intention of selling the pictures.

Inseparable from Hitchcock's desire for celebrity was his impulse to entertain, in his unique way and on as large a scale as possible. The tension between wanting to be an artist and being an entertainer who gives the people what they want lingered from his first film to his last. "Hitchcock admits to catering for the low-brow," averred one critic who wrote one of the first published reviews of a Hitchcock film, in the spring of 1926, though that same year his work was branded the "last word in screen art" by another reviewer. Eleven months later, Hitchcock pasted into one of his many scrapbooks a review of *The Lodger* that calls the movie "only for entertainment," a phrase underlined and put in quotation marks. If made by Hitchcock, these markings might be the exasperation of a young filmmaker whose artistic efforts did not get their due; more likely, Hitchcock was satisfied that a film that was initially derided by the moneymen as art-house drivel had defied its doubters. Ivor Montagu remembered that Hitchcock had once told him that canny filmmakers "make pictures for the press," because pleasing them is the only way to safeguard one's reputation—and to gain power and influence within the industry. It was for the reviewers that he stuffed his films with "the Hitchcock touches," to satisfy their desire to see cleverness on screen. Michael Balcon had different recollections of Hitchcock's attitude during his British period, saying that he and Hitchcock "were in the business of giving the public what it seemed to want in entertainment. We did not talk about art or social significance." Though Hitchcock went through phases in his career of trying to recalibrate his style and redesign the parameters in which he worked, he never swerved from the notion that his priority was to keep the public on the edge of their seats, and to find ways of lending one's artistic impulses to that end. This, he avowed, was the mark of real talent. To Truffaut he put it plainly: "You have to design your film just as Shakespeare did his plays—for an audience."

Audiences, of course, were available not only in movie theaters; Hitchcock could sniff them out anywhere. To entertain those around him, and establish himself as a mercurial personality on set, early in his career he developed a series of routines and habits—an off-camera Hitchcock touch—such as ending breaks in filming by smashing a tea-cup on the floor. Antic eccentricity was gradually replaced by something more sedate, though no less performed: the Zen-like master who pro-fessed to be bored by the business of shooting a film, and took more plea-sure in gathering cast and crew to listen to him recite a lewd joke or an anecdote about the movie business of yore. The dinner table was another space for performance, as were the countless interviews during which he repeated so many of the same quips and anecdotes, the lines of a part only he could play.

Had he possessed more confidence in his appearance, it's possible he would have pursued a more conventional type of performing; one could imagine him in the "character" parts he gave to those such as Peter Lorre, Hume Cronyn, Edmund Gwenn, and, in his silent films, Gordon Harker, actors who were never romantic leads in a Hitchcock movie, yet whose differentness he admired and relied on to add oddness and humor. In essence, this is what happened from the late fifties, when he starred in numerous trailers for his latest big-screen releases in the guise of the comedic persona from the television shows. Inhabiting a character was a process he clearly enjoyed; on at least two occasions, he posed in character for pieces in American publications, including one in which he took on all the roles in an Agatha Christie–style murder mystery.[*] Ingrid Bergman explained that although Hitchcock didn't like to talk about acting, he was given to performing dialogue from scripts, or giving practical demonstrations of how he thought an emotion should be projected. For the magazine *Pageant* he was photographed in various poses, as he acted out Bergman's part in *Notorious*, curled up coquettishly in a chair, crossing his legs in as ladylike a fashion as he could muster.

That particular piece of horseplay was self-deprecating in a way, mocking himself as a gargoyle compared to the divine Bergman. But it also poked fun at actors, the preening peacocks who Hitchcock insisted—only half-jokingly—were the bane of his professional life and whose craft he seemed genuinely ambivalent about as a form of creative endeavor. In the first couple of decades of his directing career, Hitchcock could feel threatened by big-name actors and had testy relationships with them on set. Both John Gielgud and Michael Redgrave were luminaries of the London stage when they took starring roles in Hitchcock films, Gielgud in *Secret Agent* (1936), Redgrave in *The Lady Vanishes* (1938). Both always insisted they were cinephiles. Indeed, Gielgud had first become aware of Hitchcock through London Film Society screenings of European movies, and Redgrave shared Hitchcock's love of German cinema, having spent time in Heidelberg during his youth. Films made in London, however, were a different matter. "British films before 1939 were regarded as something of a laughing-stock," explained Redgrave, and actors of his background considered movie work lucrative enough to take, but not legitimate enough to take seriously. "You sell to the cinema what you've learned in the theatre," was Ralph Richardson's dictum.

---

[*]   The other appeared in *Life* magazine, July 1942, in which Hitchcock played the part of a bartender in a six-page photo-essay, "Have You Heard?" about the potential deadly cost of wartime gossip.

Hitchcock was acutely aware of how he and his industry were viewed by thespians, and he cheekily used it in his favor when trying to convince Gielgud to sign up, telling him—misleadingly—that his part of novelist turned assassin was a modern-day version of Hamlet. Inevitably, relations were fraught between Hitchcock and actors who thought they were slumming it on his set. On the first day of filming, he told Redgrave that he hadn't been the first choice for the role, which Redgrave took as an aggressive attempt to put him in his place. Similarly, Gielgud complained that his director made him "sick with nervousness" and that he seemed intent on asserting his superiority rather than bringing the best out of his cast. For his part, Hitchcock dismissed Gielgud's background in theater as "absolutely no use to him here . . . rub out everything and start again." It wasn't only female stars Hitchcock felt he had the power to deconstruct and rebuild.

Famously, it was in Redgrave's presence that Hitchcock compared actors to cattle, as though they were dumb beasts who needed to be herded at the point of a prod. It was one of those deliberately "shocking" outbursts that helped bolster his reputation as a forceful, opinionated director, endlessly quotable. On the set of *Mr. and Mrs. Smith* in 1940, Hitchcock arrived one morning to find three calves awaiting him, each with the name of a cast member around its neck, a joke present from the movie's star, Carole Lombard. The line "actors are cattle" stuck with him for the next forty years, and he was asked about it in countless interviews. With tongue in cheek, he frequently protested his innocence. "I would never say such an unfeeling, rude thing about actors at all. What I probably said was all actors should be *treated* like cattle." As with so many of his other famous quips, Hitchcock never appeared to tire of it, nor did he express irritation when it was raised time and again in the media. It was nothing more than an opportunity to deliver a well-rehearsed comeback, followed by an inevitable giggle from his audience.

Whether or not Hitchcock said "actors are cattle"—Michael Redgrave was certain that he did—the phrase does get close to how Hitchcock regularly felt frustrated by those employed to pose before his camera. When films didn't perform at the box office, he was quick to pin the blame on bad acting performances, or the casting of an actor who had been foisted on him by studio executives. Farley Granger felt that Hitchcock had been "cold and sometimes cruel" to Ruth Roman during *Strangers on a Train* because she had been a studio pick that Hitchcock didn't want for the role of Anne Morton. He also professed to be frustrated or perplexed by what he considered to be the neediness of actors, many of whom were unsettled by the lack of feedback they received on their performance, an instance of Hitchcock's legendary stinginess with praise. Doris Day described making *The Man Who Knew Too Much* as "something that I'll never forget," though partly because of the baffling behavior of the film's director who didn't seem interested at all in working with actors. "He was very pleasant, he was very quiet, and he didn't seem to direct," recalled Day. "Jimmy [Stewart] would say, 'Now, just relax, Doris, of course he liked it. When he doesn't say anything he's okay.' . . . We would go to dinner and laugh and he was warm and loving, just really sweet. But I didn't understand him on the set." Despite his own vanity and his own need for external validation, Hitchcock had little patience for it in others.

Unlike the highly skilled people who worked in roles behind the scenes, an anxious actor like Day, or—worse still—one with ideas that didn't tally with Hitchcock's thoughts on how a part should be played, could challenge his feeling that all those around him were pulling in the direction of "Hitchcock." He made an effort to be as diplomatic as possible with actors he didn't like, but he struggled with those who brought what he perceived to be obstruction and complication to his set. He found Charles Laughton's process of discovering his character on *Jamaica Inn* almost more than he could bear, while during the filming of *I Confess*, he was infuriated by Montgomery Clift's repeated questioning of the script and his character's motivation. Particularly galling for Hitchcock was the interference of Clift's acting coach, whose constant presence on the set Clift had guaranteed in his contract. Similarly, when Paul Newman sent a long memo critiquing his scenes in *Torn Curtain*, he challenged the certainty Hitchcock needed to feel that the production was progressing according to his blueprint. Roy Thinnes sent Hitchcock a comparable—though far shorter and more diffident—note about his concerns regarding *Family Plot*, and it's possible this played a part in Hitchcock's decision to fire Thinnes, one of four leading actors in the film, very shortly after. Anthony Perkins found the experience of working with Hitchcock to be the most purely enjoyable and creatively rewarding experience of his life, gratified that Hitchcock was amenable to various suggestions about characterization. Yet Perkins's ideas—such as having Norman Bates chew candy corn throughout the movie—fit in with Hitchcock's preexisting notion of the character and what he hoped Perkins, the doe-eyed heartthrob, would bring to the role. When faced with an actor who had strong ideas about how to develop their character that deviated from his design, Hitchcock was less indulgent. William Devane, who replaced Thinnes in *Family Plot*, recalls Hitchcock's reaction when Karen Black insisted on playing scenes in a way the director didn't like, especially by improvising dialogue. "I'd look over at him," Devane recalls, "and he'd raise his fingers like a pair of scissors. . . . That was the deal with him. You said your lines, you hit your marks . . . if he didn't like something, he'd cut it." To quote Hitchcock, "do what you want, there's always the cutting room floor."

"Hitchcock" is one of those rare words that have traveled from proper noun to adjective. Perhaps taking their cue from the ideas that the man himself pressed home in his innumerable interviews, most critics invoke Hitchcock's name as shorthand for rising tension, slow but unyielding psychological torture, exquisitely unbearable suspense. Those things, of course, are vital to his work, but Hitchcock wouldn't be Hitchcock if the brooding darkness weren't undercut by humor. *The Girl on the Train*, *Split*, and *Nocturnal Animals* are among many films in recent times to have been labeled "Hitchcockian," either by reviewers or by publicists, because of their *noir* qualities—yet there's barely a laugh to be had in any of them. The undercurrent of humor in *Gone Girl*, directed by the Hitchcock aficionado David Fincher, is much closer to true Hitchcock territory. Although Jordan Peele's comedic style and thematic concerns are a long way removed from Hitchcock's, his balancing of the disturbing, the suspenseful, and the humorous puts *Get Out* in the Hitchcockian tradition, too. In Hitchcock's mind, humor wasn't simply a garnish of color or light relief; it was the silver thread that ran through most of his best work. "Next to reality," he told an interviewer in 1936, "I put the accent on comedy, which, strangely enough, makes a film more dramatic." In a self-authored exploration of his work published that same year, he suggested that he excelled as a writer and director of comedy: "I always look for a subject that has plenty of action. I introduce the comedy myself."

Corroboration of that appears in the production files of numerous Hitchcock films. To pick just one example from dozens, the well-known moment in *The Birds* in which the camera cuts to the caged love birds on the back seat of Melanie's car, swaying left and right on their perch as Melanie tears around corners was a touch Hitchcock added himself. Being tossed this way and that in a speeding car was something that tickled him, and it crops up as a moment of physical comedy in *Notorious*, *To Catch a Thief*, *North by Northwest*, and *Family Plot*.* In the latter two, he strung the joke out for so long that we seem to have left one film and entered another, as though the director had wanted to make a straight-up comedy all along. It is, though, a flourish entirely in keeping with Hitchcock, whose comedic sensibilities stayed conspicuously constant across six decades of filmmaking—in fact, it might be the most recurrent element of his artistic style, even more than the suspense on which his legend has been built.

Evidence of his early interest in comedy surfaces in several humorous pieces he wrote for the *Henley Telegraph*, published between 1919 and 1921. None evinces skilled comic writing. Yet it's remarkable to see how much of Hitchcock's core personality, his sense of humor, and the subjects of his interest were locked in at a young age. One piece was presented as a melodramatic scene of love and hate between a married couple, only for the twist at the end to reveal it to be a scene from a play, acted out before

---

* He tried to get a similar sequence into *Blackmail*, in which two bobbing heads seen in the back windows of a police van would look like a pair of giant eyeballs, shifting from side to side.

an audience. Another is a drawn-out joke about a man who unwittingly arranges for his friend to go to bed with his wife. His spoof essay "The History of Pea Eating" speaks of "a process by which a pipe was placed in the mouth and the peas drawn up by pneumatic means. But in the trials the inventor unfortunately turned on the power in the reverse direction, with the result that the victim's tongue is now much longer than hitherto." It's a bit of absurdist drollery in the wry voice that evokes the style of Hitchcock's television monologues forty years later.

Hitchcock's sense of himself as funny was utterly crucial to his identity as a public and private person. Humor was his default means of communication. Shy, and awkward around strangers, he could appear pompous and disdainful to new acquaintances, something that happened regularly in his youth. Learning how to make others laugh offered him the opportunity of "fitting in." Colleagues at Henley's remembered him as what the English people of the day would have described as a "good sort," always ready for joshing and "leg-pulling," meaning teasing and hoaxing. At Gainsborough Pictures, too, where he worked for Balcon, he was valued for his good cheer as much as for his talent and uncontainable ambition. It was in this period that he began to compile the storehouse of ribald jokes and stories from which he would draw for the rest of his life as a means of connecting with others. The bantering style of the young Hitchcock is even caught on camera. When Hitchcock set his mind to filming *Blackmail* as a sound movie, he had the problem of what to do about Anny Ondra, the film's star and one of his favorite actresses, whose strong Czech accent was deemed inappropriate for a story about the travails of a typical girl-next-door Londoner. To test her voice, Hitchcock stood with her in front of a camera and recorded an exchange in which he teased Ondra into a fit of nervous laughter, asking her whether she has "slept with men." As Ondra turns from the camera, giggling, Hitchcock tells her to "stand in your place, or it will not come out right—as the girl said to the soldier." Thus, among the first dialogue Hitchcock ever recorded was him embarrassing a woman with a quip about her sex life, topped with a double entendre. He started as he meant to continue. Thirty years later he tried something similar with

Tippi Hedren in her screen test, though Hedren navigated the joke without being thrown off track.

On film sets and at restaurant tables, Hitchcock liked to work out whether he could connect with someone based on their response to his scabrous jokes. His love of creating shock and playing with taboos played some part in this, but he also felt accepted by those who laughed at his gags, and trusted those who understood his sense of humor. When Peggy Robertson first worked with Hitchcock, as script supervisor on *Under Capricorn*, she felt entirely frozen out; he wouldn't look at her, let alone speak to her. It wasn't until she laughed at a dirty story he was telling the actress Margaret Leighton that his attitude changed. "From then on I was his pet," and part of the inner circle, invited to the end-of-day cocktail sessions in Hitchcock's office. Hitchcock even arranged for his car to pick her up on the way to collecting him from the Savoy. A quarter-century later, Bernard Cribbins broke through Hitchcock's on-set formality by reciting limericks about "sex-starved gorillas" and the like.

Hitchcock's urge to entertain through comedy was strong and self-evident. He had a catalog of party tricks, anecdotes, and rhymes. He was also very quick-witted, capable of sharp one-liners and bursts of physical comedy, impersonating people with his body and his voice. The film publicist Herb Steinberg remembered being at Chasen's one evening when Hitchcock bounced to his feet to mimic a little girl in a ballet class, a sight Steinberg recalled as both uncannily accurate and unforgettably funny as Hitchcock did fumbling pliés and pirouettes on the restaurant floor.

Gags, however, are only one part of the sense of humor that colors Hitchcock's films. Clive James once wrote that "common sense and a sense of humor are the same things moving at different speeds. A sense of humor is just common sense, dancing." That definition beautifully describes what humor typically provides in Hitchcock's work: a perspective that shifts us one step from the world as we know it. There are laughs in most Hitchcock films, plenty of them, but more important, there are layers of irony, coincidence, and uncanniness. Even the most earnest of his films can be seen as bleak jokes played on the protagonist.

Hitchcock as comedian.

The Wrong Man and *Vertigo*, for instance, torment their heroes with situations of role-playing and mistaken identity that could be taken from the text of an Elizabethan-era comedy, the audience watching as characters stumble through a maze that has sprung up around them, constructed of deceit, misunderstanding, and confusion.

Going back as far as *The White Shadow* (1924)—the recently rediscovered movie on which Hitchcock worked, about two twins who swap identities—teasing and deception, puzzles and games, feature prominently. Hitchcock's role on that film was relatively minor, reminding us that those features of his work that seem most identifiable with him may also have been influenced and nurtured by those he was reticent to credit—producers, writers, other directors, and the conventions of the culture in which he lived and worked. These influences made themselves very apparent on the first films Hitchcock directed. His nine silent movies are of surprising variety, but the ironies of masquerade and performance are prominent in most of them. For example, central characters in *Easy Virtue* and *Champagne* are—in very different ways, for very different reasons—forced to change their identities, living lives that are not their own. In the Hitchcock universe, however, it is ultimately impossible to hide one's real self, a truth that persists right up to *Family Plot* in 1976.

At times, audiences struggle to tell whether the implausible situations his characters get wrapped up in are meant to elicit gasps of horror or belly laughs. Hitchcock enjoyed perpetuating the ambiguity, even though he sometimes complained that people misconstrued his intention. When the reviews came out for *North by Northwest*, Whitney Balliett in *The New Yorker* declared it "the brilliant realization of a feat he [Hitchcock] has unintentionally been moving toward for more than a decade—a perfect parody of his own work." Hitchcock liked the "brilliant" bit, but grumbled that there was nothing unintentional about it; the allusions to his previous work were all deliberately crafted in what was intended to be the "Hitchcock picture to end all Hitchcock pictures." Rodney Ackland said that he and Hitchcock had done something similar in the 1930s with the film *Number Seventeen*, which they wanted to write "as a burlesque of all the thrillers . . . and do it so subtly that nobody at Elstree would realize the subject was being guyed." When Mel Brooks made his film *High Anxiety*, an affectionate send-up of Hitchcockian thrillers, Hitchcock was so flattered that he sent Brooks a case of Château Haut-Brion. But as many reviewers pointed out at the time, it's hard to parody something as knowing as Hitchcock, a body of work in which repetitions and clichés come off as ironic in-jokes, parodied in their very telling. Audiences sometimes detected humor in places Hitchcock didn't intend it. At a test screening for *Torn Curtain* there was laughter in several unexpected places, including the drawn-out murder scene. Hitchcock put this down to audience anxiety, a need to relieve tension. It might also have been the laughter of recognition, the audience making it known that they were wise to Hitchcock's strain of irony and self-parody, to the extent that they spotted humor where it wasn't meant to be.

When Claude Chabrol—accompanied by Truffaut—interviewed Hitchcock in 1954, he described it as a thoroughly Hitchcockian experience: compelling, disorientating, but ultimately one big joke at his expense. Hitchcock was engaging, but not quite engaged. "We don't know where to begin with this crafty dissembler," writes Chabrol, describing how he and Truffaut watched Hitchcock perform, substituting serious answers with jokes and "anecdotes that apparently have ceased to make him laugh some time ago." At the point that Hitchcock insists that he has no regard for any of his American films, Chabrol realizes that "none of this is serious; he's just taking us for a ride." To the Italian writer Oriana Fallaci, Hitchcock was pretty explicit in admitting the pleasure he took in leading journalists up the garden path, straight into a brick wall: "You have to write an article about me," he said toward the end of a playful, almost flirtatious conversation, "and you don't know anything about me." "But I do," retorted Fallaci. "With all your cordial humor, your nice round face, your nice innocent paunch, you are the most wicked, cruel man I have ever met."

The English sense of humor—more usually, but less precisely, conflated into the British sense of humor—is often spoken about, not least by the

English themselves, as some complex curiosity. In truth, there is nothing elevated about English humor, though elements of it may be distinctive. Its biggest defining feature is perhaps its ubiquity in social interactions among the English. Which is not to say that the English are funnier than any other people, just that even the least funny among them habitually revert to humor as a means of communication, often to mask emotional reserve. A case in point is Hitchcock and his mental Rolodex of daft one-liners and weak puns of which he made frequent, extensive use. Actors were told to mind the "dog's feet," meaning "pause"; "don't come pig's tail," he advised dinner guests, meaning "don't come too early"; "Hitch, without the cock" is how he sometimes introduced himself. Desmond Tester, the boy who played the hapless Stevie in *Sabotage*, was addressed as "the testicle" on set; Georgine Darcy (Miss Torso in *Rear Window*) would be asked whether she had indulged in "mastication" during her lunch break. Although such gags grated on some, Darcy adored Hitchcock and his juvenile wordplay. The same was true of Cary Grant, who bonded with Hitchcock over a shared sense of humor. Grant filled pages of notepaper with groan-inducing puns, cheesy jokes, and lightweight witticisms, including a list of spoof film credits that Hitchcock once recited to a reporter: a camera operator by the name of "Otto Focus," an editor called "Eddie Tor," and so on.

In explaining the English sense of humor, the anthropologist Kate Fox says "seriousness is acceptable, solemnity is prohibited. Sincerity is allowed, earnestness is strictly forbidden. Pomposity and self-importance are outlawed." George Orwell put it even more succinctly when he said that humor is "dignity sitting on a tintack." It's a decent working definition of a type of joke that occurs in Hitchcock films from the 1920s to the 1970s, in which Hitchcock attempts to undermine, deflate, and ridicule those who get too big for their boots—including himself, in some of the cameos in which he sends himself up as a passenger who gets bullied by a kid on the train, an exasperated photographer lurking outside a courthouse, a man who has a bus door closed in his face during the New York rush hour. In *Murder!*, Hitchcock put his lead character, Sir John Menier, through a similarly demeaning experience when he is awoken in a boardinghouse by an army of unruly children and their animals who charge into his room and leap onto his bed. At the same time as making the English version of the film, Hitchcock was filming an exact replica with a German-speaking cast, and he claimed that this scene was struck from the German version as it was deemed inappropriate for a man of such standing to have his dignity compromised for no apparent reason. Hitchcock was bemused: to him, there was nothing funnier than seeing people brought down a peg. There's even a hint of this in the famous Mount Rushmore scene in *North by Northwest*, for which Hitchcock's original idea was for Cary Grant to have a sneezing fit while inside Lincoln's nose, a funny tableau that would gently mock American reverence for the monument. The humor in Hitchcock's work might help explain why he never won an Oscar, an award that almost always favors the "serious" over the comedic. He was nominated five times, though three of those—*Rebecca*, *Lifeboat*, and *Spellbound*—are among the most earnest work he ever made, and although Hitchcock thought *Psycho* was funny, few others agreed.

On the whole, Hitchcock found a way of translating his humor for American audiences, although it took several years for him to produce work that fused menace and humor as the best of his late English work had. When he did so, it was two American writers who most effectively captured his comedic voice. One was James Allardice, the man responsible for Hitchcock's television monologues; the other was John Michael Hayes, screenwriter of *The Trouble with Harry*, a much-overlooked gem of the Hitchcock canon, valuable not only because it is well structured and highly entertaining but also because Hitchcock felt it reflected much of his personality. Adapted from the novel by Jack Trevor Story, the action in Hitchcock's film is transposed from rural England to Vermont, but its humor of ironic understatement stays decisively on the other side of the Atlantic. The eponymous Harry is a corpse, lying on the ground of an autumnal woodland. Four eccentric locals stumble on him, three of whom believe, wrongly, that they must have been responsible for his death; "the trouble with Harry" is what to do about his body without getting the law involved. As Harry is buried and dug up twice, two love affairs begin among the lead characters. The film ends with both couples planning marriage and the discovery that Harry died of natural causes, letting them all off the hook. The dead body is what Hitchcock referred to as a "Mac-Guffin," a plot device that acts as a catalyst for the action in a story but is immaterial to its substance. These are very common in Hitchcock films, and although he never intended for the audience to worry about them, the characters usually care very much, such as when Cary Grant and Ingrid Bergman go on the hunt for hidden Nazi uranium in *Notorious*. Not so in *The Trouble with Harry*. The sudden appearance of a dead body in a quaint New England hamlet doesn't trigger dread, panic, or anguish, just irritation at the amount of bother involved in covering up a homicide. This was macabre Hitchcock played strictly for laughs.

With lovers meeting and stumbling across strange secrets in the woods, *The Trouble with Harry* resembles *A Midsummer Night's Dream*; in its highly mannered comedic take on death and violence in out-of-the-way America, it has the look of an ancestor of the Coen brothers' *Fargo*. It is, though, Hitchcock's sense of humor undiluted—albeit one that must also have been very close to that of John Michael Hayes and Jack Trevor Story—and includes what Hitchcock claimed was his favorite line in any of his films, when the bashful Miss Gravely sees Captain Wiles standing over the corpse and asks, "What seems to be the trouble, Captain?" The English silliness and dark understatements were less appreciated by American critics and audiences—*The New Yorker* harrumphed about the declining quality of Hitchcock by alleging the film "skids to preposterous depths"—though it fared far better in the United Kingdom and in France. Hitchcock felt a little stung that in making a film that so thoroughly pleased himself, he had failed to entertain an audience.

Someone else who had misgivings about *The Trouble with Harry* was Thelma Ritter, who had recently performed so brilliantly in the role of Stella in *Rear Window*. Admiring her comedic talents, Hitchcock asked Ritter to take the part of Miss Gravely (ultimately given to Mildred Natwick), but in a letter to her husband, she sounded appalled at the prospect: "I must not have much vision but this one scares me. It's lewd, immoral, and for anyone without a real nasty off beat sense of humor, in

Hitchcock holding court at the Screen Directors Guild award dinner, February 1955.

very bad taste." The writer Peter Conrad once dubbed Hitchcock "everyone's wicked uncle," a homely looking man, ever ready with a barbed gag, intended to "prod at the bad conscience of the twentieth century." Hitchcock's sense of humor produced unease, even among many of those who liked and admired him. As already noted, Oriana Fallaci, an avowed fan, labeled him "the most wicked, cruel man I have ever met." Descriptions like that, whether in jest or in earnest, have been attached to Hitchcock for decades, at least since he cuffed Madeleine Carroll and had her dragged around the set of *The 39 Steps*. Her costar Robert Donat looked back on the incident with admiration for her stoicism but winced at the "weals and bruises which the handcuffs made on her delicate wrists" and the "humiliations" she endured. John Gielgud, who played alongside Carroll in *Secret Agent*, also thought Hitchcock was "beastly to her." Cruelty was something Hitchcock took very seriously—perhaps that's why he made it the subject of so many jokes.

Charles Bennett was in no doubt that Hitchcock's propulsive creative energy was sadism. When Hitchcock screened *Psycho* for him, Bennett concluded that "only a sadist could have directed that bathroom scene." Hitchcock was used to that kind of criticism. "I directed that scene for laughs," he told Bennett, and said the same to lots of others, implying that those who didn't like *Psycho* were suffering from a serious sense of humor deficiency.

If, by this, Hitchcock meant that he intended to fill auditoriums with laughter as Marion Crane's blood swirls down the shower drain, he was obviously being dishonest. If, however, he meant that he found amusement in the suffering of others—if only the suffering of the audience who he knew would leap out of their seats in fright—then he was speaking the truth, and confirming that, as Bennett charged, sadism—or at least an insistent urge to assert his control over others—was a powerful force within him.

Hitchcock found great sport in seeing others being humbled. It was there in his publicly expressed desire to "knock the ladylikeness out of chorus girls." In his films, characters are frequently shoved off their perch and lose their dignity, and in real life he seized any opportunity to pierce what he considered pretension or conceitedness. Most examples of this occurred before the move to Hollywood. When, as a young director in London, he overheard a colleague talking at length about his new, modern home, Hitchcock decided to have two tons of coal delivered to the man's front door, just desserts, Hitchcock thought, for his boasting. Shortly after Joan Harrison started working as Hitchcock's secretary in the early 1930s, she told the boss that she couldn't work late one night as she had a party to attend. The following day she was inundated with telegrams inviting her to social engagements. Hitchcock had sent them all.

Disapproval of, and ceaseless jokes about, those who get above their station is surely a function of Hitchcock's Englishness. The instinct to express that disapproval through shaming punishments, however, may well have stemmed from his experiences of corporal punishment at school, the vivid memories of which stayed with him for life. Uncomfortable with conflict, and lacking the skills to express himself in some other more constructive way, Hitchcock disguised his rebukes in the form of practical jokes—perhaps an echo of his father's behavior when he pretended to have his young son imprisoned as punishment for going missing.

"My father belongs to that hardy group that plays practical jokes as a rough and spirited game," said Pat Hitchcock in 1963. Some were ingenious and genuinely funny, such as the time he hired an elderly actress—who was in on the joke—to attend one of his dinner parties where she sat silently throughout the meal as Hitchcock pretended not to know who she was or why she had arrived, leaving the other guests bemused. At another dinner party, he arranged for all the food to be colored blue, fish, soup, and all. These are Dadaist jokes; they have no individual target, and no agenda other than to puzzle and confound. When his jokes did pick on a particular person, they were often people he liked or whose approval he sought—very often women—and they could be decidedly cruel. On the set of *Rich and Strange*, for example, he pranked his friend the actress Elsie Randolph by having her shoot a scene in a phone booth that he slowly filled with steam, knowing that Randolph would panic because of her allergy to smoke. "He was a darling, but a darling with a sadistic sense of humour," was Randolph's gracious verdict.

Of course, it's possible to see this sadism, especially where women are involved, as a further sign of his desire to control and demean. But perhaps it was the outgrowth of a sclerotic masculinity that rendered him emotionally inarticulate to such a degree that pranks and gags were another substitute for intimacy—like a little boy in the playground pulling on a girl's ponytail. At work, Hitchcock had his films into which he could pour the strong emotions he felt keenly but had no other means of processing. In his day-to-day life, especially in his twenties and thirties, he used humor as a release for these feelings: lust, fear, insecurity, disgust, even anger, that emotion he swore he hardly ever experienced.

As a successful young director, the boy who had grown up as an unusual loner also found himself in the novel position of being a dominant figure in social situations. At times he misused the power this gave him, leading to some awkward and unpleasant encounters. In his memoirs, Charles Bennett related a remarkable story about a time he and Hitchcock went out for the evening with two young ladies, one of whom was a Florence Foster Jenkins type of character who gained notoriety in London for her dreadful singing. Bennett claims that Hitchcock was giddy with the anticipation of slyly mocking her throughout the evening, only to discover that the woman was as sharp as a tack and was more than capable of keeping Hitchcock in his box. "I had never seen Hitch more unhappy," said Bennett. "The biter was bit."

Similarly, several contemporaries recall Hitchcock making young, inexperienced, or naive members of his production teams the target of his teasing, sometimes in nasty, unfunny ways. Once he offered to give the unit manager on *The 39 Steps*, Dickie Beville, a lift to the theater in London where he was due to meet his wife. A little while into the journey, Beville realized that Hitchcock was driving them out of the city altogether, heading to the Hitchcocks' cottage in Surrey. Beville's wife was to be stood up. Another, more infamous, story has a few variations, but always involves Hitchcock spiking a crew member's drink with a laxative and then conspiring to leave him on his own overnight, in handcuffs, in some public place, where the inevitable consequences of the laxative would kick in, leading to the kind of humiliation that Hitchcock himself would have found soul-destroying. Alma, who herself liked a practical joke—she once spiked Hitchcock's drink with Benzedrine—thought very dimly of her husband's extreme pranks. "Would any of Hitch's friends dare to play such jokes on him?" she once asked aloud. "Not if they wanted to remain his friends, they wouldn't." As Hitchcock said of himself, "I'm very sensitive; a sharp word . . . hurts me for days."

Hitchcock relished the power he had to effect discomfort in others, while keeping himself safe from ridicule. Having grown up with a strong sense of vulnerability because of his sense of differentness from those around him—his size and shape, his profile, his solitary nature—and anxious that he would be laughed at because of it, the ability to be the one who made others squirm and feel like outsiders had an intoxicating effect on him. Whether his behavior was sadism or simple teasing, it was ultimately about his desire for control—of his body, his emotions, his reputation—and his fear of losing it.

This unpleasant strand of his joking never entirely left him, but it diminished greatly once he moved to America. The bantering, informal sets over which he presided in London were different from those more professional environments in Hollywood, where he was unable—certainly in the first few years of his American career—to be quite the dominant figure he had been in England. More prosaically, he simply grew out of the rougher, more juvenile stuff as he aged.

Since the details of his nastier jokes have come to light following his death, a lot of those close to Hitchcock have reacted with incredulity that the man's humor could be construed as anything other than the mischievousness of a cheeky, overgrown schoolboy. His daughter has claimed that sensationalist gossip has bred a false impression that her father was a sadist. She takes particular exception to a story that during the filming of the fairground scenes in *Strangers on a Train* she took a ride on a Ferris wheel that Hitchcock ordered to have stopped at the moment her carriage was at the very top, leaving her hanging in midair for several minutes. She insists the gag lasted for a few fleeting seconds, and she was never screaming with fear, as the misreporting has it. There is no evidence to counter her recollection of the incident, nor any reason to doubt it. Yet the story to which she objects appears to have first surfaced in publicity material written by Warner Bros. and sanctioned by her father. The same is true with several tales of Hitchcock's humor; a good deal of his reputation as the dark, sadistic joker was directed by himself. Talking about a lifetime of pranking, embarrassing, and compromising people, Hitchcock told an interviewer that "the moment any opportunity occurs, I'm in there. . . . I love hearing or seeing . . . the *nice* discomfort of the recipient of the joke." As is the case with his complex relationship with women, his teasing, cruel humor wasn't an aspect of his personality that was obscured from the public, but was taken in hand and marketed as part of the Hitchcock legend. He knew how it would make him look; he enjoyed the notoriety.

When he came to write his biography of Hitchcock, Patrick McGilligan discovered that one infamous anecdote about Hitchcock's brutal sadism couldn't possibly be true. Hitherto, Robert Goold, an old boy of St Ignatius College, had maintained that during his schooldays Hitchcock had been one of two boys who had restrained him, pulled down his trousers, and attached firecrackers to his underwear, terrifying him and very nearly causing him serious and painful injury. But McGilligan's research showed that the dates didn't tally; Hitchcock had left St Ignatius before Goold had enrolled. Goold conceded that it must have been a false childhood memory; ironically Hitchcockian, in its way.

Rather than a malicious lie, Goold's story was likely the fusing of distant recollections with Hitchcock's predilection for undermining dignity in the name of entertainment. He loved to scare, disturb, and discomfort, and he based his entire career on knowing that, deep down, we yearn for these things, too. As a born entertainer, his mantra was to give the audience what they want—whether they like it or not.

10

THE PIONEER

P rominent among Alfred Hitchcock's enviable talents was his ability to reinvent himself while remaining exactly the same. It was a running joke on his television series, in which he appeared in multiple, unconvincing guises. He was Hitchcock the Pilgrim, Hitchcock the Baby, Hitchcock the Scarecrow—even Hitchcock the Beatle, wearing a mop-top wig for an episode in 1964. No matter how elaborate the costume, there was never any disguising the wearer.

As the fifties drew to a close, he used his education—and the expertise of those around him—in the swiftness and economy of television production to induce the most memorable reinvention of his career, as the maker of horrifying black-and-white slasher flicks. *Psycho* was a game changer in Hollywood, especially its sparse, expressionist score by Bernard Herrmann, and George Tomasini's quick-cut editing, both of which exerted a huge influence on other filmmakers' work. Having self-financed the production, Hitchcock had also challenged the business model of the old studio system, and made himself a phenomenal profit in the process. In the wider culture, *Psycho* was not so much a landmark as a lightning bolt. Upon its release, it was derided by establishment critics, who dismissed it as grubby melodrama. Andrew Sarris was one of a younger breed who thought very differently. "Hitchcock is the most-daring avant-garde film-maker in America," he wrote in the *Village Voice*. "Besides making previous horror films look like variations of 'Pollyanna,' 'Psycho' is overlaid with a richly symbolic commentary on the modern world as a public swamp in which human feelings and passions are flushed down the drain." At sixty, Hitchcock had made a film that kept pace with the fast-changing expectations of young audiences, those for whom violent dislocation was an increasingly familiar cultural experience.

It would be pleasingly neat if Hitchcock had always intended to follow *Psycho* with *The Birds*, a bestial nightmare that evoked the Cold War–era terror of destruction from the skies. In fact, Hitchcock came to *The Birds* rather belatedly. For a long while, he harbored hopes of getting Audrey Hepburn to play a lawyer-turned-undercover-hooker in *No Bail for the Judge*, or tempting Grace Kelly, now the Princess consort of Monaco, to take the title role in *Marnie*, turning Her Serene Highness into a kleptomaniac with a psychosexual disorder—a Hitchcockian act of reinvention if ever there was one. When neither of those worked out, he switched horses and pushed ahead with an adaptation of "The Birds," a short story by Daphne du Maurier first published in 1952. The action was transposed from du Maurier's native Cornwall to California, and the story became one of Hitchcock's trademark tales of a beautiful, independent woman stripped of her poise and dignity, beaten down by terrifying forces she can't control or comprehend. Around that familiar conceit, Hitchcock arranged a carapace of cutting-edge filmmaking that makes *The Birds* one of the most influential movies ever made.

As much as *Psycho*, *The Birds* is a prime example of Hitchcock as modernist showman, working in the tradition of impresarios and publicists such as Sergei Diaghilev and Edward Bernays, as well as groundbreaking filmmakers. With his use of advanced special effects and sound design, a marketing campaign built around his celebrity, and an attempt to create a movie star out of somebody who'd never before had a professional acting job, Hitchcock revealed himself to be a man motivated by the desire to outdo himself, to innovate, reinvent, and avoid the steady creep of boredom.

The idea of lending Hitchcock's gifts to a tale of humans besieged by the natural world had floated around for many years before *The Birds* went into production. In 1953, his friend and sometime business partner Sidney Bernstein recommended buying the rights to *The Day of the Triffids*, John Wyndham's dystopian novel about humans under attack from a species of giant plant. Bernstein and Mary Elsom—an Englishwoman engaged in scouting potential Hitchcock material—pitched the book as an H. G. Wells extravaganza, ripe for exploitation by the latest special effects, including 3D. Hitchcock didn't bite. He was wary of science fiction, and despite his enthusiasm for adopting and adapting new technology, he was never sold on the viability of 3D as a storytelling tool. When sound and color were introduced in the twenties and thirties, he instantly saw the potential of each to help build a narrative and add new layers to the Hitchcock touch. However, 3D, he believed, was just the opposite, a gimmick that reduced rather than expanded a filmmaker's options.

Another concern Hitchcock had with 3D is that it failed to deliver on its central promise. Rather than drawing the viewer into the world of the film, it reminded them of the artificiality of what they were seeing, which could only detract from a distinctive and convincing diegesis. As daring as it was, *Psycho* had forced Hitchcock back to basics, drawing on his core filmmaking principles for a black-and-white movie made on the kind of budget he hadn't handled since wartime. There were no real stars, no stunts, and no dramatic chase sequences across world-famous monuments. Faced with such constrictions, he made the most of what he had when it came to selling the film in a novel, now legendary, advertising campaign, intertwining his celebrity with the gothic dread of the film's fairy-tale universe. In an unforgettable trailer, he led cinema audiences around the Bates house, like a realtor from the Seventh Circle of Hell. His face appeared in promo posters; he, rather than Janet Leigh or Anthony Perkins, recorded radio ads. It was also he who shaped how the film should be exhibited in cinemas across the country. He insisted that nobody be allowed admission to *Psycho* once the film had begun, a break from the custom of the day that he told exhibitors was needed to extend an atmosphere of "mysterious importance" from the screen to the lobby. It was Hitchcock's likeness that moviegoers saw in cardboard-cutout form as they waited in line, pointing grimly at his watch, and it was his voice they heard in prerecorded messages warning them that any attempts to enter the auditorium once the film had started "will be met by force." Hitchcock's reputation was front and center in creating an atmosphere of specialness around the film, priming audiences for the spooky world they were about to enter. There were no preview screenings, and the cast and crew had been asked to take an oath promising not to divulge any of the awful secrets of the film's plot—a fact that was used for publicity purposes, along with the revelation that the usually press-friendly Hitchcock had ordered a closed set during filming. The ratcheting suspense had its desired effect. From the opening week, there were reports of not merely shrieking inside the auditorium, but crying, fainting, and seats wetted by patrons who had lost control of themselves.

The excitement spread across the planet. When Hitchcock embarked on a world tour to promote *Psycho*, he and his personality were exploited every bit as extensively. In Australia, he made headlines by expressing his dislike of the way in which women were treated in the antipodes. "Your women are marvellous," he told a journalist in Sydney, "yet they are so downtrodden by your men." Considering that *Psycho* is all about American women being treated horrendously by American men, that was a bold statement, indeed. Less provocatively, he also posed for photographs in his hotel room to accompany an article about his efforts to locate a missing shoe, which at least one newspaper deemed newsworthy.

The Australian leg of the tour ended with a dinner in Hitchcock's honor, on Friday, May 13, at which the creepy turned to camp. The dining room was draped in black, colored only by sprays of white lilies and chrysanthemums, and according to the Melbourne *Herald*, "sombre organ music filled the room." Hitchcock arrived by hearse, greeted by eight young women dressed all in black, while guests—several of whom were "leading psychiatrists"—posed for photographs in front of a huge copy of Hitchcock's silhouette. The publicity tour underlined what the opening of the film in the United States had demonstrated: *Psycho* was less a movie and more a cultural happening, expanding on a tradition of the riotous early performances of *Le Sacre du Printemps* in Paris, and the Armory Show exhibition in New York in 1913, which introduced the American public to cubism, fauvism, and futurism, and allied Europe's groundbreaking modern art with an American genius for marketing and working the public into a lather.

Three years later, the success of that campaign shaped the promotion of *The Birds*. "The star of this picture, as with *Psycho*, is Alfred Hitchcock," stated the shrewd Madison Avenue PR man William F. Blowitz in a memo to his colleagues. "Therefore, a pivotal element in publicity and advertising will be Hitchcock. In the notes on the magazine campaign, the trailer and ads, all of this is emphasized. The point of the campaign is to sell tickets to *The Birds*; Hitchcock will be a principal element." Hitchcock was not just placed at the center of it, he served as its propelling force. As with his work with writers, in matters of publicity he needed collaborators with skills and talents he lacked—yet the entire project was guided by his image and bursts of brilliance. Hitchcock invited the photographer Philippe Halsman to take a series of pictures that would position the director as the star of the film, and remind the audience that he looked on the mayhem in front of his camera with a twinkle in the eye. The screenwriter Evan Hunter remembers how, with hands spread wide as if framing the words on an imaginary billboard, Hitchcock pitched the movie's tagline to Universal Pictures' moneymen: "*The Birds* is coming!" A young executive in the meeting, unused to Hitchcock's sense of humor, was the first of many to raise a syntactical objection; surely it should be "The birds *are* coming"? The complaints of grammar pedants notwithstanding, the slogan was perfectly Hitchcock and set the tone for a marketing campaign that provided a seam of humor that the film itself lacks.

The campaigns for *Psycho* and *The Birds*, inspired as they were in many ways, built on practices that Hitchcock, and those who worked to publicize his movies, had been developing for years. Even in promoting *The Lodger*, there were publicity stunts designed to bring the menace of the film out into the real world, and sound rather like the kind of marketing strategies we more readily associate with our own era. In various towns, men dressed up as the Lodger/the Avenger in shrouding capes

One of Philippe Halsman's famous publicity photos for *The Birds*.

and scarves, handed out flyers, and, in one case, acted as walking bill-boards, carrying suitcases bearing messages such as "BEWARE GIRLS!" and "MEET ME AT THE GRAND," the name of the local cinema. The Balham Palladium in south London took things an inventive step fur-ther by arranging with a nearby shop to re-create a pivotal scene in the film in its window, complete with atmospheric Hitchcockian lighting. The scene caused a buzz along the High Street and "proved very success-ful as a business proposition," according to a report from the time. It's unknown whether Hitchcock had anything to do with such stunts, but he (or perhaps a clipping service in his employ) collected the press cover-age of them and pasted them into his scrapbooks, evidence at least of his awareness of and interest in how his work was promoted.

Within a few years, "Hitchcock" was a big enough name in Britain to dominate marketing campaigns. The same wasn't quite true in the United States until several years after his relocation, but the publicity staff at the studios found working with Hitchcock a delight; he was full of ideas, open to those of others, and happy to do as many interviews as could be scheduled. Other studio figures were sometimes less enam-ored of Hitchcock's brilliance for publicity. As Leonard Leff has writ-ten, "feature stories on *Spellbound* (a David O. Selznick production) somehow became feature stories on Hitchcock (distinctly *not* a David O. Selznick production)." By 1959, when audiences turned up at their local movie theater to see *North by Northwest* in its opening weeks, they were confronted—just as they would be for *Psycho* and *The Birds*—by life-size cut-outs of Hitchcock, and his name and face were incorporated into much of the marketing paraphernalia that was sent out across the United States. The hero of that movie, Cary Grant's Roger Thornhill, is a Madi-son Avenue advertising guru, a prototype of Don Draper from *Mad Men*, a devastatingly suave, cynical genius in the grips of a severe identity cri-sis. Ernest Lehman recollects that when he and Hitchcock were piecing together the ideas for the script, "advertising executive" was just one of dozens of occupations he had written down, but it seemed the perfect fit for a tale about a superficial nowhere man.

Advertising fascinated Hitchcock. It was modern, open to innovation, multidisciplinary, and it sought to manipulate human behavior by tapping into people's hopes and fears, just as he did in his films. It was in the advertising department of W.T. Henley's Telegraph Works Company that Hitchcock's creativity was given its first professional outlet. There, his strong pictorial imagination and lively wit were put to good use, sketching clever, economical designs to sell electrical cabling. He considered his strongly visual imagination to be more attuned with the disciplines of poster design, photography, and advertising layouts than with many of the traditional, figurative painters he admired. It's another reminder of the cultural environment from which he emanated. Hitchcock embodied a new type of Briton, an educated member of the urban lower-middle class thoroughly versed in new media—cinema, advertising, radio—that permeated the barriers between commerce, mass culture, and art. The material culture of that environment is strongly present in a number of Hitchcock's British films—the ads on the train that make Fred yearn for a more exciting life in *Rich and Strange*; the advertisement for a brand of tea that facilitates a crucial plot point in *The Lady Vanishes*; and the neon signs in *Blackmail*, selling West End excitement to ordinary folks on a night out. The series of billboard advertisements that Dorothy Parker worked into the script of *Saboteur*, which cleverly address the unfolding action, brought the motif into Hitchcock's American work for the first time.

The boldness and ubiquity of American advertising was of particular interest to Hitchcock. When he arrived in the US, he was fascinated to hear commercial spots on the radio; back in Britain, the BBC monopoly of radio that lasted until 1973 meant advertising was banned on the airwaves. On his television series, he gained a reputation for his withering remarks about commercial breaks, but the deprecation was deliberately crafted to draw more attention to the slots.

Hitchcock's process as a director was folded into the marketing of his films almost from the moment his name was in the public consciousness. While making *Easy Virtue* in 1927, Hitchcock and his producer gave journalists extensive access to various aspects of the production process. One wrote about his trip to Nice where a portion of the film was shot;

another described the exact replica of a London divorce court that he had built. A month later came a story detailing the various glamorous places Hitchcock had shot, such as the polo ground of the exclusive Roehampton Club. In publicity for *Downhill*, British critics raved about a scene in which Ivor Novello's character travels glumly down an escalator into the London Underground, symbolic of his descent into existential despair. Anticipating the stir that would be caused by this use of a landmark of modern London, Hitchcock made sure that several reporters and critics were invited to witness the scene being filmed. The shoot took place at night and attracted a large crowd of onlookers, many excited to see Novello, a bona fide star of the British stage and screen. Not to be outdone by a mere actor, Hitchcock made the grandest entrance of the evening, dressed in white tie and tails, as he'd come straight from the theater. Around this time, Ivor Montagu, the film's editor, was rapped on the knuckles for playing the footage to people unconnected to the production. The studio reminded Montagu that only Hitchcock had the privilege of showing rushes to those he deemed useful for publicity purposes.

Using his set as a hub of publicity was a key feature of so many Hitchcock films, including *Lifeboat*, *Rope*, and *Rear Window*, all of which were reported on as being technologically groundbreaking in one way or another. Here again, the practice was precedented by Hitchcock's pre-Hollywood career, on films such as *The Farmer's Wife* and *The Ring*, both of which attracted publicity for their ambitious and novel set designs, and the farsightedness of their pioneering director. *The Ring* featured a clever reproduction of the Albert Hall and a working fairground, which was constructed solely for the shooting of the film's opening scenes but which was made open to the public, in order that the director could capture authentic footage for the start of the film. A couple of weeks before the shoot took place, Hitchcock swore to one journalist that to ensure he remained incognito, he planned to be "thoroughly disguised as a showman wearing the traditional frockcoat, red silk handkerchief and ebullient silk hat."

Over the coming years, the line between publicizing a Hitchcock film and publicizing Hitchcock could be hazy, at least for those who oversaw the budgets. In the summer of 1935, Hitchcock received a terse letter from H. G. Boxall at the Gaumont-British studio complaining about an article Hitchcock had written that had been accompanied by a photograph of Alma and him on the set of *The 39 Steps*, none of which had been authorized and was therefore an obvious breach of contract. Not that Hitchcock was always keen for outsiders to come and see how the magic happened. The photographer Michael Powell had to finagle his way onto the set of *Champagne* to take publicity stills, because Hitchcock was so unhappy with the script that he didn't think there was anything to publicize. "I don't wish my name to be associated with this film," he said as he sat glumly in his chair. "I think this film is shit."

The older he got, the more Hitchcock professed that for him filmmaking was about the perfection of form. "As far as I'm concerned," he avowed in the 1960s, "the content is secondary to the handling; the effect I can produce on an audience rather than the subject matter" was the chief interest. This line helped him dodge questions about whether the increasingly strange subject matter of his films—from *Vertigo* onward—revealed anything about him as a person, though it's also indicative of the pleasure he took in grappling with intractable technical problems in a way not shared by all film directors. When he chose to reinvigorate his career by breaking from Selznick to make *Rope* and *Under Capricorn* through his own production company, the long-take filming method he adopted on both films posed an unwieldy bundle of complex challenges. On *Rope*, the interior of a Manhattan apartment was built, with sliding walls and props and furniture on rollers, allowing the camera to glide around on floors designed to silence the noise of all these enormous moving pieces. Each scene had to be painstakingly choreographed, leading James Stewart to complain that "the only thing that's been rehearsed around here is the camera."

In *Under Capricorn*, the same challenges presented themselves, though on a larger scale: instead of being set entirely in the reception rooms of a Manhattan apartment, the movie took place in a range of locations in colonial-era Australia, including a sprawling mansion through which the camera roamed, occupying as many as six rooms in one scene. In one of Hitchcock's most memorable dining scenes, a special table had to be made, a jigsaw of fourteen pieces that could be whipped out of shot, allowing a crane to move unfettered. Recalling how the actors in the scene were required to double as stage hands, the cinematographer Jack Cardiff said it was "positively weird to see them suddenly grab a section of a table, with a candle or a plate of food fixed on to it, and fall wildly out of picture into the perspiring melee with their own parts of the table clutched in their hands." Despite the inevitable stresses entailed in such an ambitious and minutely choreographed production, Hitchcock—who also chose these two films to be his first foray into Technicolor—was energized by the technical complexity. At the time of its release, he proclaimed *Rope* "the most exciting picture I've ever directed."

Hitchcock prided himself on knowing more about each department on a film set better than anyone other than the department heads. He enjoyed telling people that it was he who taught Jack Cox, the cinematographer on several of his British films, how to shoot on the job, as they made *The Ring*. When Cox called in sick one day, it was Hitchcock, so he claimed, who lit the day's scenes himself. It was that firsthand knowledge that spurred him to approach sequences in novel ways. Hitchcock's silent films abound with trick shots and visual inventiveness. *Easy Virtue* opens with a shot of what looks like a crop circle but is slowly revealed to be the top of a judicial wig. As the judge looks wearily across the courtroom, we see what he sees: his hand bringing his monocle slowly to his eye, the magnified image of the barrister getting ever larger in the screen. Something similarly convoluted was applied to the start of *Champagne*, in which the disembodied arm of a waiter holds a champagne bottle at the camera, the cork staring at us as if the barrel of a gun. The cork pops, and champagne runs over the lens, at which point Hitchcock cuts to a close-up of the wine being poured into a glass that is then instantly tilted back, as though the audience is downing the contents. In a single bubble at the bottom of the glass, a distant scene is magnified: a jazz band playing on stage, while a couple spins on the dance floor. It's a delightfully clever sequence, if rather empty. As Hitchcock matured, such set pieces would become more integrated into the story of the film; there are moments in his silent films that resemble the show reel of a director of commercials, rather than the work of a feature film storyteller. Unlike the authorship of Hitchcock's stories and scripts, there is little doubt from whose mind such visual sequences came; this, ultimately, is the essence of the Hitchcock touch.

As soon as sound was introduced into Hitchcock's armory, he sought ingenious ways of incorporating that, too. *Blackmail* was already in production as a silent film when its producers decided they wanted it to be a talkie. Hitchcock saw the problems this presented as an opportunity, and he found ways to use sound that few other filmmakers of that generation even attempted. Shortly after Alice kills her attacker in self-defense, we hear what she hears when her family discusses reports of the man found stabbed to death in his own bed. To Alice, guilt-ridden and panicking, the dialogue becomes babble in her ears, apart from the word "knife," each sharp utterance of which is a reminder of the stab with which she killed her attacker. Eight years after the film's release, a respected critic watched it again and was moved to write that "there is a freshness about the approach to sound in it that is positively startling in these days of stereotyped dialogue and balanced background."

The Skin Game is one of Hitchcock's most prosaically shot films, reverting to lengthy single takes with a static camera as though the action is taking place beneath the proscenium arch of a theater stage—the type of film that Hitchcock himself frequently derided as "pictures of people talking." Even here, though, he found moments to experiment: a montage of sound in the opening scene in the marketplace is followed by a shot of the darkened doorway of a house, out of which spills a conversation we can hear but cannot see. Overhearing and conversations out of earshot are a motif of the film, used to stress various social divisions in 1930s England: north and south, town and country, old money and the nouveau riche. As the film reaches its climax, Chloe Hornblower, the female protagonist, hides behind a curtain, terrified that a shameful secret from her past is about to be exposed, and eavesdrops on her

Hitchcock (with Anny Ondra) working with the latest technology on the set of *Blackmail*.

husband denouncing her—but Hitchcock shoots it in such a way that the voices seem to be in the woman's head, her guilt and shame tearing her apart from the inside, driving her to suicide.

Undoubtedly, many of the stylistic trills that ornamented his films, whether in London or in Hollywood, stemmed from Hitchcock's search for novelty, or his desire to create a problem in order that he could find its solution. It was also a means of keeping himself on screen while remaining behind the camera. At first, so he claimed, he laid his clever touches and in-jokes for critics to pick up. Later, when he was a household name and much less reliant on critical appreciation to carry his public reputation, these were things he felt duty bound to include for paying customers who had certain expectations about what constituted a Hitchcock movie. Other filmmakers weren't always impressed. For Orson Welles, the elaborate shots were clever but hollow, stunts to distract from Hitchcock's essential vacuity. "His contrivances remain contrivances," said Welles in 1967, "no matter how marvelously they're conceived and executed. I don't honestly believe Hitchcock is a director whose pictures will be of any interest a hundred years from now."

Welles's criticism was uncharitable, but not without foundation. There are certainly examples of Hitchcock putting on film clever bits of business mainly because it had never been done before. Equally, there are many stunning moments in Hitchcock when his thirst for novelty meets the needs of storytelling and characterization, resulting in the visceral expression of physical and emotional experience. At some point during the twenties or thirties, Hitchcock attended the Chelsea Arts Ball in London, where he drank too much and experienced the peculiar "sensation that everything was going away from me." For years he thought about how he might express that feeling with the camera. He'd wanted to incorporate it into *Rebecca* as a means of communicating the disorientation and fear experienced by Joan Fontaine's character, but he and his crew were unable to find a way of achieving the shot. The idea sat with him for a further fifteen years until he began planning *Vertigo* and wanted to express Scottie's sudden wooziness when looking down. At last, a solution was found: by moving the camera away from James Stewart's face at the same time as zooming in on him with the lens, that strange, dizzying sensation that Hitchcock had first experienced when drunk could be achieved. The only problem, Hitchcock's cameraman told him, was that to do this at the top of the staircase would be enormously expensive, around fifty thousand dollars. As Hitchcock told Truffaut, he came up with a neat solution: he laid a miniature model of the staircase on its side, performing a tracking shot and a zoom flat on the ground. The pride and satisfaction at having thought his way through the problem was palpable: "So that's the way we did it, and it only cost us nineteen thousand dollars." He tried for something similarly inventive in the beautiful sequence in *Shadow of a Doubt* in which young Charlie, on her own in the library, reads about her uncle's horrific crimes. The camerawork and lighting help make this a dramatic high point of the film, but Hitchcock had originally planned an extra element: at the precise moment of revelation, the camera would jolt upward, as though experiencing a sharp intake of breath along with Charlie. Try as they might, Hitchcock and his director of photography, Joseph Valentine, could not find an adequate method. A sanguine Hitchcock apparently brushed it off, telling colleagues that "if I get fifty percent of what I want to get I feel lucky."

Trial and error, and the toleration of failure, were built into the Hitchcock operation. Considering his reputation for preproduction planning and his stated dislike of on-set experimentation, it might sound surprising that Hitchcock welcomed compromise and disappointment as part of the filmmaking process. Rather than an artist's studio in which he strove for visionary perfection, his workspaces were more like a technician's laboratory, where hypotheses were formulated and tested, and valuable lessons were learned. Just as he aimed at playing his audience like an organ, pressing the keys and the pedals at the right times to induce particular emotions, so he used his films as a way of exploring the potentialities and limitations of the technology at his disposal, making it more expressive, closing the gap between our willingness to be moved and the camera's ability to emote.

Nowhere is this more apparent than in *The Birds*. The film has myriad obvious flaws. Much of the intended humor falls flat; certain characters appear to have wandered in from some other corner of the Hitchcock universe. What nobody can criticize is the scale of the film's ambition. In attempting to realize that ambition, Hitchcock assembled a remarkable team of artists and technicians, many of whom were Hitchcock veterans, including Bernard Herrmann, George Tomasini, production designer Robert Boyle, and director of photography Robert Burks. Hitchcock never spoke dismissively of technicians in the way he could do of actors and writers. Partly, this must be because camera operators and set designers represented less threat to his public profile as a sun king in charge of his court. But it's also because he had such esteem for their skill sets. Gregory Peck felt that Hitchcock regarded actors as animate props, or bits of equipment, in the manner of a camera or a lighting rig. He didn't so much give "notes" to his cast as command words in order to switch them from one acting mode to another. On one occasion, he is reported to have prepared Norman Lloyd for a dramatic close-up with the instruction, "Please start sweating now." James Stewart never heard him call actors cattle, but he agreed that Hitchcock had an essentially technocratic approach to filmmaking in which actors were a cog in a machine. "Hitch believed you were hired to do your job . . . know your lines and carry your part."

When Hitchcock encountered a director of photography, set designer, illustrator, or any other member of production staff he liked and trusted, he kept hold of them. He was "extremely possessive of people who worked for him," remembered his secretary Carol Shourds, "especially the crew." Not that it was always obvious whether one was in favor or not. Hilton Green, an assistant director on Hitchcock's television shows who filled the same position on *Psycho*, recalls that Hitchcock didn't speak a word to him when they worked together the first time. Assuming he had fallen short of the director's high standards, Green was stunned when he got a call asking if he'd like to work on future projects, so pleased had Hitchcock been with his work.

Green was of a mind with other of Hitchcock's off-camera collaborators who found the experience of working with him stimulating but infuriating. Robert Burks, one of the great Hollywood cinematographers of his era, was frequently exasperated with the late nights spent working through some convoluted technical challenge set by Hitchcock's desire for a particular effect. "This is the last one I'm going to do for Hitch," his colleague Robert Boyle recalls him saying on several occasions, "it's just too much." Boyle shared the frustration, remembering that seemingly every day on a Hitchcock film "you had to solve a problem, and if you were on location, Hitch would come out in a big black limousine, drive up, lower the window about an eighth of an inch, look out the window and ask you a couple of questions, and then leave!" However, Burks, Boyle, and others stuck with Hitchcock because of the creative latitude he gave them and the respect he paid to their expert opinions. It was "the most collaborative of all the working relationships I had," was Boyle's ultimate assessment.

The Birds demonstrates Hitchcock's understanding of suspense as well as any film he made. The famous scene outside the school in which the birds are seen to gradually amass on the jungle gym was filmed precisely as storyboarded by the illustrator Harold Michelson, but Michelson had taken his cue from Hitchcock's own vision for the scene: each time the gaze of the camera cuts to the playground, more birds have amassed, the tension rising inexorably. From the beginning, however, Hitchcock knew that the finely wrought suspense would be ruined if the special effects were not adequately convincing. To assuage this, Hitchcock—on the advice of Robert Boyle—pulled in the artist Ub Iwerks, Walt Disney's longtime collaborator, to lend his expertise on the sodium vapor process, a method of color separation that allows the merging of separately shot backgrounds and foregrounds, and that was used to create the attack scenes.* Following the example set by Bernard Herrmann's remarkable score for *Psycho*, Hitchcock also wanted to do something radical with sound in *The Birds*, and was excited to learn of Oskar Sala and Remi Gassmann, two German pioneers of electronic music, who had demonstrated to other members of the Hitchcock team that they had the ability to create, electronically, an enormous range of sounds, thereby providing limitless options for film soundtracks. The introduction of electronic sounds into his toolbox was a great boon to Hitchcock. When he heard a demonstration of the sounds Sala and Gassmann could create, he was delighted, and recalled to others how impressed he had been by a film of a tank battle in which all the sound had been created electronically. Ultimately, though, it was the capacity to conjure new, expressive sounds—new possibilities for the evocation of atmosphere and emotion—that most motivated him. As Sala and Gassmann created their soundtrack in Berlin, Hitchcock issued directions, asking them to

---

* Two years after *The Birds* was released, Iwerks won an Academy Award for his special effects work on *Mary Poppins*, which used the same sodium vapor process.

give sonic form to abstract concepts such as menace, anger, and confusion. For the final sequence of the film, he asked for "electronically the equivalent of brooding silence. Naturally, to achieve some effect like this will necessitate some experimentation."

Correspondence with Hitchcock's office suggests Sala and Gassmann were stressed by the workload but happy that Hitchcock trusted their ability to interpret his ideas. He was very satisfied with their labors and enjoyed seeing them work up close when he accompanied Bernard Herrmann to Berlin just before Christmas 1962. Back in Germany among avant-garde technologists, exposing himself to new elements of his craft, the trip was a homecoming of sorts. The machine that Sala and Gassmann used was a Mixtur-Trautonium, an electronic instrument based on the Trautonium, one of the world's first synthesizers, which had been invented by Friedrich Trautwein in the late 1920s, and which Hitchcock had supposedly heard during a visit to Berlin around that time. As much as *The Birds* was an ambitious leap for Hitchcock, it was also a reinforcement of a core aspect of his identity as a filmmaker—a drive to realize a creative ambition through the exploitation of technology and technique.

The link with the German avant-garde is also a reminder of the milieu from which Hitchcock had emerged as a Hollywood director of note more than twenty years earlier. He had been part of a pioneering wartime generation of European filmmakers who came to Hollywood, what has been described as "an eruption of film talent" matched only by the arrival of the New Hollywood generation of the sixties and seventies. As a leading member of that wave of émigrés, Hitchcock's first few American films helped to set patterns that would proliferate over the ensuing two decades. His focus on the trials of complexly alluring female characters, suspense, psychological themes, and expressionist filming techniques are the key elements of film noir, and they exerted a huge influence on the era of classical Hollywood cinema.

Hitchcock grumbled that he was forever being copied, which made it difficult for him to remain fresh and distinctive—though he often conveniently forgot the many debts that he owed to the directors from whom he borrowed, especially contemporaries such as Welles, Clouzot, and Antonioni. A sense that he needed to keep a step ahead of his imitators was surely behind his periodic reinventions, such as when he took on the multiple challenges of *Rope* and *Under Capricorn*, his flirtation with social realism in *The Wrong Man*, or the darker, more arthouse territory he entered with *The Birds* and *Marnie*. At every stage, the Hitchcock publicity machine—the man himself, allied with the producers, distributors, and promoters of his movies—stressed the daring inventiveness of these ventures. In promotional material published for *Rope*, Jack Warner, an establishment figure who thought of himself as a rebel and a rule breaker, hailed the film as "real pioneering on the part of Mr. Hitchcock and it foreshadows great potential improvements in motion picture production." The same booklet contained a section that placed Hitchcock and *Rope* in the same rarified space as *The Cabinet of Dr. Caligari*, *The Great Train Robbery*, and the best work of Griffith and Méliès. Rather than selling the story of the film, Warner Bros. focused on the technological wonders involved in its production: the moving set that allowed the camera to rove without cuts; the electronic control boards from which technicians could control their equipment "with split-second accuracy"; the radical ways in which Hitchcock was using sound, lighting, and color to give a vivid sense of time and place. Hitchcock publicly boasted that *Rope* featured "the most revolutionary technique Hollywood had ever seen." Given all this, it's ironic that, to safeguard public morals, *Rope* was banned for a time in Germany, cradle of Hitchcock's cinematic technique and of the Nietzschean philosophy that provides Phillip and Brandon with their chilling motivation. It wasn't until 1963 that the ban was permanently lifted, just as *The Birds*, Hitchcock's most technologically advanced film of all, was let fly.

In certain ways, *The Birds* was ahead of its time. Indeed, in its depiction of a panicked community sheltering in place against the assault of benign nature suddenly turned savage, it could be said that *The Birds* is a film more of our times than of Hitchcock's. Yet this was also the last

Hitchcock film to feel urgently relevant to the wider world. Some critics would dispute this, making the case that *Marnie* is the zenith of Hitchcock's career, a forerunner of the emerging New Hollywood, and powerfully engaged with important issues that shape our society. However, key members of Hitchcock's production team maintained that *Marnie* fell short of what they had hoped for. In particular, various technical aspects of the film undermine its impact, especially the backdrop of a ship looming at the end of a Baltimore street, and the close-up shots of Marnie riding her horse. Some will have us believe that these were not blunders, but evidence of *Marnie*'s artistic purity, augmenting the dreaminess of the film, just as Hitchcock intended, though not as he admitted to. Sounding embarrassed about the criticism the film received, Hitchcock blamed a "technical mixup, and something of which I did not approve." If he'd had the opportunity, he would have redone several sequences from scratch. Burks and Boyle, the technicians responsible for the effects, had a different recollection. They agreed that they had both made serious mistakes with the ship backdrop, and said they asked Hitchcock if they could have another attempt. But, according to Boyle, "Hitchcock wouldn't reshoot it. He would reshoot it if Tippi Hedren's hair or dress was awry, but not that."

Hitchcock primed us for the sixties, but as it swept through our culture, it left him behind. He'd always enjoyed prodding at the limits of what censors had deemed acceptable, and by the time the Motion Picture Production Code was formally dismantled in 1968, he had already prepared himself for a new era of permissiveness with a script that would make *Psycho* look quaint. *Kaleidoscope* (also known as *Frenzy*, though not to be confused with Hitchcock's 1972 film of that name) proposed to take Hitchcock's demonstrable interest in sexually motivated murder to graphic new heights—or depths, depending on one's perspective. The story was loosely inspired by the real-life crimes of English murderer Neville Heath in the 1940s, though Hitchcock intended to set his film among the hippies of 1960s New York. The screenplay—one draft of which Hitchcock wrote himself—and the film tests he carried out in 1967 indicate that he planned a bracing new iteration of a Hitchcock film, with more nudity, sex, and violence than ever before. But his pitch was rejected by his studio of the time, Universal. Had it been made, it's possible that *Kaleidoscope* might have taken its place alongside *Bonnie and Clyde*, *Easy Rider*, *The Wild Bunch*, and other daring classics of the era. As Dan Auiler succinctly puts it, "This project was an intended turning point in Hitchcock's career—a turn that the studio denied him."

In a sense, he had become a victim of his own wild success. By the mid-sixties, Hitchcock was a cultural institution, an establishment figure who had hosted Lyndon Johnson's inaugural gala and had lunched with Henry Kissinger. Moreover, after his agent and friend Lew Wasserman negotiated the purchase of Universal Pictures by his company MCA in 1962, Hitchcock signed lucrative deals with Universal in which he exchanged the rights to Shamley Productions, his production company, the television shows, and various of his movies, including *Psycho*, for a colossal amount of corporate stock, making him one of the wealthiest people in Hollywood, bolstered by his substantial investments in oil and livestock. He had always been acutely interested in the business side of the movies. Rodney Ackland recalled that when Hitchcock returned to England during the forties, his "conversation was of finance, mergers between Hollywood film companies, problems of distribution, how much his last picture had taken and so on." Thirty years later, nothing much had changed when Hitchcock wrote to another old acquaintance in England about industry news that was of immense interest to him and his bank manager, but one wonders how much it would have excited distant friends across the pond: MCA's huge slush fund, for example, "which they don't know what to do with. The shares stand at $40, higher than anyone else. All of this, of course, has been given a lift by the film JAWS. Now I think that the next thing liable to happen in a lesser degree is Fox, whose shares have jumped 5 or 6 points in the last few days, following the release of a picture called STAR WARS."

Unfortunately for him, executives at Universal were unable to reconcile Hitchcock the venerable shareholder with Hitchcock the artistic defiler of public morals. When the studio signed him, the hope and expectation was that Hitchcock would bring prestige and critical acclaim to their brand, along with box-office clout. They looked to him for another *North by Northwest*, not a leap into the mind of—as he himself put it—the "questionable old man of the later movies, who occupied himself dispassionately with sex matters."

Ultimately, the two films Universal did allow him to make in the second half of the sixties were among the biggest failures of his Hollywood career, artistically and commercially. *Torn Curtain* is a diverting but uninspired revisitation of earlier Hitchcock spy thrillers. In that same genre, *Topaz* (1969) is a disjointed, meandering mess, the high point of which is Karin Dor's death scene, in which her dress spreads around her as she falls to the gleaming tiled floor, like a flowing pool of purple blood. Both were attempts to engage with the state of the world in the Cold War era—as his classics *The Man Who Knew Too Much*, *The 39 Steps*, and *The Lady Vanishes* had engaged with the atmosphere of 1930s Europe—but neither feels urgently topical. *Torn Curtain* caused the implosion of Hitchcock's association with Bernard Herrmann, who failed to provide the pop score that Universal wanted. A year earlier Hitchcock had lost another vital collaborator, when George Tomasini died of a heart attack. The unraveling had begun.

Hitchcock remained fascinated by the times in which he lived, collecting files' worth of newspaper clippings about hippies, the Black Power movement, anti-apartheid and anticolonialism across Africa, the Weather Underground, the "opening-up" in China, and third-wave feminism. Nothing came of them. To François Truffaut, he complained that he was "completely desperate" for new material.

Now, as you realize, you are a free person to make whatever you want. I, on the other hand, can only make what is expected of me; that is, a thriller, or a suspense story, and that I find hard to do. So many stories seem to be about the neo-Nazis, Palestinians fighting Israelis, and all that kind of thing. And, you see, none of these subjects has any human conflict.

By "human conflict" Hitchcock presumably meant conflict within the human mind, the psychological struggles of the individual. Ideology, religion, and the wounds of history held no intrinsic interest to Hitchcock the filmmaker.

Hitchcock felt "typed" and unable to shake himself loose from the straitjacket of his own reputation. "I'm in competition with myself," he complained. The last two films of his career were *Frenzy*—a variation on the Ripper theme—and *Family Plot*, an enjoyable caper that lacks the sharp edges of Hitchcock at his best. The critical response to the final two films was markedly more generous than that afforded the previous three. At this advanced stage, Hitchcock was yogi-like, beyond praise or disparagement as meted out to other directors. As Truffaut observed, "a director who is over seventy years old and still working enjoys what might be defined as critical immunity."

Attempting to make sense of "late style," the work of great artists in their final years, Edward Said contrasted those whose efforts display a serene wisdom, with those such as Beethoven whose final works are defined by "intransigence, difficulty and unresolved contradiction," a challenge to the idea that art can ever bring resolution and harmony, "a sort of deliberately unproductive productiveness." The academic Mark Goble contends that this description fits *Psycho*, *The Birds*, and *Marnie*, in which Hitchcock pursued outsized commercial ambition with films that were darker, more ambiguous, and more provocative than any he had made, each one featuring a different sort of technical complexity, and challenging expectations of what a mainstream Hollywood movie could or should be. But no matter how pioneering or provocative Hitchcock thought himself, he was wedded to the movie business, and therefore incapable of using his films as a form of self-exile in the way Said believes Beethoven did with his final compositions. After Hitchcock's late style came a post-late style—or "too-late style," in Goble's words—a heavily self-referential period in which the master exhibited some of his enviable skills, but to no great effect. In trying to re-create the magic of times past, he drifted further from the present.

As Hitchcock was wont to say, style is the act of self-plagiarism. For his entire career, he returned to, and then innovated on, a tradition he—with vital contributions from his collaborators—created for himself. This is why a Hitchcock film becomes more fascinating the more one watches other Hitchcock films; each of his works is in deep conversation with the rest. After *Marnie*, the conversation became more of a circular monologue about the Hitchcock canon rather than an attempt to take it somewhere new. The clever elaborations that allowed Hitchcock to revisit old ground while staying fresh and vital had vanished. Finally, the master had run out of reinventions.

11

THE LONDONER

Hitchcock preferred to begin his fairy tales by giving the audience a sense of time and place—"once upon a time in a land far, far away." Sometimes, these openings were performed with real style and imagination, of a piece with the rest of the film. The opening sequence of *North by Northwest*, for instance, has Saul Bass's Mondrian-like graphics, beautiful in their clever, sleek economy, appearing on the side of a Madison Avenue skyscraper; the yellow cabs reflected in its glass panes tell us we could be nowhere else but 1950s New York. It was only Hitchcock's overspending that prevented him from realizing the opening he first devised, in which the camera would float through a window into the office of Roger Thornhill's advertising firm, where the credits would appear as designs for a new ad campaign, immersing us in Thornhill's world of pretense and artifice before a single line of dialogue was spoken.

It was a simple matter of story structure, said Hitchcock: begin in wide shot, and by degrees allow the audience to get closer and closer, until nestled right inside the heads of the characters. Repeatedly, he tried to take that principle to its conclusion, starting up in the clouds and homing in on a small pocket of action, some tiny scene that would turn out to be something scandalous. It wasn't until his penultimate film, *Frenzy*, that he managed to do it just as he'd envisaged. Against a stirring orchestral score, the camera swoops down a great stretch of the Thames, showing London, new and old, magisterial and modern. As the music fades, the camera zooms in on the bankside, where a pompous official boasts to a small crowd that the dank stretch of water on which the city's fortunes have been built will soon be "clear of industrial effluent, clear of detergents, clear of the waste products of our society." Then, a startled bystander points out a naked floating corpse, quickly identified as another victim of the "necktie murderer," a serial killer who strangles women with his own clothing before disposing of their bodies. Staring at the dead woman, the crowd gossips about the psychopath and his victims, with a mixture of morbid curiosity and terror.

For anyone with a knowledge of London's past, it's an obvious evocation of Jack the Ripper; for anyone with a knowledge of Hitchcock's past, it's a revival of *The Lodger*, which begins with the discovery of a female corpse by the side of the Thames and the reactions of gawking locals. Now in his seventies, Hitchcock was back on his old turf, the city that made him, telling the world that despite all this talk of a new, swinging London, this was the same glorious and rotten place it had always been, the greatest shithole on earth.

Like many before and since, Hitchcock was frequently guilty of eliding "British" with "English," using them interchangeably, saying one when he really meant the other. In his book *English Hitchcock*, Charles Barr astutely asserts that we get a better grasp of Hitchcock, either side of his move to Hollywood, by thinking of him and his work as more English than British. With few exceptions, the British characters in his films are from the south of England, reflecting a particular version of Englishness with which Hitchcock himself identified. To be more specific, Hitchcock was a Londoner, denizen of a global capital that was brasher, more cosmopolitan, and more outward-looking than anywhere else in the country.

The significance of London to Hitchcock can be parsed into two sections. First is Hitchcock in London: the life he had there prior to his relocation to Hollywood in 1939, where he developed the craft, skills, and reputation that facilitated his stellar rise in the United States—all greatly assisted by the talents of those in the London film industry with whom he worked.

Second is London in Hitchcock. Pre-Hollywood, Hitchcock used the British Isles as the precinct for most of his work. London was a notable setting in eleven films: *The Pleasure Garden*, *The Lodger*, *Downhill*, *The Ring*, *Blackmail*, *Murder!*, *Rich and Strange*, *Number Seventeen*, *The Man Who Knew Too Much*, *The 39 Steps*, and *Sabotage*. None of them are gritty, social tracts; some are as phantasmagorical as *North by Northwest* and *Psycho*. Yet all are wonderfully evocative of the London he knew—an environment that never left him. At the time of his death, he'd lived in California more than half his life. But he never knew that place, or anywhere else on the planet, in the way he knew London. His films are set in locations across the globe, but it's only London that appears to be in the bones of his characters, rather than as the backdrop of their existence. A notable exception could be made for the San Francisco of *Vertigo*. Even then, there's something of Hitchcock's London about it: a city of mists and winding streets, where history piles up on itself and, for all their nosiness, no one really knows anyone else.

Arguably, Hitchcock was not a native Londoner, as the Essex town of Leytonstone in which he was born would have then been too far east to have been enveloped by the city sprawl. He was touched when, late in life, he received a letter from the vice chancellor of the University of Essex, referring to him as "a son of Essex" in his offer of an honorary doctorate. These days, Leytonstone has another world-famous son, David Beckham, who embodies a type of emotionally expressive, seemingly classless Englishness that Hitchcock would have barely recognized as English at all. Yet Hitchcock still has a home there: tiled to the walls of the local Tube station are mosaics of legendary Hitchcock scenes, a kitsch but fitting tribute to a man whose lifelong interest in travel and transport began here as a boy, transfixed by the tram service that ran from Leytonstone into the wheezing city to the west, the place that became the Hitchcocks' home when Alfred was around six years old.

Through the years, Hitchcock's social awkwardness and his sense of himself as an outsider may have encouraged some to have spotted "otherness" in his life where it didn't exist. True, the family's Catholicism made them anomalous in a nation where followers of the Roman Catholic Church had faced centuries of persecution. Yet Limehouse, Poplar, and Stepney, the East London communities in which the family lived and worked, were among the most diffuse mix of ethnicities and religions to be found anywhere in western Europe. Moreover, it is inaccurate to suggest, as one biographer has, that the family was "not socially respectable." The Hitchcocks were an unremarkable lower-middle-class family, whom only the tiniest, most elite percentage of British society would have considered anything other than respectable. Likewise, though it's true that Hitchcock was sensitive about his relative lack of formal learning, he would have had a quality of education superior to most in the East End. It was only in the year of his birth that the age for leaving school was raised to twelve, but Hitchcock attended school until the eve of his fourteenth birthday, after which he studied engineering, followed by classes in art at the University of London, acquiring diverse skills that stayed with him for life. If his American friend John Houseman was correct in saying that Hitchcock bore "scars from a social system against which he was in perpetual revolt," it was not because he was a member of the downtrodden proletariat, but because of a frustration about the narrow existence prescribed to those from any particular class background, the sense that one must know one's place, which has long been the ambient hum of English life.

Accordingly, referring to Hitchcock as a Cockney (a label widely applied to him but never used by himself) is not without complication. His childhood London homes were in traditional Cockney terrain, but as with "Scouser" in Liverpool and "Geordie" in Newcastle, "Cockney" is loaded with social complexity. The word is often a designation of class identity as well as geographic location, and the Hitchcocks perhaps considered themselves a little too well-to-do to qualify as true "Cockney." Unquestionably, Hitchcock was an East Ender who grew up immersed in Cockney culture, felt kinship with it, and recognized all the associated attitudes, traits, and character types—but he was more among them than of them. England being a place where accents carry heavy associations, it's worth regarding that several of those who worked with him in London found his speech interesting because it was difficult to pin down. When Jack Cardiff first met him in 1930, Hitchcock spoke in a "plummy, posh-cockney voice." Four years earlier, according to June Tripp, he "spoke in a curious mixture of Cockney and North Country accents with a laboured stress on elusive aitches."

The primary way in which London shaped Hitchcock's Englishness, and his identity as a filmmaker, was that it instilled in him a thoroughly urban, modern outlook. The year 1899, when Hitchcock was born, fell in the middle of what have been described as the thirty most transformative years in London's history. Between the mid-1880s and the outbreak of World War I, the city experienced a rush of self-conscious modernity: "electrification, motorization, socialism, secularism, feminism, cosmopolitanism, family planning, suburbanization, mass entertainment, modern retailing, democracy, state intervention," as well as the arrival of London's notorious tabloid press, and panics about the uncontrollable spread of moral turpitude. The most obvious symptom of this rapid change was the thicket of humanity that clogged London's streets, particularly in the East End in which the young Hitchcock grew up and the West End in which he sought entertainment as an adult. During these three decades, the population soared by two and a half million; there were more than seven million Londoners in 1914, rising to eight and a half million by 1939—the year Hitchcock moved to Los Angeles—a figure unsurpassed until 2015. One East End resident of the early 1900s recalled its profusion of markets that "swarmed with people . . . you could have walked on the people's heads all the way from Commercial Road to Cable Street." That Hitchcock remembers the dense throng is viscerally evident in almost every film he set in London—down by the Thames in *The Lodger*; under the neon dazzle in *Blackmail*; in an overcrowded train on an unpleasant commute in *Rich and Strange*; amid the bustle of hustlers, hawkers, and shoppers in *Sabotage*.

In the 1950s, Hitchcock reflected on the impact of England's high-density population on the national character, and he concluded that it fostered an "inordinate regard for personal privacy." That was something he knew intimately well; Hitchcock, the inveterate self-publicist, performed a conjurer's trick of disappearing in plain sight, being constantly present while remaining aloof. Like Londoners of both his day and ours, he learned the trick of guarding his privacy in a pack, living cheek by jowl with countless people but connecting with barely any of them. It's a long-standing English style of disengagement, raised to Olympian heights in London, what Ralph Waldo Emerson called a "stony neglect, each of every other." Emerson observed that a happy product of this obsessive minding of one's own business was the English tolerance of eccentricity, but it made chipping through the cladding to reach the human being beneath a fearsome challenge. "In short," he wrote, "every one of these islanders is an island in himself, safe, tranquil, incommunicable. In a company of strangers, you would think him deaf; his eyes never wander from his table and newspaper." Aloofness and secrecy were part of Hitchcock's DNA, and he passed that on to his most intriguing urbanites. The inscrutable Roger Thornhill; the chic, mysterious drifters played by Tippi Hedren; the Manhattanites in *Rope* with their scandalous, secret lives; Jeff and his neighbors in *Rear Window*, all together and all alone in Greenwich Village. Islanders, these city dwellers, every one.

The need to keep oneself to oneself in the world's most populous city could result in explosions of indignity of a sort that fascinated, and horrified, Hitchcock, who was chilled by the prospect of public embarrassment. In his movies, he favored scenes of what one might term "an ecstasy of fumbling," to borrow Wilfred Owen's description of the panicked rush of bodies in the trenches of World War I. The climax of *The Lodger*, with a baying crowd squashed together in violent pursuit of a man they believe to be a murderer is the earliest example. Away from London, the awkward pressing of bodies is used for comic effect in the original version of *The Man Who Knew Too Much*, when a sudden accident on a Swiss ski slope knocks over a dozen people, creating an undignified jumble of limbs, noses in armpits, boots up arses. In a moment of tension rather than comedy, Paul Newman and Julie Andrews are pulled this way and that in *Torn Curtain* by an amorphous panicking crowd, rushing from a cry of "Fire!" in a crowded Berlin theater, a reprisal of a scene in *The 39 Steps* when a gunshot causes a stampede from an East End music hall of the type Hitchcock frequented as a child.

Sudden, shocking violence was a feature of the East End. The district was notorious for its pub fights and street brawls. An exact contemporary of Hitchcock's named Eileen Bailey recalled that in their neighborhoods violence broke out so frequently that locals "developed a kind of instinct, an embryo ability to tell when a fight was going to peter out or flare up into a scrap worth watching." Sometimes the fights were between women, who would "use their long hat-pins on each other's eyes." On the walls of his second home in Santa Cruz, Hitchcock hung five pictures by Thomas Rowlandson, an eighteenth-century artist who depicted the most scabrous, frenzied scenes of London life, two of which detail women grappling and clawing at each other in the street. Here is a London Hitchcock recognized: a rowdy place of endless entertainment in which an act of spontaneous violence was only ever a dodgy look away.

The London neighborhoods of Hitchcock's youth showed a double face to the world. On the one hand, they were insular and guarded, filled with intensely parochial communities that were conscious of a certain separateness, even from the rest of the city. On the other hand, the East End was the opening to a world beyond England. Limehouse had prodigiously busy docks and was home to many ethnic groups, including London's Chinatown, an enclave that inspired the fictional character Fu Manchu and D. W. Griffith's movie *Broken Blossoms* in the 1910s. Stepney was the center of the East End's Jewish community, one of the largest populations of Jews in western Europe. In the vicinity of both places ran the River Lea and the Thames, the historic conduit between London and the rest of the globe. If his recollections can be trusted, Hitchcock the child was acutely aware that the lazy old river was a superhighway of possibility. During the filming of *Frenzy* he recounted to the critic Charles Champlin that as a child of about nine, back in the days when his father

Opposite: Hitchcock beside the River Thames with Ingrid Bergman, October 1948.

supplied fish and poultry to ocean steamers, he was allowed to ride the steamboats all the way to Gravesend, at the mouth of the river, before climbing down the rope ladder with the pilot. Returning to the city had rekindled his old feelings for the ships: "The Royal Albert Docks, now there is romance." In a similarly nostalgic mood a year later, he told the journalist Margaret Pride that as a boy he became so obsessed with ships from all over the world that he could recognize them in silhouette, and would track their movements with pins stuck into a world map he kept in his bedroom.

Once Hitchcock entered the movie business, his horizons grew even wider, and his social circles ever more cosmopolitan. It was, after all, at the London branch of the American firm Famous Players-Lasky that he got his first job in the film industry, working alongside the American women who dominated the writing department. Michael Balcon, the man Hitchcock credited with launching his career, was the son of east European–Jewish émigrés and was married to a South African woman of Polish ancestry. When Balcon gave Hitchcock his chance to direct, it was in Germany not England that he did so, gaining a grasp of the German language along the way. Around this time, Hitchcock was part of the London Film Society, recently established by (among others) his friends and sometime collaborators Ivor Montagu and Sidney Bernstein as a forum in which to exhibit and discuss the best cinema from across Europe and to promote "the production of really artistic films" in Britain, "those which the trade deemed uncommercial or which the censor refused." The society announced itself to London on the front page of the *Daily Express* in May 1925, the same month that Hitchcock left for Germany to begin shooting his debut feature film. For Montagu, too, Germany was a beacon of cinematic art, and his initial aim was to screen titles that are now considered modernist classics, including Murnau's *Nosferatu*. Over time, though, it was Soviet cinema that really enthused him, and it was through Montagu and the Film Society that Hitchcock got to examine the "pure cinema" techniques of Russian filmmakers including Sergei Eisenstein and Vsevolod Pudovkin.

Montagu was also the man whom Balcon brought in to help refine *The*

Lodger, the film in which Hitchcock took all that he had absorbed in Germany and made a film in London about London, its people, and its menacing "fog," literal and metaphorical, under which this enormous beast of a city spluttered. It is a vivid projection of London, full of its humor, its dangers, and its folklore, and it provided a template for the Hitchcockian city: the glitter of civilization resting on a cesspit of human frailty. Decades after *The Lodger*, Hitchcock outlined the idea of a film he'd always wanted to make: "twenty-four hours in the life of a city . . . full of incidents, full of backgrounds." Uniting his ambivalent feelings about people, consumption, and urban life, the film would be "an anthology on food, showing its arrival in the city, its distribution, the selling, buying by people, the cooking, the various ways in which it's consumed. . . . So there's a cycle, beginning with the gleaming fresh vegetables and ending with the mess that's poured into the sewers. . . . Your theme might almost be the rottenness of humanity. You could take it through the whole city, look at everything, film everything." The film was never realized—though aspects of it appear in *Frenzy*—because Hitchcock couldn't find a way of hanging a story on the structure that would appeal to not just "the first row in the balcony or for a few seats on the aisle. It would have to be geared toward two thousand seats in the theater." Raised in a family of London merchants, Hitchcock knew full well the importance of catering to the customer.

The reaction to *The Lodger* from the British press could not have been more effusive. Hitchcock was lionized as the great hope of British cinema, "an English director of genius." The film elevated to the status of "mystery and magic what might easily have proved merely a sordid record of crime," wrote one reviewer. But what most enthused critics was that the setting for this dark fantasy was a place they recognized as home—the pockmarked capital of the British Empire. The apparent lack of authentically British subjects in British films was a constant source of worry in the interwar period. In December 1925, the film section of the *Daily Herald* reported on Hitchcock's trip to Germany to make *The Plea-*

sure Garden and The Mountain Eagle. In the same article, it was noted that Hitchcock's peer, the director Adrian Brunel, was slated to begin work on a film called London, "which will centre around life in the metropolis. It is good that at last someone should exploit the material in our own back-garden."

It wasn't only critics who were chomping for more homemade fare. The Cinematograph Films Act of 1927 was one of many measures designed to spur the production of more British films and wean the nation's picturegoers off Hollywood imports. The effort was part of a broader, existential panic about Britain and its empire in an age of rapid American growth. One of the several polemics about the threat of Americanization published in Britain in the 1920s was Americanism: A World Menace, published in 1922, the same year in which the BBC was founded, itself a project designed, in part, to inoculate its colonies from American culture, which was talked of as a virus.

Hollywood films were regarded as especially dangerous. Four weeks after The Lodger was released, G. A. Atkinson, a film reviewer for the Daily Express and the BBC, issued a stark warning about how young Britons were being turned into Americans, one Gloria Swanson flick at a time. "They talk America, think America, and dream America. We have several million people, mostly women, who, to all intent and purpose, are temporary American citizens." Serious public voices even raised the possibility of having the British film industry funded by the Ministry of Defence, as though Hollywood were a threat to national security.

Consequently, when Hitchcock began making imaginative and stylish films that dealt with life as lived on his home turf, he was lauded in some quarters as not just a wunderkind who had brought together the British, American, and German traditions in an exciting way but as a national hero; he was even name-checked by Lord Burnham in a speech in the Houses of Parliament about the importance of cinema to the continued strength of the empire. Downhill, the follow-up to The Lodger, appears risible today, with a thirty-something Ivor Novello playing a teenage schoolboy, but it drew praise from reviewers for its presentation of distinctive features of British life, including the London Underground and a public school. The following year, 1928, saw the release of *The Farmer's Wife*, Hitchcock's silent adaptation of a play about a rural widower in search of love. It's a charming film of visual imagination, technical accomplishment, and gentle comedy—but some reviewers were struck by its potential as propaganda. "Americans, I am sure, would pay money to see the beautiful Devonshire woodlands" after seeing the film, wrote the *Daily Mirror*. "It's been left to Alfred Hitchcock to put England on screen," added London's *Evening Standard*. "He has done so gloriously."

When *Blackmail* arrived in 1929, it solidified Hitchcock's status as a soldier at the front line in the battle against Americanization. Since the introduction of the talkies two years earlier, the threat from Hollywood was deemed to have worsened. From converting young Britons to the fashions and habits of Americans, the motion pictures were now encouraging them to ditch the King's English. But in *Blackmail*, the nation's brightest film talent had delivered a tale of modern London in accents and dialects that wouldn't make one's ears bleed. "Hear English as it should be spoken," ran an advertisement for the film. Among the reviews in Hitchcock's scrapbook were those by the *Daily Mail*, which declared his film a "British Triumph" and a "shock for the Americans," while the *London Evening News* praised it for being "All British—and with a London setting" and judged it equal to "anything Germany or America has achieved." A reviewer for *The Times* exceeded them all, congratulating Hitchcock for having made a British *Tosca*, and for "sweeping aside American traditions of speed and glamour."

The irony was that Hitchcock had embraced the "speed and glamour" of American popular culture as gleefully as anyone in Britain. Indeed, as a filmmaker, he considered himself to be working in a furrow plowed by Americans, from Edwin Porter to Cecil B. DeMille, via D. W. Griffith. "I'm American trained. . . . I never learned in the British studios," he told one interviewer, proudly recalling that a review of one of his early films praised it for its thoroughly American qualities. In the 1920s, Hitchcock was a member of the jokingly named Hate Club, in which he and others in the industry would gather to review—and usually lambast—the latest British releases.

Hitchcock riding the London Underground in *Blackmail*.

When we think of Hitchcock in this context, his cultural significance extends beyond film, and we can identify connections with other
English or British popular artists whose work was a manifestation of,
and a response to, American cultural influence. There's an interesting
parallel with the Beatles. Like Hitchcock, they served a creative apprenticeship in Germany at a time of cultural renewal following a cataclysmic
war. Both injected their crowd-pleasing work with esoteric or avant-
garde influences, greedily absorbed from around the world; and both
used American popular culture as a means of circumventing the stric-

tures of the class system at moments of imperial decline when old ideas about British identity were thrown into flux.

The introduction of sound immediately allowed Hitchcock to deepen his depiction of life in the British Isles. Though he always insisted that he remained, at root, a silent filmmaker, accents, jokes, rhythms of speech, and ambient noise enabled him to create more rounded characters and textured settings in his 1930s films that domestic audiences would instantly recognize—whether it was the jury room of a murder trial, a crowded market, or a family dining table. He tackled weightier themes, too, issues of pressing topicality. *The Skin Game* dealt with class dynamics in the industrialized north of England, and *Juno and the Paycock* adapted Sean O'Casey's celebrated play about an impoverished Dublin family struggling its way through the Irish Civil War.

Neither of those films, however, quite have the brilliant flashes of social observation found in Hitchcock's London-bound talkies, three of which were scripted by Charles Bennett, who helped Hitchcock use his eye and ear for authentic background detail as a storytelling tool. The action in *The 39 Steps*, for example, is catalyzed by a music-hall audience of wisecracking Londoners, smoking, smirking, and heckling as they shout out sarcastic questions to the performer Mr. Memory, who holds explosive secrets in the depths of his encyclopedic mind. When a gunshot suddenly turns the place into a scene of mass panic, a couple of young strangers, a man and a woman, are brought together and end up back at the man's home, hinting at the kind of illicit, unexpected liaisons that can happen in a megacity at night. In the murky London of *The Man Who Knew Too Much*, the action leads us—with grinning irony—into a sun worshippers' temple, and it climaxes in a scene inspired by the 1911 Siege of Sidney Street, a dramatic event instantly familiar to Londoners of the time, in which Winston Churchill joined armed police in a gunfight battle against anarchist revolutionaries holed up in a house in the East End. The characters, too, seem plucked from the London of Hitchcock's experience: loud, jocular Cockneys; plodding police constables; eccentric shopkeepers; sardonic smart-asses more adept at keeping secrets than showing emotion; a smattering of ethnically indeterminate "foreign-ers," expressing the truth that London was the capital of Britain but also a gateway to the rest of the planet.

Hitchcock undercut any tub-thumping jingoism by pointing out that in putting his homeland on screen in such a way, he was emulating his con-temporaries abroad, especially in America, that supposed scourge of Brit-ish culture. The key to developing first-rate, distinctively British films, he said, was to follow Hollywood's lead in producing commercial films about ordinary, everyday people. He complained that London film cul-ture focused almost exclusively on grinding poverty or the wealthy elite. Instead, he wanted to see people from his background, "men who leap on buses, the girls who pack into the Tube, the commercial travellers . . . the cinema queues, the *palais de danse* crowds . . . the fellows who love gar-dening, the chaps who lounge in pubs . . . girls who catch their fingers in doors and say what they feel." Unlike "stodgy" British films, "Ameri-cans use imaginative backgrounds. They give us pictures about telephone exchanges, icemen, newspaper reporters, police cars, repair gangs," all "with a freshness that is lacking in our drawing room school of drama."

Hitchcock's interest in social authenticity coincided with the British Documentary Film Movement of the 1930s. Unofficially led by the pro-ducer and director John Grierson, the movement was cinema's iteration of a wider British trend of the interwar years, in which wealthy middle-class figures dedicated themselves to exposing the truth about the lives of working people. A documentarian, remarked one of those within the movement, "must be a gentleman, a Socialist, have a university edu-cation, [and] a private income." This was not Hitchcock, who was only a couple of rungs up the ladder from the working-class people being documented. Within London's cultural establishment, the documen-tary films of Grierson et al. came to be regarded as the gold standard of British cinema; Hitchcock's thrillers of the 1930s were recognized for their inventiveness but dismissed as inconsequential. Grierson himself sneered at Hitchcock as "the best director, the slickest craftsman . . . of unimportant films."

But Hitchcock's influences, objectives, and achievements were closer to the highbrow, polemical documentarians than is often acknowledged. As with Hitchcock's best London films, the documentaries Grierson directed—*Drifters* (1929); *Granton Trawler* (1934)—rely on montage and inventive use of sound, have an interest in juxtaposing tradition and modernity, and exhibit the inspiration of the "city symphony" film genre of the 1920s. Grierson, not averse to staging scenes in his documentaries, used fiction to underpin his portrayal of authenticity; Hitchcock used authenticity to underpin his fiction. The overlap between the documentarians' interests and Hitchcock's is smartly summed up by *Housing Problems*, a revelatory documentary produced by Ruby Grierson, John's sister, about the slums of the East End, which featured working-class people talking candidly, straight to the camera, about their lives. Hitchcock had never lived in the slums, but he had grown up with them on his doorstep, and thirteen years earlier he'd attempted to make what would have been his debut feature, *Number Thirteen*, a work of fiction about the experiences of people living in a building created by the Peabody Trust, a philanthropic organization committed to tackling London's housing crisis. It's healthy to be skeptical of claims Hitchcock made in the thirties about earnestly wanting to work in documentary. This may have been a way of trying to assuage feelings of insecurity about his escapist fantasies when compared to the weighty, "serious" business of the documentarian intellectuals. However, it's worth noting that, in 1969, Hitchcock hosted a Scottish television documentary honoring Grierson's life and work, suggesting a genuine admiration for the aims and methods of the documentary movement, which sought to make British film distinctive by turning to the lived experiences of its population.

In his career as a director in London, Hitchcock did his best to put the world he knew on the screen: pet shops, theaters, buses, boxing matches, fairgrounds, museums, churches, cinemas, pubs, marketplaces, railway carriages, boardinghouses, dentists' offices, prison cells, tearooms, tenement houses, and artists' studio flats—all were intrinsic parts of his plots. He avoided addressing the meaty issues of the day head-on, yet his London had authenticity in both large ways and small. Raymond Durgnat, who grew up in London in the 1930s, thought Hitchcock's projection of the city, despite its adventures and fancies, was sharper and more truthful than anything produced by the famous Ealing Studios' films of the 1950s. In an age when one "couldn't just point a T.V. camera in the street" to capture reality, Hitchcock's gimlet eye brought details of contemporary urban England to life. "He had first to notice certain details, love them enough to remember and to recreate them, and lastly to slide them deftly into a thriller context. . . . They are in no sense pebbles; they are cherished like jewels." Even among the relatively small but ardent batch of Hitchcock fans in America at the time, the evocation of this gray city of eccentric people and surprising jolts of action was part of the fascination. As Norman Lloyd remembered, "You would go to these little theaters in New York, you know, the Thalia or someplace and see a Hitchcock film in black and white on a rainy day in New York; you'd come out thinking you were wearing a trench coat and all of that."

Having been so championed by the popular press, and even by some avant-garde outlets, as the embodiment of a great British cinema, Hitchcock's move to America caused no little irritation, even some hurt. The timing of his departure, in 1939, just before Britain declared war on Germany, only exacerbated the sense of betrayal. Michael Balcon, the man who had done so much to nurture Hitchcock's talent, took out space in a London newspaper to flay his former protégé for apparently deserting his country in its hour of need, referring to him haughtily as a "plump young junior technician." Most refrained from making the issue personal, but the critic C. A. Lejeune observed that a lot of her peers believed Hitchcock "had sold his soul to Hollywood. . . . There would be no more Hitchcock pictures, only Hollywood pictures made by Hitchcock." London Hitchcock, so the thinking went, had been a bespoke maker of exquisite Swiss watches, each with his hallmark engraved on the back; Hollywood Hitchcock was bound to be a factory foreman, churning out Model Ts on a relentless production line. Both were remarkable objects, but only one was a thing of beauty bearing the soul of its creator.

There is merit in that argument, as Hitchcock's first Hollywood movie, *Rebecca*, shows. In many ways, the film was a professional triumph. Lejeune said Hitchcock's detractors in London would have to eat their words: "his first Hollywood picture is in every way his best." Although Hitchcock's opinion on the film's quality vacillated, he recognized that it was a crucial step in developing his career. In his words, it was "a completely British picture," with an all-English cast, set mainly in England, and based on source material by an English author. Yet it was not like the depictions of England that audiences back home had come to expect from Hitchcock. Finely observed authenticity had slunk to the background, replaced by a more generic sense of Englishness, all stately home sternness and patrician hauteur. Hitchcock put this down to the demands of Selznick, and the influence of the film's American screenwriter Robert Sherwood, who gave the script a "broader viewpoint than it would have had if made in Britain." In fact, *Rebecca* was of a piece with Hollywood fashions. English and British films, such as the ones Hitchcock had been making since the silent days, tended to do modest business at the US box office, but romantic American fantasies about life across the Atlantic—almost always set in the past—were hugely popular with the public and the critics. Britons themselves could be unkind about these films. Graham Greene mocked Twentieth Century-Fox's *Lloyd's of London* (1937) by remarking that the "name of England is so freely on the characters' lips that we recognize at once an American picture." According to one scholar, between 1930 and 1945, Hollywood churned out more than one hundred and fifty "British" films. Hitchcock made a significant contribution to the genre: three of his first four Hollywood films were set in his homeland, including *Foreign Correspondent*, in which a straight-shooting American journalist battles an anti-British spy ring as the grip of war tightens on the sceptered isle. The movie helped bolster the wartime myth of London's "Blitz spirit," and was nominated for Best Picture at the Academy Awards in 1941, a category won by *Rebecca*.

Eighty years later, it seems little has changed. Britain's place in the film world is still to present tales of kings and queens, a vanished past, or fantasy worlds that have never existed. The first British film to win an Oscar was *The Private Life of Henry VIII* in 1933. The travails of English aristocrats remain Academy Award catnip—*The Queen*, *Darkest Hour*, *The King's Speech*, *The Favourite*, all spring to mind. The chances of a British version of *Moonlight*, *Manchester by the Sea*, or *Three Billboards Outside Ebbing, Missouri* receiving the same attention are remote. Those from communities whose lives are underrepresented on British screens—Idris Elba, John Boyega, Thandie Newton, for example—often leave for Hollywood in order to reinvent themselves as on-screen Americans. In Hitchcock's day, the Londoner Charles Chaplin made the same journey, as did Bristolian Archie Leach, metamorphosizing into a magnificent, rootless alien who went by the name Cary Grant.

So much of what Hitchcock learned and developed during his two decades in the London film industry he took with him to America, and repurposed it for Hollywood with stunning results—from the narrative formula of the Hitchcock chase thriller and the MacGuffin plot device to his manipulation of the press. One thing he left at home was his sharp take on place and the characters who inhabit them. Shortly before he left for Hollywood, Hitchcock said, "You've got to live twenty years in a country before you can express its idiom." It didn't take him that long to engage with American society in his films, but when he did, it came from the perspective of a perceptive outsider, not from somebody whose pores had been clogged with the place since the day he was born.

In front of American audiences, Hitchcock exploited his Englishness. The displays of deadpan reserve—almost flamboyant in their denial of emotion—the sharp-tongued drollery, the fastidious attention to doing things *properly*, these all played upon his Old World origins. At times, it was knowing parody: he appeared on television with a bowler hat and umbrella, and posed for photographs reading *The Times* or taking tea on set. In interviews and articles he explained himself, often rather plausibly, in terms of his nationality. His understanding of violence, sex, food, humor, art, literature, clothing, child-rearing, home furnishings, sports, politics, world history, all derived from the central, inescapable fact of his Englishness, he said. Curiously, in her biography of her mother, Pat Hitchcock wrote that while Alma kept her native accent, Hitchcock lost his. Perhaps she meant that the glottal stop and rounded vowels of East London became diminished in his speech over time. Or, maybe in private, as an off-duty professional Britisher, he sounded more American. Either way, most who heard him speak on late-night talk shows or in the weekly skits on his television programs would identify him as he encouraged them to: a gray, old-fashioned Englishman amusingly out of place in the ceaseless sunshine of California.

Even as he wore his Englishness on his sleeve, Hitchcock resisted unalloyed patriotism. As with his size and shape, being English was a stubborn fact of his existence, but not necessarily a source of pride. He was happy to poke fun at the English for their cult of tradition, their cage of class, and their knee-jerk anti-American prejudices. In this, the Londoner in Hitchcock reappeared: the cosmopolitan, skeptical piss-taker, individualistic to the point of contrariness, rooted as an oak tree in the English soil, but wary of flags, salutes, and oaths of allegiance. This ambivalence about national identity manifested itself in his eventual decision to swap his British citizenship for American, which he did in 1955, five years after Alma had done so. To the friend who drove him there, he explained that he was nervous about the ceremony because "the Hitchcock name goes back almost to the beginning of the British Empire. It isn't easy giving up a lifetime surrounded with British tradition and history."

Still, lightening oneself of a little of that baggage could be liberating; he was quietly proud to be an American citizen, because, to him at least, it meant being a citizen of the world. He loved that America is a "polyglot country. I often tell people, there are no Americans, it's full of foreigners."

A world full of foreigners rather neatly describes a feeling that works its way through Hitchcock's Hollywood canon, in which location and identity are regularly smudged to a blur, and accents roam freely, sometimes absurdly so. In *The Birds*, the first person Melanie meets in the tiny, insular Californian community of Bodega Bay sounds so much like a New Englander that it seems deliberately disorienting. In *Foreign Correspondent*, Laraine Day and Joel McCrea encounter the Latvian ambassador in London who, inconceivably, speaks not a word of English, German, or French, so Day talks to him in his mother tongue; handily she knows "just enough Latvian to get about." Later in the film, a little Dutch girl assists some of her compatriots by translating English into their native language, but does so with such a strong American accent that one wonders whether she might be better off having a stab at Latvian herself. The Rutland family in *Marnie* is an upper-crust Philadelphian clan as old as the Liberty Bell, but its eldest son, played by Sean Connery, speaks like a born-and-bred Edinburgher. Ingrid Bergman had kittens trying to modulate her Swedish-American-English into an Irish brogue for the Australian-based *Under Capricorn*. Her on-screen husband, Joseph Cotten, didn't bother; Hitchcock was happy for the script to be altered, switching the character's origins from Dublin to Virginia, Cotten's home state.

Topaz is a bad picture, but it's the ultimate example of Hitchcock's cosmopolitan and internationalist outlook, with its united nations of cast and characters. Indeed, the United Nations was a topic of great interest to Hitchcock. It was at the site of the UN building in New York that Cary Grant's Roger Thornhill—the apotheosis of Hitchcock's unplaceable globalist—witnesses the murder that sends him on the run in *North by Northwest*. But Hitchcock had toyed with the idea of designing a film around the United Nations several years earlier, when he exchanged letters, and had at least one meeting, with Mogens Skot-Hansen, a UN representative from Denmark, about the ways in which Hitchcock could lend his talents to depicting the organization's work on screen. Thirteen years later, in the spring of 1964, he agreed to direct one of six feature-length episodes of an ambitious television drama series designed to sell the United Nations to the American public. Press reports of the time suggest it was a surprising move for a commercial, nonpolemical director such as Hitchcock, on account of the "widespread organized opposition to the U.N. in this country."[*]

---

[*] Hitchcock's episode was to celebrate the work of the World Health Organization. He dropped out over scheduling pressures and concerns regarding the quality of the script written by Richard Condon. Ultimately, four episodes were made by other directors and aired on ABC.

Of course, Hitchcock did cling to his English cultural roots in the making of his Hollywood movies. He turned time and again to English source material, English screenwriters, and English actors. He also returned to London as a venue for production, and three of his 1950s movies were set in the city. In *Stage Fright*, a little of the Hitchcock feel for Londoners comes back: Kay Walsh is deliciously good as the sour, dyspeptic Nellie, a pub gossip and resentful maid for a sultry cabaret star (played by Marlene Dietrich), who seems like the kind of character that Hitchcock and Alma had encountered a hundred times before. But, on the whole, an authentic reflection of London ceased to be a key part of Hitchcock's films and public image. Neither has Hitchcock's take on London and England left much of a cinematic legacy. The best of the Bond films—an obvious heir to Hitchcock—have something of the wit of early Hitchcock, but the franchise has only ever offered a flattened, thinned-out version of Englishness, akin to Hitchcock's Hollywood years, devoid of the beautifully observed gems that punctuate *The Man Who Knew Too Much*, *Sabotage*, and *The Lady Vanishes*.

Perhaps it's understandable, then, that as Hitchcock's Hollywood legend has mushroomed and obscured the earlier chapters of his career, acknowledgment of his role in the story of twentieth-century London has dwindled. Today, at the site of Gainsborough Studios, where he made some of his earliest films, sits an enormous bust of Hitchcock. But it's not the head of the young Londoner who toiled to make his name, rather the older, jowly, glum-looking man from California who came to define the popular idea of Hitchcock. The importance of his London years, to Hitchcock's career as well as to the history of the city, is consistently overlooked, even among those who know a vast amount about both. In recent social and cultural histories of interwar London, Hitchcock barely makes an appearance, despite being one of the city's most famous, commercially successful, and influential creative figures of the last hundred years. Amid a galaxy of other Londoners—from Aldous Huxley and the Kinks to Peter Stringfellow and Leon Trotsky—Jerry White's enthralling book, *London in the Twentieth Century* (2001), carries not a single mention of Hitchcock's name. Juliet Gardiner's equally riveting chronicle of

A Londoner to his bones. Hitchcock, 1972.

British life, *The Thirties: An Intimate History* (2010), mentions Hitchcock in one paragraph, less than the space given to John Grierson and the Left Book Club, and about the same as Hitchcock's sometime collaborator, Charles Laughton, who won an Oscar for his star turn in *The Private Life of Henry VIII*. In other works, aristocratic socialites, such as the Mitford sisters and the so-called Bright Young People, are used as ciphers of the interwar decades, while Hitchcock, whose best London films filled cinemas and, in their idiosyncratic way, engaged with the reality of modern urban life as lived by millions, is thought of as an entity unto himself, somehow not entirely plugged into the life of the city. It seems that even to scholars of cultural history, there is an assumption that Hitchcock's London period was merely the apprenticeship of a master craftsman whose work tells us little, if anything, about the times in which he lived, or the more celebrated work he would go on to create.

It's redolent of the kind of marginalization that he experienced first-hand. Laurence Olivier was eight years younger than Hitchcock, yet he received a knighthood "for services to stage and film" in 1947, just two weeks after his fortieth birthday. Similarly, David Lean, who made his name in epics about heroes and adventurers of the British Empire, and in adaptations of Dickens novels, was nine years Hitchcock's junior and didn't direct his first film until 1942, yet he was elevated to Commander of the British Empire in 1953. When Hitchcock was offered the same honor in 1962 (a year after John Grierson had been given his), he declined it, probably because he felt insulted that it did not sufficiently recognize his achievements. Back in London on the filming of *Frenzy* in 1971—a few months after receiving the Légion d'honneur from the French government—he told Charles Champlin that after thirty years out of the country, the British honors system seemed as baffling to him as ever. "I've never really understood titles. You become Sir George. But who ever really calls you Sir George? Waiters in good restaurants and your servants at home. To your friends, you're still good old Stinky." Still, that didn't prevent him from accepting a knighthood a few months before his death, even though the fact that he was no longer a subject of the Crown meant he was not technically entitled to call himself "Sir." When asked by reporters why he thought it had taken the queen so long to honor him, he shrugged that she probably had other things on her mind.

Despite his self-exile, Hitchcock never took his eye off Britain's film industry. During the fifties and sixties, he watched the "kitchen-sink" films such as *Saturday Night and Sunday Morning*, *Room at the Top*, *Look Back in Anger*, *A Taste of Honey*, and *Billy Liar*, which put working-class and lower-middle-class life on screen in a way that Hitchcock had fantasized about many years earlier. *Frenzy* attempted to capture something of that atmosphere, set in a version of the London Hitchcock had grown up in, one of greengrocers and market traders, publicans and barmaids, coarse humor and an edge of menace. Yet *Frenzy* also shows us how the London in Hitchcock's core was not quite the city of 1972, the home of Marc Bolan and *Spare Rib* magazine. During the scripting of the remake of *The Man Who Knew Too Much* in 1955, Hitchcock noted certain small inaccuracies that had strayed into John Michael Hayes's script, including in the sections set in London: the conduct of the receptionists at Claridge's, the finer points of English reserve, the demeanor of MI6 agents. He also questioned the Americanisms Hayes had put in the mouths of the English characters and recommended changing them—but then added the caveat, "I am out of touch with the English." That is plainly evident in *Frenzy*. The London here is like an alternate reality, one in which the fog has lifted, fashions and technology have moved on, but in every other respect it has been frozen in 1939. Arthur La Bern, the author of the novel *Goodbye Piccadilly, Farewell Leicester Square*, on which the film was based, found *Frenzy* "distasteful," and watching it was a "most painful experience." He groaned at the dialogue, too, an "amalgam of an old Aldwych farce" and various hackneyed British television series. He lamented the absence of his "authentic London characters."

Barbara Leigh-Hunt, the last of Hitchcock's slaughtered London blondes, agrees that there was a discrepancy between the London of the 1970s and the city that Hitchcock attempted to evoke: "England had changed since he had lived and worked here. The club that my character was supposed to go to, that sort of thing didn't happen anymore, and women didn't dress like that anymore. I felt it was dated." But reviewing the film in 2018, she was no longer bothered by the clunky anachronisms. "So much time has passed, it doesn't matter now." As the seventies drift into the waters of distant memory, what Hitchcock's farewell to London gives us isn't an accurate record of that moment in its history, but something equally vital: a concentrate of Hitchcock's London, a feeling of the city untethered from time.

12

THE MAN OF GOD

In the final year of his life, Hitchcock's health declined precipitously. For Alma and him, the previous decade had been increasingly testing. During the filming of *Frenzy* in 1971, Alma suffered a stroke, followed by another, far more debilitating attack in 1976, the year Hitchcock's final film, *Family Plot*, was released. Her ill-health left her largely housebound and in need of round-the-clock nursing. Hitchcock was devastated. For fifty years Alma had been his closest friend, constant collaborator, and emotional counterbalance. Her decline had him fretting for her well-being but also scared of his own vulnerability. He did his best to tend to her but was burdened by his problems with arthritis, his heart, and, lately, his kidneys, all likely exacerbated by excessive drinking, which made him tired, confused, and irritable. As his mortality came into ever sharper focus, the familiar pose of equanimity shattered. Several family members, colleagues, and friends saw him cry in fear that Alma might be slipping away; he asked some of them how much longer they thought he had left to live.

During those years of Hitchcock's physical and creative decline, his presence in contemporary cinema was maintained by his disciples. So many classic seventies films bear his thumbprint, from *Don't Look Now* to *Jaws* to *Carrie* and the Bond franchise. Martin Scorsese, arguably the most accomplished American filmmaker of the last fifty years, credits Hitchcock as a key influence, especially on *Taxi Driver*, released a matter of weeks before *Family Plot* opened in theaters.[*] Travis Bickle might be an East Coast cousin of Norman Bates, or perhaps the charmless, estranged son of Uncle Charlie; the New York he inhabits is as dangerous and sordid as the London of *The Lodger*, oozing with violent misogyny, male rage, and disgust for the filth of the city. Beneath the patina of character and setting, Hitchcock's commitment to showing over telling is also shared by Scorsese. "The Hitchcock pictures I like looking at repeatedly, repeatedly, repeatedly," Scorsese told Roger Ebert, "often without the sound." On *Taxi Driver*, it was Hitchcock's ability to silently express the emotional experience of Catholic identity that most influenced him. "*The Wrong Man* . . . has more to do with the camera movements in *Taxi Driver* than any other picture I can think of. It's such a heavy influence because of the sense of guilt and paranoia."

In May 1979 it became obvious, even to Hitchcock, that making another film was an unreachable fantasy. He abruptly closed his office at Universal, leaving his devoted, long-serving staff suddenly unemployed. Life away from work proved an oxymoron. After a short while, he began turning up as though he'd never left, always in the same suit-and-tie uniform, pushing bits of paper around a desk, getting a haircut and a shoeshine, receiving the odd guest to hear his patter. On January 3, 1980, he received his knighthood in a special ceremony arranged, fittingly, on a Universal sound stage. The following day, the biographer Gilbert Harrison dropped by to interview him about Thornton Wilder. Afterward, Harrison reflected that he'd encountered "Alfred Hitchcock," the myth rather than the man:

> His face was florid. He was balding but not entirely bald. The main thing about him is his bulk. He seemed like a tuskless walrus dressed in a well-cut black suit with vest, white shirt and tie, propped up in a high-back swivel desk chair. And, out of that bulk

[*] Coincidentally, the male lead in *Family Plot* is also a disgruntled cab driver, George Lumley, played by Bruce Dern.

which remained largely immobile during the interview, came this low, carefully modulated, middle-class English accent. There was little spontaneity in what he said. He chose his words carefully, and it seemed to me he had said them all before. It was as if he was remembering some script that he had written earlier. It was a little difficult to keep him on Wilder, who I think did not much interest him, and off of himself and his work.

Hitchcock died of renal failure on the morning of April 29, 1980. His funeral took place at the Church of the Good Shepherd in Beverly Hills. A few days later he was cremated, his ashes scattered over the Pacific Ocean, a conspicuously unconventional farewell for a Catholic born in the nineteenth century. Though the Vatican had allowed cremations since 1963, the idea was that one's ashes should still be interred; to do otherwise would be a denial of the Resurrection. On June 3, a memorial Requiem Mass was held at Westminster Cathedral, the mother church of the Roman Catholic Church in England and Wales. The first hymn was the signal anthem of England's late nineteenth-century Catholic revival, "Firmly I Believe and Truly." Quite how firm or true was Hitchcock's belief is an enduring mystery.

The severe discipline of his school days may have filled Hitchcock with fears and dark fixations, but he admitted that his time at St Ignatius College left more constructive legacies, too. Above all, he believed that a Jesuitical education had a profound influence on his ability to think, as it "shapes the mind into given reasoning powers." Echoing James Joyce, who thought his Jesuit teachers taught him how "to arrange things in such a way that they become easy to survey and to judge," Hitchcock said that St Ignatius College bequeathed him "organization, control, and, to some degree, analysis." By "reasoning powers" and "analysis," he was presumably referring to his enviable ability for thinking through a problem and learning lessons from it. The Jesuits' reliance on casuistry—a method of moral reasoning in which one seeks to extract broad principles from specific cases—is apparent in Hitchcock's theories on how to manipulate an audience. The death of Stevie in *Sabotage*, for example, taught Hitchcock that it is okay to murder a child in a film, but not when the audience is expecting the kid to be saved. His rules for creating suspense, developing character, using montage, and all the other tenets of the filmmaking gospel according to Alfred around which he built his public image had a casuistic stem.

Biographers have pointed out that St Ignatius College would almost certainly have inculcated in Hitchcock the lengthy tale of Catholic persecution in England, which might have dampened his patriotism and intensified his fascination with torture, pain, and suffering. Equally, he would have been versed in the astonishing history of the Jesuits' long mission to spread the word of the Bible, which led its members to faraway lands. Exotic tales of the Jesuit missionaries who made scientific breakthroughs, won favor in the court of the Chinese emperor, mapped the Mississippi, and trekked through the Amazon were precisely the kinds of stories that would have fired the imagination of a young Alfred Hitchcock daydreaming of a world away from Leytonstone and Limehouse. To be a part of the Jesuitical mission was to be part of an exciting adventure that sought to explode mysteries and open up new vistas. Simon Callow, the actor and author, was educated at Catholic schools in London during the fifties and sixties and envied those boys taught by the Jesuits. "They epitomized the romance of the priesthood which still held such a seductive power for the young and religiously inclined," he says. "They were fearless explorers, both geographically and intellectually . . . fiercely intelligent, practical, effective, radical," adjectives that could easily be used to describe Hitchcock and his approach to moviemaking.

The sense of corporate belonging embraced an artistic sensibility, too. One Jesuit critic believes that Hitchcock's connection with German expressionism did not come as a thunderbolt revelation after watching the films of Lang and Murnau, or from visiting Munich and Berlin at the zenith of the Weimar renaissance; rather, it flowed naturally from "the religious and educational atmosphere of St Ignatius College prior to World War One," which was "heavily baroque and was congruent with the new wave of Expressionism." One should add that English cultural life in the years of Hitchcock's childhood and young adulthood was more informed by Catholicism than at any moment since the early seventeenth century, especially in London. In 1850, the Catholic hierarchy in England had been reestablished after an absence of nearly three hundred years, coinciding with a famous Royal Academy exhibition of paintings by the Pre-Raphaelite Brotherhood, which shocked establishment critics with their unapologetic "Romishness." The Pre-Raphaelites fed into a broad revival of Catholic influence in English art that rumbled throughout the late nineteenth and early twentieth centuries, discernible in painting, neo-Gothic architecture, and the Arts and Crafts movement, as well as in the numbers of prominent artistic figures who converted to the Catholic faith, among them G. K. Chesterton (one of Hitchcock's favorite writers), Gerard Manley Hopkins, Evelyn Waugh, Graham Greene, Aubrey Beardsley, and, on his deathbed, Oscar Wilde. In Hitchcock's home city, this Anglo-Catholic influence, with its notes of ornamentation, theatricality, and otherworldliness, gradually asserted itself from the mid-nineteenth century, and flourished in locations such as the interiors of the Houses of Parliament (designed by the Catholic convert Augustus Pugin); Westminster Cathedral (the location of an attempted murder in *Foreign Correspondent*), completed in 1903; and the Brompton Oratory, the capital's second-largest Catholic church, where Alfred and Alma were married in 1926.

In the most superficial sense, many of Hitchcock's films certainly have a *look* that could be described as Catholic. In the 1950s and '60s, his use of color as symbol bordered on the liturgical, especially in the way he selected colors for his leading ladies' outfits. He explained how he designed a color scheme for Grace Kelly in *Dial M for Murder* that expressed her descent from vibrant soul of femininity to nervous and broken victim. She first appeared in "a bright red dress, her face in full natural makeup. From there, her clothes went to brick red, then to pale brown shades. Her face kept pace, becoming paler and paler until at the end her face and clothes were completely drab." The following four films he made for Paramount in the 1950s—*Rear Window*, *To Catch a Thief*,

The Trouble with Harry, and *The Man Who Knew Too Much*—are similarly crammed with symbolic use of color. With the autumnal colors of Vermont, and Shirley MacLaine's vivid purple outfit, there are shots in *The Trouble with Harry* that look like moving stained-glass windows. Several scenes in *To Catch a Thief*, bursting with the colors of the Côte d'Azur, put one in mind of Henri Matisse's "cut-outs" from the 1940s and '50s, which were inspired by the same region of France, and by Matisse's reawakening to God and the Catholic Church.

A partiality for the vibrant, the dramatic, and the baroque are features of a recognizably Catholic aesthetic, but they are only surface, the same visual elements of Catholicism harvested by Madonna for her videos and Dolce & Gabbana for their handbags. Gauging the depth of Hitchcock's faith is a trickier matter. Unquestionably, he was, as boy and man, gripped by the ceremonial aspects of religion, the liturgies and sacraments, which appealed to each of his senses, as well as his adoration of the dramatic and the spectacular. Elements of this crop up in his film work; religious vestments, ceremonies, and places of worship appear in numerous Hitchcock movies that don't have any explicit religious subject. In a neat bit of bookending, Hitchcock placed a prayer scene early in his first movie, *The Pleasure Garden*, and made the abduction of a bishop during a church service a pivotal moment in his final film, *Family Plot*, a movie about births, deaths, marriages, and knotted connections between this world and the next. In the intervening fifty-one films (and hundreds of television episodes), the appurtenances of religion are brought into the frame at the slightest opportunity, evidence of their prominence in Hitchcock's experience of the world, and in the public's perception of him. In his ill-fated television collaboration with Hitchcock, Richard Condon had crowbarred some nuns into the script because he thought it seemed suitably Hitchcockian. Hitchcock said he appreciated the gesture but that on this occasion the wimples and cinctures detracted from the story. In his youth, Hitchcock was an enthusiastic participant in Catholic ceremonies, to the extent that he became an acolyte, assisting with the service of the altar, despite not knowing the correct Latin responses to recite during Mass. It was the tactile, sensual drama of the ceremony that captivated him: the surplice, the candles, the bells, and the incense, all deployed before a captive audience in an atmospheric setting that he loved, like the cinema, the theater, the courtroom, and the dining room of a good restaurant. The Jesuit priest George Tyrrell would have understood. Tyrrell was raised Protestant but began a conversion to Catholicism in 1879 when he experienced Mass, among a mainly Irish congregation, at a Catholic church in London. Through the ragged theater of the ceremony, Tyrrell felt connected to the early Christians: "The sense of reality! Here was the old business, being carried on by the old firm, in the old ways; here was continuity, that took one back to the catacombs." There's something pleasingly Hitchcockian about this "sense of reality" that isn't fastened to the dry world of fact, but has the power to transport one through time and space.

This is the identifiably Catholic idea that can be found in Hitchcock's aesthetic sensibility: surface beauty is transcendental, a gateway to another dimension of experience. "Catholics live in an enchanted world," explains Father Andrew Greeley in his description of the Catholic imagination, in which all objects—not just rosary beads and bottles of holy water—are sacramental, "a revelation of the presence of God." Some of the most famous shots in Hitchcock's films display objects that seem to be imbued with forces, good and evil, beyond the physical realm. Think of the moment in *Notorious* in which Hitchcock's camera swoops down across a vast hallway to close in on the key Ingrid Bergman holds in her hand, or when Johnnie Aysgarth (Cary Grant's rogue in *Suspicion*) walks portentously upstairs with a magically luminescent glass of milk, carrying it as a young Hitchcock would have carried a votive candle in church. *Strangers on a Train* has enough possessed objects to fill the Lourdes Grotto: the two pairs of shoes that bring about Guy and Bruno's chance meeting; the cigarette lighter that ties them together; the women's glasses that arouse and enrage Bruno. In *Psycho*, it seems that every-

Opposite: Hitchcock with a nun (the actress Carol Lynley) during the filming of *The Alfred Hitchcock Hour* episode "The Final Vow" (1962).

thing from a stuffed owl to a scrap of paper bobbing in a toilet bowl hums with the supernatural.

Across the Hitchcock canon, various inanimate objects, such as scissors, eyeglasses, keys, and jewelry, crop up repeatedly, as though relics floating from one locale of the Hitchcock universe to the next, and all with the power to bring harmony or wreak havoc. Mrs. Danvers, the terrifying housekeeper in *Rebecca*, keeps the first Mrs. de Winter's bedroom as a shrine, filled with her clothing, including underwear "made especially for her by the nuns at the convent of St Claire," as though they were the Turin Shroud or fragments of the true cross. In *The Ring*, the bracelet Bob gifts to Mabel is a symbol of their illicit love—which Hitchcock agreed could be read as an allusion to original sin—that bores into Mabel's conscience and that she attempts to conceal, just as other Hitchcock characters hide handcuffs that have been placed on them to restrain, punish, and shame. One might locate Hitchcock's pre-adolescent encounters with the ferule as the start of his fascination with the artifacts of restraint and chastisement, especially ligatures and handcuffs, which he conceded had strong fetishistic properties. In *The Lodger*, Ivor Novello finds himself dangling from a bridge above the Thames, his cuffed hands above his head, both sexually prone and Christ-like as a baying crowd urges his mortal punishment for deviant crimes he has not committed. Like Bernini and his design of the *Ecstasy of Saint Teresa*, Hitchcock stands in a long line of Catholic artists who relish blurring the lines between the sexual and the spiritual, the sacred and the profane. Yet this is another of Hitchcock's preoccupations that speaks to our time perhaps more clearly than it did to his. In the early 1980s, when Donald Spoto published his theories about Hitchcock's sadomasochism, it elicited twenty years of pushback by those who insisted that the Master had no such grubby fixations. In a post-*Secretary*, post–*Fifty Shades of Grey* world, where conversations about submission and domination are mainstream, Hitchcock's handcuffs and humiliations seem less like one aberrant man's twisted perversions and more like further evidence of his ability to point us to our future, with a nudge and a sly wink.

The magical elements of Catholic teaching to which Hitchcock was drawn were defended fiercely by the Vatican in the years of Hitchcock's creative life as a bulwark against modernity—a condition that Hitchcock not only grasped but embodied. In the fall of 1910, the very season in which Hitchcock began his education at St Ignatius College, Pope Pius X issued the "Oath Against Modernism," an attempt to insulate the Catholic faith from the insistent rush of a changing world, the hyper-urban and individualistic place that Hitchcock took such delight in exploring and exposing. The oath wasn't rescinded until July 1967, by which point his decline as a filmmaker was well advanced. Between those poles, Hitchcock found a way to fuse the two contradictory traditions of the magical and the modern. He had a fixation with technique and precision planning, but this was used to create a filmic world that slipped the grasp of science, technology, and rational thought. In its way, this mirrors an experience with which many Catholics of the twentieth century could identify in their daily lives: reconciling the dogma of their church and the spirituality of their faith with the secular world.

When the Hitchcocks wed, Alma converted to Catholicism, just as William Hitchcock had converted to the faith when he married Alfred's mother. When Pat arrived into the world, she was raised Catholic, too. As opposed to her father's upbringing, it was not insisted that she confess her sins to her parents each night, but she did have a painting of the Virgin Mary above her bed. Her mother and father also ensured that she was a regular churchgoer and was confirmed in the faith. Among the lunches, production meetings, and sessions in the projection room, a space was cleared in Hitchcock's diary to attend his granddaughters' confirmation in December 1966. Five years later, Pat joined her daughter Mary on a trip to Europe, which included a private papal audience, a privilege Hitchcock had been granted as early as the summer of 1935. When Pat and Mary were announced before his Holiness Pope Paul VI, one of the papal guards began to hum the theme tune to *Alfred Hitchcock*

Presents, suggesting that the flow of influence between Hitchcock and the Vatican wasn't *entirely* one way.

In an arm's-length kind of way, Hitchcock kept in touch with his alma mater, too. A history of the school, published to celebrate its centenary in 1994, named Hitchcock as one of the school's alumni who had "given greater glory to God by their life's work." It concedes that "his admiration for his old school was not unbounded" but also confirms that it was he who provided the lion's share of funds for new buildings on the school site. He was similarly giving to Catholic causes in California, even though his attendance at Mass became fitful after a few years in America. He formed a close bond with the Jesuit priest Thomas Sullivan, whose various charitable endeavors Hitchcock supported. It was to Sullivan that he wrote in 1966 to decline a request to give a speech at a function, telling Sullivan that such events caused him great anxiety, likening it to the drain he felt from making a film: "I go through hell and get no pleasure at all from the fact that it succeeds. I'm only relieved that it wasn't a complete failure." Not a confession as such, but few people received such emotional honesty from the man who publicly claimed to feel nothing but soporific boredom on a production once the script was finished.

Hitchcock's knowledge of being a practicing Catholic is unequivocally present in *I Confess*, his most explicitly Catholic film, released in 1952. Not only is its protagonist a priest, but its plot depends on the detail of sacrament, a rare example of a Hollywood movie that shows its audience the priesthood from inside the Church. The action takes place in Quebec City, in which Father Michael Logan (Montgomery Clift) hears the confession of his caretaker, Otto Keller (O. E. Hasse), who reveals that, while disguised as a priest, he has just killed a wealthy local man by the name of Villette, whose home Keller was attempting to burgle. In a characteristic twist, we soon learn that Villette was blackmailing Ruth Grandfort (Anne Baxter), the wife of a high-profile politician, over a secret relationship she had with Logan before he took orders. When the police investigate the murder, Ruth confesses her past romance with Logan, while Keller plays innocent, knowing that the rules of the sacrament prohibit Logan from revealing what he has heard in confession.

Logan is arrested and tried for Villette's murder but refuses to reveal the truth, honoring spiritual authorities over civil ones. By a whisker, he avoids a guilty verdict, to the fury of the public. Racked with guilt, Keller's wife runs to Logan to apologize. In desperation, Keller shoots her and runs away, at which point the police fathom their mistake. In a final scene, Keller is killed by a police officer's gunfire, and is cradled by Logan who reads him his last rites.

I Confess is not in the first rank of Hitchcock movies, but it treats its subject with intelligence; the complex character dynamics belie the idea that Hitchcock films relegate characterization to playful afterthought. Hitchcock himself, however, was not a fan. Dissatisfaction with casting, lack of humor, frustrations with Clift, and underwhelming box-office takings, led him to speak coolly of the film in later years. He was also frustrated that people identified the central premise of the movie— Logan's refusal to divulge what Keller tells him in confession—as the latest example of Hitchcock's war against narrative plausibility. Not only does the film reflect a truth about the sacredness of sacrament, it is rooted in the real-world experience of many Catholics of the time who felt the push and pull of competing bases of truth. The tussle between the rule of law and the rule of God is one that was particularly pertinent to the film's setting—Quebec of the 1950s—which was still a place where "the Holy Church cherished quotidian control over the prospects of men," to quote one Canadian writer who lived through the period.

The two other Hitchcock films in which the practice of Catholicism plays an explicit part likewise sprang from factual events, and speak to moments when the Catholic faith conflicts with the secular institutions of the modern world. *The Wrong Man* is based on the true story of a man who clings to his Catholicism when the law convicts him of a crime he has not committed; *Juno and the Paycock* is set amid the Irish Civil War, when the old religion provides succor to those caught up in the battles of nationalism and imperialism. At the end of the latter film, Juno, played by Sara Allgood, pleads with statues of Christ and the Virgin Mary to help her rise above the violence that has torn her family apart. In his own pit of despair, Manny Balestrero clutches rosary beads and prays before a portrait of Jesus in *The Wrong Man*. Though Hitchcock expressed regret that his editing might imply that Manny's eventual exculpation resulted from his prayers—a trill that deviated from the strict recitation of fact that had been the director's stated aim—it is the ritualistic adherence to Catholicism that provides a mystical counterpoint to the equally proscriptive rituals of the criminal justice system. The rule of law is meant to be an objective, rational process, but its capriciousness bewilders Manny and crushes Rose, whose faith in law and God cracks. She tells her husband, "No matter what you do they've got it fixed so that it goes against you. No matter how innocent you are or how hard you try, they'll find you guilty." She could be talking about policemen or priests. But Manny's mother, an older woman from the old country, implores her son to pray for strength. She has faith that absolution is always available from a priest in the confessional. New York City cops can't be relied on in the same way.

What Hitchcock whispered in his own prayers, or what sins he might have felt moved to confess, is unknown. He spoke publicly about his Catholic background but rarely gave any indication as to the precise nature of his beliefs. One of the many areas in which he surprised and disappointed André Bazin when they met was the director's inability to unpick what Bazin thought were the obviously Catholic themes of his films: guilt, shame, penitence, and vengeance. Bazin floated the idea that the Hitchcock universe was governed by a Jansenist God. "What's a Jansenist?" asked Hitchcock. The answer is a Catholic who subscribes to the austere ideas of the Dutch theologian Cornelius Jansen, who focused on original sin, predestination, and the depravities of the flesh. Jansenism thrived in Ireland after the famines of the mid-nineteenth century, communicating a disgust for bodily functions and stressing the need to repress sexual urges. One can see why Bazin detected a strain of Jansen in Hitchcock. Bad things almost always befall the unchaste and immodest in his movies, and in his own life he went out of his way to claim—unconvincingly—that away from filmmaking he had no interest in sex, and he boasted about the white, gleaming cleanliness of his home bathroom, which looked perpetually unused. As a matter of routine, he would use paper towels to dry a sink once he had washed his hands, lest any trace of his body be left in that place of unmentionable activities. For similar reasons, he would always lift his feet off the floor if he were forced to use a public toilet cubicle. Embarrassment about bodily functions is far from a Jansenist preserve, however, and, as Patrick McGilligan has pointed out, it could as easily be labeled an English pathology, the flip side of a scatological sense of humor, something Hitchcock also possessed. In any event, Jansenist severity only goes so far in Hitchcock, who spent at least as much of his life celebrating fleshly indulgences as he did denying them; he was a voluptuary and an aesthete, the wearer of silk pajamas and tailored suits, not burlap and hair shirts.

About the closest Hitchcock ever got to expressing his own sense of faith was in a brief interview with the St Ignatius College magazine in the 1970s. When asked whether he was religious, Hitchcock suggested that though he considered himself a Catholic, he was not necessarily a man of God. "[A] claim to be religious rests entirely on your own conscience, whether you believe or not. A Catholic attitude was indoctrinated into me. After all, I was born a Catholic, I went to a Catholic school, and I now have a conscience with lots of trials over belief." Considering that the interviewer was a teenage schoolboy, it's forgivable that this enticing morsel was not pursued; the follow-up question was about Hitchcock's love of maps.

What did he mean by "trials over belief"? Did he lie awake at night plagued by worries for his eternal soul? Did he question how God could exist in a world of such arbitrary injustice and pervasive cruelty, that subtext of his darkest films? Were the images of violence and sadism that he projected from his mind onto our screens a reflection of his belief in man's inherent evil? Could he find the strength to admit to his priest things about himself that he said he found impossible to tell a psychiatrist, a friend, Alma, or even himself?

The definitive answers to those questions went with Hitchcock's ashes into the Pacific Ocean, and perhaps into a realm beyond our own. But many of those who worked with him—in particular, his writers—believe that Hitchcock, consciously or not, used his films as a means of "concocting a moral vision of the universe," one in which evil doers are exposed and punished, and almost everyone is in need of expiation for something. In a gloomy frame of mind in old age, he told an interviewer that "today to a great extent evil *has* spread, every little town has had its share of evil," although why that had happened or when it started, he didn't say. In this world of ever-present wrongdoing, guilt can appear to be contagious, passed from one sinner to the next as easily as the common cold. "Transference of guilt" is what some critics call it, and it's supposedly observable in manifold places: in *Dial M for Murder* and *Blackmail*, when the female protagonists inadvertently kill men who are attacking them; in *Shadow of a Doubt*, when young Charlie absorbs the guilt of Uncle Charlie, her "twin"; in *Strangers on a Train*, when Bruno commits a horrific crime that appalls Guy but that he has secretly willed. There are even readings of *North by Northwest* that state the hellish absurdity into which Roger Thornhill falls is cosmic payback for his stealing a cab in the opening scene.

This would be to mistake harlequinade irony for theological severity. Ambiguity in all things was Hitchcock's preferred way of looking at the world, but his films don't equate the violence of rape and murder with the violence of self-defense, nor small acts of selfishness with psychopathic thuggery and unpleasant thoughts with unpleasant acts. The feeling of guilt sloshes around the Hitchcock universe; it envelops his characters the way the swamp claims Marion Crane's car—slowly, inexorably, completely. Yet this is because the human conscience is a punishing taskmaster, especially among the goodhearted and the God-fearing. It's Hitchcock's supreme joke that the men and women most burdened by their conscience tend to be those with the least to feel guilty about. Perhaps that's how he felt about himself.

Whether it's Barry Kane's struggle to maintain his freedom and his faith in democracy in *Saboteur*, Dr. Petersen's attempt to find the exonerating truth about the man she loves in *Spellbound*, or Iris's attempt to rediscover the lost memories that will save Miss Froy in *The Lady Vanishes*, Hitchcock created testing rituals that his characters must endure in order to come out strengthened and absolved, their good names intact. Seen in this light, the master of modernism becomes the designer of medieval ordeals, tales of chivalric struggle from a pre-Reformation world. In Hitchcock's land of birth, that tradition is dominated by the legend of Camelot and the Round Table; the deadly love triangle between Arthur, Guinevere, and Lancelot, swaddled in lust, deceit, guilt, shame, and vengeance, would have been terrific source material for a Hitchcock thriller. According to the critic Father Neil Hurley, such travails are the root of Jesuit spirituality, too. St Ignatius adhered to "the principle that a study of moral disease was a step toward health and happiness," a notion that Hurley also sees at work in films such as *Marnie* and *The Birds*, in which the characters played by Tippi Hedren are put through the wringer in order to deal with the moral flaws that have led them to dissipation and unhappiness. "The soul of man prevails," notes Hurley of Hitchcock's films, "but only when moral struggle is present. Hope is there, but it must be activated by human initiative."

Perhaps, then, Hitchcock's religious background helped him develop the narrative structure for his picaresque adventure stories. Yet it's not clear whether Hitchcock felt that the ordeals he put his characters through were morally just. In the Tippi Hedren films, the audience is always meant to be on her side, and her transgressions do not warrant the punishments that befall her, nearly killed by birds in one case; tormented, blackmailed, raped, and suicidal in the other. In *Psycho*, Marion realizes the moral responsibility she has to hand back the money she has stolen—at which point she's knifed to death. Hitchcock conceded that one could discern allusions to original sin throughout his filmography. But one might say that his films engage with the idea of original sin by protesting the injustice of the concept rather than endorsing its reality. The burdens carried by his heroes and heroines are given to them unfairly, sometimes arbitrarily; the fatiguing work of shedding that weight of paranoia, guilt, and shame is a waking nightmare.

To judge him by his films, Hitchcock was a man who believed in such things as good and evil, and whose mind had been captivated by the rituals and iconography of Catholicism. Yet God flits in and out of his movies as though communicating through a weak AM radio signal, as it seems to have done in his personal life. Many of Hitchcock's heroes ultimately survive because they act as individuals—albeit ones who realize that individualism won't save the day. It is by letting Daisy into his cell of internal anguish that the Lodger is saved from ruin; Jeff in *Rear Window* finds justice and happiness by putting his trust in Lisa; Michael's noble mission in *Torn Curtain* is completed only once he accepts Sarah's undying love. Hitchcock's films suggest that the world is a baffling place, filthy and dangerous. People aren't always who they appear to be; they can betray us and hurt us, destroy us, if they so wish. Yet they're all we have. The best we can do is to be brave and reach out to them— something Hitchcock found very hard to do but had, sometimes, been rewarded richly for doing so, his marriage to Alma being the definitive case in point.

Perhaps he would have found sense in Oscar Wilde's ideas on the subject. After his public ruination, Wilde wrote that sin and suffering were "beautiful, holy things" because they allowed one to reach within oneself to begin the painful, arduous process of spiritual growth, which in turn allowed one to form closer bonds with one's fellow man. Though Wilde said this was an act of self-realization, not dependent on an unseen deity, he recognized the importance of Catholic materiality—"what one can touch, and look at"—in finding spiritual peace. He imagined "an order for those who cannot believe: the Confraternity of the Faithless, one might call it, where on an altar, on which no taper burned, a priest, in whose heart peace had no dwelling, might celebrate with unblessed bread and a chalice empty of wine." With Hitchcock's strident individualism and his "trials of belief," allied with his love of routine, spectacle, and performance, perhaps beautifully ritualized agnosticism was a religious idea to which he could have turned. God, in the end, was to be found only in the inexplicable mysteries of each human heart.

For fifty years, Hitchcock was the god of the universe he brought to life on film. At times, he was a beneficent giver of love and the hope of rebirth. At others, he threw down Old Testament punishments of plagues and avenging angels. No matter which iteration of the supreme creator he assumed, the mortality of his subjects was never in doubt. Nobody on planet Hitchcock was more than one wrinkle of fate away from the end—nobody, that is, except for the majestic instigator himself, who popped up for a brief moment in each film, seemingly immutable and everlasting.

In the 1970s, that began to change. In a publicity stunt for *Frenzy*, Hitchcock arranged for a life-size mannequin of himself to be sailed down the Thames, a floating corpse to signal the return of the "boy director" as he still liked to call himself. Four years later, the distributers of *Family Plot* attempted to compensate for the movie's lack of bankable stars by putting Hitchcock's face on the promotional posters. At the bottom of the frame, his disembodied head appears in a crystal ball, winking at us in reference to the final shot of the movie, but also, it seems, a cheeky acknowledgment of both his age and his apparent omnipotence—even from the next world he would be playing tricks on us. His cameo in the movie was equally playful, but more explicit, about his advancing years: in that famous silhouette, he is seen remonstrating with someone behind a door marked "Registrar of Births and Deaths."

These jokes aside, Hitchcock labored in the final stretch. The glee he took in murder was counterbalanced by a genuine terror of death. He had attempted to perfect living by approaching it as art and craft; dying had no stimulating form or soothing routine. He searched for a consolatory epilogue; the final page gave him nothing beyond "THE END."

In Donald Spoto's biography, he says Hitchcock, oscillating between terror and anger in his last days, told various people that he had cut his ties with the Church and would not receive absolution. Patrick McGilligan reports it differently, writing that Father Thomas Sullivan "insisted on coming to Bellagio Road once a week to say Mass for him and Alma," making it sound as though Hitchcock's final connection with Catholicism had more to do with his old-fashioned English manners, and his fear of confrontation with an authority figure, rather than a sincere desire for closer communion with God.

Mark Henninger, a young priest who accompanied Sullivan on many of his visits in Hitchcock's last few weeks, suggests that it was in fact Hitchcock who requested their attendance. Henninger never knew the

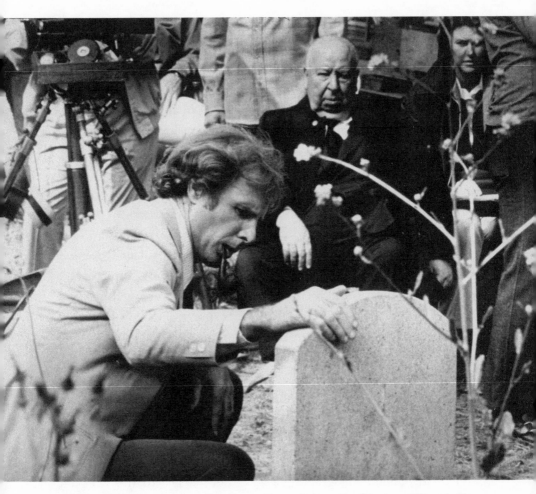

Hitchcock in a graveyard with Bruce Dern during the filming of *Family Plot*.

precise reasons why Hitchcock wanted the Church back in his life after so many years away from it, and he suspects it may not have been entirely clear to Hitchcock either. "But something whispered in his heart, and the visits answered a profound human desire, a real human need."

On Henninger's first visit with Sullivan, they found Hitchcock dressed in black pajamas, asleep in a living room chair. Fatigue, old age, and ill-health hadn't eradicated his sense of humor. "Hitch," Sullivan said as Hitchcock came to, "this is Mark Henninger, a young priest from

Cleveland." Looking up, a sleepy Hitchcock replied, "Cleveland? Disgraceful!" During Mass, it became apparent that the old ways of his religion hadn't left him, either; he gave his responses in Latin, as he would have done as a boy, rather than in English as had been the practice since Vatican II. "But the most remarkable sight," says Henninger, "was that after receiving communion, he silently cried, tears rolling down his huge cheeks." Whether moved by the grace of God, fear of His judgment, fear of the unknown, or simply sadness at the nearness of death, Henninger couldn't say.

When Hitchcock died, Alma struggled to comprehend the loss and spent the remaining two years of her life believing he was still with them. In one sense, she was right. The further we get from the twentieth century, the more importance to its story Hitchcock assumes. His variegated legacies, buttressed by his phenomenal talent and unconventional personality, make him a codex of his times, usually complex, often troubling, but always vital. Not long before he passed, he was asked by an interviewer for his plans for the future. More of the same, he said; years and years more Hitchcock. "I have lots of ideas . . . and something always comes up, some new story. . . . I warn you, I mean to go on forever!"

Acknowledgments

I owe special thanks to the Alfred J. Hitchcock Trust for kindly allowing me to reproduce excerpts from various sources. Numerous other estates have provided similar cooperation, and I am grateful to them all.

In conducting my research, I was helped by many people and institutions: Lisa Hilton and the extremely welcoming staff at the Margaret Herrick Library; Brendan Coates at the Academy of Motion Picture Arts and Sciences, Oral History Projects department; JC Johnson and his colleagues at the Howard Gotlieb Archival Research Center, Boston University; the Charles E. Young Research Library, UCLA; Terre Heydari at the DeGloyer Library, Southern Methodist University; Gaila Sims at the Harry Ransom Center, University of Texas at Austin; Susan Krueger at the Wisconsin Historical Research Society; the Rare Books and Manuscripts Division, and the Billy Rose Theatre Division at the New York Public Library; the Beinecke Rare Books and Manuscript Library at Yale University; the Butler Library at Columbia University; the Bodleian Library at the University of Oxford; Victoria Bennett and colleagues at the British Film Institute; and all the staff at the magnificent British Library.

I am indebted to various Hitchcock scholars whose work has informed my own in many ways. These include—but are not limited to—Charles Barr, Jane Sloan, Sidney Gottlieb, John Russell Taylor, Donald Spoto, Dan Auiler, Tania Modleski, and Peter Conrad. Patrick McGilligan also belongs to this group, and I owe him extra thanks for kindly assisting me in my research, as did Sue Jones, Tabitha Machin, David Freeman, Barbara Leigh-Hunt, Peter Bogdanovich, Tim Kirby, William Devane, Mariette Hartley, Bernard Cribbins, Nick Wright, Cornelia Parker, Gus Van Sant, Donna Ranieri, Andrew Bainbridge, Sophie Sweet, and Chris Levy.

Thanks to Nancy Palmquist and everybody at W. W. Norton, but especially my editor John Glusman, and Helen Thomaides who has been a model of efficiency and forbearance in fielding my endless, annoying queries. The guidance and assistance of Melissa Flamson and Janet Woods at With Permission was invaluable, while Chris Parris-Lamb was, as always, a great source of advice and encouragement. Thanks also to Sarah Bolling and the rest of the Gernert Company.

The unfailing patience and support of my family was, and is, much needed and cherished.

Alfred Hitchcock Filmography

English-language feature films directed solely by Alfred Hitchcock. There is some debate about the dating of Hitchcock's earliest films; the dates below give the year of the first UK screening for films up to 1939, and the first US screening of all subsequent films, following Hitchcock's move to Hollywood.

The Pleasure Garden (1926)

The Mountain Eagle (1926)

The Lodger: A Story of the London Fog (1926)

Downhill (1927)

Easy Virtue (1927)

The Ring (1927)

The Farmer's Wife (1928)

Champagne (1928)

The Manxman (1929)

Blackmail (1929)

Juno and the Paycock (1930)

Murder! (1930)

The Skin Game (1931)

Rich and Strange (1931)

Number Seventeen (1932)

Waltzes from Vienna (1934)

The Man Who Knew Too Much (1934)

The 39 Steps (1935)

Secret Agent (1936)

Sabotage (1936)

Young and Innocent (1937)

The Lady Vanishes (1938)

Jamaica Inn (1939)

Rebecca (1940)

Foreign Correspondent (1940)

Mr. and Mrs. Smith (1941)

Suspicion (1941)

Saboteur (1942)

Shadow of a Doubt (1943)

Lifeboat (1944)

Spellbound (1945)

Notorious (1946)

The Paradine Case (1947)

Rope (1948)

Under Capricorn (1949)

Stage Fright (1950)

Strangers on a Train (1951)

I Confess (1953)

Dial M for Murder (1954)

Rear Window (1954)

To Catch a Thief (1955)

The Trouble with Harry (1955)

The Man Who Knew Too Much (1956)

The Wrong Man (1956)

Vertigo (1958)

North by Northwest (1959)

Psycho (1960)

The Birds (1963)

Marnie (1964)

Torn Curtain (1966)

Topaz (1969)

Frenzy (1972)

Family Plot (1976)

Abbreviations

AH	Alfred Hitchcock
AHC MHL	Alfred Hitchcock Collection, Margaret Herrick Library, Academy of Motion Picture Arts and Sciences
BFI	British Film Institute
MHL	Margaret Herrick Library, Academy of Motion Picture Arts and Sciences
Kirby	Transcripts of interviews by Tim Kirby, Patrick McGilligan Collection, Wisconsin Historical Society
DSP UCLA	Donald Spoto Papers, Department of Special Collections, Charles E. Young Library, University of California, Los Angeles
HGARC	Howard Gotlieb Archival Research Center at Boston University
OHP	Academy of Motion Picture Arts & Sciences Oral History Projects
PMC WHS	Patrick McGilligan Collection, Wisconsin Historical Society
SMU	DeGolyer Library, Southern Methodist University, Ronald L. Davis Oral History Collection

Notes

INTRODUCTION

xi *It appears he . . . 1921:* Patrick McGilligan, *Alfred Hitchcock: A Life in Darkness and Light* (New York: HarperCollins, 2010), loc. 1062 of 20272, Kindle.

xii *According to Hitchcock . . . present:* Andy Warhol, "Hitchcock," *Andy Warhol's Interview,* September 1974, 7.

xii *"an economical way . . . cinema":* Paula Marantz Cohen, "Alfred Hitchcock: modest exhibitionist," *TLS* (September 5, 2008), https://www.the-tls.co.uk/articles/private/alfred-hitchcock-modest-exhibitionist/.

xiv *The economist David Galenson . . . either:* David Galenson, *Old Masters and Young Geniuses: The Two Life Cycles of Artistic Creativity* (Princeton and Oxford: Princeton University Press, 2006).

xvi *"I've never known . . . should be":* Norman Lloyd, interview by Fletcher Markle, "A Talk with Hitchcock, Part Two," *Telescope,* on the DVD *A Talk with Hitchcock,* 2000. Originally broadcast by CBC, 1964.

1: THE BOY WHO COULDN'T GROW UP

2 *"This eerie and . . . scuttles":* "Our Captious Critic: 'Mary Rose,' at the Haymarket Theatre," review of *Mary Rose* by J. M. Barrie, Haymarket Theatre, London, *Illustrated Sporting and Dramatic News,* May 15, 1920.

2 *"slice of a delightful cake":* "'Mary Rose' at the Haymarket," review of *Mary Rose* by J. M. Barrie, Haymarket Theatre, London *Common Cause,* May 7, 1920.

2 *It so influenced . . . inspiration:* Herbert Coleman to Kay Selby, May 9, 1957, Paramount Pictures Production Records, MHL.

3 *"the man is not different from the boy":* Charlotte Chandler, *It's Only a Movie—Alfred Hitchcock: A Personal Biography* (London: Pocket Books, 2006), 34.

3 *"A wonderful character . . . line":* Patricia Hitchcock O'Connell, in "Reputations," *Hitch: Alfred the Great,* BBC Two, May 30, 1999.

5 *"lamb without a spot":* François Truffaut, *Hitchcock* (London: Faber & Faber, 2017), 25.

5 *Society of Jesus . . . God:* For a useful narrative history of the Jesuits, see Jonathan Wright, *God's Soldiers: Adventure, Politics, Intrigue, and Power—A History of the Jesuits* (London: Doubleday, 2005).

5 *"highly dramatic . . . going for execution":* John O'Riordan, "Interview with Alfred Hitchcock," *Ignatian*, summer 1973, reprinted in Neil Hurley, *Soul in Suspense: Hitchcock's Fright and Delight* (Metuchen, NJ, and London: Scarecrow Press, 1993), 290.

6 *"spread it over . . . strokes":* Ibid.

6 *He told some . . . work:* Donald Spoto, *The Dark Side of Genius: The Life of Alfred Hitchcock* (London: Collins, 1983), 28, citing an interview with Hitchcock in *TV Guide*, May 29, 1965.

6 *"If you don't . . . id":* Bill Mumy, interview by Archive of American Television, September 3, 2013, Television Academy Foundation, https://interviews.televisionacademy.com/interviews/bill-mumy.

7 *"I don't remember ever having a playmate":* "The Elderly Cherub That Is Hitchcock," *TV Guide*, May 29, 1965, 15.

7 *schoolmates tended to . . . fish:* McGilligan, *Darkness and Light*, loc. 485 of 20272, Kindle.

7 *"An alarm clock . . . inside":* Hedda Hopper, "Hitchcock: He Runs on Fear," *Los Angeles Times*, August 17, 1958, part V, 1.

7 *"It was amazing . . . screen":* Robert Boyle, OHP.

7 *"a visual poet of anxiety and accident":* Spoto, *Dark Side of Genius*, 9.

8 *"I think he . . . nerve-wracking":* Chandler, *It's Only a Movie*, 37.

8 *"I must have . . . boys":* Truffaut, *Hitchcock*, 25.

8 *John Russell Taylor . . . events:* John Russell Taylor, *Hitch: The Life and Times of Alfred Hitchcock* (London: Bloomsbury Reader, 2013), loc. 147 of 5468, Kindle.

8 *the journalist Oriana Fallci . . . eleven:* Oriana Fallaci, "Mr. Chastity," in *The Egotists: Sixteen Surprising Interviews*, trans. Pamela Swinglehurst (Chicago: Henry Regnery, 1968), 249. The interview took place in May 1963. See also McGilligan, *Darkness and Light*, loc. 137 of 20272, Kindle.

8 *"I'm told I . . . thrills":* "Hitchcock in Sydney on PR Visit," *The Advertiser*, May 5, 1960, AHC MHL.

9 *"perhaps he was . . . about me":* Chandler, *It's Only a Movie*, 31.

9 *"There he was . . . time":* Spoto, *Dark Side of Genius*, 340.

9 *One time he . . . returned:* Ibid., 18–19.

9 *he explained that . . . "Boo!":* Hitchcock told the yarn to various interviewers, including Fletcher Markle and Dick Cavett. See Markle, "A Talk with Hitchcock, Part Two," and *The Dick Cavett Show*, ABC, June 8, 1972.

10 *"a clear horizon . . . plate":* AH, Markle, "A Talk with Hitchcock, Part Two."

10 *"a tidy mind":* AH, interview by George Angell, *Time of My Life: Alfred Hitchcock*, BBC Home Service, August 28, 1966.

10 *"I believe it's . . . pictures"*: Chandler, *It's Only a Movie*, 13.

10 *"mind of an . . . abstractions"*: Russell Maloney, "What Happens After That?" Profiles, *New Yorker*, September 10, 1938, 24.

11 *"I was very . . . child"*: Patrick McGilligan, *Backstory 2: Interviews with Screenwriters of the 1940s and 1950s* (Berkeley: University of California Press, 1991), 138.

11 *"My wife says . . . child"*: Hopper, "Hitchcock: He Runs on Fear," 1.

11 *"the sadness of . . . films"*: Alfred Hitchcock, "Why I Am Afraid of the Dark," in *Hitchcock on Hitchcock, Volume 1*, ed. Sidney Gottlieb, trans. Claire Marrone (London: University of California Press, 1997), 143. Originally published as "Pourquoi J'ai Peur la Nuit," *Arts: Lettres, Spectacles*, no. 777 (June 1–7, 1960): 1, 7.

11 *huge impact on Hitchcock:* Alfred Hitchcock, "Columbus of the Screen," *Film Weekly*, February 21, 1931, 9.

11 *San Francisco Bay Area Transit system:* Hitchcock's interest in working the Bay Area rail network into the script of *Family Plot* is evident in the transcript of his story conferences with the film's screenwriter, Ernest Lehman. Ernest Lehman Collection, Harry Ransom Center, University of Texas at Austin.

11 *the distance between . . . filmed:* Discussion of these issues occurs in various letters and memos in the folder relating to *The Short Night*, AHC MHL.

13 *"Your problem, Hitch . . . adult"*: Herbert Coleman, *The Man Who Knew Hitchcock: A Hollywood Memoir* (Lanham, MD; Toronto; Plymouth, UK: Scarecrow Press, 2007), 220.

13 *"I really don't . . . arms?"*: *The Birds* story conference, February 24, 1962, AHC MHL.

13 *"pretty little fat . . . realistic"*: Vicky Lebeau, *Childhood and Cinema* (London: Reaktion Books, 2008), 37.

14 *per the critic Michael Walker:* Michael Walker, *Hitchcock's Motifs* (Amsterdam: Amsterdam University Press, 2005), 98–110.

15 *"I loved the . . . stuff"*: Rex Reed, "Film Violence," *Calgary Herald*, June 17, 1972, 65.

16 *"The bomb is . . . wish?"*: F. S. Jennings, "Master of Suspense," *The Era*, December 9, 1936, 13.

16 *"there is a . . . code"*: James Chapman, *Hitchcock and the Spy Film* (London: Bloomsbury, 2017), 102, citing Anthony Lejeune, ed., *The C.A. Lejeune Film Reader* (Manchester, UK: Carcanet, 1991), 107.

17 *"Had the audience . . . outraged"*: Alfred Hitchcock, "The Enjoyment of Fear," *Good Housekeeping*, February 1949, 243.

17 *"The boy was . . . deliberately"*: Truffaut, *Hitchcock*, 109.

17 *The director Gus Van Sant . . . heart:* Gus Van Sant in discussion with the author, October 17, 2018.

18 *From the television . . . filmography:* Ibid.

18 *"a 3 foot . . . neck"*: Donald Du Pre to AH, undated, AHC MHL.

20 *"Not too much . . . reasonable":* Truffaut, *Hitchcock*, 259.

20 *About a year . . . smash:* Jay Presson Allen, interviewed by Tim Kirby for *Reputations*, BBC, PMC WHS.

20 *"solid, unblurred images":* Truffaut, *Hitchcock*, 51.

22 *In an earlier . . . mother:* notes on script, "MELANIE—FINAL SEQUENCE," April 9, 1962, AHC MHL.

22 *"I would go . . . before":* William Baer, *Classic American Films: Conversations with the Screenwriters* (Westport, CT; London: Praeger, 2008), 81.

22 *"I said to Hitchcock . . . stopping him":* "Everyone's Wicked Uncle," BBC Radio 3, 1999.

23 *"I think I . . . people":* Taylor, *Hitch*, loc. 199 of 5468, Kindle.

24 *"Your father's dead . . . dissociation":* Ibid., loc. 483 of 5468, Kindle.

24 *Sixteen thousand Londoners . . . 1918:* Mark Honigsbaum, *Living with Enza: The Forgotten Story of Britain and the Great Flu Pandemic of 1918* (London: Macmillan, 2009), 105.

24 *"Londoners almost without . . . everything":* Jerry White, *Zeppelin Nights: London in the First World War* (London: Bodley Head, 2014), i.

25 *"relentless disruption and . . . night":* Ibid., 215.

25 *"did not impinge much on him":* Taylor, *Hitch*, loc. 488 of 5468, Kindle.

26 *"inspired by a . . . look":* "Westcliff Cine Club Visits Mr Hitchcock in Hollywood," https://player.bfi.org.uk/free/film/watch-westcliff-cine-club-visits-mr-hitchcock-in-hollywood-1963-online

2: THE MURDERER

28 *"passion for films . . . learn":* Michael Balcon, *Michael Balcon Presents: A Lifetime of Films* (London: Hutchinson, 1969), 19.

28 *"I'm sure that . . . to do so":* Ibid.

28 *"a twilight of . . . landscapes":* Lottie Eisner, *The Haunted Screen: Expressionism in the German Cinema and the Influence of Max Reinhardt* (Davis: University of California Press, 2008), 8.

28 *"know-it-all son of a bitch":* Chandler, *It's Only a Movie*, 51.

28 *"I can smile . . . ghastly":* Alfred Hitchcock, "My Screen Memories—I: I Begin with a Nightmare," *Film Weekly*, May 2, 1936, 16.

30 *"the suddenness of . . . blue":* Truffaut, *Hitchcock*, 268.

30 *"a rotting corpse . . . knifed":* Keith Brace, "The Trouble with Alfred," *Birmingham Daily Post*, August 5, 1960, 3.

30 *"reflect in any . . . mind":* Alfred Hitchcock and Frederic Wertham, "A *Redbook* Dialogue," in Gottlieb, ed., *Hitchcock on Hitchcock, Volume 1*, 152. Originally published in *Redbook* 120 (April 1963): 71, 108, 110–12.

30 "sadism, perversion, bestiality... dangerous": Alfred Hitchcock, "Why 'Thrillers' Thrive," *Picturegoer*, January 18, 1936, 15.

30 *Staff of his... pale:* Peggy Robertson, OHP.

30 "I did what... home": Spoto, *Dark Side of Genius*, 311.

31 "people will immediately... corpse": Fallaci, "Mr. Chastity," in *The Egotists*, 243.

31 "I've spent so... hold of": John Russell Taylor, "Surviving: Alfred Hitchcock," *Sight & Sound* 46 (Summer 1977): 174.

31 "I would have... court": Ivor Davis, "Alfred Hitchcock Abhors Violence, Prefers Suspense": *Los Angeles Times*, September 7, 1969, 26.

32 "Many great English... English": Hitchcock and Wertham, "A *Redbook* Dialogue," in Gottlieb, ed., *Hitchcock on Hitchcock, Volume 1*, 152.

32 "crime mystique in... everyone": R. Allen Leider, "Interview: Alfred Hitchcock," in Sidney Gottlieb, ed., *Hitchcock on Hitchcock, Volume 2* (Oakland: University of California Press, 2015), 260.

32 "Much perturbation appears... weeks": "From the archive, 24 January 1920: Is there a crime wave in the country?" *Guardian*, January 24, 2012, https://www.theguardian .com/theguardian/2012/jan/24/crime-wave-uk-1920. Originally published in the Manchester *Guardian*, January 24, 1920.

32 *he claimed to... lessons:* Taylor, *Hitch*, loc. 285 of 5468, Kindle.

34 "an ingrained racial sense of drama": Alfred Hitchcock, "Murder—with English on It," *New York Times Magazine*, March 3, 1957, 17.

34 *American gangsters and... crimes:* AH to Anita Colby, May 1, 1957, AHC MHL.

34 "it's a matter... criminals don't": Leider, "Interview: Alfred Hitchcock," in Gottlieb, ed., *Hitchcock on Hitchcock, Volume 2*, 260.

34 "people get blasted... style": Ibid.

35 "the evident trend... films": Bosley Crowther to AH, December 1, 1960, AHC MHL.

36 "within living memory... crime": George Orwell, "The English People," *I Have Tried to Tell the Truth: 1943–1944* (London: Secker & Warburg, 1998), 201.

36 "great period in... 1925": George Orwell, "Decline of the English Murder," in *Decline of the English Murder* (London: Penguin, 2009), 15.

37 "I am out... 'shake-up'": "Alfred Hitchcock Reveals His Methods," *Midland Daily Telegraph*, July 14, 1936, 6.

37 "grow sluggish and... firsthand": Hitchcock, "Why 'Thrillers' Thrive," 15.

37 "To him, the... ovation": Joseph Cotten, *Vanity Will Get You Somewhere* (London: Columbus Books, 1987), 64.

38 *He said that... his dreams:* Chandler, *It's Only a Movie*, 19.

38 "those aspects of... at all": Harold Hayes to AH, December 28, 1960, AHC MHL.

38 "for amusement, choose... Man": Alfred Hitchcock, "The Sophistication of Violence," *Esquire*, July 1961, 108.

39 *David Thomson writes . . . footage:* David Thomson, *The Moment of* Psycho: *How Alfred Hitchcock Taught America to Love Murder* (New York: Basic Books, 2009).

40 *"first good film":* Leider, "Interview: Alfred Hitchcock," in Gottlieb, ed., *Hitchcock on Hitchcock, Volume 2*, 259.

40 *"the first time . . . picture":* Truffaut, *Hitchcock*, 44.

40 *To Truffaut he . . . Paris:* Ibid., 47.

41 *"All murderers regard . . . mean":* "Alfred Hitchcock Murders a Blonde," in Gottlieb, ed., *Hitchcock on Hitchcock, Volume 2*, 87. Originally published in *Weekend Magazine, Ottawa Citizen* 8, no. 22 (May 31, 1958): 6, 7, 33, 44.

41 *"another Hyde":* Simon Joyce, "Sexual Politics and the Aesthetics of Crime: Oscar Wilde in the '90s," *ELH* 69, no. 2 (Summer 2002): 501–23.

41 *Such reporting promoted . . . Hyde:* Ibid.

42 *In 2002 and . . . Group:* Before Cornwell's second book was published, Patrick McGilligan noted the connection. See McGilligan, *Darkness and Light*, loc. 12019 of 20272, Kindle. Cornwell's books are *Portrait of a Killer: Jack the Ripper, Case Closed* (New York: Little, Brown, 2002), and *Ripper: The Secret Life of Walter Sickert* (Seattle: Thomas & Mercer, 2017).

42 *he bought one . . . wall:* Inventory of Hitchcock's art, AHC MHL.

45 *"The program seems . . . for it":* Alfred Hitchcock, *Alfred Hitchcock Presents Music to Be Murdered By*, 1958.

45 *"the master, Uncle Alfred":* @Eminem, Twitter, January 17, 2020, https://twitter.com/Eminem/status/1218044393736822786

46 *"My parents were not political":* Patricia Hitchcock O'Connell and Laurent Bouzereau, *Alma Hitchcock: The Woman Behind the Man* (New York: Berkley Books, 2003), 203.

46 *"violent things . . . use them":* J. Danvers Williams, "The Censor Wouldn't Pass It," *Film Weekly*, November 5, 1938, 6.

46 *"I was both . . . life":* Truffaut, *Hitchcock*, 159.

47 *according to one . . . conflict:* Charles Barr and Alain Kerzoncuf, *Hitchcock Lost and Found: The Forgotten Films* (Lexington: University Press of Kentucky, 2015), 126.

47 *Contrary to later . . . received:* Ibid., 158.

47 *"We realized that . . . conflicts":* Truffaut, *Hitchcock*, 161.

48 *Originally designed to . . . the Camps:* Kay Gladstone, "Separate Intentions: The Allied Screening of Concentration Camp Documentaries in Defeated Germany in 1945–46: *Death Mills and Memory of the Camps*," in *Holocaust and the Moving Image: Representations in Film and Television since 1933*, ed. Toby Haggith and Joanna Newman (London: Wallflower, 2005), 50–64.

48 *Only in 2014 . . . Survey:* The film is stored in the archives of the Imperial War Museum, but members of the public can view some of the footage that was in the cut of the documentary that Hitchcock worked on in the 2014 documentary, *Night Will Fall*, which tells the story of the making of the *German Concentration Camps Factual Survey*. The PBS *Frontline* documentary is also available online.

48   *"thought he, a . . . he had"*: Sidney Bernstein speaking in *Night Will Fall*, 2014.

48   *"was very careful . . . any way"*: Elizabeth Sussex, "The Fate of F3080," *Sight & Sound* 53, no. 2 (Spring 1984): 92.

48   *"juxtaposition of what . . . themes"*: Jean-Louis Comolli, "Fatal Rendezvous," in *Cinema and the Shoah: An Art Confronts the Tragedy of the Twentieth Century*, ed. Jean-Michel Frodon, trans. Anna Harrison and Tom Mes (Albany: State University of New York Press, 2010), 62.

49   *"One cannot contemplate . . . horrors"*: Robin Wood, *Hitchcock's Films Revisited* (New York: Columbia University Press, 1989), 150.

50   *"He seemed genuinely . . . Jews"*: Peter Bogdanovich, "Hitchcock High and Low," *New York*, May 6, 1974, 75.

50   *"here we are . . . brutality"*: Alfred Hitchcock, interview by Richard Schickel, *The Men Who Made the Movies: Alfred Hitchcock*, PBS, November 4, 1973.

50   *"sponge, eager to . . . design"*: Jane Sloan, *Alfred Hitchcock: A Filmography and Bibliography* (Berkeley: University of California Press, 1995), 37.

51   *"nauseating . . . stomach-turning . . . unnecessarily tasteless"*: Hitchcock at the NFT, BBC One, December 30, 1969. Viewed at the BFI Southbank Mediatheque, London.

51   *"I would say . . . business"*: Ibid.

51   *"people die without . . . pain"*: Quoted in Robert Sklar, "Death at Work: Hitchcock's Violence and Spectator Identification," in *After Hitchcock: Influence, Imitation, and Intertexuality*, ed. David Boyd and R. Barton Palmer (Austin: University of Texas Press, 2010), 219. Original source is "Le Devoir" interview, folder no. 96, Sam Peckinpah Collection, MHL.

51   *"Just another day . . . this"*: Barry Foster, speaking in *The Story of Frenzy*, DVD extra on *Frenzy*, 2005.

51   *"the effect is . . . there"*: Ibid.

3: THE AUTEUR

53   *"but Hitch didn't . . . thing"*: Ronald Neame, interviewed by Tim Kirby for *Reputations*, BBC, PMCWHS.

53   *"I saw Hitchcock . . . head"*: Ibid.

53   *"I really hate the word artistic"*: Gerald Pratley, "Alfred Hitchcock's Working Credo," *Films in Review* 3, no. 10 (December 1952): 502.

53   *"I have too . . . critics"*: Ibid., 503.

54   *"prodigiously bored"*: André Bazin, "Hitchcock vs. Hitchcock," in *The Cinema of Cruelty: From Buñuel to Hitchcock* (New York: Seaver Books, 1982), 144. Originally appeared in *Cahiers du Cinéma*, no. 39, October 1954.

54   *"No, the light . . . tomorrow"*: Ibid., 145.

54   *"one's first reaction . . . foolish"*: Richard Roud, "The French Line," *Sight & Sound* 29, no. 4 (Autumn 1960): 167.

55 *"this Hitchcock idolatry"*: Ibid., 169.

55 *Hitchcock arranged for . . . days:* Peggy Robertson to Jean Douchet, June 14, 1963, AHC MHL.

55 *excepting a night . . . paid:* Suzanne Gauthier to Miss Minotto at the Fairmont Hotel, San Francisco, June 28, 1963, AHC MHL.

55 *"They are their . . . man"*: Alfred Hitchcock, "Films We Could Make," *London Evening News*, November 16, 1927, 13.

56 *"Fresh from Berlin . . . patent"*: June Tripp, *The Glass Ladder* (London: William Heinemann, 1960), 156.

57 *"began to tell . . . Woolf"*: Balcon, *Michael Balcon Presents*, 26.

57 *"as humiliating for . . . other"*: Ivor Montagu, *The Youngest Son* (London: Lawrence and Wishart, 1970), 349.

57 *"in the nature . . . light"*: Ivor Montagu, "Working with Hitchcock," *Sight & Sound* 49, no. 3 (Summer 1980): 190.

58 *"what the film . . . qualities"*: Ibid.

58 *"observation of familiar . . . compositions"*: Montagu, *The Youngest Son*, 349.

58 *"a born celebrity"*: Hitchcock O'Connell and Bouzereau, *Alma Hitchcock*, 3.

58 *"seamy side of film life" . . . "cutter"*: Joan Weston Edwards, "Making Good in the Film Trade," unknown publication, February 26, 1927, AHC MHL.

58 *A variety of . . . Griffith:* Hitchcock O'Connell and Bouzerau, *Alma Hitchcock*, 25.

59 *"unthinkable for a . . . position"*: Alma Reville Hitchcock, "My Husband Hates Suspense," *Everywoman's Family Circle*, June 1958, 37.

59 *"extremely self-conscious . . . education"*: Hitchcock O'Connell and Bouzereau, *Alma Hitchcock*, 19.

59 *Alma even had . . . crowds:* Ibid., 17.

60 *"groaned, nodded her head, and burped"*: Alfred Hitchcock, "The Woman Who Knows Too Much," *McCall's*, March 1956, 12.

60 *As observed by . . . fantasy:* McGilligan, *Darkness and Light*, loc. 1656 of 20272, Kindle.

60 *"sweet soul, gave . . . marvelously"*: Hitchcock, "I Begin with a Nightmare," 17.

60 *"Like a man . . . work"*: Ibid.

60 *"standing four-foot-eleven . . . pyjamas"*: Alfred Hitchcock, "Life Among the Stars," *News Chronicle*, March 1, 1937, 15.

60 *It's been said . . . Germany:* Patrick McGilligan and Peter Ackroyd both make this point in their biographies of Hitchcock.

61 *"one or two . . . ended"*: A. J. Hitchcock, "Titles—Artistic and Otherwise," *Motion Picture Studio*, July 23, 1921, 6.

61 *"my most interesting . . . fascinating"*: Alfred Hitchcock, "My Spies," *Film Weekly*, May 30, 1936, 27.

61 *"I have some . . . mother"*: Alfred Hitchcock, "Lecture at Columbia University," in

Gottlieb, ed., *Hitchcock on Hitchcock, Volume 1*, 267. Full transcript of the lecture in AHC MHL.

63 *"We don't show . . . show"*: John P. Shanley, "Lady Producer of Thrillers," *New York Times*, May 29, 1960, 11.

63 *"Let 'em suffer . . . turning"*: Gilbert Millstein, "Harrison Horror Story," *New York Times*, July 21, 1957, 23.

63 *"Alfred Hitchcock was . . . shots"*: Janet Leigh with Christopher Nickens, *Psycho: Behind the Scenes of the Classic Thriller* (London: Pavilion Books, 1995), 67.

63 *"spontaneous, not something . . . attention"*: "Hitchcock's Shower Scene: Another View," *Cinefantastique* 16, no. 4 (October 1986): 66. Saul Bass Collection, MHL.

64 *"Hitch was always . . . not"*: Ibid.

64 *"This is our . . . sell"*: Evan Hunter to Scott Meredith, October 27, 1961, Evan Hunter Collection, HGARC.

64 *"No, you didn't . . . Hitchcock did"*: Evan Hunter, *Me and Hitch* (London: Faber & Faber, 1997), 4.

64 *"about 99.44-percent Hitchcock"*: Maloney, "What Happens After That?" 25.

64 *"I dictate the picture . . . Hitchcock"*: Pamela Robertson Wojcik, "The Author of This Claptrap: Cornell Woolrich, Alfred Hitchcock, and *Rear Window*," in *Hitchcock at the Source: The Auteur as Adaptor*, ed. R. Barton Palmer and David Boyd (Albany: State University of New York Press, 2011), 218. Quoting from AH's deposition in the case of *Stewart v. Abend*. See also http://www.writingwithhitchcock.com/ontherecord.html.

65 *"biggest trouble is . . . lines"*: Gerald Clark, "Here's Hitchcock's Recipe for Suspense," *Weekend Magazine, The Standard*, December 22, 1951, 11.

65 *"I can't really . . . picture"*: Auiler, *Hitchcock's Secret Notebooks*, 24.

65 *Original scripts were . . . Vidal:* Such lists and correspondence are located in various parts of Hitchcock's papers, AHC MHL.

65 *"I never read . . . book"*: Alfred Hitchcock, "How I Make My Films," *News Chronicle*, March 5, 1937, 14.

65 *"a very lucky . . . on it"*: "Story Conference for *Family Plot*," 44, Ernest Lehman Collection, Harry Ransom Center, University of Texas at Austin. See also McGilligan, *Darkness and Light*, loc. 16344 of 20272, Kindle.

66 *Certainly, he had . . . studios:* See Leonard J. Leff, *Hitchcock and Selznick: The Rich and Strange Collaboration of Alfred Hitchcock and David O. Selznick in Hollywood* (London: Weidenfeld & Nicholson, 1987).

66 *"The first scene . . . novel"*: Baer, *Classic American Films*, 61.

67 *"Certain writers want . . . play"*: Peter Bogdanovich, "Alfred Hitchcock (1899–1980)," in *Who the Devil Made It: Conversations with Legendary Film Directors* (New York: Ballantine Books, 1997), loc. 9300 of 15740, Kindle.

67 *"unrealized ambition is . . . Rushmore"*: Lawrence Greene, "He Is a Camera," *Esquire*, August 1952, 110.

67   *"They were all ... them":* Baer, *Classic American Films*, 63.

68   *"tried to develop ... like him":* Ibid., 71.

68   *"a Hitchcock picture ... pictures":* Spoto, *Dark Side of Genius*, 392.

68   *"very special kind ... Hitchcock":* Ernest Lehman, "Screen Writer's Recipe for 'Hitch's Brew,'" *New York Times*, August 2, 1959, 5.

69   *"writing a bitter ... except me":* Ernest Lehman, Kirby.

69   *"My God, how ... lists":* Transcript of *Family Plot* story conference, Ernest Lehman Collection, Harry Ransom Center, University of Texas at Austin.

70   *"too many scripts ... theme":* Charles Barr, *English Hitchcock* (Moffat, Scotland: Cameron and Hollis, 1999), 23.

70   *"the master of ... missing":* Samuel Taylor, speaking in *Omnibus: It's Only Another Movie*, BBC One, September 26, 1986.

70   *"completely vain ... director":* Charles Bennett, *Hitchcock's Partner in Suspense: The Life of Screenwriter Charles Bennett*, ed. John Charles Bennett (Lexington: University of Kentucky, 2018), 205.

70   *"We were a ... himself":* Ibid., 67.

71   *"'Thank you' was ... vocabulary":* Coleman, *The Man Who Knew Hitchcock*, 181.

71   *"I'm not being ... good":* Bennett, *Hitchcock's Partner in Suspense*, 52.

71   *"cheerful side is ... experience":* Evan Hunter to Scott Meredith, September 30, 1961, Evan Hunter Collection, HGARC.

71   *"the script has ... total":* AH to Evan Hunter, November 30, 1961, AHC MHL. Published in Auiler, *Hitchcock's Secret Notebooks*, 206.

71   *"stuck his finger ... door":* Hunter, *Me and Hitch*, 56.

72   *"He essentially left ... them":* Chris Wehner, "Chris Wehner: Interview with REAR WINDOW scribe John Michael Hayes," http://www.screenwritersutopia.com/article/d14ec43e. Originally published in *Screenwriter's Monthly*, December 2002.

72   *"You know they ... material":* Spoto, *Dark Side of Genius*, 361.

72   *"Young man, you ... Times":* Ibid.

73   *"He wasn't for ... own":* Wehner, "Chris Wehner: Interview."

73   *"credit where credit was due":* Ibid.

73   *"I had a ... resented it":* John Michael Hayes, interview by Steven DeRosa, https://www.youtube.com/watch?v=l981MGsT9n4.

74   *Unthinkable, said Hitchcock ... classic:* Truffaut, *Hitchcock*, 71.

74   *"For hours Hitchcock ... employer":* Thornton Wilder to Isobel Wilder, May 26, 1942, *The Selected Letters of Thornton Wilder*, eds. Robin G. Wilder and Jackson R. Bryer (New York: HarperCollins, 2008), 395.

74   *"He wasn't like ... for that":* Bogdanovich, *Who the Devil Made It*, loc. 9798 of 15740, Kindle.

74   *"My relationship with ... have been":* AH, interview by Gilbert Harrison, January 4, 1980, Gilbert A. Harrison Papers Relating to Thornton Wilder, Beinecke Rare Book and Manuscript Library, Yale University.

77 *"incredible English middle class . . . people"*: John Steinbeck to Annie Laurie Williams, February 21, 1944, in *Steinbeck: A Life in Letters*, ed. Elaine Steinbeck and Robert Wallsten (London: Penguin, 2001), 267.

77 *"hard to work with"*: Frank MacShane, *The Life of Raymond Chandler* (London: Hamish Hamilton, 1986), 175.

77 *"sarcastic and disagreeable . . . bastard"*: Ibid., 171.

77 *"trying to make . . . happened"*: Ibid., 173. Quote from Chandler's notes in his personal files.

77 *Ormonde recalled that . . . trash*: McGilligan, *Darkness and Light*, loc. 10195 of 20272, Kindle.

78 *"a flabby mass . . . characters"*: Raymond Chandler to AH, December 6, 1950, in *The Raymond Chandler Papers: Selected Letters and Non-Fiction, 1909–1959*, eds. Tom Hiney and Frank MacShane (London: Hamish Hamilton, 2000), 142.

78 *"camera angles, stage . . . story"*: Ibid.

78 *"there must be . . . written"*: Raymond Chandler to Sol Siegal, April 27, 1951, in Hiney and MacShane, eds., *Raymond Chandler Papers*, 162.

78 *However, in postproduction Hitchcock . . . executives*: Charles Barr, *Vertigo*, 2nd ed. (London: BFI, 2012), 11. See also Dan Auiler, *Vertigo: The Making of a Hitchcock Classic* (London: Titan, 1999).

79 *"the type of . . . suspense"*: AH to Vladimir Nabokov, November 19, 1964, AHC MHL.

79 *"As I indicated . . . story-teller"*: Ibid.

80 *"symbolized the more . . . symbolism"*: Hunter, *Me and Hitch*, 24.

80 *"we are going . . . doing it?' "*: AH to Evan Hunter, November 30, 1961, AHC MHL. Published in Auiler, *Hitchcock's Secret Notebooks*, 209.

80 *"It's those damned . . . reality"*: Baer, *Classic American Films*, 70.

80 *"shot at, caged . . . longer!"*: March 9, 1969, Sandee to AHC MHL.

80 *"Why should I . . . omnipotent"*: Cited in Robert Kapsis, *Hitchcock: The Making of a Reputation* (Chicago and London: University of Chicago Press, 1992), 68. A form of those words appears in numerous letters from Hitchcock's office to members of the public during the 1960s, AHC MHL. Kapsis's book reproduces various letters from members of the public who were confused, curious, and angered by the film's oblique ending and the lack of apparent reason for the birds' attack, 64–68.

4: THE WOMANIZER

81 *"Hitchcock's genius . . . pettiness"*: G. A. Atkinson, "The Authenticity of Alfred," *The Era*, December 16, 1931, 10.

82 *"Too big and . . . looking"*: AH to David O. Selznick, July 19, 1939, AHC MHL, reprinted in Auiler, *Hitchcock's Secret Notebooks*, 308.

82 *"Grotesque"*: AH to David O. Selznick, July 21, 1939, AHC MHL, reprinted in Auiler, *Hitchcock's Secret Notebooks*, 309.

82 *"We liked each . . . about it"*: Joan Fontaine, *No Bed of Roses* (London: W.H. Allen, 1978), 116.

82 *"I did . . . bawling"*: Leff, *Hitchcock and Selznick*, 74. Originally printed in *Photoplay*, September 1979, 57.

82 *"gorgeous genius . . . demands!"*: "Exposing Weaknesses of Top Ranking Stars," *Modern Screen*, December 1940, 24. Joan Fontaine Collection, HGARC.

83 the *"suffragette outrages" . . . ladylike:* For an excellent overview of Britain's suffragette movement, see Diane Atkinson, *Rise Up Women!: The Remarkable Lives of the Suffragettes* (London: Bloomsbury, 2018).

83 *When the American . . . director:* Anthony Slide, *The Silent Feminists: America's First Women Directors* (Lanham, MD, and London: Scarecrow Press, 1996), xvii.

84 *identified in some . . . Codd:* John Russell Taylor in his authorized biography *Hitch* names the writer as Anita Ross; in an unpublished part of an interview with Peter Bogdanovich, Hitchcock called her Elsie Codd.

84 *Hitchcock's writing work . . . Morton:* Bryony Dixon, "The White Shadow," http://www.screenonline.org.uk/film/id/1423007/index.html.

84 *"caught on the hop":* Balcon, *Michael Balcon Presents*, 16.

85 *"without a soul":* Title card from *The White Shadow* (1923).

85 *"to please women . . . audience":* Alfred Hitchcock, "How I Choose My Heroines," in Langford Reed and Hetty Spiers, eds., *Who's Who in Filmland* (London: Chapman and Hall, 1931), xxi.

85 *"80 percent of . . . choice":* Huw Weldon, "Alfred Hitchcock on His Films," *The Listener*, August 6, 1964, 189.

86 *"never had the gift of friendship":* Donald Spoto, *Spellbound by Beauty: Alfred Hitchcock and His Leading Ladies* (London: Arrow, 2009), loc. 3777 of 4805, Kindle.

87 *"fruitful kind of . . . opinions":* Joseph McBride, "Mr. and Mrs. Hitchcock," *Sight & Sound* 45, no. 4 (Autumn 1976): 225.

87 *"Although I think . . . them":* Tony Lee Moral, *Hitchcock and the Making of* Marnie (Lanham, MD; Toronto; Plymouth, UK: Scarecrow Press, 2013), 100.

87 *Hitchcock told some . . . conceived:* McGilligan, *Darkness and Light*, loc. 4009 of 20272, Kindle.

88 *"to tell me . . . life!":* Truffaut, *Hitchcock*, 34.

89 *"not a backward . . . century":* Spoto, *Spellbound by Beauty*, loc. 276 of 4805, Kindle.

89 *"exactly how male and female joined":* E. M. Forster, diary entry, cited in Wendy Moffatt, *A Great Unrecorded History: A New Life of E. M. Forster* (New York: Farrar, Straus & Giroux, 2010), 39.

89 *"women with sex . . . baubles":* Roderick Mann, "Hitchcock: Show Must Go On," *Los Angeles Times*, August 8, 1978, part IV, 7.

89   *"a woman who . . . air"*: Alfred Hitchcock, "Elegance Above Sex," in Gottlieb, ed., *Hitchcock on Hitchcock, Volume 1*, 95. Originally published in *Hollywood Reporter*, November 1962, 172.

89   *"Anything could happen . . . taxi"*: American Film Institute, "Dialogue on Film: Alfred Hitchcock," in Sidney Gottlieb, ed., *Alfred Hitchcock Interviews* (Jackson: University Press of Mississippi, 2003), 93.

89   *a real-life experience . . . thirties*: Evan Hunter, Kirby.

90   *"typical American woman . . . mother"*: Bogdanovich, *Who the Devil Made It*, loc. 10034 of 15740, Kindle.

90   *"the snow princess . . . writer"*: Bryan Mawr, quoted in Robert Lacey, *Grace* (London: Sidgwick & Jackson, 1994), 138.

90   *Hitchcock's view of . . . women*: Steven DeRosa, *Writing with Hitchcock: The Collaboration of Alfred Hitchcock and John Michael Hayes* (New York and London: Faber & Faber, 2001).

90   *In each of . . . characters*: For a brilliant description of Lisa's "alien presence" in *Rear Window*, see Tania Modleski, *The Women Who Knew Too Much: Hitchcock and Feminist Theory*, 2nd ed. (New York and London: Routledge, 2005), 73.

91   *women, as Richard Allen . . . intuition*: Richard Allen, *Hitchcock's Romantic Irony* (New York: Columbia University Press, 2007), 81.

92   *"very well known . . . breasts"*: Arthur Knight, "Conversation with Alfred Hitchcock," in Gottlieb, ed., *Alfred Hitchcock Interviews*, 175. Originally published in *Oui*, February 1973, 67–68, 82, 114, 116–21.

92   *"A woman who . . . you"*: "Women," in Gottlieb, ed., *Hitchcock on Hitchcock, Volume 2*, 226. Originally published in *Picture Show and TV Mirror*, September 12, 1959, 15.

93   *there were multiple . . . judging*: Including, Eric D. Morley (Miss World) to AH, October 15, 1963; George J. Cavalier (Miss California) to AH, April 4, 1963; Maureen Dragone (Miss Zodiac) to AH, July 29, 1972, AHC MHL.

94   *sounded out about . . . 1978*: Jason Frankfort, Women's Basketball Association to AH, October 24, 1978, AHC MHL.

94   *"It's easy for . . . again"*: June Morfield, "The One Man Grace Kelly Couldn't Say 'No' To," *TV Radio Mirror*, July 1962, 89.

94   *"Hitchcock Gives Free . . . Sex"*: "Hitchcock Gives Free Rein to the Gentle Sex," *TV Guide*, May 10, 1958, 12.

95   *"it was very . . . ideas"*: Rui Nogueira and Nicoletta Zalaffi, "Hitch, Hitch, Hitch, Hurrah!" in Gottlieb, ed., *Hitchcock Interviews*, 123. Originally published in *Écran*, July-August 1972, 2–8.

95   *"rich man who . . . detail"*: Ibid.

95   *"I took a . . . dissipated"*: Hedda Hopper, "Papa Hitchcock," *Chicago Sunday Tribune Magazine*, April 29, 1962, C16, DSP UCLA.

96   *"you go to . . . wasted":* "Hitchcock on Truffaut," in Gottlieb, ed., *Hitchcock on Hitch-cock, Volume 2*, 133.

96   *In her book . . . naivete:* Lois Banner, *American Beauty* (New York: Alfred A. Knopf, 1983), 284.

97   *In a draft . . . script:* Draft of *The Trouble with Harry,* July 27, 1954, written by John Michael Hayes, AHC MHL.

97   *"poor Marilyn had . . . face":* transcript of AH interview with Peter Bogdanovich, 1962, AHC MHL.

97   *"high-style, lady-like . . . Colbert":* Moral, *Making of* Marnie, 17. Transcripts of the Hitchcock-Truffaut interviews, AHC MHL.

97   *"Shortly after our . . . gasped":* Tippi Hedren, *Tippi: A Memoir* (New York: William Morrow, 2016), loc. 614–25 of 3653, Kindle.

98   *"Tippi started to . . . eyes":* Hitchcock O'Connell and Bouzereau, *Alma Hitchcock,* 189.

98   *"eyes were dry . . . himself":* Hedren, *Tippi,* loc. 625 of 3653, Kindle.

98   *"It was brutal . . . relentless":* Ibid., loc. 791 of 3653, Kindle.

99   *"very hard for . . . watch it":* Kyle Counts, "The Making of Alfred Hitchcock's *The Birds,"* *Cinemafantastique,* Fall 1980, 33.

99   *Even when Hedren . . . her:* Notes on Edwin Miller's interview with Tippi Hedren and Alfred Hitchcock, March 20, 1963, Edwin Miller Interviews for *Seventeen* Magazine, Rare Books and Manuscript Division, New York Public Library.

99   *"He was not . . . fabulous":* Peter Anthony Holder, *Great Conversations* (Albany, NY: BearManor Media, 2017), loc. 3273 of 3562, Kindle.

100   *"threw himself on . . . memory":* Hedren, *Tippi,* loc. 709 of 3653, Kindle.

100   *"referred to my* weight": Taylor, *Hitch,* loc. 221 of 5468, Kindle.

100   *"I've never gone . . . repulsed":* Hedren, *Tippi,* loc. 989–1001 of 3653, Kindle.

100   *Hedren contends that . . . untrue:* Tony Lee Moral, "How Accurate is *The Girl?"* *Broadcast,* December 14, 2012, http://www.broadcastnow.co.uk/comment/how-accurate-is-the-girl/5050231.article.

102   *"How else is . . . Hitchcock?":* John Russell Taylor, "Alfred Hitchcock: Fact and Fiction by John Russell Taylor," April 8, 2013, https://bloomsburyreader.wordpress.com/2013/04/08/alfred-hitchcock-fact-and-fiction-by-john-russell-taylor/.

102   *"It was an . . . different":* McGilligan, *Darkness and Light,* loc. 12557 of 20272, Kindle.

103   *"capable of questionable . . . mouth":* Ibid., loc. 3993 of 20272, Kindle.

103   *"ugly, intimate demands":* Spoto, *Dark Side of Genius,* 550.

103   *"I'm being erotic . . . Hitchcock":* David Freeman in discussion with the author, October 6, 2018.

103   *"a god of cinema":* This form of words, and similar terms, have been used to describe Hitchcock by multiple actors, directors, and critics, including Barbara Leigh-Hunt and William Devane, who both used it in interviews with the author.

103 *"It was a . . . knowing this":* David Freeman in discussion with the author, October 6, 2018.

104 *"lots of laughs . . . boy":* Peggy Robertson, OHP.

104 *"absolutely charming. He . . . right":* Marcella Rabwin, interviewed by Tim Kirby for *Reputations*, BBC. Courtesy BBC / Tim Kirby.

104 *"He was sarcastic . . . overlooked it":* Ibid.

104 *"Every relationship my . . . required":* Jean Stein, *West of Eden* (London: Jonathan Cape, 2016), 178.

104 *"the vanity of . . . cold, too":* Elspeth Grant, "Converted to Beatledom," *Tatler*, July 22, 1964, 183.

105 *"glaringly fake cardboard . . . script":* Eugene Archer, "Hitchcock's 'Marnie,' with Tippi Hedren and Sean Connery," *New York Times*, June 23, 1964, 19.

105 *"If you don't . . . cinema":* Robin Wood, in *The Trouble with Marnie*, DVD extra on *Marnie*, 2005.

106 *"Evan, when he . . . face!":* Hunter, *Me and Hitch*, 75.

106 *"reason for making the movie,"* Ibid.

106 *"I'm very fond . . . rape":* Richard Allen, "An Interview with Jay Presson Allen," in *Framing Hitchcock: Selected Essays from the Hitchcock Annual*, eds. Sidney Gottlieb and Christopher Brookhouse (Detroit: Wayne State University Press, 2002), 208.

106 *"didn't bother me . . . [Mark]":* Jay Presson Allen, interviewed by Tim Kirby for *Reputations*, BBC, PMC WHS.

106 *"full-on misogyny . . . apologism":* Bidisha, "What's Wrong with Hitchcock's Women," *Guardian*, October 21, 2010, https://www.theguardian.com/film/2010/oct/21/alfred-hitchcock-women-psycho-the-birds-bidisha.

106 *"has a singular . . . himself":* William Rothman, *Hitchcock: The Murderous Gaze*, 2nd ed. (Albany: State University of New York Press, 2002), 360.

106 *"whose will, if . . . whom":* Ibid., 414.

106 *"so-called rape":* Ibid., 411.

106 *"gives him grounds . . . her":* Ibid., 416.

106 *"entranced, turned inward":* Ibid.

107 *In the 1980s . . . much:* Wood, *Hitchcock's Films Revisited*, 241–22.

107 *"portrait of a . . . graceful":* Truffaut, *Hitchcock*, 155.

107 *"carnal qualities . . . brassiere":* Ibid., 248.

108 *"her dignity and glamour":* Barbara J. Buchanan, "Alfred Hitchcock Tells a Woman that Women Are a Nuisance," *Film Weekly*, September 20, 1935, 10.

108 *"a nuisance . . . girls!":* Ibid.

108 *"entered into the . . . her!":* Alfred Hitchcock, "Making 'The Thirty-Nine Steps,'" *Film Weekly*, May 23, 1936, 29.

108 *"torture the women!":* Cited in Spoto, *Dark Side of Genius*, 458. Quoting Stephen Rebello, "Plotting with Hitchcock," *The Real Paper*, February 16, 1980, 30–31.

108   *"sooner or later... humiliated":* Roger Ebert, *"Vertigo,"* October 13, 1996, https://www.rogerebert.com/reviews/great-movie-vertigo-1958.

109   *"When one is... 'yes, but...'":* Modleski, *The Women Who Knew Too Much,* 3.

5: THE FAT MAN

110   *"I don't know... disgracefully":* AH to Darryl F. Zanuck, August 30, 1943, in Auiler, *Hitchcock's Secret Notebooks,* 131.

110   *"It has tempo... level":* Darry F. Zanuck to AH, September 4, 1943, ibid., 132.

110   *"Hitch knows more... know":* Walter Slezak, *What Time's the Next Swan?* (Garden City, NY: Doubleday, 1962), 219.

111   *"there's no law... comfortable":* Hume Cronyn, *A Terrible Liar: A Memoir* (New York: William Morrow, 1991), 163.

112   *"accidentally swallow... away":* Alfred Hitchcock, "The Woman Who Knows Too Much," *McCall's,* March 1956, 12.

113   *"I don't feel... fat":* John D. Weaver, "The Man Behind the Body," *Holiday,* September 1964, 85.

114   *"I have all... fat":* Robert Boyle, OHP.

114   *"The casting department... self":* Alfred Hitchcock, "The Real Me (The Thin One)," *Daily Express,* August 9, 1966, 8.

115   *"funny-looking":* Chandler, *It's Only a Movie,* 33.

115   *"You'll grow out of it":* Ibid.

116   *"You're sitting on it":* Emerson Batdorf, "Let's Hear It for Hitchcock," in Gottlieb, ed., *Hitchcock Interviews,* 78. Originally published in *Cleveland Plain Dealer,* February 1, 1970, 28–31.

116   *"in England, everyone... on it":* David Freeman, *Last Days of Alfred Hitchcock* (Woodstock, NY: Overlook Press, 1984), 6.

116   *"was not one... food":* Coleman, *The Man Who Knew Hitchcock,* 253.

116   *"his pleasure was... efficiency":* David Freeman, interviewed by Tim Kirby for *Reputations,* BBC, PMC WHS.

116   *When he threw... 1892:* Chandler, *It's Only a Movie,* 233.

117   *"He is much... ice-cream":* Rita Grosvenor, "I don't scare easily, says Mrs Hitchcock," *Sunday Express,* January 30, 1972, 3.

117   *"feet planted firmly... hand":* Spike Hughes, "Coarse Cricket," *Daily Herald,* July 30, 1938, 8.

118   *"Hitch insists on... time!":* Hitchcock O'Connell and Bouzereau, *Alma Hitchcock,* 151.

118   *Whitfield Cook recalled... "watched":* Ibid.

118   *"He does not... most":* T.H.E., "Meet the Strong, Silent Director!" *Sunderland Daily Echo and Shipping Gazette,* February 16, 1935, 10.

118 *"sprawl artistically on . . . gleaming":* Frank S. Nugent, "Assignment in Hollywood," *Good Housekeeping,* November 1945, 12.

118 *The turn against . . . more:* Daniel Delis Hill, *Advertising to the American Woman, 1900–1999* (Columbus: Ohio State University Press, 2002).

119 *Male bodies were . . . bodybuilding:* Peter Stearns, *Fat History: Bodies and Beauty in the Modern West* (New York: New York University Press, 1997), 20.

119 *William Howard Taft . . . weight:* Alexis Coe, "William Howard Taft Is Still Stuck in the Tub," *New York Times,* September 15, 2017, https://www.nytimes .com/2017/09/15/opinion/william-howard-taft-bathtub.html.

119 *In 1909, Lillian Russell . . . workout:* Stearns, *Fat History,* 20.

119 *When the German . . . shape:* Toni Bentley, *Sisters of Salome* (Lincoln: University of Nebraska Press, 2005), 38.

119 *A few years later . . . singers:* Edward White, *The Tastemaker: Carl Van Vechten and the Birth of Modern America* (New York: Farrar, Straus & Giroux, 2014), 79.

119 *"Working with Hitch . . . him":* Shirley MacLaine, *I'm Over All That: And Other Confessions* (New York: Atria, 2012), 70.

119 *"I wasn't blonde . . . me":* Shirley MacLaine, interview by James Corden, *The Late Late Show with James Corden,* CBS, March 1, 2017.

119 *"breakfast was pancakes . . . soufflés":* MacLaine, *I'm Over All That,* 70.

120 *If Smith's account . . . brandy:* H. Allen Smith, "Hitchcock Likes to Smash Cups," *New York World-Telegram,* August 28, 1937, 7.

120 *He was reported . . . debut:* McGilligan, *Darkness and Light,* loc. 4666 of 20272, Kindle.

120 *"His free-floating, unconfined . . . another":* "Falstaff in Manhattan," *New York Times,* September 5, 1937, 122.

120 *"Alfred Hitchcock has . . . flee":* Lawrence Greene, "He Is a Camera," *Esquire,* August 1952, 43.

120 *"forepart of a . . . chins":* Walter Ross, "Murder in the Mezzanine," *Esquire,* January 1954, 75.

121 *"The newcomer was . . . suit":* Alva Johnston, "300-Pound Prophet Comes to Hollywood," *Saturday Evening Post,* May 22, 1943, 12.

121 *"holds two distinctions . . . cords":* Bill Davidson, "Alfred Hitchcock Resents," *Saturday Evening Post,* December 15, 1962, 62.

121 *"comply with their . . . arose":* Casey McKittrick, *Hitchcock's Appetites: The Corpulent Plots of Desire and Dread* (New York and London: Bloomsbury, 2016), 30.

121 *he had caught . . . image:* Leff, *Hitchcock and Selznick,* 107.

122 *he was experiencing . . . enlarged:* McKittrick, *Hitchcock's Appetites,* 27.

123 *Joel McCrea, the . . . 1940:* Ibid., 28. See also Spoto, *Dark Side of Genius,* 31.

123 *Around the same . . . Suspicion:* Ibid. See also McGilligan, *Darkness and Light,* loc. 6331 of 20272, Kindle.

123 *Anthony Shaffer, the screenwriter... again:* McGilligan, *Darkness and Light*, loc. 15965 of 20272, Kindle.

123 Life *magazine, which... an eight-week period:* "Speaking of Pictures... Alfred Hitchcock Reduces as Plant Expands," *Life*, March 13, 1944, DSP UCLA.

124 *"Hitchcock countenance will... building":* Alfred Hitchcock, "My Most Exciting Picture," in Gottlieb, ed., *Hitchcock on Hitchcock, Volume 1*, 282. Originally published in *Popular Photography*, November 1948. See also George E. Turner, "Rope—Something Different," *American Cinematographer*, 1985.

124 *"one of the... century":* Jan Olsson, *Hitchcock à la Carte* (Durham, NC, and London: Duke University Press, 2015), 1.

126 *"the breast ballet":* Whitfield Cook, diary, April 1, 1945, Whitfield Cook Collection, HGARC.

126 *"the whistling sailor... expression":* Rodney Ackland and Elspeth Grant, *The Celluloid Mistress, or The Custard Pie of Dr. Caligari* (London: Allan Wingate, 1954), 38.

126 *As originally written... obese: Torn Curtain* script, October 6, 1965, AHC MHL.

126 *"I don't look... garret":* Chandler, *It's Only a Movie*, 11.

126 *"simply but a lot":* Ben Wickham, "Hitchcock Co., Horror Unlimited," unknown publication, 1940, AHC MHL.

126 *By the 1950s... martini:* Clark, "Here's Hitchcock's Recipe for Suspense," 11.

127 *"that turkey and eggnog waistline":* "It's Time Now to Start Taking Off That Turkey and Eggnog Waistline," *Los Angeles Times*, January 18, 1955, B2.

127 *the paper's West... sophistication:* Telegram from AH to Mary Reinholz, September 13, 1967, AHC MHL.

127 *For the popular... fifties:* Olsson, *Hitchcock à la Carte*, 54, citing Selma Robinson, "Alfred Hitchcock in the Hundred-Pound Mystery," *McCall's*, April 1958, 58, 150, 152–53.

127 *he suggested, they... fact:* Chandler, *It's Only a Movie*, 118.

127 *"I don't get... off":* Richard Gehman, "Chairman of the Board," in Gottlieb, ed., *Hitchcock on Hitchcock, Volume 2*, 235. Article found in the Film Study Center, Museum of Modern Art, Hitchcock clippings folder #2. No publication or page number.

127 *"He used to... about it":* Donald Spoto, *High Society: Grace Kelly and Hollywood* (London: Hutchinson, 2005), 138, citing Roderick Mann, "Princess Grace: How a Royal Beauty Stays Beautiful," *Ladies Home Journal*, May 1970.

127 *"We would gather... more":* Oleg Cassini, *In My Own Fashion: An Autobiography* (London: Simon & Schuster, 1987), 252–53.

128 *"It was a meticulously timed event":* Marcella Rabwin, interviewed by Tim Kirby for *Reputations*, BBC, courtesy BBC / Tim Kirby.

128 *His expenditure on... liquor:* Report made by Carol Stevens of AH's income and expenditure for 1939, February 6, 1940, AHC MHL.

128   *"Grace was never . . . so":* Edith Head, *The Dress Doctor* (Kingswood, UK: World's Work, 1960), 151.

128   *"I loved to . . . dessert":* Charlotte Chandler, *Ingrid: Ingrid Bergman, A Personal Biography* (London: Simon & Schuster, 2007), 124.

129   *Pat remembers that . . . wife:* Hitchcock O'Connell and Bouzereau, *Alma Hitchcock*, 228.

129   *"They took their . . . dishes":* Ibid., 230.

129   *which apparently cost . . . house:* Martin Abramson, "What Hitchcock Does with His Blood Money," *Cosmopolitan*, January 1964, 74.

129   *In his excellent . . . 1963:* Olsson, *Hitchcock à la Carte*, 57–61.

129   *Olsson points out . . . kitchens:* Ibid., 57.

129   *"Food, like pure . . . something":* Marilyn Kaytor, "The Alfred Hitchcock Dinner Hour," *Look*, August 27, 1963, DSP UCLA.

130   *From the mid-sixties . . . maintain:* Olsson, *Hitchcock à la Carte*, 57.

130   *In 1966, he . . . issued:* AH to Geoffrey Watkins, May 13, 1966, AHC MHL.

130   *the decade in . . . began:* Greg Critser, *Fat Land: How Americans Became the Fattest People in the World* (Boston and New York: Houghton Mifflin, 2003).

130   *Weekly check-ups with . . . week:* AH appointment books, AHC MHL.

131   *He'd ask a . . . vodka:* Ernest Lehman, Kirby.

131   *the maid knew . . . medicinal:* AH to Elsie Randolph, December 6, 1978, AHC MHL.

131   *he'd find a . . . swigs:* David Freeman in discussion with the author, October 6, 2018.

132   *"Lunch usually consists . . . week":* AH to Gladys Hitching, June 15, 1978, AHC MHL.

132   *While his television . . . lip:* See McKittrick, *Hitchcock's Appetites*, for a more thorough exploration of how Hitchcock used his body to build his brand in various ways.

132   *David O. Selznick . . . re-release:* David O. Selznick to AH, August 28, 1956, DSP UCLA.

132   *Hitchcock refused:* Herman Citron to David O. Selznick, August 30, 1956, DSP UCLA.

132   *Later, a PR executive . . . design:* Bill Blowitz to AH, March 21, 1963, AHC MHL.

132   *Again, Hitchcock said no:* Ibid. Annotation at the top of Blowitz's letter states that Hitchcock rejected the idea of changing his silhouette.

6: THE DANDY

134   *"It's inherently uncinematic . . . movie":* David Fincher in *Rope: Pro and Con*, DVD extra on *Hitchcock/Truffaut*, 2016.

135   *"a man unduly . . . dandy":* Search result from google.com, March 1, 2019.

135   *Wilde, the unignorable . . . imagination:* For more on the self-invention of Wilde's dandy persona as a key to his celebrity, see David M. Friedman, *Wilde in America: Oscar Wilde and the Invention of Modern Celebrity* (New York: W. W. Norton, 2014).

136   *Under his influence . . . existence:* For a vivid and entertaining biography of Brummell, see Ian Kelly, *Beau Brummell: The Ultimate Dandy* (London: Hodder & Stoughton, 2005).

136 *"We can't recall . . . affection":* Frank S. Nugent, "The Screen in Review," *New York Times*, October 12, 1939, 33.

136 *"virtually unwatchable":* Barr, *English Hitchcock*, 204.

136 *"Laughton's picture, not Hitchcock's":* Peter Ackroyd, *Alfred Hitchcock* (London: Chatto & Windus, 2015), 81.

136 *The film features . . . performance: Jamaica Inn* shooting script, Alfred Hitchcock Collection, BFI.

137 *While still working . . . Strand:* Taylor, *Hitch*, loc. 779 of 5468, Kindle.

137 *"the kind of . . . to be":* Samuel Taylor, in "Reputations," *Hitch: Alfred the Great*, BBC Two, May 30, 1999.

138 *"the Hollywood people . . . combination":* Transcript of Hitchcock's interview with Peter Bogdanovich, AHC MHL.

138 *"a form of . . . months":* Oscar Wilde, "The Philosophy of Dress," *New York Tribune*, April 19, 1885, 9.

139 *One Hitchcock biographer . . . Sternberg:* Taylor, *Hitch*, loc. 2683 of 5468, Kindle.

139 *"The dandy does . . . living":* Philip Mann, *The Dandy at Dusk: Taste and Melancholy in the Twentieth Century* (London: Head of Zeus, 2017), 5.

139 "always *wore them . . . Marrakesh":* Thomas Elsaesser, "The Dandy in Hitchcock," in Richard Allen and S. Ishii Gonzales, eds., *Alfred Hitchcock: Centenary Essays* (London: British Film Institute, 1999), 4.

139 *One friend, permitted . . . weight:* Chandler, *It's Only a Movie*, 2.

140 *Hitchcock sometimes said . . . proportions:* Ibid., 1.

140 *"uniform in its . . . details":* Mann, *The Dandy at Dusk*, 33.

140 *Appointment books kept . . . tailor:* AH appointment books, AHC MHL.

140 *"Whenever I need . . . "Make that!'":* Judy Klemsrud, "Men's Clothes: Here Comes the Liberace Look," *New York Times*, March 4, 1970, 50.

140 *"dramatic and emotional . . . thought":* Thornton Delehanty, "A Liberated Hitchcock Dreams Gaudy Dreams in Technicolor," *New York Herald Tribune*, April 22, 1945, AHC MHL.

141 *"red drops of . . . strongly":* "Some Thoughts on Color by Alfred Hitchcock," *Adelaide Advertiser*, September 4, 1937, 13.

141 *"smears her lips . . . on it":* Delehanty, "A Liberated Hitchcock Dreams Gaudy Dreams in Technicolor."

141 *"Hitchcock thinks in . . . color":* Edith Head and Jane Kesner Ardmore, *The Dress Doctor* (Kingswood, Surrey: World's Work, 1960), 159.

141 *"an education in restraint":* Edith Head and Paddy Calistro, *Edith Head's Hollywood* (New York: Dutton, 1983), 58.

141 *"She's an extraordinarily . . . colour":* Head and Kesner Ardmore, *Dress Doctor*, 160.

142 *"Hitch paints a . . . suit":* Ibid., 21.

142 *"helped me stand . . . Madeleine":* Auiler, *Vertigo*, 68.

142 *"I think Hitchcock . . . camera"*: Eva Marie Saint, OHP.

142 *"He had such . . . Kendall"*: Ibid.

143 *"Martin, put on . . . surroundings"*: Tim Burrows, "Martin Landau: 'I chose to play Leonard as gay,'" *Daily Telegraph*, October 12, 2012, https://www.telegraph.co.uk/culture/film/starsandstories/9601547/Martin-Landau-I-chose-to-play-Leonard-as-gay.html.

143 *"Excuse me, Mr.Landau . . . impossible"*: Tom Mankiewicz and Robert Crane, *My Life as a Mankiewicz: An Insider's Journey through Hollywood* (Lexington: University Press of Kentucky, 2012), 109.

143 "North by Northwest . . . suit": Todd McEwen, "Cary Grant's Suit," in *How Not to Be American: Misadventures in the Land of the Free* (London: Aurum, 2013), 147.

145 *"it would be . . . sadism"*: Ibid., 151.

145 *"gone to any . . . taste"*: Cary Grant, "Cary Grant on Style," *GQ*, April 15, 2013, https://www.gq.com/story/cary-grant-on-style. Originally published in *GQ*, Winter 1967–68.

145 *"She's wearing a . . . slacks?"*: Head and Kesner Ardmore, *Dress Doctor*, 156.

145 *"the only actor I ever loved"*: Nancy Nelson, *Evenings with Cary Grant* (New York: Warner, 1993), 211.

145 *"a rapport and . . . words"*: Grant McCann, *Cary Grant: A Class Apart* (New York: Columbia University Press, 1996), 180.

146 *"have the privilege . . . know"*: AH to Cary Grant, March 13, 1979, Cary Grant Papers, MHL.

146 *"Hitch thinks it . . . casually"*: Hunter, *Me and Hitch*, 15.

146 *"Real directors wear ties"*: Hitchcock O'Connell and Bouzereau, *Alma Hitchcock*, 83.

147 *"I was so thrilled . . . tell"*: Peggy Robertson, OHP.

147 *A look in . . . homes*: Appraisal of property at 10957 Bellagio Road, Bel Air, by John J. Donahue and Associates, 1962, AHC MHL.

148 *"Someone should bring . . . saucer"*: Walter Raubicheck, "Working with Hitchcock: A Collaborators' Forum with Patricia Hitchcock, Janet Leigh, Teresa Wright, and Eva Marie Saint," in *Hitchcock Annual*, 2002–03, 33.

148 *More indecorous behavior . . . can*: Taylor, *Hitch*, loc. 4777 of 5468, Kindle.

148 *"I've come to . . . us"*: Alfred Hitchcock, "Would You Like to Know Your Future?" in Gottlieb, ed., *Hitchcock on Hitchcock, Volume 1*, 140–41. Originally published in *Guideposts Magazine* 14, no. 8 (October 1959): 1–4.

149 *"Let's play"*: Bogdanovich, *Who the Devil Made It*, loc. 9300 of 15740, Kindle.

149 *"knows more about . . . job"*: Coleman, *The Man Who Knew Hitchcock*, 236.

149 *"to keep the . . . in him"*: Spoto, *Dark Side of Genius*, 406–7.

150 *"protest, the triumph . . . art"*: Elsaesser, "The Dandy in Hitchcock," 5.

150 *"unshakable resolve not . . . moved"*: Mann, *Dandy at Dusk*, 30.

151 *"negative acting, the . . . nothing"*: "Film Crasher Hitchcock," *Cue*, May 19, 1951, DSP UCLA.

151 *"The screen actor . . . well":* Alfred Hitchcock, "Direction," in Charles Davy, ed., *Footnotes to the Film* (London: Lovat Dickson, 1937), 9.

151 *"You have got . . . over it":* Bogdanovich, *Who the Devil Made It*, loc. 10166 of 15740, Kindle.

152 *"One cannot become . . . man":* Chandler, *It's Only a Movie*, 309.

152 *John Landis was . . . bearing:* Ibid.

152 *"You hear about . . . afresh":* Freeman, *The Last Days of Alfred Hitchcock*, 5.

152 *"I don't give . . . weeks":* Bruce Dern with Christopher Fryer and Robert Crane, *Things I've Said, But Probably Shouldn't Have: An Unrepentant Memoir* (Hoboken, NJ: Wiley, 2007), 143.

152 *Apparently, the brazenness . . . unapproachability:* Bruce Dern, Kirby.

153 *"A lot of . . . they are":* AH, interview by Richard Schickel, *The Men Who Made the Movies: Alfred Hitchcock*, PBS, November 4, 1973.

153 *Laurents was as . . . 1940s:* See Arthur Laurents, *Original Story By: A Memoir of Broadway and Hollywood* (New York: Alfred A. Knopf, 2000).

153 *harassment and criminalization . . . wars:* see George Chauncey, *Gay New York: The Making of the Gay Male World, 1890–1940* (London: Flamingo, 1995).

153 *"built sexual ambiguity . . . material":* Farley Granger, *Include Me Out: My Life from Goldwyn to Broadway* (New York: St. Martin's Press, 2007), 69.

154 *"According to Hitchcock . . . attack":* Laurents, *Original Story By*, 131.

154 *"always sexual":* Ibid.

154 *"Not once was . . . do it":* David Thomson, "Charms and the Man," *Film Comment*, February 1984, 61.

155 *"a new kind . . . at all?":* McCann, *Cary Grant*, 121.

155 *"It was just . . . while":* Ackland and Grant, *The Celluloid Mistress*, 35.

155 *"a soft baby-face . . . effeminate":* Ernest Lehman, *North by Northwest* (New York: Viking Press, 1972), 11.

155 *"if there is . . . Code":* Geoffrey M. Shurlock to Robert Vogel, of the Motion Picture Association of America, August 21, 1958, AHC MHL.

155 *Yet Landau intentionally . . . infatuated:* Burrows, "Martin Landau: 'I chose to play Leonard as gay.'"

156 *"Martin," he assured . . . "role":* Ibid.

156 *An "odd, weird, little faggish man":* McGilligan, *Darkness and Light*, loc. 6342 of 20272, Kindle.

156 *"become a poof":* Taylor, *Hitch*, loc. 190 of 5468, Kindle.

156 *"sapphic overtones":* McGilligan, *Darkness and Light*, loc. 1476 of 20272, Kindle.

158 *"In the hotel . . . anything":* Truffaut, *Hitchcock*, 39.

158 *"They are all . . . trousers":* Batdorf, "Let's Hear It for Hitchcock," in Gottlieb, ed., *Alfred Hitchcock Interviews*, 77.

158 *Once, he did . . . 1957:* Alfred Hitchcock, "Alfred Hitchcock Presents: The Great Hitchcock Murder Mystery," *This Week*, August 4, 1957, 8–9, 11.

7: THE FAMILY MAN

159 *"Florence we just . . . badly"*: Alma Reville to Carol Shourds, April 18, 1951, AHC MHL. Published in Hitchcock O'Connell and Bouzereau, *Alma Hitchcock*, 156.

160 *"Journal of Mr. Hitchcock. . . . of it"*: AH to Carol Shourds, May 21, 1951, AHC MHL.

163 *"like a town without neon signs"*: Bogdanovich, *Who the Devil Made It*, loc. 9801 of 15740, Kindle.

163 *Throughout research and . . . perfect:* AH to Maxwell Anderson, March 15, 1956, AHC MHL.

164 *"cutting and continuity . . . capital 'A'"*: Alma Reville, "Cutting and Continuity," *Motion Picture News*, January 13, 1923, 10.

165 *"Alma in Wonderland . . . married!"*: "Alma in Wonderland: A woman's place is not always in the home," *Picturegoer*, December 1925, 48.

165 *prompting some researchers . . . career:* See Christiana Lane and Josephine Botting, " 'What Did Alma Think?' Continuity, Writing, Editing, and Adaptation," in *Hitchcock and Adaptation: On the Page and Screen*, ed. Mark Osteen (Lanham, MD, and Plymouth, UK: Rowman and Littlefield, 2014).

165 *"Be interested . . . country"*: Weston Edwards, "Making Good in the Film Trade," AHC MHL.

166 *"utmost value so . . . girls?"*: Roger Burford, "A New "Chair" Which a Woman Might Fill," *The Gateway for Women at Work*, July 1929, 102.

166 *"the product of . . . likely to"*: Alfred Hitchcock, "Making *Murder!*" *Cassell's Magazine*, August 1930, in Gottlieb, ed., *Hitchcock on Hitchcock, Volume 2*, 165. *NB: The author was unable to locate this piece in the edition of* Cassell's *given by Gottlieb in his anthology.*

166 *"who is two . . . coppice"*: Ibid., 164.

167 *"imbued with the . . . days"*: Alan Warwick, "Alfred Hitchcock's Tudor Cottage," *Home Chat*, February 27, 1932, AHC MHL.

167 *"delightfully vivacious and . . . garden"*: Mary Benedetta, "A Day with Hitchcock," unknown publication, undated, AHC MHL.

168 *"there is no . . . hall"*: Cyril Connolly, *Enemies of Promise* (Chicago: University of Chicago Press, 2008), 116.

168 *"I have a . . . cook"*: Jeffrey Meyers, *The Enemy: A Biography of Wyndham Lewis* (London: Routledge, 1980), 100. Originally published in Geoffrey Grigson, "Recollections of Wyndham Lewis," *The Listener*, May 16, 1957, 786.

168 *Hitchcock's affectionate public . . . highbrows:* See John Carey, *The Intellectuals and the Masses: Pride and Prejudice Among the Literary Intelligentsia, 1880–1939* (London: Faber & Faber, 1992), 152–81, for a discussion on Bennett's take on family life.

168 *"chaos world"*: The phrase was first used by Robin Wood in 1965. See Wood, *Hitchcock's Films Revisited*.

169 *As Donald Spoto . . . Hill:* Spoto, *Dark Side of Genius*, 132–33.

169 *"In front of . . . abroad!"*: Truffaut, *Hitchcock*, 80.

169 *"After it's all . . . movie"*: Bogdanovich, *Who the Devil Made It*, loc. 9534 of 15740, Kindle.

169 *as pointed out . . . Barr*: Barr, *English Hitchcock*, 122.

170 *"What I want . . . here"*: Geoffrey T. Hellman, "Alfred Hitchcock," *Life*, November 20, 1943, 43.

170 *Alma's green thumb . . . baskets*: Hitchcock O'Connell and Bouzereau, *Alma Hitchcock*, 99–100.

171 *The blurry snapshots . . . shirt*: Frederick Knott Collection, Beinecke Rare Book and Manuscript Library, Yale University.

171 *"When Hitchcock liked . . . family"*: Laurents, *Original Story By*, 125.

171 *felt like an adopted child*: Arthur Laurents, interview by Donald Spoto, October 19, 1981, DSP UCLA.

171 *"it was lovely . . . other"*: Laurents, *Original Story By*, 126.

171 *"Oh God, I . . . Daddy's"*: McGilligan, *Backstory 2*, 138–39.

171 *"It wasn't like . . . to do"*: Peggy Robertson, OHP.

172 *"He had very . . . personality"*: Chandler, *It's Only a Movie*, 256.

172 *Cook's agent wrote . . . role*: Jacques Chambrun to Whitfield Cook, November 17, 1944, Whitfield Cook Collection, HGARC.

172 *"Papa Hitchcock will . . . trouper"*: "Film Director's Daughter Scores in New Comedy," *Hartford Times*, October 13, 1944, Whitfield Cook Collection, HGARC.

173 *"her mother does . . . daughter"*: Marjory Adams, "Hitchcock, En Route Overseas, Stops Off for Daughter's Play," *Boston Morning Globe*, October 17, 1944, Whitfield Cook Collection, HGARC.

174 *In 1948, Cook . . . party*: December 24, 1948, and December 31, 1948, Whitfield Cook diary, Whitfield Cook Collection, HGARC.

174 *prior to engaging . . . Temple*: December 30, 1945, ibid. Cook's diary entry says David Selznick was interested in having Temple star in a remake of an old Hitchcock movie, but doesn't state which one.

174 *"late-Victorian sense of . . . smile"*: Whitfield Cook, "Happy Ending," Whitfield Cook Collection, HGARC.

174 *"gin and menstrual . . . beamish"*: Laurents, *Original Story By*, 126.

175 *"Unexpected evening!"*: Whitfield Cook Diary, September 20, 1948, Whitfield Cook Collection, HGARC.

175 *"Chez moi later"*: Whitfield Cook Diary, October 9, 1948, Whitfield Cook Collection, HGARC.

175 *"Dinner with A . . . call"*: Whitfield Cook Diary, October 1, 1948, Whitfield Cook Collection, HGARC.

175 *McGilligan also notes . . . together*: McGilligan, *Darkness and Light*, loc. 9739 of 20272, Kindle.

175 *In a diary . . . "Tears later":* Whitfield Cook Diary, October 7, 1948, Whitfield Cook Collection, HGARC.

176 *"married life was . . . of it":* Bennett, *Partner in Suspense*, 71.

176 *"very lonely this . . . arrived":* Alma Reville to Whitfield Cook, August 23, 1949, Whitfield Cook Collection, HGARC.

176 *"unintentionally hilarious":* Richard Coe, "Bergman Sobers Up Down Under," *Washington Post*, October 7, 1949, C12.

176 *"extremely attractive . . . and her warmth":* Hitchcock O'Connell and Bouzereau, *Alma Hitchcock*, 149.

176 *"Her First Island . . . protection":* Whitfield Cook, "Her First Island," Whitfield Cook Collection, HGARC.

177 *"affection, appreciation, encouragement, . . . collaboration":* AH speech at AFI Lifetime Achievement Award ceremony, March 7, 1979, "Alfred Hitchcock Accepts the AFI Life Achievement Award in 1979," American Film Institute YouTube channel, https://www.youtube.com/watch?v=pb5VdGCQFOM.

177 *"There was a . . . ahead":* Hitchcock O'Connell and Bouzereau, *Alma Hitchcock*, 7.

178 *Hitchcock said he . . . career:* Hitchcock, *The Woman Who Knows Too Much*, 14.

178 *With John Buchan's . . . blank:* Alma Reville's script notes, *The Three Hostages*, September 16, 1964, AHC MHL.

179 *"I had Mrs . . . quality":* AH to Richard Condon, December 8, 1964, Richard Condon Collection, HGARC.

179 *"that shot of . . . awful":* Freeman, *The Last Days of Alfred Hitchcock*, 19.

179 *"Alma hates the film":* Peggy Robertson, OHP.

179 *"weeping and shaking convulsively":* Taylor, *Hitch*, loc. 4233 of 5468, Kindle.

179 *In 1966 a . . . demurred:* Denis Gifford of the Central Office of Information, to Alma Reville, August 8, 1966, AHC MHL.

180 *"Mrs Hitchcock and . . . sense":* AH to Madeline Warren, February 20, 1974, AHC MHL.

180 *"will never be . . . too":* Hitchcock, "The Woman Who Knows Too Much," 14.

180 *"It was like . . . years":* David Freeman, in discussion with the author, October 6, 2018.

180 *"I think he . . . approval":* Freeman, *The Last Days of Alfred Hitchcock*, 19.

8: THE VOYEUR

182 *In 1915, Audrey Munson . . . years later:* James Bone, *The Curse of Beauty: The Scandalous & Tragic Life of Audrey Munson, America's First Supermodel* (New York: Simon & Schuster, 2016).

182 *evoking Duchamp's seminal . . . 1885:* Calvin Tomkins, *Duchamp: A Biography* (London: Pimlico, 1996), 78.

183   *"into this upper . . . films"*: Warhol, "Hitchcock," 8.

183   *"had been entirely . . . Dyson"*: Alfred Hitchcock, "The Chloroform Clue: My Favorite Mystery," in Gottlieb, ed., *Hitchcock on Hitchcock, Volume 2*, 47. Originally published in *American Weekly*, March 22, 1953, 18–20.

183   *"making violent love . . . looked on"*: Truffaut, *Hitchcock*, 206.

183   *In the first . . . love*: Draft script of *The Trouble with Harry*, July 27, 1954,
AHC MHL.

184   *Hitchcock imagined a . . . hair*: Notes from meeting about *The Short Night* between
AH, David Freeman, and Peggy Robertson, December 26, 1978.

184   *"male gaze"*: Laura Mulvey, "Visual Pleasure and Narrative Cinema," in *Film Theory and Criticism: Introductory Readings*, eds. Leo Braudy and Marshall Cohen
(New York: Oxford University Press, 1999), 833–44.

184   *"the little people . . . lives"*: Krohn, *Hitchcock at Work*, 141.

187   *"more concerned with . . . narration"*: John Belton, "Introduction: Spectacle and
Narrative," in *Alfred Hitchcock's* Rear Window, ed. John Belton (Cambridge, UK:
Cambridge University Press, 2000), 3.

187   *"Hitchcock taught me . . . silently"*: Patrick McGilligan, *Backstory 3: Interviews with
Screenwriters of the 1960s* (Berkeley: University of California Press, 1997), 181.

187   *"Of all the . . . cinematic"*: Alfred Hitchcock, *"Rear Window,"* in Gottlieb, ed.,
Hitchcock on Hitchcock, Volume 2, 95. Originally published in *Take One* 2, no.2
(November-December 1968), 18–20.

187   *"Galloping horses in . . . film"*: Ibid., 96.

187   *"Show a man . . . person"*: Alfred Hitchcock, "Film Production," in Gottlieb, ed.,
Hitchcock on Hitchcock, Volume 1, 215. Originally published in *Encyclopaedia Bri-
tannica*, vol. 15, 1965, 907–11.

187   *"What is he . . . man"*: AH, Markle, "A Talk with Hitchcock, Part One."

188   *"largely consisted of . . . bored"*: Roger Ebert, *Awake in the Dark: The Best of Roger
Ebert*, 2nd ed. (Chicago: University of Chicago Press, 2017), 11.

189   *"I watch, I . . . Hitchcock"*: Tippi Hedren, SMU.

189   *"the British disease"*: Vincent, David, *The Culture of Secrecy: Britain, 1832–1998*
(Oxford, UK: Oxford University Press, 1998), 10.

189   *"secrecy is as . . . society"*: Ibid.

189   *"always felt that . . . you"*: AH to Carol Shourds, May 21, 1951, AHC MHL.

190   *"a fake masterspy"*: Otis L. Guernsey to AH, October 14, 1957, in Auiler, *Hitchcock's
Secret Notebooks*, 205.

190   *Ernest Lehman was . . . Northwest*: Baer, *Classic American Films*, 66.

190   *"he had an . . . sense"*: Peggy Robertson, OHP.

190   *"It was as . . . eerie"*: Susan Royal, "Steven Spielberg in His Adventures on Earth,"
in *Steven Spielberg Interviews*, eds. Lester D. Friedman and Brent Notbohm (Jackson: University Press of Mississippi, 2000), 102.

191   *"never look at . . . done"*: Arthur Knight, "Conversation with Alfred Hitchcock," in
        Gottlieb, ed., *Alfred Hitchcock Interviews*, 178. Originally printed in *Oui*, February
        1973, 67–68, 82, 114, 116–21.

191   *"The general method . . . floor"*: Alfred Hitchcock, "Director's Problems," *The Lis-
        tener*, February 2, 1938, 241.

191   *"Films," he said, "are made before they are shot"*: David Lewin, "Alfred Hitchcock,"
        CinemaTV Today, August 19, 1972, 4.

191   *assistant production manager . . . hoof*: Hugh Brown notes, June 7, 1955, Paramount
        Production Records, MHL.

192   *"Hitchcock is a . . . over"*: Robert Benchley to Gertrude Benchley, March 25, 1940,
        Robert Benchley Collection, HGARC.

192   *"tracings of each . . . storyboard"*: Krohn, *Hitchcock at Work*, 13.

192   *Krohn posits that . . . methodology*: Ibid. See also "Campaign ideas for 'SABO-
        TEUR' " notes (undated) in AHC MHL.

192   *"a Pattern Designer"*: Duncan Underhill, "Hitchcock Is Like a Pattern Designer,"
        New York World-Telegram, April 6, 1940, AHC MHL.

192   *Many years later . . . wrapped*: Robert Boyle, OHP.

192   *"Every wall was . . . script"*: Granger, *Include Me Out*, 67.

193   *"But he never . . . dialogue"*: Krohn, *Hitchcock at Work*, 12.

193   *"He hardly ever . . . mind"*: Jack Cardiff, *Magic Hour* (London: Faber & Faber, 1996), 107.

193   *"He had his . . . reel"*: Ibid.

194   *"They were expecting . . . helpless"*: AH, interview by Mike Scott, *Cinema: Alfred
        Hitchcock*, DVD extra on *Hitchcock: The British Years*, DVD, 2008.

194   *"Not enough people . . . screen"*: Anthony Macklin, "It's the Manner of Telling: An
        Interview with Alfred Hitchcock," *Film Heritage* 11 (1976): 18.

194   *"because he knew . . . few"*: Peter Bogdanovich in discussion with the author, Sep-
        tember 11, 2018.

194   *His appointment books . . . directors*: AH appointment books, 1956–78, AHC MHL.

195   *"These Italian directors . . . technique!"*: Spoto, *Dark Side of Genius*, 495.

195   *"I'm not self-indulgent . . . painter"*: Charles Thomas Samuels, *Encountering Directors*
        (New York: G. P. Putnam's Sons, 1972), 239.

195   *"he has indicated . . . Hitchcock"*: Ibid., 233.

195   *"very good"*: Ibid., 235.

196   *"was actually an . . . manuscript"*: Dolly Haas, SMU.

196   *"could be titled . . . Shower"*: Chris Hodenfield, "Alfred Hitchcock: Muuuurder by
        the Babbling Brook," *Rolling Stone*, July 29, 1976, https://www.rollingstone.com/
        movies/movie-features/alfred-hitchcock-muuuurder-by-the-babbling-brook
        -59347/.

196   *Parker says that . . . Sacrilege*: Royal Academy of Arts, *Transitional Object [Psycho-
        Barn]: Cornelia Park* (London: Royal Academy Publications, 2018), 44.

197 *Hitchcock's own inspiration . . . Hopper:* Stephen Rebello, *Alfred Hitchcock and the Making of* Psycho, (New York: St. Martin's Press, 1998), 68.

197 *Parker watched* Psycho . . . *facade:* Cornelia Parker in discussion with the author, April 2019.

197 *It was Hitchcock's . . . moviemaking:* Robert Boyle, OHP.

197 *"I avoid out-and-out . . . banal":* Truffaut, *Hitchcock*, 103.

197 *"fairytales played against . . . environment":* Robert Boyle, OHP.

198 *Doc Erickson, the . . . compass:* Mac Johnson to Doc Erickson, October 5, 1953, Paramount Pictures Production Records, MHL.

198 *Hitchcock insisted on . . . detail:* Gordon Cole to Frank Caffey, July 11, 1953, Paramount Pictures Production Records, MHL.

198 *The sounds of . . . film:* Frank Caffey to Hiller Innes, November 11, 1953, Paramount Pictures Production Records, MHL.

198 *"eliminate the blemishes . . . neck":* Herbert Coleman to Luigi Zaccardi, July 11, 1956, Paramount Pictures Production Records, MHL.

198 *the director requested . . . operation:* AH's notes for dubbing on *Frenzy*, October 14, 1971, Peggy Robertson Papers, MHL.

199 *"the hidden meanings and symbols":* Andrew Sarris, "The Movie Journal," *Village Voice*, June 11, 1960, 8.

199 *Before he published . . . about it:* Barr, *Vertigo*, 22.

199 *"sometimes a corpse is just a corpse":* Walker, *Hitchcock's Motifs*, 131.

200 *"semi-unconscious mode of viewing":* D. A. Miller, *Hidden Hitchcock* (Chicago and London: University of Chicago Press, 2017), 45.

200 *"mistake, confusion, and . . . cinema":* Ibid., 17.

200 *"the too-close viewer . . . there?":* Ibid., 107.

200 *Among the hidden . . . anthologies:* Ibid., 28, 35.

200 *"amused him, and . . . way":* Peter Bogdanovich in discussion with the author, September 11, 2018.

200 *In the early . . . a C:* Patricia Hitchcock, interviewed by Anwar Brett, "Patricia Hitchcock and James C. Katz Interviews," February 27, 1997, Anwar Brett tapes, Sound and Moving Images Archive, British Library.

201 *In 2012, Vertigo . . . years:* Peter Matthews, "*Vertigo* rises: the greatest film of all time?" *Sight & Sound*, September 2012, https://www.bfi.org.uk/news-opinion/sight-sound-magazine/polls-surveys/greatest-films-all-time/vertigo-hitchcock-new-number-one

201 *"Our lives are lonely but not private":* Raymond Durgnat, *The Strange Case of Alfred Hitchcock* (London: Faber & Faber, 1974), 236.

9: THE ENTERTAINER

203 *"that degrading side . . . actor"*: AH, Markle, "A Talk with Hitchcock, Part Two."

204 *According to figures . . . 1960:* Peter Lev, *Transforming the Screen, 1950–1959* (Berkeley: University of California Press, 2003), 7.

204 *"People swarmed out . . . Presley"*: Leigh and Nickens, *Psycho*, 5.

205 *"French, German, English, and American"*: Barbara Goldsmith, "Bristol-Meyers' Alfred Hitchcock: His 'personality' sells what he derides," *Printers' Ink*, July 18, 1958, 68, Barbara Goldsmith Papers, Manuscripts and Archives Division, The New York Public Library, Astor, Lenox, and Tilden Foundations.

205 *Herbert Coleman and . . . diner:* Coleman, *The Man Who Knew Hitchcock*, 360; Samuel Taylor, interviewed by Tim Kirby for *Reputations*, BBC, PMC WHS.

205 *Mindful of not . . . pictures:* Coleman, *The Man Who Knew Hitchcock*, 238.

205 *"Hitchcock admits to . . . low-brow"*: "Seen on the Screen," *Daily Herald*, April 17, 1926, 9.

205 *"last word in screen art"*: " 'The Lodger,' the Last Word in Screen Art," *Leeds Mercury*, October 2, 1926, 6.

205 *"only for entertainment"*: *Ely Herald*, September 22, 1927, AHC MHL.

206 *"make pictures for . . . screen:* Montagu, "Working with Hitchcock," 190.

206 *"were in the . . . significance"*: Balcon, *Michael Balcon Presents*, 27.

206 *"You have to . . . audience"*: Truffaut, *Hitchcock*, 283.

207 *Ingrid Bergman explained . . . projected:* Transcript of Donald Spoto's interview with Ingrid Bergman, DSP UCLA.

207 *For the magazine . . . muster:* "Ingrid Bergman—as played by Alfred Hitchcock," *Pageant*, March 1946, 38–41.

207 *"British films before . . . laughing-stock"*: Michael Redgrave, *In My Mind's Eye: An Autobiography* (London: Weidenfeld & Nicolson, 1983), 9.

207 *"You sell to . . . theatre"*: Alan Strachan, *Secret Dreams: The Biography of Michael Redgrave* (London: Weidenfeld & Nicolson, 2004), 161.

208 *"sick with nervousness . . . again"*: Sheridan Morley, *John Gielgud: The Authorized Biography* (London: Simon & Schuster, 2010), 151.

208 *"I would never . . . cattle"*: AH, Cavett, *The Dick Cavett Show*.

208 *Michael Redgrave was . . . did:* Redgrave, *In My Mind's Eye*, 125.

208 *"cold and sometimes cruel"*: Granger, *Include Me Out*, 109.

209 *"something that I'll . . . set"*: Doris Day, SMU.

209 *Roy Thinnes sent . . . after:* Roy Thinnes to AH, May 25, 1976, AHC MHL. See also McGilligan, *Darkness and Light*, loc. 16537 of 20272, Kindle.

210 *"I'd look over . . . cut it"*: William Devane in discussion with the author, November 25, 2018.

210 *"do what you . . . floor"*: June Morfield, "The One Man Grace Kelly Couldn't Say 'No' To," *TV Radio Mirror*, July 1962, 90.

211 *"Next to reality . . . dramatic"*: "Alfred Hitchcock Reveals His Methods," *Midland Telegraph*, July 14, 1936, 6.

211 *"I always look . . . myself"*: Alfred Hitchcock, "My Spies," *Film Weekly*, May 30, 1936, 27.

212 *"a process by . . . hitherto"*: Alfred Hitchcock, "The History of Pea Eating," *Henley Telegraph*, December 1920, reprinted in McGilligan, *Darkness and Light*, loc. 963 of 20272, Kindle.

212 *"slept with men . . . soldier"*: *"Blackmail* Test Take," BFI YouTube Channel, https:// www.youtube.com/watch?v=7Z8mSwzSQQk

213 *"From then on I was his pet"*: Peggy Robertson, OHP.

213 *"sex-starved gorillas"*: Bernard Cribbins in discussion with the author, July 13, 2018.

213 *The film publicist . . . floor:* Herb Steinberg, Kirby.

213 *"common sense and . . . dancing"*: Clive James, "Exploring the Medium," in *Clive James on Television* (London: Picador, 1991), 307.

215 *"the brilliant realization . . . work"*: Whitney Balliet, "Hitchcock on Hitchcock," *The New Yorker*, August 8, 1959, https://www.newyorker.com/magazine/1959/08/15/ hitchcock-on-hitchcock

215 *"as a burlesque . . . guyed"*: Ackland, *The Celluloid Mistress*, 36.

216 *When Mel Brooks . . . Haut-Brion:* AH to Mel Brooks, March 1, 1979, AHC MHL.

216 *At a test . . . scene:* "Audience Reactions at CAMELBACK THEATRE, SCOTTS-DALE, ARIZONA," June 10, 1966, AHC MHL.

216 *"We don't know . . . dissembler"*: Claude Chabrol, "Story of an Interview," in Gottlieb, ed., *Alfred Hitchcock Interviews*, 39 (trans. James M. Vest). Originally appeared as "Histoire d'une Interview," *Cahiers du Cinéma*, no. 39 (October 1954): 39–44.

216 *"anecdotes that apparently . . . ago"*: Ibid., 40.

216 *"none of this . . . ride"*: Ibid., 39.

216 *"You have to . . . met"*: Fallaci, "Mr. Chastity," in *The Egotists*, 256.

217 *Actors were told . . . himself:* These, and other similar remarks, have been recorded plentifully. See the Hitchcock biographies by Spoto, McGilligan, and Chandler. In discussion with the author, William Devane, Bernard Cribbins, and Barbara Leigh-Hunt also mentioned this quirk of Hitchcock's.

217 *"the testicle"*: McGilligan, *Darkness and Light*, loc. 4288 of 20272, Kindle.

217 *Georgine Darcy . . . break:* Georgine Darcy, Kirby.

217 *Grant filled pages . . . "Eddie Tor"*: Batdorf, "Let's Hear It for Hitchcock," in Gottlieb, ed., *Alfred Hitchcock Interviews*, 82. See also "Hitchcock Comedy Crew," Cary Grant Papers, MHL.

217 *"seriousness is acceptable . . . outlawed"*: Kate Fox, *Watching the English: The Hidden Rules of English Behaviour* (London: Hodder & Stoughton, 2004), 62.

217   *"dignity sitting on a tintack"*: George Orwell, "Funny But Not Vulgar," in *The Collected Essays, Journalism and Letters of George Orwell, Volume 3* (London: Penguin), 1970, 325.

218   *he claimed that this . . . peg*: Bob Thomas, "Alfred Hitchcock: The German Years," *Action* (January-February 1973), 23–25, in Gottlieb, ed., *Alfred Hitchcock Interviews*, 159.

219   *includes what Hitchcock . . . "Captain?"*: Truffaut, *Hitchcock*, 227.

219   *"skids to preposterous depths"*: John McCarten, "The Current Cinema," *The New Yorker*, October 29, 1955, 145.

219   *"I must not . . . taste"*: Thelma Ritter to Joseph Moran, August 1954, Thelma Ritter and Joseph Aloysius Moran Papers, MHL.

220   *"everyone's wicked uncle . . . century"*: "Everyone's Wicked Uncle," BBC Radio 3, July 27, 1999.

221   *"weals and bruises" . . . endured*: Spoto, *Spellbound by Beauty*, loc. 882 of 4,805, Kindle, quoting Donat in Kenneth Barrow, *Mr Chips: The Life of Robert Donat* (London: Methuen, 1985), 75–76.

221   *"beastly to her"*: Ibid., loc. 953 of 4805, Kindle.

221   *"only a sadist . . . laughs"*: Bennett, *Hitchcock's Partner in Suspense*, 63.

221   *overheard a colleague . . . boasting*: Spoto, *Dark Side of Genius*, 110.

221   *Shortly after Joan Harrison . . . all*: Selznick International Pictures biographical materials on AH, AHC MHL

222   *"My father belongs . . . game"*: Marya Saunders, "My Dad, the Jokester," *Family Weekly*, July 21, 1963, 8.

222   *"He was a . . . humour"*: Spoto, *Dark Side of Genius*, 132.

223   *In his memoirs . . . "was bit"*: Bennett, *Hitchcock's Partner in Suspense*, 66.

223   *"Would any of . . . wouldn't"*: Mrs Alfred Hitchcock as told to Martin Abramson, "My Husband Alfred Hitchcock Hates Suspense," *Coronet*, August 1964, 17.

224   *"I'm very sensitive . . . days"*: AH, Markle, "A Talk with Hitchcock, Part Two."

224   *Yet the story . . . father*: Donald Spoto's notes on a Warner Bros. draft press release, November 30, 1950, DS UCLA.

225   *"the moment any . . . joke"*: AH, interview by George Angell, "Time of My Life," BBC Home Service, August 28, 1968.

225   *Patrick McGilligan discovered . . . enrolled*: McGilligan, *Darkness and Light*, loc. 439 of 20272, Kindle.

10: THE PIONEER

226   *"Hitchcock is the . . . drain"*: Sarris, "The Movie Journal," 8.

228   *In 1953, his . . . 3D*: Sidney Bernstein to AH, July 31, 1953, AHC MHL.

228   *"mysterious importance"*: Rebello, *Making of Psycho*, 149.

229   *"will be met by force"*: Ibid., 151.

229 *"Your women are . . . men"*: "Hitchcock: 'Treat Your Wives Better,' " *The Sun*, May 16, 1960, AHC ML.

229 *he also posed . . . newsworthy:* "Case of the Missing Shoe," *Sydney Morning Herald*, May 5, 1960, AHC MHL.

229 *The Australian leg . . . silhouette:* "Everything Went Black," *The Herald*, May 14, 1960, AHC MHL.

230 *"The star of . . . element":* Kapsis, *Making of a Reputation*, 83.

230 *Hitchcock invited the . . . eye:* Tony Lee Moral, *The Making of Hitchcock's* The Birds (Harpenden, UK: Kamera Books, 2013), loc. 3141 of 3812, Kindle.

230 *"The Birds is coming!":* Hunter, *Me and Hitch*, 77.

230 *"The birds are coming":* Ibid.

232 *"BEWARE GIRLS!" . . . "THE GRAND": Kinematograph Weekly*, March 31, 1927, AHC MHL.

232 *"proved very successful . . . proposition":* "Impersonating 'The Lodger,' " *The Bioscope*, March 17, 1927, 70.

232 *"feature stories on . . . production)":* Leff, *Hitchcock and Selznick*, 168.

232 *Ernest Lehman recollects . . . man:* Ernest Lehman, interview by Julian Schlossberg, "[Interview]," Sound and Moving Images Archive, British Library.

233 *On his television . . . slots:* Folders regarding the advertising agency Young and Rubicam in the Thelma Ritter and Joseph Aloysius Moran Papers, MHL, indicate what a commercial asset Hitchcock's "lead-ins" and "lead-outs" were thought to be.

233 *One wrote about . . . shot:* "Film-Making Problems," *Daily Mail*, March 31, 1927, AHC MHL.

234 *another described the . . . built:* "Talk of the Trade," *The Bioscope*, April 21, 1927, 20.

234 *A month later . . . Club:* "Talk of the Trade," *The Bioscope*, May 26, 1927, 31.

234 *the grandest entrance . . . theater:* See various clippings in the *Downhill* scrapbook, AHC MHL.

234 *The studio reminded . . . purposes:* Studio Manager (unidentified) to Ivor Montagu, February 22, 1927, Ivor Montagu Collection, BFI.

234 *"thoroughly disguised as . . . hat":* "All the Fun of the Fair—Free," *Evening Standard*, June 15, 1927, AHC MHL.

235 *In the summer . . . contract:* H. G. Boxall to AH, June 6, 1935, Ivor Montagu Collection, BFI.

235 *"I don't wish . . . shit":* Thelma Schoonmaker, Peter Von Bagh, and Raymond Durgnat, "Midnight Sun Film Festival," in David Lazar, ed., *Michael Powell: Interviews* (Jackson: University Press of Mississippi, 2003), 146.

235 *"As far as . . . matter":* Bogdanovich, *Who the Devil Made It*, loc. 9117 of 15740, Kindle.

235 *"the only thing . . . camera":* Laurents, *Original Story By*, 128.

236 *"positively weird to . . . hands":* Jack Cardiff, "The Problem of Lighting and Photographing *Under Capricorn*," *American Cinematographer*, October 1949, 382.

236   *"the most exciting . . . directed"*: Hitchcock, "My Most Exciting Picture," 276.

237   *"there is a . . . background"*: Harry Watt, "Re-Seeing Blackmail," *World Film News*, April 1937, 15.

239   *"His contrivances remain . . . now"*: David Bordwell, *Reinventing Hollywood: How 1940s Filmmakers Changed Movie Storytelling* (Chicago and London: Chicago University Press, 2017), 442. Quote originally in *Playboy*, March 1967.

239   *"sensation that everything . . . me"*: Truffaut, *Hitchcock*, 246.

239   *"So that's the . . . dollars"*: Ibid.

240   *Hitchcock had originally . . . "feel lucky"*: Robert Boyle, OHP.

241   *"Please start sweating now"*: Nugent, "Assignment in Hollywood," 13.

241   *"Hitch believed you . . . part"*: Marc Eliot, *James Stewart: A Biography* (London: Aurum, 2006), 29.

241   *"extremely possessive of . . . crew"*: Leff, *Hitchcock and Selznick*, 190.

241   *Hilton Green, an . . . work:* Hilton Green, Kirby.

241   *"This is the . . . much"*: Robert Boyle, OHP.

241   *"you had to . . . leave!"*: Ibid.

242   *"the most collaborative . . . I had"*: Ibid.

242   *The famous scene . . . inexorably:* Moral, *Making of Hitchcock's* The Birds, loc. 1525 of 3812, Kindle.

242   *When he heard . . . electronically:* Transcript of AH interview with Steve Rubin, December 1976, *Cinefantastique* magazine records, MHL.

243   *"electronically the equivalent . . . experimentation"*: Moral, *Making of Hitchcock's* The Birds, loc. 2733 of 3812, Kindle. See also AH notes on sound for *The Birds*, October 23, 1962, AHC MHL.

243   *Correspondence with Hitchcock's . . . ideas:* See the correspondence in *The Birds* folders, AHC MHL.

243   *The machine that . . . time:* Moral, *Making of Hitchcock's* The Birds, loc. 2676 of 3812, Kindle.

243   *"an eruption of film talent"*: Pells, *Modernist America*, 238.

244   *In promotional material . . . place: A Photographic Production Notebook on Alfred Hitchcock's ROPE,* Warner Bros., 1957, AHC MHL.

244   *"the most revolutionary . . . seen"*: Hitchcock, "My Most Exciting Picture," 276.

245   *"technical mixup, and . . . approve"*: Samuels, *Encountering Directors*, 237.

245   *"Hitchcock wouldn't reshoot . . . not that"*: Moral, *Making of* Marnie, 99. Quoting from Robert Boyle, American Film Institute seminar, 1977.

246   *"This project was . . . denied him"*: Auiler, *Hitchcock's Secret Notebooks*, 549.

246   *his "conversation was . . . so on"*: Ackland, *The Celluloid Mistress*, 39.

246   *"which they don't know . . . WARS"*: AH to Michael Balcon, October 6, 1977, AHC MHL.

247 *"questionable old man . . . matters":* AH notes on the manuscript of *Hitch* by John Russell Taylor, 1974, 12.

247 *Hitchcock remained fascinated . . . feminism:* See clippings folders, AHC MHL.

247 *"completely desperate . . . conflict":* AH to François Truffaut, October 20, 1976, in Truffaut, *Hitchcock*, 342.

248 *"I'm in competition with myself":* Bogdanovich, *Who the Devil Made It*, loc. 9196 of 15740, Kindle.

248 *"a director who . . . immunity":* Truffaut, *Hitchcock*, 341.

248 *"intransigence, difficulty and unresolved contradiction":* Edward Said, *On Late Style: Music and Literature Against the Grain* (London: Bloomsbury, 2017), 3.

248 *"a sort of deliberately unproductive productiveness":* Ibid., 4.

248 *"too-late style":* Mark Goble, "Live Nude Hitchcock: Final Frenzies," in Jonathan Freedman, ed., *The Cambridge Companion to Alfred Hitchcock* (New York: Cambridge University Press, 2015), 208.

11: THE LONDONER

252 *"son of Essex":* AH to A. E. Sloman, March 26, 1975, AHC MHL.

253 *"not socially respectable":* Spoto, *Dark Side of Genius*, 22.

253 *"scars from a . . . revolt":* John Houseman, *Unfinished Business: Memoirs, 1902–1988* (New York: Applause Theatre Books, 1989), 235.

254 *"plummy, posh-cockney voice":* Cardiff, *Magic Hour*, 19.

254 *"spoke in a . . . aitches":* Tripp, *The Glass Ladder*, 156.

254 *"electrification, motorization, socialism . . . state intervention":* Stephen Inwood, *City of Cities: The Birth of Modern London* (London: MacMillan, 2005), xv.

254 *During these three . . . 2015:* Greater London Authority, "Population Change 1939–2015," https://data.london.gov.uk/dataset/population-change-1939–2015.

254 *"swarmed with people . . . Street":* Peter Ackroyd, *London: The Concise Biography* (London: Vintage Books, 2012), 560. Quoting Horace Thorogood's memoir *East of Aldgate* (London: Allen and Unwin, 1935).

254 *"inordinate regard for personal privacy":* Alfred Hitchcock, "Murder—With English on It," *New York Times*, March 3, 1957, 199.

255 *"stony neglect, each . . . newspaper":* Ralph Waldo Emerson, *English Traits* (London and New York: Tauris Parke, 2011), 77.

256 *"an ecstasy of fumbling":* Wilfred Owen, "Dulce et Decorum Est," 1915, in Wilfred Owen, *Anthem for Doomed Youth* (London: Penguin, 2015), 2.

256 *"developed a kind . . . eyes":* Jerry White, *London in the Twentieth Century: A City and Its People* (London: Vintage Books, 2008), 313. Quoting Eileen Bailey's memoir, *The Shabby Paradise: The Autobiography of a Decade* (London: Hutchinson & Co., 1958), 17ff.

258 *"The Royal Albert . . . romance":* Charles Champlin, "What's It All About, Alfie?" *Los Angeles Times,* June 7, 1971, 12.

258 *In a similarly . . . bedroom:* Margaret Pride, "Your Fears Are My Life," *Reveille,* September 23, 1972, 7, AHC MHL.

258 *"the production of . . . refused":* Henry K. Miller, "Film Society, The (1925–39)," http://www.screenonline.org.uk/film/id/454755/index.html.

259 *"twenty-four hours . . . everything":* Truffaut, *Hitchcock,* 320.

259 *"the first row . . . theater":* Ibid.

259 *"an English director of genius":* "From Our London Correspondent," *Western Morning News,* May 29, 1926, 6.

259 *"mystery and magic . . . crime":* "British Films Booming," *Daily Herald,* September 15, 1926, 2.

260 *"which will centre . . . back-garden":* "To Be Seen on the Screen," *Daily Herald,* December 5, 1925, 7.

260 *The effort was . . . virus:* Genevieve Abravanel, *Americanizing Britain: The Rise of Modernism in the Age of the Entertainment Empire* (New York: Oxford University Press, 2012), 8.

260 *"They talk America . . . citizens":* G. A. Atkinson, "'British' Films Made to Please America," March 18, 1927, cited in Mark Glancy, *Hollywood and the Americanization of Britain: From the 1920s to the Present* (London and New York: I.B. Tauris, 2013), 14.

260 *he was even . . . empire:* "The British Film," *Western Morning News,* October 19, 1926, 4.

261 *"Americans, I am . . . woodlands":* "The Farmer's Wife," *Daily Mirror,* March 5, 1928, AHC MHL.

261 *"It's been left . . . gloriously":* "Putting England on the Screen," *Evening Standard,* March 5, 1928, AHC MHL.

261 *"Hear English as . . . spoken":* Advertising poster for *Blackmail,* AHC MHL.

261 *"British Triumph . . . Americans":* *Daily Mail,* June 24, 1929, AHC MHL.

261 *"All British—and . . . achieved":* London *Evening News,* June 22, 1929, AHC MHL.

261 *"sweeping aside American . . . glamour":* *The Times,* June 24, 1929, AHC MHL.

261 *"I'm American trained" . . . qualities:* Batdorf, "Let's Hear It for Hitchcock," in Gottlieb, ed., *Alfred Hitchcock Interviews,* 82.

264 *"men who leap . . . feel":* Alfred Hitchcock, "More Cabbages, Fewer Kings: A Believer in the Little Man," *Kinematograph Weekly,* January 14, 1937, 30.

264 *Unlike "stodgy" British films, "American . . . drama":* Alfred Hitchcock, "Stodgy British Pictures," *Film Weekly,* December 14, 1934, 14.

264 *"must be a . . . income":* *Britain Through a Lens: The Documentary Film Mob,* BBC Four, July 19, 2011.

264 *"the best director . . . films":* John Grierson, "Two Reviews," in Forsyth Hardy, ed., *Grierson on Documentary* (Berkeley: University of California Press, 1971), 71–72.

265   *in 1969, Hitchcock . . . movement:* Barr and Kerzoncuf, *Lost and Found*, 209–10.

266   *"couldn't just point . . . jewels":* Durgnat, *The Strange Case of Alfred Hitchcock*, 30.

266   *"you would go . . . that":* Norman Lloyd, SMU.

266   *"plump young junior technician":* Michael Balcon, "DESERTERS!" *Sunday Dispatch*, August 25, 1940, 6.

266   *"had sold his . . . Hitchcock":* C. A. Lejeune, "Cinema Cameos," *The Sketch*, July 10, 1940, 52.

267   *"his first Hollywood . . . best":* Ibid.

267   *"a completely British picture":* Truffaut, *Hitchcock*, 128.

267   *"broader viewpoint than . . . Britain":* Ibid.

267   *"name of England . . . picture":* H. Mark Glancy, *When Hollywood Loved Britain: The Hollywood 'British' Film, 1930–1945* (Manchester and New York: Manchester University Press, 1999), 3, citing *The Spectator* (May 7, 1937).

267   *According to one . . . films:* Ibid., 1.

268   *"You've got to . . . idiom":* Leslie Perkoff, "The Censor and Sydney Street," *World Film News*, March 12, 1938, 5.

268   *Curiously, in her . . . lost his:* Hitchcock O'Connell and Bouzereau, *Alma Hitchcock*, 167.

269   *"the Hitchcock name . . . history":* Coleman, *The Man Who Knew Hitchcock*, 217.

269   *"polyglot country. I . . . foreigners":* Ian Cameron and V. F. Perkins, "Interview with Hitchcock," *Movie*, no. 6 (January 1963): 6.

270   *he exchanged letters . . . screen:* Mogens Skot-Hansen, UN Representative to the Motion Picture Industry, to AH, February 5, 1951, AHC MHL.

270   *"widespread organized opposition . . . country":* Peter Bart, "Advertising: TV series on U.N. Stirs Debate," *New York Times*, April 10, 1964, AHC MHL.

271   *Amid a galaxy . . . name:* White, *London in the Twentieth Century*.

271   *Juliet Gardiner's equally . . . Henry VIII:* Juliet Gardiner, *The Thirties: An Intimate History* (London: Harper Press, 2010).

273   *"I've never really . . . Stinky":* Champlin, "What's It All About, Alfie?" 12.

274   *During the fifties . . . earlier:* Viewings of all these British films—and many others— are listed in Hitchcock's appointment books, AHC MHL.

274   *"I am out . . . English":* AH notes on draft script of *The Man Who Knew Too Much*, April 27, 1955, AHC MHL.

274   *Arthur La Bern . . . characters":* Arthur La Bern, "Letters to the Editor: Hitchcock's 'Frenzy,' from Mr Arthur La Bern," *The Times*, May 29, 1972, 7. See also Taylor, *Hitch*, loc. 4900 of 5468, Kindle.

274   *"England had changed . . . now":* Barbara Leigh-Hunt in discussion with the author, December 15, 2018.

12: THE MAN OF GOD

276   *Several family members . . . live:* Hitchcock O'Connell and Bouzereau, *Alma Hitchcock*, 216; Spoto, *Dark Side of Genius*, 550.

277   *"The Hitchcock pictures . . . paranoia":* Roger Ebert, "Scorsese Learns from Those Who Went before Him," January 11, 1998, https://www.rogerebert.com/interviews/scorsese-learns-from-those-who-went-before-him.

277   *"His face was . . . work":* Gilbert Harrison's spoken notes on his meeting with AH, January 4, 1980, Gilbert A. Harrison papers relating to Thornton Wilder, 1956–1985, Beinecke Rare Book and Manuscript Library, Yale University.

278   *"shapes the mind . . . powers":* O'Riordan, "Interview with Alfred Hitchcock," 289.

278   *"to arrange things . . . judge":* Bruce Bradley, *James Joyce's Schooldays* (Dublin: Gill and MacMillan, 1982), 7.

278   *"organization, control, and . . . analysis":* Bogdanovich, *Who the Devil Made It*, loc. 9287 of 15740, Kindle.

279   *"They epitomized the . . . radical":* Simon Callow, "The Spiritual SAS," *Guardian*, January 31, 2004, https://www.theguardian.com/books/2004/jan/31/featuresreviews.guardianreview6.

279   *One Jesuit critic . . . "Expressionism":* Neil Hurley, *Soul in Suspense: Hitchcock's Fright and Delight* (Metuchen, NJ, and London: Scarecrow Press, 1993), 13.

280   *"a bright red . . . drab":* Jon Whitcomb, "Master of Mayhem," *Cosmopolitan*, October 1959, 24.

281   *In his ill-fated . . . story:* AH to Richard Condon, November 3, 1964, Richard Condon Collection, HGARC.

281   *In his youth . . . Mass:* Spoto, *Dark Side of Genius*, 20.

282   *"The sense of . . . catacombs":* Anthony M. Maher, *The Forgotten Jesuit of Catholic Modernism: George Tyrrell's Prophetic Theology* (Minneapolis, MN: Fortress Press, 2017), 26.

282   *"Catholics live in . . . God":* Andrew Greeley, *The Catholic Imagination* (Berkeley and London: University of California Press, 2000), 1.

285   *she did have . . . bed:* Ackland, *The Celluloid Mistress*, 37.

285   *his granddaughters' confirmation . . . 1966:* AH appointment books, AHC MHL.

285   *When Pat and . . . Presents:* Hitchcock O'Connell and Bouzereau, *Alma Hitchcock*, 213.

286   *"given greater glory . . . work":* Bernard Parkin S.J., *St Ignatius College, 1894–1994* (Enfield, UK: St Ignatius Press, 1994), viii.

286   *"his admiration for . . . unbounded":* Ibid., 146.

286   *"I go through . . . failure":* AH to Reverend Thomas J. Sullivan, S.J., October 20, 1966, AHC MHL. See also McGilligan, *Darkness and Light*, loc. 15188 of 20272, Kindle.

286   *a rare example . . . Church:* see Berry C. Knowlton and Eloise R. Knowlton, "Murder Mystery Meets Sacred Mystery: The Catholic Sacramental in Hitchcock's *I Confess*," in Regina Hansen, ed., *Roman Catholicism in Fantastic Film: Essays on Belief, Spectacle, Ritual and Imagery* (Jefferson, NC: McFarland, 2011), 196.

287   *Dissatisfaction with casting . . . years:* Truffaut, *Hitchcock*, 200–202.

287   *He was also . . . plausibility:* Ibid., 203.

287   *"the Holy Church . . . men":* Murray Pomerance, *An Eye for Hitchcock* (New Brunswick, NJ, and London: Rutgers University Press, 2004), 173.

288   *"What's a Jansenist?":* Bazin, *Cinema of Cruelty*, 152.

288   *As a matter . . . activities:* Weaver, "The Man Behind the Body," 88.

288   *For similar reasons . . . cubicle:* Spoto, *Dark Side of Genius*, 385.

289   *"[A] claim to . . . belief":* O'Riordan, "Interview with Alfred Hitchcock," 290.

289   *"concocting a moral . . . universe":* David Freeman, in discussion with the author, October 6, 2018.

290   *"today to a . . . evil":* Alfred Hitchcock, interview by Richard Schickel, *The Men Who Made the Movies: Alfred Hitchcock*, PBS, 1973.

290   *"Transference of guilt":* Eric Rohmer and Claude Chabrol were the first to discuss this. See Eric Rohmer and Claude Chabrol, *Hitchcock: The First Forty-Four Films*, trans. Stanley Hochman (Oxford: Roundhouse, 1992).

291   *"the principle that . . . happiness":* Hurley, *Soul in Suspense*, 72.

291   *"The soul of . . . initiative":* Ibid., 199.

291   *Hitchcock conceded that . . . filmography:* Truffaut, *Hitchcock*, 54.

292   *"beautiful, holy things":* Oscar Wilde, "De Profundis," *De Profundis: The Ballad of Reading Gaol and Other Writings* (London: Wordsworth Editions, 1999), 83.

292   *"what one can . . . at":* Ibid., 59.

292   *"an order for . . . wine":* Ibid.

293   *In Donald Spoto's . . . absolution:* Spoto, *Dark Side of Genius*, 551.

293   *"insisted on coming . . . Alma":* McGilligan, *Darkness and Light*, loc. 16939 of 20272, Kindle.

294   *"But something whispered . . . need":* Mark Henninger, "Alfred Hitchcock's Surprise Ending," *Wall Street Journal*, June 12, 2012, https://www.wsj.com/articles/SB10001424127887323401904578159573738040636.

294   *On Henninger's first . . . "cheeks":* Ibid.

295   *Alma struggled to . . . them:* Hitchcock O'Connell and Bouzereau, *Alma Hitchcock*, 222.

295   *"I have lots . . . forever!":* Taylor, "Surviving," 176.

Selected Bibliography

A NOTE ON PRIMARY SOURCES

In researching the life and work of Alfred Hitchcock, the Alfred Hitchcock Collection at the Margaret Herrick Library, Academy of Motion Picture Arts and Sciences, Los Angeles, is an indispensable resource. Numerous other collections at the Library—including those of the various Hollywood studios for which Hitchcock worked, his writers, technicians, actors, and friends—are similarly important. The Academy's oral history collections contain transcripts of lengthy interviews with key names from Hitchcock's Hollywood years. Also in Los Angeles, the Special Collections at the Charles E. Young Research Library, UCLA, provided many very useful materials in the research of this book.

The Howard Gotlieb Archival Research Center at Boston University has collections of papers belonging to several of Hitchcock's associates and collaborators. Texas has some excellent resources, including the Ernest Lehman and David O. Selznick collections at the Harry Ransom Center at the University of Texas, Austin, and the Ronald Davis Oral History Collection at the Southern Methodist University in Dallas. In New York, the Museum of Modern Art, and the Rare Books and Manuscripts Division and the Billy Rose Theatre Division at the New York Public Library have limited but useful resources about various writers who wrote with and about Hitchcock. The Beinecke Rare Books and Manuscript Library at Yale University has jewels scattered through its capacious archives, including a recording of Gilbert Harrison's interview with Hitchcock in 1980, one of the last he ever did.

In London, the British Film Institute (BFI) holds the best primary materials for studying Hitchcock's career and milieu before his departure for Hollywood. Beyond its invaluable store of film periodicals, the BFI's Reuben Library also has vast collections of photographs and film footage that help to shine light on Hitchcock's work. North of the Thames, the British Library's comprehensive collections of periodicals helped me locate original copies of dozens of articles by and about Hitchcock from the 1920s onward, and its audiovisual archives have a trove of Hitchcock interviews and documentaries. The Library's magnificent online newspaper database also allowed me to stumble across many Hitchcock-related articles that I would not have otherwise encountered.

I am indebted to the outstanding work of the scholars Sidney Gottlieb and Jane Sloan for bringing so much material by and about Hitchcock to my attention. Sloan's bibliography and Gottlieb's anthologies of Hitchcock's writing and interviews are indispensable to any Hitchcock researcher.

PERIODICAL ARTICLES AND WEBSITES

"Alfred Hitchcock Reveals His Methods." *Midland Daily Telegraph*, July 14, 1936.

"All the Fun of the Fair—Free." *Evening Standard*, June 15, 1927.

"Alma in Wonderland: A Woman's Place Is Not Always in the Home." *Picturegoer*, December 1925.

"The British Film." *Western Morning News*, October 19, 1926.

"British Films Booming." *Daily Herald*, September 15, 1926.

"Case of the Missing Shoe." *Sydney Morning Herald*, May 5, 1960.

"The Elderly Cherub That Is Hitchcock." *TV Guide*, May 29, 1965.

"Everything Went Black." *The Herald*, May 14, 1960.

"Exposing Weaknesses of Top Ranking Stars." *Modern Screen*, December 1940.

"Falstaff in Manhattan." *New York Times*, September 5, 1937.

"The Farmer's Wife." *Daily Mirror*, March 5, 1928.

"Film Crasher Hitchcock." *Cue*, May 19, 1951.

"Film Director's Daughter Scores in New Comedy." *Hartford Times*, October 13, 1944.

"Film-Making Problems." *Daily Mail*, March 31, 1927.

"From Our London Correspondent." *Western Morning News*, May 29, 1926.

"From the archive, 24 January 1920: Is there a crime wave in the country?" *Guardian*, January 24, 2012, https://www.theguardian.com/theguardian/2012/jan/24/crime-wave -uk-1920. Originally published in the *Manchester Guardian*, January 24, 1920.

"Hitchcock Gives Free Rein to the Gentle Sex." *TV Guide*, May 10, 1958.

"Hitchcock in Sydney on PR Visit." *The Advertiser*, May 5, 1960.

"Hitchcock's Shower Scene: Another View." *Cinefantastique* 16, no. 4 (October 1986): 4–5, 64–67.

"Hitchcock: 'Treat Your Wives Better.'" *The Sun*, May 16, 1960.

"Impersonating 'The Lodger.'" *The Bioscope*, March 17, 1927.

"Ingrid Bergman—As Played by Alfred Hitchcock." *Pageant*, March 1946.

"'The Lodger,' the Last Word in Screen Art." *Leeds Mercury*, October 2, 1926.

"'Mary Rose' at the Haymarket." *Common Cause*, May 7, 1920.

"Our Captious Critic: 'Mary Rose.'" *Illustrated Sporting and Dramatic News*, May 15, 1920.

"Putting England on the Screen." *Evening Standard*, March 5, 1928.

"Seen on the Screen." *Daily Herald*, April 17, 1926.

"Some Thoughts on Color by Alfred Hitchcock." *Adelaide Advertiser*, September 4, 1937.

"Talk of the Trade." *The Bioscope*, April 21, 1927.

"Talk of the Trade." *The Bioscope*, May 26, 1927.

"To Be Seen on the Screen." *Daily Herald*, December 5, 1925.

Abramson, Martin. "What Hitchcock Does with His Blood Money." *Cosmopolitan*, January 1964.

Adams, Marjory. "Hitchcock, En Route Overseas, Stops Off for Daughter's Play." *Boston Morning Globe*, October 17, 1944.

Archer, Eugene. "Hitchcock's 'Marnie,' with Tippi Hedren and Sean Connery." *New York Times*, June 23, 1964.

Atkinson, G. A. "The Authenticity of Alfred." *The Era*, December 16, 1931.

Balcon, Michael. "DESERTERS!" *Sunday Dispatch*, August 25, 1940.

Balliet, Whitney. "Hitchcock on Hitchcock." *The New Yorker*, August 8, 1959. https://www.newyorker.com/magazine/1959/08/15/hitchcock-on-hitchcock.

Bart, Peter. "Advertising: TV series on U.N. Stirs Debate." *New York Times*, April 10, 1964.

Benedetta, Mary. "A Day with Hitchcock." Unknown publication, undated. AHC MHL.

Bidisha. "What's Wrong with Hitchcock's Women." *Guardian*, October 21, 2010. https://www.theguardian.com/film/2010/oct/21/alfred-hitchcock-women-psycho-the-birds-bidisha.

Bogdanovich, Peter. "Hitchcock High and Low." *New York*, May 6, 1974.

Brace, Keith. "The Trouble with Alfred." *Birmingham Daily Post*, August 5, 1960.

Buchanan, Barbara J. "Alfred Hitchcock Tells a Woman that Women Are a Nuisance." *Film Weekly*, September 20, 1935.

Burford, Roger. "A New 'Chair' Which a Woman Might Fill." *Gateway for Women at Work* 1, no. 3 (July 1929): 100–103.

Burrows, Tim. "Martin Landau: 'I chose to play Leonard as gay.'" *Daily Telegraph*, October 12, 2012. https://www.telegraph.co.uk/culture/film/starsandstories/9601547/Martin-Landau-I-chose-to-play-Leonard-as-gay.html.

Callow, Simon. "The Spiritual SAS." *Guardian*, January 31, 2004. https://www.theguardian.com/books/2004/jan/31/featuresreviews.guardianreview6.

Cameron, Ian, and V. F. Perkins. "Interview with Hitchcock." *Movie*, no. 6 (January 1963): 4–6.

Champlin, Charles. "What's It All About, Alfie?" *Los Angeles Times*, June 7, 1971.

Clark, Gerald. "Here's Hitchcock's Recipe for Suspense." *Weekend Magazine, The Standard*, December 22, 1951.

Coe, Alexis. "William Howard Taft Is Still Stuck in the Tub." *New York Times*, September 15, 2017. https://www.nytimes.com/2017/09/15/opinion/william-howard-taft-bathtub.html.

Coe, Richard. "Bergman Sobers Up Down Under." *Washington Post*, October 7, 1949.

Cohen, Paula Marantz. "Alfred Hitchcock: Modest Exhibitionist." *TLS*, September 5, 2008. https://www.the-tls.co.uk/articles/private/alfred-hitchcock-modest-exhibitionist/.

Counts, Kyle. "The Making of Alfred Hitchcock's *The Birds*." *Cinefantastique* 10, no. 2 (Fall 1980): 15–35.

Davidson, Bill. "Alfred Hitchcock Resents." *Saturday Evening Post*, December 15, 1962.

Davis, Ivor. "Alfred Hitchcock Abhors Violence, Prefers Suspense." *Los Angeles Times*, September 7, 1969.

Delehanty, Thornton. "A Liberated Hitchcock Dreams Gaudy Dreams in Technicolor." *New York Herald Tribune*, April 22, 1945.

Dixon, Bryony. "The White Shadow." http://www.screenonline.org.uk/film/id/1423007/index.html.

Ebert, Roger. "Scorsese Learns from Those Who Went Before Him." January 11, 1998. https://www.rogerebert.com/interviews/scorsese-learns-from-those-who-went-before-him.

——. "*Vertigo*." October 13, 1996. https://www.rogerebert.com/reviews/great-movie-vertigo-1958.

Goldsmith, Barbara. "Bristol-Meyers' Alfred Hitchcock: His 'Personality' Sells What He Derides." *Printers' Ink* (July 18, 1958): 63–68.

Grant, Cary. "Cary Grant on Style." *GQ*, April 15, 2013. https://www.gq.com/story/cary-grant-on-style. Originally published in *GQ*, Winter 1967–68.

Grant, Elspeth. "Converted to Beatledom." *Tatler*, July 22, 1964.

Greene, Lawrence. "He Is a Camera." *Esquire*, August 1952.

Grosvenor, Rita. "I Don't Scare Easily, Says Mrs Hitchcock." *Sunday Express*, January 30, 1972.

Hellman, Geoffrey T. "Alfred Hitchcock." *Life*, November 20, 1943.

Henninger, Mark. "Alfred Hitchcock's Surprise Ending." *Wall Street Journal*, June 12, 2012. https://www.wsj.com/articles/SB10001424127887323401904578159573738040636.

Hitchcock, A. J. "Titles—Artistic and Otherwise." *Motion Picture Studio*, July 23, 1921.

Hitchcock, Alfred. "Alfred Hitchcock Presents: The Great Hitchcock Murder Mystery." *This Week*, August 4, 1957.

——. "Columbus of the Screen." *Film Weekly*, February 21, 1931.

——. "Director's Problems." *The Listener*, February 2, 1938, 241.

——. "Films We Could Make." *London Evening News*, November 16, 1927.

——. "How I Make My Films." *News Chronicle*, March 5, 1937.

——. "It's Time Now to Start Taking Off That Turkey and Eggnog Waistline." *Los Angeles Times*, January 18, 1955.

——. "Life Among the Stars." *News Chronicle*, March 1, 1937.

——. "Making 'The Thirty-Nine Steps.'" *Film Weekly*, May 23, 1936.

——. "More Cabbages, Fewer Kings: A Believer in the Little Man." *Kinematograph Weekly*, January 14, 1937.

——. "Murder—with English on It." *New York Times Magazine*, March 3, 1957.

——. "My Screen Memories—1: I Begin with a Nightmare." *Film Weekly*, May 2, 1936.

——. "My Screen Memories—2: The Story Behind 'Blackmail.'" *Film Weekly*, May 9, 1936.

——— . "My Spies." *Film Weekly*, May 30, 1936.

——— . "My Strangest Year." *Film Weekly*, May 16, 1936.

——— . "The Real Me (The Thin One)." *Daily Express*, August 9, 1966.

——— . "The Sophistication of Violence." *Esquire*, July 1961.

——— . "Stodgy British Pictures." *Film Weekly*, December 14, 1934.

——— . "The Woman Who Knows Too Much." *McCall's*, March 1956.

Hitchcock, Alma Reville. "My Husband Hates Suspense." *Everywoman's Family Circle*, June 1958.

Mrs Alfred Hitchcock, as told to Martin Abramson. "My Husband Alfred Hitchcock Hates Suspense." *Coronet*, August 1964.

Hodenfield, Chris. "Alfred Hitchcock: Muuuurder by the Babbling Brook." *Rolling Stone*, July 29, 1976. https://www.rollingstone.com/movies/movie-features/alfred -hitchcock-muuuurder-by-the-babbling-brook-59347/.

Hopper, Hedda. "Hitchcock: He Runs on Fear." *Los Angeles Times*, August 17, 1958.

——— . "Papa Hitchcock." *Chicago Sunday Tribune Magazine*, October 13, 1944.

Hughes, Spike. "Coarse Cricket." *Daily Herald*, July 30, 1938.

Jennings, F. S. "Master of Suspense." *The Era*, December 9, 1936.

Johnston, Alva. "300-Pound Prophet Comes to Hollywood." *Saturday Evening Post*, May 22, 1943.

Joyce, Simon. "Sexual Politics and the Aesthetics of Crime: Oscar Wilde in the '90s." *ELH* 69, no. 2 (Summer 2002): 501–23.

Kaytor, Marilyn. "The Alfred Hitchcock Dinner Hour." *Look*, August 27, 1963.

Klemsrud, Judy. "Men's Clothes: Here Comes the Liberace Look." *New York Times*, March 4, 1970.

La Bern, Arthur. "Letters to the Editor: Hitchcock's 'Frenzy,' from Mr Arthur La Bern." *The Times*, May 29, 1972.

Lehman, Ernest. "Screen Writer's Recipe for 'Hitch's Brew.'" *New York Times*, August 2, 1959.

Lejeune, C. A. "Cinema Cameos." *The Sketch*, July 10, 1940.

Lewin, David. "Alfred Hitchcock." *CinemaTV Today*, August 19, 1972.

Macklin, Anthony. "It's the Manner of Telling: An Interview with Alfred Hitchcock." *Film Heritage* 11 (1976): 15–32.

Maloney, Russell. "What Happens After That?" Profiles, *The New Yorker*, September 10, 1938.

Mann, Roderick. "Hitchcock: Show Must Go On." *Los Angeles Times*, August 8, 1978.

Matthews, Peter. "*Vertigo* rises: the greatest film of all time?" *Sight & Sound*, September 2012. https://www.bfi.org.uk/news-opinion/sight-sound-magazine/polls-surveys/ greatest-films-all-time/vertigo-hitchcock-new-number-one.

McBride, Joseph. "Mr. and Mrs. Hitchcock." *Sight & Sound* 45, no. 4 (Autumn 1976): 224–25.

McCarten, John. "The Current Cinema." *The New Yorker*, October 29, 1955.

Miller, Henry K. "Film Society, The (1925–39)." http://www.screenonline.org.uk/film/id/454755/index.html.

Millstein, Gilbert. "Harrison Horror Story." *New York Times*, July 21, 1957.

Montagu, Ivor. "Working with Hitchcock." *Sight & Sound* 49, no. 3 (Summer 1980): 189–93.

Moral, Tony Lee. "How Accurate is *The Girl*?" *Broadcast*, December 14, 2012. http://www.broadcastnow.co.uk/comment/how-accurate-is-the-girl/5050231.article.

Morfield, June. "The One Man Grace Kelly Couldn't Say 'No' To." *TV Radio Mirror*, July 1962.

Nugent, Frank S. "Assignment in Hollywood." *Good Housekeeping*, November 1945.

——. "The Screen in Review." *New York Times*, October 12, 1939.

Perkoff, Leslie. "The Censor and Sydney Street." *World Film News*, March 12, 1938.

Pratley, Gerald. "Alfred Hitchcock's Working Credo." *Films in Review* 3, no. 10 (December 1952): 500–503.

Pride, Margaret. "Your Fears Are My Life." *Reveille*, September 23, 1972.

Reed, Rex. "Film Violence." *Calgary Herald*, June 17, 1972.

Reville, Alma. "Cutting and Continuity." *Motion Picture News*, January 13, 1923.

Ross, Walter. "Murder in the Mezzanine." *Esquire*, January 1954.

Roud, Richard. "The French Line." *Sight & Sound* 29, no. 4 (Autumn 1960): 166–71.

Sarris, Andrew. "The Movie Journal." *Village Voice*, June 11, 1960.

Saunders, Marya. "My Dad, the Jokester." *Family Weekly*, July 21, 1963.

Shanley, John P. "Lady Producer of Thrillers." *New York Times*, May 29, 1960.

Smith, H. Allen. "Hitchcock Likes to Smash Cups." *New York World-Telegram*, August 28, 1937.

Sussex, Elizabeth. "The Fate of F3080." *Sight & Sound* 53, no. 2 (Spring 1984): 92–97.

Taylor, John Russell. "Alfred Hitchcock: Fact and Fiction by John Russell Taylor." *Bloomsbury Reader*, April 8, 2013. https://bloomsburyreader.wordpress.com/2013/04/08/alfred-hitchcock-fact-and-fiction-by-john-russell-taylor/.

——. "Surviving: Alfred Hitchcock." *Sight & Sound* 46, no. 3 (Summer 1977): 174–75.

Turner, George E. "Rope—Something Different," *American Cinematographer* 66, no. 2 (February 1985): 34–40.

T.H.E. "Meet the Strong, Silent Director!" *Sunderland Daily Echo and Shipping Gazette*, February 16, 1935.

Thomson, David. "Charms and the Man," *Film Comment* 20, no. 1 (February 1984): 58–65.

Underhill, Duncan. "Hitchcock Is Like a Pattern Designer." *New York World-Telegram*, April 6, 1940.

Warhol, Andy. "Hitchcock." *Andy Warhol's Interview*, September 1974.

Warwick, Alan. "Alfred Hitchcock's Tudor Cottage." *Home Chat*, February 27, 1932.

Watt, Harry. "Re-Seeing Blackmail." *World Film News* 2, no. 1 (April 1937): 15.

Weaver, John D. "The Man Behind the Body." *Holiday*, September 1964.

Wehner, Chris. "Chris Wehner: Interview with Rear Window scribe John Michael Hayes."

http://www.screenwritersutopia.com/article/d14ec43e. Originally published in *Screenwriter's Monthly*, December 2002.

Weldon, Huw. "Alfred Hitchcock on His Films." *The Listener*, August 6, 1964.

Weston Edwards, Joan. "Making Good in the Film Trade." Unknown publication, February 26, 1927. AHC MHL.

Whitcomb, Jon. "Master of Mayhem." *Cosmopolitan*, October 1959.

Wickham, Ben. "Hitchcock Co., Horror Unlimited." Unknown publication, 1940. AHC MHL.

Wilde, Oscar. "The Philosophy of Dress." *New York Tribune*, April 19, 1885.

Williams, J. Danvers. "The Censor Wouldn't Pass It." *Film Weekly*, November 5, 1938.

TELEVISION, RADIO, AND FILM

"Alfred Hitchcock Accepts the AFI Life Achievement Award in 1979." American Film Institute, March 7, 1979. https://www.youtube.com/watch?v=pb5VdGCQFOM.

Bill Mumy, interview by Archive of American Television, September 3, 2013, Television Academy Foundation, https://interviews.televisionacademy.com/interviews/bill-mumy.

"*Blackmail* Test Take," BFI YouTube Channel, https://www.youtube.com/watch?v=7Z8mSwz SQQk.

Britain Through a Lens: The Documentary Film Mob. BBC Four, July 19, 2011.

British Film Institute. "Westcliff Cine Club Visits Mr Hitchcock in Hollywood," https://player.bfi.org.uk/free/film/watch-westcliff-cine-club-visits-mr-hitchcock-in-hollywood-1963-online.

Cinema: Alfred Hitchcock. DVD extra on *Hitchcock: The British Years*, UK: Network, 2008. DVD. Originally broadcast, ITV, 1966.

The Dick Cavett Show. ABC, June 8, 1972.

Everyone's Wicked Uncle. BBC Radio 3, July 27, 1999.

John Michael Hayes, interview by Steven DeRosa, https://www.youtube.com/watch?v=l981MGsT9n4.

Hitchcock at the NFT. BBC One, December 30, 1969.

Hitchcock/Truffaut. Directed by Kent Jones. USA: Dogwoof, 2016. DVD.

The Men Who Made the Movies, "Alfred Hitchcock." PBS, November 4, 1973.

Omnibus, "It's Only Another Movie." BBC One, September 26, 1986.

Reputations, "Hitch: Alfred the Great." BBC Two, 1999.

Reputations, "Hitch: Alfred the Auteur." BBC Two, 1999.

Rope: Pro and Con. DVD extra on *Hitchcock/Truffaut*, 2016.

The Story of Frenzy. DVD extra on *Frenzy.* Directed by Alfred Hitchcock. UK: Universal, 2005. DVD.

A Talk with Hitchcock. USA: Image Entertainment, 2000. DVD. Originally broadcast as *Telescope*, "A Talk with Hitchcock," 1964, CBC.

Time of My Life, "Alfred Hitchcock." BBC Home Service, August 28, 1966.

"Why Oscar-winner Eva Marie Saint Never Went Hollywood." CBS News, March 2, 2014, https://www.cbsnews.com/news/why-oscar-winner-eva-marie-saint-never-went -hollywood/.

BOOKS

Abramson, Leslie H. *Hitchcock and the Anxiety of Authorship*. New York: Palgrave Mac- Millan, 2015.

Abravanel, Genevieve. *Americanizing Britain: The Rise of Modernism in the Age of the Enter- tainment Empire*. New York: Oxford University Press, 2012.

Ackland, Rodney, and Elspeth Grant. *The Celluloid Mistress, or The Custard Pie of Dr. Caligari*. London: Allan Wingate, 1954.

Ackroyd, Peter. *Alfred Hitchcock*. London: Chatto & Windus, 2015.

——. *London: The Concise Biography*. London: Vintage Books, 2012.

Allen, Richard. *Hitchcock's Romantic Irony*. New York: Columbia University Press, 2007.

Atkinson, Diane. *Rise Up Women!: The Remarkable Lives of the Suffragettes*. London: Blooms- bury, 2018.

Auiler, Dan. *Hitchcock's Secret Notebooks*. London: Bloomsbury. 1999.

——. *Vertigo: The Making of a Hitchcock Classic*. London: Titan, 1999.

Badmington, Neil. *Hitchcock's Magic*. Cardiff: University of Wales Press, 2011.

Baer, William. *Classic American Films: Conversations with the Screenwriters*. Westport, CT, and London: Praeger, 2008.

Balcon, Michael. *Michael Balcon Presents: A Lifetime of Films*. London: Hutchinson, 1969.

Banner, Lois. *American Beauty*. New York: Alfred A. Knopf, 1983.

Barr, Charles. *English Hitchcock*. Moffat, Scotland: Cameron and Hollis, 1999.

——. *Vertigo*. London: BFI, 2012.

Barr, Charles, and Alain Kerzoncuf. *Hitchcock Lost and Found: The Forgotten Films*. Lexing- ton: University Press of Kentucky, 2015.

Bazin, André. *The Cinema of Cruelty: From Buñuel to Hitchcock*. New York: Seaver Books, 1982.

Belton, John, ed. *Alfred Hitchcock's* Rear Window. Cambridge, UK: Cambridge University Press, 2000.

Bennett, Charles. *Hitchcock's Partner in Suspense: The Life of Screenwriter Charles Bennett*, ed. John Charles Bennett. Lexington: University of Kentucky, 2014.

Bentley, Toni. *Sisters of Salome*. Lincoln: University of Nebraska Press, 2005.

Bogdanovich, Peter. "Alfred Hitchcock (1899–1980)," *Who the Devil Made It: Conversations with Legendary Film Directors*. New York: Ballantine Books, 1997. Kindle.

Bone, James. *The Curse of Beauty: The Scandalous & Tragic Life of Audrey Munson, America's First Supermodel*. New York: Simon & Schuster, 2016.

Bordwell, David. *Reinventing Hollywood: How 1940s Filmmakers Changed Movie Storytelling*. Chicago and London: Chicago University Press, 2017.

Bradley, Bruce. *James Joyce's Schooldays*. Dublin: Gill and MacMillan, 1982.

Brill, Lesley. *The Hitchcock Romance: Love and Irony in Hitchcock's Films*. Princeton, NJ: Princeton University Press, 1988.

Cardiff, Jack. *Magic Hour*. London: Faber & Faber, 1996.

Carey, John. *The Intellectuals and the Masses: Pride and Prejudice among the Literary Intelligentsia, 1880–1939*. London: Faber & Faber, 1992.

Cassini, Oleg. *In My Own Fashion: An Autobiography*. London: Simon & Schuster, 1987.

Chandler, Charlotte. *Ingrid: Ingrid Bergman, A Personal Biography*. London: Simon & Schuster, 2007.

——. *It's Only a Movie—Alfred Hitchcock: A Personal Biography*. London: Pocket Books, 2006.

Chapman, James. *Hitchcock and the Spy Film*. London: Bloomsbury, 2017.

Chauncey, George. *Gay New York: The Making of the Gay Male World, 1890–1940*. London: Flamingo, 1995.

Cohen, Paula Marantz. *Alfred Hitchcock: The Legacy of Victorianism*. Lexington: University Press of Kentucky, 1995.

Coleman, Herbert. *The Man Who Knew Hitchcock: A Hollywood Memoir*. Lanham, MD; Toronto; Plymouth, UK: Scarecrow Press, 2007.

Comolli, Jean-Louis. "Fatal Rendezvous." In *Cinema and the Shoah: An Art Confronts the Tragedy of the Twentieth Century*, ed. Jean-Michel Frodon, trans. Anna Harrison and Tom Mes. Albany: State University of New York Press, 2010.

Connolly, Cyril. *Enemies of Promise*. Chicago: University of Chicago Press, 2008.

Conrad, Peter. *The Hitchcock Murders*. London: Faber & Faber, 2000.

Cotten, Joseph. *Vanity Will Get You Somewhere*. London: Columbus Books, 1987.

Critser, Greg. *Fat Land: How Americans Became the Fattest People in the World*. Boston and New York: Houghton Mifflin, 2003.

Cronyn, Hume. *A Terrible Liar: A Memoir*. New York: William Morrow, 1991.

Davy, Charles. *Footnotes to the Film*. London: Lovat Dickson, 1937.

Dern, Bruce, with Christopher Fryer and Robert Crane. *Things I've Said, But Probably Shouldn't Have: An Unrepentant Memoir*. Hoboken, NJ: Wiley, 2007.

DeRosa, Steven. *Writing with Hitchcock: The Collaboration of Alfred Hitchcock and John Michael Hayes*. New York; London: Faber & Faber, 2001.

Durgnat, Raymond. *The Strange Case of Alfred Hitchcock*. London: Faber & Faber, 1974.

Ebert, Roger. *Awake in the Dark: The Best of Roger Ebert*, 2nd ed. Chicago: University of Chicago Press, 2017.

Eisner, Lottie. *The Haunted Screen: Expressionism in the German Cinema and the Influence of Max Reinhardt*. Davis: University of California Press, 2008.

Eliot, Marc. *James Stewart: A Biography*. London: Aurum, 2006.

Emerson, Ralph Waldo. *English Traits*. London and New York: Tauris Parke, 2011.

Fallaci, Oriana. *The Egotists: Sixteen Surprising Interviews*, trans. Pamela Swinglehurst. Chicago: Henry Regnery, 1968.

Fishgall, Gary. *Gregory Peck: A Biography*. New York: Scribner, 2002.

Fontaine, Joan. *No Bed of Roses*. London: W.H. Allen, 1978.

Fox, Kate. *Watching the English: The Hidden Rules of English Behaviour*. London: Hodder & Stoughton, 2004.

Freedman, Jonathan, ed. *The Cambridge Companion to Alfred Hitchcock*. New York: Cambridge University Press, 2015.

Freedman, Jonathan, and Richard Millington, eds. *Hitchcock's America*. New York and Oxford: Oxford University Press, 1999.

Freeman, David. *Last Days of Alfred Hitchcock*. Woodstock, NY: Overlook Press, 1984.

Friedman, David M. *Wilde in America: Oscar Wilde and the Invention of Modern Celebrity*. New York: W. W. Norton, 2014.

Galenson, David. *Old Masters and Young Geniuses: The Two Life Cycles of Artistic Creativity*. Princeton, NJ, and Oxford: Princeton University Press, 2006.

Gardiner, Juliet. *The Thirties: An Intimate History*. London: Harper Press, 2010.

Gehring, Wes D. *Hitchcock and Humor: Modes of Comedy in Twelve Defining Films*. Jefferson, NC: McFarland, 2019.

Gladstone, Kay. "Separate Intentions: The Allied Screening of Concentration Camp Documentaries in Defeated Germany in 1945–46: *Death Mills and Memory of the Camps*." In *Holocaust and the Moving Image: Representations in Film and Television since 1933*. Toby Haggith and Joanna Newman, eds., 50–64. London: Wallflower, 2005.

Glancy, Mark. *Hollywood and the Americanization of Britain: From the 1920s to the Present*. London and New York: I.B. Tauris, 2013.

———. *When Hollywood Loved Britain: The Hollywood "British" Film, 1930–1945*. Manchester and New York: Manchester University Press, 1999.

Glick, Elisa. *Materializing Queer Desire: Oscar Wilde to Andy Warhol*. Albany: State University of New York Press, 2009.

Gottlieb, Sidney, ed. *Alfred Hitchcock Interviews*. Jackson: University Press of Mississippi, 2003.

———. *Hitchcock on Hitchcock, Volume 1*. London: University of California Press, 1997.

———. *Hitchcock on Hitchcock, Volume 2*. Oakland: University of California Press, 2015.

Gottlieb, Sidney, and Christopher Brookhouse, eds. *Framing Hitchcock: Selected Essays from the Hitchcock Annual*. Detroit: Wayne State University Press, 2002.

Grams, Martin, Jr., and Patrik Wikstrom. *The Alfred Hitchcock Presents Companion*. Churchville, MD: OTR, 2001.

Granger, Farley. *Include Me Out: My Life from Goldwyn to Broadway*. New York: St. Martin's Press, 2007.

Greeley, Andrew. *The Catholic Imagination*. Berkeley and London: University of California Press, 2000.

Greven, David. *Intimate Violence: Hitchcock, Sex, and Queer Theory*. New York: Oxford University Press, 2017.

Grierson, John. "Two Reviews." In *Grierson on Documentary*, ed. Forsyth Hardy, 71–72. Berkeley: University of California Press, 1971.

Griffin, Susan M., and Alan Nadel, eds. *The Men Who Knew Too Much: Henry James and Alfred Hitchcock*. Oxford and New York: Oxford University Press, 2012.

Haeffner, Nicholas. *Alfred Hitchcock*. Harlow: Longman, 2005.

Harding, James, *Ivor Novello*. London; W.H. Allen, 1987.

Head, Edith, and Jane Kesner Ardmore. *The Dress Doctor*. Kingswood, UK: World's Work, 1960.

Head, Edith, and Paddy Calistro. *Edith Head's Hollywood*. New York: Dutton, 1983.

Hedren, Tippi. *Tippi: A Memoir*. New York: William Morrow, 2016. Kindle.

Hill, Daniel Delis. *Advertising to the American Woman, 1900–1999*. Columbus: Ohio State University Press, 2002.

Hiney, Tom, and Frank MacShane, eds. *The Raymond Chandler Papers: Selected Letters and Non-Fiction, 1909–1959*. London: Hamish Hamilton, 2000.

Holder, Peter Anthony. *Great Conversations*. Albany, NY: BearManor Media, 2017.

Honigsbaum, Mark. *Living with Enza: The Forgotten Story of Britain and the Great Flu Pandemic of 1918*. London: Macmillan, 2009.

Houseman, John. *Unfinished Business: Memoirs, 1902–1988*. New York: Applause Theatre Books, 1989.

Hunter, Evan. *Me and Hitch*. London: Faber & Faber, 1997.

Hurley, Neil. *Soul in Suspense: Hitchcock's Fright and Delight*. Metuchen, NJ, and London: Scarecrow Press, 1993.

Inwood, Stephen. *City of Cities: The Birth of Modern London*. London: MacMillan, 2005.

James, Clive. *Clive James on Television*. London: Picador, 1991.

Jorgensen, Jay. *Edith Head: The Fifty-Year Career of Hollywood's Greatest Costume Designer*. Philadelphia and London: Running Press, 2010.

Kapsis, Robert. *Hitchcock: The Making of a Reputation*. Chicago and London: University of Chicago Press, 1992.

Kelly, Ian. *Beau Brummell: The Ultimate Dandy*. London: Hodder & Stoughton, 2005.

Knowlton, Berry C., and Eloise R. Knowlton. "Murder Mystery Meets Sacred Mystery: The Catholic Sacramental in Hitchcock's *I Confess*." In *Roman Catholicism in Fantastic Film: Essays on Belief, Spectacle, Ritual and Imagery*, ed. Regina Hansen, 196–208. Jefferson, NC: McFarland, 2011.

Kraft, John, and Aaron Leventhal. *Footsteps in the Fog: Alfred Hitchcock's San Francisco*. Santa Monica, CA: Santa Monica Press, 2002.

Krohn, Bill. *Hitchcock at Work*. London: Phaidon Press, 2000.

Lacey, Robert. *Grace*. London: Sidgwick & Jackson, 1994.

Laurents, Arthur. *Original Story By: A Memoir of Broadway and Hollywood*. New York: Alfred A. Knopf, 2000.

Lawrence, Amy. *The Passion of Montgomery Clift*. Berkeley and London: University of California Press, 2010.

Lebeau, Vicky. *Childhood and Cinema*. London: Reaktion Books, 2008.

Leff, Leonard J. *Hitchcock and Selznick: The Rich and Strange Collaboration of Alfred Hitchcock and David O. Selznick in Hollywood*. London: Weidenfeld & Nicholson, 1987.

Lehman, Ernest. *North by Northwest*. New York: Viking Press, 1972.

Leigh, Janet, with Christopher Nickens. *Psycho: Behind the Scenes of the Classic Thriller*. London: Pavilion Books, 1995.

Lev, Peter. *Transforming the Screen, 1950–1959*. Berkeley: University of California Press, 2003.

MacLaine, Shirley. *I'm Over All That: And Other Confessions*. New York: Atria, 2012.

MacShane, Frank. *The Life of Raymond Chandler*. London: Hamish Hamilton, 1986.

Maher, Anthony M. *The Forgotten Jesuit of Catholic Modernism: George Tyrrell's Prophetic Theology*. Minneapolis, MN: Fortress Press, 2017.

Mankiewicz, Tom, and Robert Crane. *My Life as a Mankiewicz: An Insider's Journey through Hollywood*. Lexington: University Press of Kentucky, 2012.

Mann, Philip. *The Dandy at Dusk: Taste and Melancholy in the Twentieth Century*. London: Head of Zeus, 2017.

McCann, Grant. *Cary Grant: A Class Apart*. New York: Columbia University Press, 1996.

McEwen, Todd. *How Not to Be American: Misadventures in the Land of the Free*. London: Aurum, 2013.

McGilligan, Patrick. *Alfred Hitchcock: A Life in Darkness and Light*. HarperCollins, 2010. Kindle.

———. *Backstory 2: Interviews with Screenwriters of the 1940s and 1950s*. Berkeley: University of California Press, 1991.

———. *Backstory 3: Interviews with Screenwriters of the 1960s*. Berkeley: University of California Press, 1997.

McKittrick, Casey. *Hitchcock's Appetites: The Corpulent Plots of Desire and Dread*. New York and London: Bloomsbury, 2016.

Meyers, Jeffrey. *The Enemy: A Biography of Wyndham Lewis*. London: Routledge, 1980.

Miller, D. A. *Hidden Hitchcock*. Chicago and London: University of Chicago Press, 2017.

Modleski, Tania. *The Women Who Knew Too Much: Hitchcock and Feminist Theory*. New York and London: Routledge, 2005.

Moffatt, Wendy. *A Great Unrecorded History: A New Life of E. M. Forster*. New York: Farrar, Straus & Giroux, 2010.

Montagu, Ivor. *The Youngest Son*. London: Lawrence and Wishart, 1970.

Moorehead, Caroline. *Sidney Bernstein: A Biography*. London: Jonathan Cape, 1984.

Moral, Tony Lee. *Hitchcock and the Making of* Marnie. Lanham, MD; Toronto; Plymouth, UK: Scarecrow Press, 2013.

———. *The Making of Hitchcock's* The Birds. Harpenden, UK: Kamera Books, 2013. Kindle.

Morley, Sheridan. *John Gielgud: The Authorized Biography.* London: Simon & Schuster, 2010.

Mulvey, Laura. "Visual Pleasure and Narrative Cinema." In *Film Theory and Criticism: Introductory Readings*, eds. Leo Braudy and Marshall Cohen, 5th ed. New York: Oxford University Press, 1999.

Nelson, Nancy. *Evenings with Cary Grant.* New York: Warner, 1993.

Norman, Will. *Transatlantic Aliens: Modernism, Exile, and Culture in Midcentury America.* Baltimore: Johns Hopkins University Press, 2016.

O'Connell, Pat Hitchcock, and Laurent Bouzereau. *Alma Hitchcock: The Woman Behind the Man.* New York: Berkley Books, 2003.

Olson, Debbie. "The Hitchcock Imp: Children and the Hyperreal in Alfred Hitchcock's *The Birds*." In *Lost and Othered Children in Contemporary Cinema*, eds. Debbie Olson and Andrew Scahill, 287–306. Plymouth, UK: Lexington, 2014.

Olsson, Jan. *Hitchcock à la Carte.* Durham, NC, and London: Duke University Press, 2015.

Orr, John. *Hitchcock and Twentieth-Century Cinema.* London and New York: Wallflower Press, 2005.

Orwell, George. *The Collected Essays, Journalism and Letters of George Orwell*, vol. 3. London: Penguin, 1970.

———. *Decline of the English Murder.* London: Penguin, 2009.

———. *I Have Tried to Tell the Truth: 1943–1944.* London: Secker & Warburg, 1998.

Osteen, Mark, ed. *Hitchcock and Adaptation: On the Page and Screen.* Lanham, MD, and Plymouth, UK: Rowman and Littlefield, 2014.

Palmer, R. Barton, and David Boyd, eds. *Hitchcock at the Source: The Auteur as Adaptor.* Albany: State University of New York Press, 2011.

Parkin S. J., Bernard. *St Ignatius College, 1894–1994.* Enfield, UK: St Ignatius Press, 1994.

Pells, Richard. *Modernist America: Art, Music, Movies, and the Globalization of American Culture.* New Haven and London: Yale University Press, 2011.

Pomerance, Murray. *An Eye for Hitchcock.* New Brunswick, NJ, and London; Rutgers University Press, 2004.

Raubicheck, Walter. "Working with Hitchcock: A Collaborators' Forum with Patricia Hitchcock, Janet Leigh, Teresa Wright, and Eva Marie Saint." In *Hitchcock Annual: 2002–03*, eds. Sidney Gottlieb and Richard Allen, 32–66. New York: Columbia University, 2003.

Rebello, Stephen. *Alfred Hitchcock and the Making of* Psycho. New York: St. Martin's Press, 1998.

Redgrave, Michael. *In My Mind's Eye: An Autobiography.* London: Weidenfeld & Nicolson, 1983.

Reed, Langford, and Hetty Spiers, eds. *Who's Who in Filmland*. London: Chapman and Hall, 1931.

Rohmer, Eric, and Claude Chabrol. *Hitchcock: The First Forty-Four Films*, trans. Stanley Hochman. Oxford: Roundhouse, 1992.

Rothman, William. *Hitchcock: The Murderous Gaze*. Albany: State University of New York Press, 2002.

Royal, Susan. "Steven Spielberg in His Adventures on Earth." In *Steven Spielberg Interviews*, eds. Lester D. Friedman and Brent Notbohm. Jackson: University Press of Mississippi, 2000.

Royal Academy of Arts. *Transitional Object [PsychoBarn]: Cornelia Parker*. London: Royal Academy Publications, 2018.

Said, Edward. *On Late Style: Music and Literature Against the Grain*. London: Bloomsbury, 2017.

Samuels, Charles Thomas. *Encountering Directors*. New York: G. P. Putnam's Sons, 1972.

Schoonmaker, Thelma, Peter Von Bagh, and Raymond Durgnat. "Midnight Sun Film Festival." In *Michael Powell: Interviews*, ed. David Lazar. Jackson: University Press of Mississippi, 2003.

Sharff, Stefan. *The Art of Looking in Hitchcock's* Rear Window. New York: Limelight Editions, 1997.

Sklar, Robert. "Death at Work: Hitchcock's Violence and Spectator Identification." In *After Hitchcock: Influence, Imitation, and Intertexuality*, eds. David Boyd and R. Barton Palmer. Austin: University of Texas Press, 2010.

Slezak, Walter. *What Time's the Next Swan?* Garden City, NY: Doubleday, 1962.

Slide, Anthony. *The Silent Feminists: America's First Women Directors*. Lanham, MD, and London: Scarecrow Press, 1996.

Sloan, Jane. *Alfred Hitchcock: A Filmography and Bibliography*. Berkeley: University of California Press, 1995.

Smit, David. *Ingrid Bergman: The Life, Career and Public Image*. Jefferson, NC: McFarland, 2012.

Smith, Susan. *Hitchcock: Suspense, Humour and Tone*. London: BFI, 2000.

Spoto, Donald. *The Art of Alfred Hitchcock: Fifty Years of His Motion Pictures*. London: W. H. Allen, 1977.

——. *The Dark Side of Genius: The Life of Alfred Hitchcock*. London: Collins, 1983.

——. *High Society: Grace Kelly and Hollywood*. London: Hutchinson, 2005.

——. *Spellbound by Beauty: Alfred Hitchcock and His Leading Ladies*. London: Arrow, 2009. Kindle.

Stearns, Peter. *Fat History: Bodies and Beauty in the Modern West*. New York: New York University Press, 1997.

Stein, Jean. *West of Eden: An American Place*. London: Jonathan Cape, 2016.

Steinbeck, Elaine, and Robert Wallsten, eds. *Steinbeck: A Life in Letters*. London: Penguin, 2001.

Strachan, Alan. *Secret Dreams: The Biography of Michael Redgrave*. London: Weidenfeld & Nicolson, 2004.

Taylor, John Russell. *Hitch: The Life and Times of Alfred Hitchcock*. London: Bloomsbury Reader, 2013. Kindle.

Thomson, David. *The Moment of* Psycho*: How Alfred Hitchcock Taught America to Love Murder*. New York: Basic Books, 2009.

Tomkins, Calvin. *Duchamp: A Biography*. London: Pimlico, 1996.

Tripp, June. *The Glass Ladder*. London: William Heinemann, 1960.

Truffaut, François. *Hitchcock*. London: Faber & Faber, 2017.

Vincent, David. *The Culture of Secrecy: Britain, 1832–1998*. Oxford: Oxford University Press, 1998.

Walker, Michael. *Hitchcock's Motifs*. Amsterdam: Amsterdam University Press, 2005.

White, Edward. *The Tastemaker: Carl Van Vechten and the Birth of Modern America*. New York: Farrar, Straus & Giroux, 2014.

White, Jerry. *London in the Twentieth Century: A City and Its People*. London: Vintage Books, 2008.

———. *Zeppelin Nights: London in the First World War*. London: Bodley Head, 2014.

Wilde, Oscar. *De Profundis: The Ballad of Reading Gaol and Other Writings*. London: Wordsworth Editions, 1999.

Wood, Robin. *Hitchcock's Films Revisited*. New York: Columbia University Press, 1989.

Wright, Jonathan. *God's Soldiers: Adventure, Politics, Intrigue, and Power—A History of the Jesuits*. London: Doubleday, 2005.

Youngkin, Stephen D. *The Lost One: A Life of Peter Lorre*. Lexington: University Press of Kentucky, 2005.

Credits

TEXT CREDITS

Jay Presson Allen, interviewed by Tim Kirby for *Reputations*, BBC. Courtesy BBC / Tim Kirby. Manuscript from Patrick McGilligan Collection, University of Wisconsin. Used with permission of Brooke Allen.

Robert Benchley quote used by permission (of the Estate of Robert Benchley, Nat Benchley, Executor).

William F. Blowitz, memo to colleagues at Universal Pictures, 19 March 1962. Used with permission of John Blowitz, for the William F. Blowitz Estate.

Whitfield Cook, "Happy Ending" and "Her First Island," unpublished short stories, and entries from 1 April 1945, 20 September 1948, 1 October 1948, 7 October 1948, and 9 October 1948, Whitfield Cook diary. From the Whitfield Cook Collection, Howard Gotlieb Archival Research Center, Boston University. Reprinted by permission of Harold Ober Associates and the Estate of Whitfield Cook.

Doris Day, Oral History transcript. Courtesy of DeGolyer Library, Southern Methodist University, Ronald L. Davis Oral History Collection.

David Freeman, interviewed by Tim Kirby for *Reputations*, BBC. © David Freeman, courtesy BBC / Tim Kirby. Manuscript from Patrick McGilligan Collection, University of Wisconsin.

Dolly Haas, Oral History transcript. Courtesy of DeGolyer Library, Southern Methodist University, Ronald L. Davis Oral History Collection.

Gilbert Harrison, spoken notes at the end of his audio recording of his interview with Alfred Hitchcock (for Harrison's biography of Thornton Wilder), 4 January 1980, Gilbert A. Harrison papers relating to Thornton Wilder, 1956–1985, Beinecke Library, Yale University. Used with permission of the Estate of Gilbert A. Harrison.

Harold Hayes, letter to Hitchcock, 1963. Alfred Hitchcock Collection, Margaret Herrick Library. Used with permission of the author's estate.

Howard Gotlieb Archival Research Center at Boston University. Used with permission of Alfred J. Hitchcock Trust.

Transcripts from interviews with Peggy Robertson, Eva Marie Saint, and Robert Boyle. Material courtesy of the Academy's Oral History Projects department. Copyright © Academy of Motion Picture Arts and Sciences.

Samuel Taylor interviewed by Tim Kirby for *Reputations*, BBC. Manuscript from Patrick McGilligan Collection, University of Wisconsin.

ILLUSTRATION CREDITS

Index

Page numbers in *italics* refer to photographs.
Page numbers beginning with 303 refer to endnotes.